TENTH EDITION

Human Resources Administration in Education

Ronald W. Rebore
Saint Louis University

PEARSON

Boston   Columbus   Indianapolis   New York   San Francisco   Upper Saddle River
Amsterdam   Cape Town   Dubai   London   Madrid   Milan   Munich   Paris   Montreal   Toronto
Delhi   Mexico City   São Paulo   Sydney   Hong Kong   Seoul   Singapore   Taipei   Tokyo

Vice President and Editorial Director: Jeffery W. Johnston
Senior Acquisitions Editor: Meredith Fossel
Vice President, Director of Marketing: Margaret Waples
Senior Marketing Manager: Darcy Betts Prybella
Senior Marketing Assistant: Sophia Rester
Project Manager: Jennifer Gessner
Development Project Management: Aptara®, Inc.
Procurement Specialist: Pat Tonneman
Art Director: Jayne Conte
Cover Designer: Karen Salzbach
Cover Art: ©mlklekwoods, Fotolia
Media Project Manager: Noelle Chun
Full-Service Project Management: Munesh Kumar, Aptara®, Inc.
Composition: Aptara®, Inc.
Printer/Binder: LSC Communications
Cover Printer: LSC Communications
Text Font: Times Roman

Credits and acknowledgments borrowed from other sources and reproduced, with permission, in this textbook appear on appropriate page within the text.

Every effort has been made to provide accurate and current Internet information in this book. However, the Internet and information posted on it are constantly changing, so it is inevitable that some of the Internet addresses listed in this textbook will change.

This work was previously published under the title *Human Resources Administration in Education: A Management Approach.*

Library of Congress Cataloging-in-Publication Data

Rebore, Ronald W.

  Human resources administration in education / Ronald W. Rebore.—10th ed.
    p. cm.
  ISBN-13: 978-0-13-335193-4
  ISBN-10: 0-13-335193-9
  1. School personnel management—United States. I. Title.
  LB2831.58.R4295   2015
  371.2'010973—dc23

                                                                    2013033231

8 17

ISBN 13: 978-0-13-335193-4
ISBN 10:   0-13-335193-9

*I dedicate this book to my wife, Sandy;
to my two adult children, Ron and Lisa;
and my six grandchildren,
Will, Luke, Joe, Henry, Tessa, and Max.
From the beginning, they have been
my inspiration in this endeavor.*

BRIEF CONTENTS

CONTENTS

3   Recruitment   103

4   Selection   130

5 *Placement and Induction   161*

8 *Compensation*   *248*

9 *Collective Negotiations*   *303*

10   *Legal, Ethical, and Policy Issues in the Administration of Human Resources*   336

PREFACE

New to This Edition

The evolving culture of our contemporary society continues to have an ongoing and profound effect on the practice of human resources administration in schools and school districts that has necessitated a revision of the previous edition. An example of this evolving culture is set forth in a new section in each chapter concerning how technology affects the various dimensions of human resources administration. The use of technology has enriched the human resources function in virtually every public school and school district. Technology affects not only central office administration but also every level of instruction and learning.

Further, the American Recovery and Reinvestment Act of 2009 set aside billions of dollars for education that are beneficial to many public school districts adversely affected by the economic downturn. This is particularly true of many small- and medium-size school districts, which appear to have been more severely affected.

The tenth edition of *Human Resources Administration in Education* sets forth information relative to human resources administration that has surfaced since the publication of the ninth edition. Among other updated material, this edition:

- Incorporates throughout the text the effects of the economic downturn on human resources administration
- Uses more stories and personal examples in the form of focus scenarios at the beginning of each chapter
- Ends each chapter with a reflective question on the focus scenario
- Updates all endnotes to provide graduate students with the most up-to-date resources relevant to each chapter
- Updates all selected bibliographic material to give the graduate student access to the latest information on best practices in human resources administration
- Includes a section on value-added evaluations in Chapter 7
- Provides more extensive information on win–win collective negotiations in Chapter 8
- Weaves technology information throughout the text in terms of general language such as *social media*
- Moves crisis management to Chapter 10 because of legal and ethical considerations
- Emphasizes culture as a significant factor in dealing with human resources issues through stories and personal examples

Continuing Issues That Enhance the Tenth Edition

Legislation continues to have an impact on human resources management. The U.S. Congress enacted Title V of the Rehabilitation Act of 1973 and the Americans with

Disabilities Act of 1990, which is the most comprehensive legislation ever passed protecting the rights of individuals with disabilities. Furthermore, the Civil Rights Act of 1991 has the potential of costing violators punitive damages through the decisions of jury trials. In 1993, Congress also passed the Family and Medical Leave Act, which gives eligible employees the right to leave employment under certain circumstances. Testing for alcohol and controlled substances is now mandated for particular occupations, such as school bus drivers, by the Omnibus Transportation Employee Testing Act of 1991. The Health Insurance Portability and Accountability Act of 1996 assures employees that they, their spouses, and their dependents cannot be denied health insurance coverage because of an illness. In 2002, the No Child Left Behind Act ushered in the most extensive changes in federal law concerning public school education since the early 1970s. Beginning in 2001, military reserves and National Guard units have been mobilized into active duty as a consequence of the wars in Afghanistan and Iraq. This has prompted most human resources administrators to create policies and procedures that address school districts' responsibilities to those employees who have been called up for duty in the armed services.

Sexual harassment in the workplace has gained the attention of school district personnel across the United States as the media have presented coverage of the consequences of this inappropriate and illegal behavior. In addition, the phenomenon of collaborative bargaining as an alternative to the traditional model of negotiations has become more prevalent in school districts.

Health risks in the workplace, an issue that is related to the ever-increasing cost of workers' compensation, are seriously affecting school district budgets. Likewise, the costs of fringe benefits continue to rise, prompting managed healthcare as an alternative to traditional medical and hospital insurance programs.

The ethical responsibilities of human resources administrators have become a focus in light of the national concern over the honesty of employees in all levels of business, government, religion, and public education. The underlying cause of the "reform" movement is the level of accountability or lack thereof in public schools. Taxpayers in general and parents in particular believe that they are not receiving their proper entitlement. The problem of accountability is a "people" problem, and, thus, it is a human resources administration problem. An important response to this lack of accountability is to make transparent all of the financial transactions of the school district. Such transparency enhances accountability, which ensures equality of opportunity in all human resources policies and procedures.

It is evident that school district administration parallels that of corporations and other organizations in U.S. society. Fiscal management, curriculum development, physical plant management, employee supervision, and human resources administration have become specialties that require educationally sophisticated administrators.

The tenth edition of this book should be of interest to three categories of individuals: professors of educational administration, who have the responsibility of teaching courses in school human resources administration; practicing central office administrators and building principals, who want to become more familiar with the field of human resources management; and school board members and superintendents, who may be searching for a model in order to establish a central office human resources administrative position.

Chapter 1 establishes the rationale and organizational structure that support effective human resources administration. Chapters 2 through 5 are concerned with the acquisition of personnel, and Chapters 6 through 9 focus on personnel retention. Each chapter addresses a major dimension of the human resources management function and identifies the processes, procedures, and techniques necessary to carry out these dimensions. Finally, Chapter 10 considers the legal, ethical, and policy implications of human resources administration.

Acknowledgment

I give my sincere thanks to my professorial colleagues and their students who reviewed *Human Resources Administration in Education* and made valuable suggestions for improvement. I continue to incorporate as many of their suggestions as possible. I particularly want to thank the reviewers of this edition: Clay Baulch, Sul Ross State University–Rio Grande College; Edward P. Cox, University of South Carolina; Marla Israel, Loyola University Chicago; Ruthie S. Stevenson, Mississippi College; and Alan Vaughan, Cambridge College and Troy University. Also, my research assistant, Lina Harati, was most helpful as I prepared the material for the tenth edition.

R. W. R.

CHAPTER 1

Organizational Dimensions

Focus Scenario

You have just been hired as the assistant superintendent for human resources in a school district with four elementary schools, a middle school, and one high school. There is one other assistant superintendent responsible for curriculum development. The human resources department consists of just you and a secretary. The department has been functioning only in the areas of personnel recruitment and selection. Given the fact that no additional personnel will be added to the department, you have decided that the human resources function must become a shared responsibility with other administrators, teachers, and staff members in the district.

The school district has one hundred professional employees, which includes building-level administrators, teachers, counselors, and media specialists. There are thirty support personnel, including secretaries, bus drivers, maintenance workers, and housekeeping staff. There are approximately two thousand students in the school district.

The major issue facing the school district is the lack of financial resources. Over the past five years, the district has tried to increase the tax levy through two referendums, both of which failed. In addition, the new furniture factory in town has drawn many migrant workers and their families, necessitating the opening of additional classrooms and the hiring of additional language arts teachers who can instruct children in English as a second language.

Even though you meet all the requirements of the job description, the superintendent of schools and the members of the board of education are concerned as to whether you or, in fact, anyone will be able to develop an efficient and effective human resources department given the lack of resources in the school district. Also, you have had minimum experience in administering human resources from a central office perspective. However, they were impressed with your eagerness to try innovative methods. Obviously, the superintendent and the board members are particularly concerned about the way in which you intend to organize the department and engage other administrators, teachers, and staff members in carrying out the dimensions of the human resources function.

Please use both the "Discussion Questions and Statements" and "Suggested Activities" at the end of this chapter to help you develop a way of addressing the issues in this section.

Structural Framework of Public Education

The system of free and universal elementary and secondary education in the United States is one of our nation's unique and distinguishing characteristics. It is generally considered to be our greatest safeguard of freedom, and the best guarantee for the economic and social welfare of our citizens.

As an institution, the school receives its mandate from the society it serves. It is, however, only one of many institutions. The government, the family, and the church also play roles in our society, and these institutions have complementary purposes. Each provides for the advancement of society in general and the individual citizen in particular. The school's educational programs would be ineffective without the support of the government, the family, and the church. A hallmark, however, of modern-day society and these institutions is change, which is set forth dramatically in the book *Microtrends: The Small Forces Behind Tomorrow's Big Changes*, by Mark Penn and E. Kinney Zalesne. The authors identify seventy-five trends that are very powerful forces in our society, all emerging without the understanding of most members of our society but drastically changing our lives. The implication is that 1 percent of the population can have a significant effect on the lives of all Americans because of the impact of the Internet and other mass communication media on developing public attitudes and values.[1]

These notions focus on communicative and technological advancement, but in the complexity of any given society, infinite streams of change occur simultaneously. The family, the church, the school, and the government, with all their subcomponents, are not static institutions, but rather evolving entities. Change is not only continual but also accelerative, and it is further complicated by the fact that it occurs unevenly. Technology may be currently undergoing mutations faster than educational programs can make this new knowledge available, which in turn leaves students possibly years behind in learning about new advances.

Our perception of reality and how it relates to societal and individual needs determines the content of our educational programs. Although fundamental principles such as individual freedom, individual responsibility, and democratic government must be taught continuously in our schools, the accelerating rate of change in areas such as technology demands that our schools be flexible enough to adjust to new developments and conditions. Education cannot be static in the dynamic milieu of reality.

Responsibilities of Federal and State Governments

Carrying out the goals of American education is the responsibility of the individual states. The U.S. Constitution is conspicuous in its omission of any provision on or specific reference to education. The Tenth Amendment to the Constitution, ratified in 1791, states, "the powers not delegated to the United States by the Constitution, nor prohibited by it to the States, are reserved to the States respectively, or to the people." Thus, education has consistently been considered a state function.

Experience shows, however, that the federal government has been involved; in fact, its involvement has been extensive. Through the legislative branch, Congress provides funds that support special services and programs in local school districts. Through the U.S. Office of Education, the executive branch of the government first exercised authority over educational matters. The creation of a Cabinet-level Department of Education exemplifies the extent of this involvement. The many Supreme Court decisions affecting education testify to the influence of the judicial branch of the federal government on our schools.

In an ever-shrinking world and nation, the goals of U.S. education cannot be left solely to the discretion of the states. The involvement of the federal government, however, should not supplant the jurisdiction of state governments, but rather should complement and enrich those efforts.

The authority of the states to create and govern public schools is embodied in the state constitutions and exercised through the state legislatures. All state legislatures have delegated certain aspects of this authority to local units—boards of education. To ensure some control over local units, state legislatures have established minimum educational program and teacher certification requirements and have provided state funds to help finance education.

The administrative arm of most state legislatures is a state department of education, which is usually governed by a board and administered by a commissioner or state superintendent. Figure 1.1 illustrates the relationship between the state and local boards of education.

The National Council of Chief State School Officers and all other national associations of school board members, superintendents of schools, and other administrator organizations emphasize the state's educational responsibility and the state's relationship to local and federal agencies.

The organizational structure of educational governance in the United States is predicated on the constitutional premise that public education is a function of state government. Thus, through its constitution and legislation, each state is responsible for the organization and administration of public education and for general supervision of nonpublic schools. It is common practice for state boards of education to delegate the authority to organize and operate schools to various types of local governance and administrative structures. Local boards of education create the policies that govern school districts, and such boards hire superintendents of schools to administer the educational services and implement the policies of their respective boards. However, there is a shared interest in public education among local, state, and federal governments because of the importance of an educated citizenry. It is our safeguard of freedom to have citizens who understand the structure of government and who participate in our representative form of government.

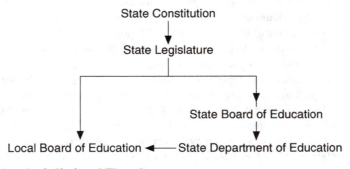

FIGURE 1.1   Jurisdictional Flowchart

Further, each branch of government must provide the services that are under its jurisdiction in order to support the total educational responsibility. Thus, the local boards of education initiate the educational enterprise, whereas the states provide the funding and monitoring necessary to achieve equality of educational opportunity. The federal government must provide funds and support to safeguard the interests of the United States.[2]

No Child Left Behind and School Reform

President George W. Bush signed the No Child Left Behind Act (NCLB) into law in January 2002; this new law reauthorized the Elementary and Secondary Education Act. NCLB ushered in the most extensive changes in federal law concerning public school education in forty years. It is the first time that federal legislation mandated student success; all other federal legislation mandated opportunity rather than success.

The law requires all children to be proficient in reading and mathematics by 2014. Other provisions of the law mandate improved communications with parents and improved safety at school for children. Although NCLB has certain provisions that apply only to Title I schools, the law clearly requires all states to develop a single system of accountability so there are uniform standards for all children. Further, schools are required to make adequate yearly progress (AYP) toward the 2014 goal. Thus, each state must develop student testing programs that demonstrate satisfactory student improvement each year. States are also required to pay particular attention to the progress of children from minority groups such as African Americans, Asians, and Hispanics. Children with disabilities form another identifiable group whose progress must be monitored for AYP.

The consequences of not achieving AYP vary from being designated as a school needing improvement to, after five years of not achieving AYP, being a school facing severe repercussions, such as having school personnel replaced or the school year extended. Further, if a student is a victim of a violent crime, that student must be allowed to transfer to another school in the district. Of course, problems with this provision arise if there is only one school with the appropriate grade level in the district, or if other schools are far from the student's home school.[3]

For human resources administration, the provisions of NCLB require serious attention. First, the requirement to hire highly qualified teachers who are capable of helping students meet the proficiency requirement places a significant responsibility on all administrators, faculty, and staff members involved in the human resources function.[4] Chapter 2 of this text, "Human Resources Planning," sets forth a planning process that places a high priority on identifying the present and future goals of a school district as they relate to the current and future qualifications needed in employees. Chapter 3, "Recruitment," explains the methods that can be used to locate and attract the best possible candidates for administrative, faculty, and support positions in a school district. Chapter 4, "Selection," outlines the steps that can be used to hire the most qualified applicants.

The provision that students must demonstrate AYP has serious implications for teacher performance evaluation and staff development. Chapter 7, "Performance Evaluation," explains best practice in the evaluation of school district employees such as administrators, teachers, and support personnel. Chapter 6, "Staff Development," sets forth a critical dimension of the human resources function because a continual upgrade of knowledge and skills is required to meet the ever-changing needs of students. Further, research is constantly improving our subject-matter knowledge base and pedagogical methodologies.

Finally, the consequences for noncompliance with AYP for five years may result in the replacement of administrators, teachers, or staff members. Chapter 7, "Performance Evaluation," also contains an extended section on how to ensure due process for those administrators, teachers, and staff members who are not meeting expectations, which could lead to termination of employment.

Highlighting these particular chapters is meant to focus attention to specific processes and procedures. However, the human resources function, as laid out in this text, is a seamless function with various dimensions. It would be a mistake to think that the various provisions of NCLB affect only certain aspects of the human resources function; rather, the law affects all interrelated dimensions of this function.

NCLB is a particular manifestation of school reform. The reform movement is always present in education because change and improvement are embedded in the education profession. The development of each child's potential to his or her maximum capacity is the goal of education. The culture of society is the milieu within which administrators, teachers, and staff members must carry out their responsibilities. Thus, school reform occupies the attention of all administrators, particularly human resources administrators, because people are the initiators and implementers of reform.

There are certain directions that are prevalent in the present reform movement. Perhaps the most evident is the *learning community approach*, which views learning as the major focus of all endeavors. Not only students but also educators are encouraged to learn from each other. This situates schools and school districts in such a manner that the organization itself, as a system and in a corporate sense, begins to learn. Thus, schools and school districts become reframed.

Reform begins with a vision formalized in individual schools through the leadership of the principal and the teachers. Evidence-based decisions must be made by the leadership team, the principal, and teachers to formulate objectives and strategies to improve student performance. Today, this assessment and the formulation of objectives and strategies can be significantly enhanced through technology.

Thus, formulas for successful reform have some common elements, including the following:

- Vision that uses a learning community approach and leads to organizational reform[5]
- Establishment, in each school, of a leadership team that includes teachers in consort with the principal[6]
- Importance placed on making decisions based on evidence
- Beneficial use of technology in management and instructional strategies

These factors clearly recognize the significance of establishing a human resources function capable of planning, recruiting, and retaining the best educators possible; reform is dependent on the quality of the people hired to carry it out.

Responsibilities of the Board of Education

School districts are perhaps the most democratically controlled of any agencies of government. The citizens of a local community elect school board members who are charged with formulating policies for the governance and administration of the schools. State departments of education exercise some regulatory authority, assuring that a minimum educational program is provided in every school district, but the citizens of the local districts maintain control of the schools through locally elected boards.

As the duties and responsibilities of school boards are considered, it is essential to bear in mind that education is a state function. The courts have consistently upheld this principle. By virtue of the authority delegated to school boards from each state legislature, boards represent the state even though the members are locally elected. Board members, as individuals, exercise no authority outside a legally constituted meeting. Policies can be agreed on only in an official meeting, and individual members cannot commit the board to any definite action except as authorized by the board at a legal meeting.

In exercising their authority to govern schools, boards of education should formulate and adopt policy statements carefully. This difficult task cannot be accomplished successfully without guidance from the professional educational staff and, at times, an attorney. Board policies must not conflict with the U.S. Constitution, federal law, or federal court decisions. In like manner, policies must not conflict with the appropriate state constitution, statutes, and court decisions. Regulations issued by a state department of education should be considered by a board in creating policies but may be ignored. However, penalties such as loss of state aid make it impractical for a school board to create policies in conflict with such regulations. Local traditions, opinions, and goals should also be taken into consideration because policies objectionable to the local community will weaken citizen support. There are many more influences in our contemporary society that affect board decisions today than there were even five years ago. Figure 1.2 illustrates some of these influences on policy formulation.

Some advantages of developing policies are outlined in the book *The School and Community Relations* and may serve as a rationale for school boards:

- Policy facilitates the orientation of new board members regarding relations between the school and the community.
- Policy facilitates a similar orientation for new employees, both professional and nonprofessional, in the school system.
- Policy acquaints the public with the position of the school board and encourages citizen involvement in educational affairs.
- Policy provides a reasonable guarantee that there will be consistency and continuity in the decisions that are made under it.

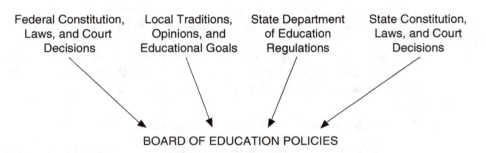

FIGURE 1.2   Influences on Policy Making

- Policy informs superintendents what they may expect from the board and what the board may expect from them.
- Policy creates the need for developing a detailed program in order to implement it.
- Policy provides a legal reason for the allocation of funds and facilities in order to make the policy work.
- Policy establishes an essential division between policy making and policy administration.[7]

School board policies should not be confused with administrative rules and regulations, which constitute the detailed manner by which policies are implemented. Rules and regulations delineate who does what, when, and where. In fact, many rules and regulations may be required to implement one policy.

Board of education policies should be stated in broad, general terms but be clear enough to allow for executive direction and interpretation. The policies reveal the philosophy of the board of education and provide the rationale for the subject about which a policy is being made. The policy may also suggest how it is to be carried out, but it should never be executive in substance or tone. Policies treat situations that are likely to occur repeatedly and are subject to continual review by the board so as to be sensitive to changing conditions. In like manner, policies authorize all school programs and activities, and provide stability when there is a change in personnel. In format, policies should be brief, clear, concise, and complete.

After the board of education establishes its policies, the superintendent of schools and his or her staff are responsible for establishing administrative processes and procedures that implement the board policies. These policies are usually also incorporated into a manual that can easily be consulted by administrators, teachers, and citizens.

There are four popular formats used in writing policies, the most common of which is the resolution style, on which the school board votes to take action. Equal employment opportunity and affirmative action policies are usually adopted in this resolution style. A second format sets forth the rationale for the policy and establishes broad goals. The third style incorporates an identification of who is responsible for implementing the policy. This is a common practice in formulating policies that address a specific function such as collective bargaining. For example, the policy might identify the director of employee relations as the chief negotiator for the school board and establish the confines within which he or she will function. A fourth format is used when the school board wants to eliminate possible misunderstanding about how the policy is to be implemented. This type of style, therefore, incorporates administrative rules and regulations.

Administrative Process

Theoretical Considerations

Administration is an indispensable component of all institutions in organized society, yet it is often taken for granted. The need for administration becomes evident whenever a task has to be performed by two or more people. Many ancient records of significant events describe administrative activities. Building the pyramids, supervising medieval feudal domains, and governing colonies in distant hemispheres have demanded a degree of administrative skill and knowledge of the administrative process.

Our understanding of the nature of administration has evolved. The earliest concepts centered on the action model. Administrators were those who took charge of an activity and accomplished a task. The formal study of administration is a recent phenomenon that has found its most fertile climate in the business world, where much study is devoted to the execution of managerial leadership.

The need for the formal study of administration in public education grew out of the increased complexity of urban school districts. The illusion that anyone with a good general education could become an effective administrator was quickly shattered during the urbanization period.

Administration is the social process of managing human, financial, and material resources toward the fulfillment of a mission. The school administrator fulfills these requisites by developing and establishing administrative processes, procedures, and techniques that harness human, financial, and material energies. The importance of administrative leadership stems from its potential for converting these energies within an organization into the fulfillment of educational objectives.

This definition of *administration* views it as an executive activity, distinct from policy making. Administration is primarily concerned with the implementation, not the making, of policy. More specifically, the administration of a district is responsible for carrying out the policies of the board of education.

The systems approach to administration has gained steadily in popularity ever since President Lyndon B. Johnson mandated its implementation in federal agencies and the outcry for accountability in the public sector advanced its use. In the systems approach, the school is viewed as a network of interrelated subsystems. Emphasis is given to formulating short- and long-range objectives that can be translated into operational activities that are implemented and evaluated.

The approach followed in this text focuses on the human resources function as a function. Thus, administration is viewed as an all-encompassing process composed of various functions. Three of the most critical functions in a school system are human resources administration, instructional programs administration, and support services administration. Support services include transportation, food services, and financial administration. Each of these functions has goals that are implemented through administrative processes, procedures, and techniques, which are collectively referred to as *management*. This text, of course, centers on the human resources function and its management.

Functions are carried out by administrators within a given organizational framework. The remaining portion of this section delineates and clarifies the role of the superintendent of schools and major central office administrators.

Organization of the Central Office

Historically and, in most states, by statutory mandate, school boards have delegated the responsibility for implementing policies to a chief executive officer—the superintendent of schools. The superintendent assumes full control of all operations. As school districts grow in size and complexity, it becomes necessary to develop specialized functions, and the central office staff comes into being. However, school district employees, professional and otherwise, ultimately report to the superintendent and are subordinate to him or her. The superintendent is the only employee who deals with the board of education on a regular and direct basis.

The superintendent's role can be described in terms of the three major roles incorporated into this one position: chief advisor, executive officer, and educational leader.

Chief Advisor

The superintendent is the main consultant and advisor to the school board on all matters concerning the school district. As such, he or she is expected to contribute to the board's deliberations by furnishing reports, information, and recommendations, both on request of the board and through self-directed initiative. A list of the superintendent's duties and functions as the board's chief advisor includes the following:

- Formulate and recommend human resources policies necessary for the efficient functioning of the school staff.
- Provide information to the school board on vital matters pertaining to the school system.
- Prepare and submit to the board a preliminary budget.
- Provide employment recommendations for candidates. (Candidates should be employed only on recommendation of the superintendent even though the board has the authority to reject specific candidates.)
- Submit an annual report to the board on the operations of the school system.

Executive Officer

Once the board of education establishes a policy decision, it becomes the responsibility of the executive officer of the board and the district's staff to execute that decision. The administration should implement board policies via rules and regulations. As the chief executive officer of the district, the superintendent sets the tone for the entire system. In performing this function, the duties and responsibilities of the superintendent are as follows:

- Carry out policies and regulations established by the board. (In matters not specifically covered by board policies, the superintendent should take appropriate action and report the action to the board no later than the next meeting.)
- Prepare regulations and instruct school employees as necessary to make effective the policies of the board.
- Direct purchases and expenditures in accordance with the policies of the board.
- Formulate and administer a program of supervision for the schools.
- Develop a program of maintenance and improvement or expansion of buildings and site.

Educational Leader

The superintendent's educational leadership role should be exercised not only with other professional educators within the district but also with regional, state, and national professional educators, organizations, and agencies. As the educational leader within the community, the superintendent will be called on to keep the public informed as to the activities, achievements, needs, and directions of the school system. The superintendent should also keep the members of the board informed of new trends in education and their implications for the local district. A leadership role must also be assumed among the staff members of the school district. Without the support and understanding of the employees, the goals and objectives set by the district cannot be achieved.[8]

An ongoing reality in school administration, particularly in the superintendency, is the administrative team approach to central office and building-level management. In most districts, the administrative team is a group of administrators who oversee certain responsibilities of the superintendent of schools. Each administrator usually has the title of *deputy*, *associate*, or *assistant superintendent*. In most school districts, personnel having the title of *director* or *coordinator* are not members of the administrative team, but rather support personnel to the team.

Members of the administrative team are formally designated by appointment to the superintendent's cabinet, which is a strategy-planning and decision-making body. The heads of human resources administration, instructional programs administration, and support services administration are typically included in the cabinet.

This formal organization of the superintendent's cabinet is not meant to imply that the superintendent should confine the "team" effort only to the highest levels of school district administration. Rather, the establishment of a cabinet is an attempt to share the strategy-planning process with key administrators. The issues and problems facing school districts are so far-reaching today that the superintendent must have continual and effective counsel in making decisions.

Because school districts need to identify various echelons in the administrative organization, it is recommended that the title of *director* or *coordinator* be attached to administrative positions reporting to an assistant superintendent in charge of a particular function. Although not meant to be all inclusive, Figure 1.3 represents a possible central office organization that incorporates a line authority from superintendent to assistant superintendents (cabinet positions) to directors. The number of central office administrators shown suggests that this could be the organizational structure for a school district with a student population of approximately 25,000. Please note that the director of affirmative action and director of community relations report directly to the superintendent, which is a common practice.

Human Resources Administration

Human Resources Function

In every school district, people must be recruited, selected, placed, evaluated, and compensated, whether by a central human resources office or by various administrators within the school district.

The goals of the human resources function are basically the same in all school systems: to hire, retain, develop, and motivate personnel to achieve the objectives of the school district; to assist individual members of the staff to reach the highest possible levels of achievement; and to maximize the career development of personnel. These goals must be implemented through the following dimensions of the human resources function:

- *Human resources planning.* Establishing a master plan of long- and short-range human resources requirements is a vital part of the school district's curricular and fiscal planning processes.

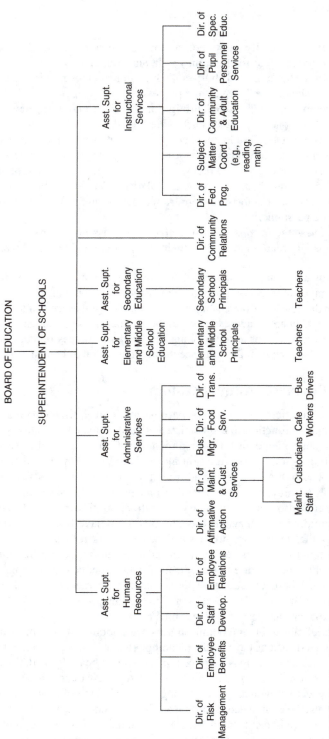

FIGURE 1.3 Possible Central Office Organization

11

- *Recruitment.* Quality personnel, of course, are essential for the delivery of effective educational services to children, youth, and adults.
- *Selection.* The long- and short-range human resources requirements are implemented through selection techniques and processes.
- *Placement and induction.* Through appropriate planning, new personnel and the school district accommodate each other's goals.
- *Staff development.* Development programs help personnel meet school district objectives, and also provide individuals with the opportunity for personal and professional growth.
- *Performance evaluation.* Processes and techniques for evaluation help the individual grow professionally and help the school district attain its objectives.
- *Compensation.* Establishing programs that compensate quality performance helps motivate personnel.
- *Collective negotiations.* The negotiating process gives personnel an opportunity to participate in matters that affect their professional and personal welfare.

Unfortunately, many school districts still see the human resources function only as the hiring of competent teachers. The eight dimensions of the human resources function discussed here are not discrete and isolated entities, but rather integral aspects of the same function. Each of the next eight chapters addresses one of these dimensions. Administrative processes, procedures, and techniques for accomplishing the human resources function are reviewed. Also, major issues that significantly influence the administration of human resources are addressed.

Human Resources Administrators

Many school districts have more recently seen the need to delegate a major share of the human resources function to a specialized central office unit. In this type of organization, an assistant superintendent for human resources (or director of human resources) administers the human resources function and aids the superintendent in solving personnel problems. The human resources administrator is usually a staff position that exists to service line administrators. Line positions include the assistant superintendents for secondary education and elementary education, administrators of certain support services, and building principals. These administrators have been granted authority to make decisions in the supervisory process as it relates to staff, faculty, and students.

The human resources function not only has an impact on the continual staffing of positions, which in turn directly affects the quality of educational programs, but it also has a significant effect on the budget. Approximately 80 percent of school district expenditures are for salaries and benefits. Inefficiency in the human resources function can potentially cost the taxpayer unnecessarily large sums of money.

Boards of education and administrators are seldom fully aware of the pervasive effect their personnel decisions have on the planning process. Every position within a school system generates a series of decisions as to the type of work to be performed, the qualities needed for its proper performance, and its economic value. A variety of actions is required for the proper recruiting, selecting, inducting, developing, and evaluating of personnel. Policies and procedures must also be established regarding academic freedom, tenure, health, grievances, leaves of absence, and retirement. In all but the very smallest districts, the movement of personnel into and out of a school district requires the attention of human resources specialists.

The number of strikes by public school teachers has remained relatively constant since the early 2000s. Salaries, fringe benefits, and working conditions constitute the major issues that may lead to an impasse at the table and result in a strike. Education, however, is a relative newcomer to the negotiations process.

Collective negotiation is traditionally a human resources function and correctly belongs under the jurisdiction of the assistant superintendent for human resources. Because of the magnitude of the issues involved with this process, most school districts should consider establishing the position of director of employee relations. The American Association of School Administrators sponsored the publication of a monograph entitled *Helping Administrators Negotiate*, with the prophetic subtitle of *A Profile of the Emerging Management Position of Director of Employee Relations in the Administrative Structure of a School System*.

The knowledge explosion and the constantly changing social milieu have also produced a major issue in the area of human resources administration. In the past, staff development was viewed primarily from the in-service training model, which concentrated on providing a few workshops on instructional materials. The past quarter century, however, has ushered in federal legislation and litigation that have more clearly defined the rights of racial minorities, women, students, older workers, and people with disabilities. This, coupled with the deluge of new instructional technologies, the differing attitudes of the new professionals entering teaching, and the changing values of our society as manifested by parents and students, has created a need for an ongoing staff development program for administrators and teachers alike. This function is so specialized that, like collective negotiations, it requires the attention of a human resources specialist—the director of staff development.

The avalanche of federal legislation and litigation concerning human rights has made it necessary to establish a central office administrative position, usually entitled *director of affirmative action*. Most federal legislation contains an equal opportunity clause, which in turn dictates the organization of a detailed program for carrying out the intent of the law in all phases of the human resources function. This organized program is more commonly called *affirmative action*. Chapter 2 presents a complete explanation of major civil rights legislation and the concept of affirmative action. A unique feature of this administrative position in the organizational structure of a school district is the fact that the director of affirmative action usually reports directly to the superintendent of schools. This provides integrity in the school district's compliance with civil rights legislation because the director is thus protected from the influences of other administrators.

The escalating cost of healthcare is an issue facing every school district that provides healthcare and related benefits to employees. Most school districts have undertaken drastic measures in an attempt to control costs, which has led to what is commonly referred to as *managed care*. Along with the many innovations under way is the need to hire human resources staff members who not only have experience but also have academic credentials in healthcare management. Further, the rising cost of workers' compensation reinforces the need to hire human resources staff members who have experience with and understand the nuances of risk management. Most school districts use the title *director of employee benefits* to designate the staff member who is responsible for managing the employee benefits and workers' compensation programs. The administrator, of course, reports to the assistant superintendent for human resources.

Contemporary society is fraught with risks to personal security and safety. This has been graphically embedded in the consciousness of all Americans because of the enormous loss of life in schools over the past decade due to student violence perpetrated against other students, teachers, staff members, and administrators. People from outside the school community have also entered school buildings and committed violent acts against students and employees. In addition, there is the ever-present risk of injury to students and employees because of accidents stemming from school facilities and equipment. Finally, risk also arises from the potential breach of confidentiality in relation to student and employee records. Safety and security audits, rules, and procedures must be developed in order to ensure, as much as possible, a risk-free environment for both students and employees. This has prompted school districts to create the position of director of risk management.

The job description for the director of employee relations was modeled on the description in *Helping Administrators Negotiate* published by the American Association of School Administrators, which is out of print (see Exhibit 1.1).

EXHIBIT 1.1   Six Major Human Resources Specialists

Personal abilities and characteristics are universal for all administrators. The superintendent, assistant superintendents, directors, and building principals must have good human relations skills; good writing skills; work well with details; and must be self-starters. The descriptions provided here should be seen as building on this foundation.

Job Description for the Assistant Superintendent for Human Resources

Job Summary

The assistant superintendent for human resources (or director of human resources) is responsible for managing the school district's human resources program, including the establishment and maintenance of effective two-way communications between the various organizational levels, as well as the formulation, recommendation, and administration of the school district's human resources policies.

Organizational Relationships

The assistant superintendent has a line relationship with and reports directly to the superintendent of schools. He or she serves as the superintendent's chief advisor on human resources matters and has a staff relationship with other administrative personnel. The assistant superintendent for human resources has a line relationship with his or her immediate staff, which includes the director of employee relations, the director of staff development, the director of employee benefits, and the director of risk management. These administrators report directly to the assistant superintendent.

Organizational Tasks

The assistant superintendent for human resources is directly responsible for establishing administrative processes, procedures, and techniques for human resources planning, recruitment of staff, selection of personnel, the placement and induction of personnel, staff evaluation, and compensation programs. He or she is further responsible for supervising the director of employee relations, the director of staff development, the director of employee benefits, and the director of risk management.

Job Qualifications

In terms of education and experience, the assistant superintendent for human resources should possess the following:

- Appropriate state administrator certification
- A doctorate in educational administration
- Formal course work in the areas of curriculum, finance, school law, human resources administration, and collective negotiations
- Classroom teaching experience and five years as a building-level administrator

EXHIBIT 1.1

Job Description for the
Director of Employee Relations

Job Summary

The director of employee relations is responsible for the administration of the school district's management–employee relations program. This includes establishing and maintaining effective two-way communications between the various organizational levels; formulating, recommending, and administering the school district's management–employee relations policies, as well as administering the collective negotiations process.

Organizational Relationships

The director of employee relations has a line relationship with and reports directly to the assistant superintendent for human resources. He or she serves as the assistant superintendent's chief advisor on employee relations. He or she has a staff relationship with other administrative personnel. The director of employee relations has a cooperative–professional relationship with non-administrative personnel with whom he or she negotiates. Of course, the director has a line relationship with his or her immediate staff, and they report directly to the director.

Organizational Tasks

In preparing for negotiations, the director of employee relations shall

- Develop negotiations strategies for management
- Prepare proposals and counterproposals for management
- Analyze and evaluate employee proposals and advise management accordingly
- Know state laws and court decisions relevant to professional negotiations
- Secure input from all administrative personnel prior to developing management's proposals

In at-the-table negotiations, the director of employee relations shall

- Serve as the chief negotiator for the school district

- Direct the school district's negotiations team
- Keep administrative personnel informed during negotiations
- Draft negotiated agreements reached with unions
- Maintain records of proposals and counterproposals presented by all parties during negotiations

In administering the negotiated agreement, the director of employee relations shall

- Serve as the school district's chief advisor in the interpretation of adopted agreements
- Serve as the school district's chief advisor in all grievance matters
- Consult with principals and other supervisors concerning their understanding of and compliance with the adopted agreements
- Initiate management's grievances and mediation activities

Job Qualifications

In terms of education and experience, the director of employee relations should possess

- Appropriate state administrator certification
- Master's degree (minimum)
- Formal course work in the areas of educational administration, with exposure to courses in curriculum, finance, school law, collective negotiations, and human resources administration
- Classroom teaching experience and at least two years as a building principal

Job Description for the
Director of Staff Development

Job Summary

The director of staff development is responsible for the management of the school district's staff development program. This includes the establishment and maintenance of effective two-way communications between the various organizational levels, as well as the formulation, recommendation, and administration of the school district's staff development policies.

Continued

EXHIBIT 1.1 *Continued*

Organizational Relationships

The director of staff development has a line relationship with and reports directly to the assistant superintendent for human resources. He or she serves as the assistant superintendent's chief advisor on staff development matters. The director of staff development has a staff relationship with other administrative personnel and has a cooperative–professional relationship with nonadministrative personnel with whom he or she works. The director has a line relationship with his or her immediate staff, and they report directly to him or her.

Organizational Tasks

In planning and implementing a staff development program, the director shall

- Establish and implement ongoing needs assessment techniques with all personnel
- Analyze and evaluate assessment instruments
- Secure input from administrative personnel concerning the most desirable time and place for program presentation
- Evaluate program presentations

Job Qualifications

In terms of education and experience, the director of staff development should possess

- Master's degree (minimum)
- Formal course work in the areas of testing and measurement, statistics, curriculum, and supervision
- A minimum of two years professional experience as a teacher or building administrator

Job Description for the Director of Affirmative Action

Job Summary

The director of affirmative action is responsible for administering the school district's affirmative action program. This includes establishing and maintaining effective two-way communications between organizational levels, as well as formulating, recommending, and administering the school district's affirmative action policies.

Organizational Relationships

The director of affirmative action has a line relationship with and reports directly to the superintendent of schools. He or she serves as the superintendent's chief advisor on affirmative action matters. The director of affirmative action has a staff relationship with other administrative personnel, and has a cooperative–professional relationship with nonadministrative personnel with whom he or she works. Of course, the director has a line relationship with his or her immediate staff, and they report directly to the director.

Organizational Tasks

The director of affirmative action is responsible for the following tasks:

- Studying affirmative action problems and suggesting solutions to the superintendent, if possible
- Using school district data in reviewing the qualifications of all employees, with particular emphasis on minorities, women, older workers, and people with disabilities as the data relate to fair employment practices
- Developing and updating goals and timetables for correcting identifiable deficiencies
- Advising the superintendent on recruitment of minorities, women, older workers, and people with disabilities for those classified, and positions in which they may be falling short of the district's affirmative action goals
- Assuming the role of compliance officer and making all contacts with state and federal agencies
- Reviewing all job announcements, job descriptions, and selection criteria to ensure compliance with affirmative action requirements
- Briefing the superintendent on the nature, purpose, and intent of all laws, executive orders, policies, regulations, and reports of external agencies that affect the school district's affirmative action program
- Helping district administrators investigate formal complaints of alleged discrimination

EXHIBIT 1.1

relating to fair employment practices, and recommending corrective measures to the superintendent

- Maintaining liaison with local, state, and federal agencies and with organizations concerned with promoting fair employment practices
- Representing the school district at meetings, conferences, and other gatherings pertaining to the affirmative action program
- Working with appropriate individuals and agencies in ascertaining correct population characteristic data for the district
- Compiling an annual report to the superintendent on the progress of the school district's affirmative action program

Job Qualifications

In terms of education and experience, the director of affirmative action should possess

- A master's degree (minimum)
- Formal course work in the areas of educational administration, with exposure to school law, collective negotiations, and human resources administration
- Classroom teaching experience, two years as a building principal, and two years as a central office administrator

Job Description for the Director of Employee Benefits

Job Summary

The director of employee benefits is responsible for the management of the school district's benefits program, including the establishment and maintenance of effective two-way communication between the various organizational levels, as well as the formulation, recommendation, and administration of the school district's employee benefits policies.

Organizational Relationships

The director of employee benefits has a line relationship with and reports directly to the assistant superintendent for human resources. He or she serves as the assistant superintendent's chief advisor on employee benefits and has a staff relationship

with other administrative personnel. The director of employee benefits has a cooperative–professional relationship with nonadministrative personnel with whom he or she works. Of course, the director has a line relationship with his or her immediate staff, and they report directly to him or her.

Organizational Tasks

In planning and implementing the employee benefits program, the director shall

- Establish and implement ongoing monitoring techniques to evaluate the cost effectiveness and efficient management of the benefits program
- Establish and chair the employee benefits committee, which is charged with reviewing employee benefits, making suggestions for improving benefits, making suggestions for containing costs, reviewing specifications for bidding benefits insurance, reviewing the analysis of bids, and annually making recommendations to the superintendent of schools
- Collaborate with personnel from the procurement department in developing specifications for bidding benefits insurance
- Develop, implement, and evaluate an annual survey of employee perceptions concerning the scope and effectiveness of the benefits program
- Serve as the liaison between the district and those companies providing healthcare and related insurance
- Develop informational materials and provide presentations to employees about the district's benefits program

In planning and implementing the workers' compensation program, the director shall

- Establish and implement ongoing monitoring techniques to evaluate the cost effectiveness and efficient management of the workers' compensation program
- Collaborate with personnel from the procurement department in developing specifications for bidding workers' compensation insurance
- Serve as the liaison between the district and the company providing workers' compensation insurance

Continued

EXHIBIT 1.1 *Continued*

Job Qualifications

In terms of education and experience, the director of employee benefits should possess

- A bachelor's degree (minimum)
- Formal course work in the areas of human resources administration, benefits management, risk management, insurance management, and workers' compensation
- Three years' experience in at least one of the following areas: human resources administration, benefits management, insurance management, or workers' compensation management

Job Description for the Director of Risk Management

Job Summary

The director of risk management is responsible for administering the school district's risk management program, including establishing and maintaining effective two-way communications between organizational levels, as well as formulating, recommending, and administering the school district's risk management policies.

Organizational Relationships

The director of risk management has a line relationship with and reports directly to the assistant superintendent for human resources. He or she serves as the assistant superintendent's chief advisor on risk management matters. The director of risk management has a staff relationship with other administrative personnel and has a cooperative–professional relationship with nonadministrative personnel with whom he or she works. The director has a line relationship with his or her immediate staff, and they report directly to him or her.

Organizational Tasks

In planning and implementing the risk management program, the director shall

- Establish and chair the employee safety and security committee, which is charged with reviewing safety and security rules and procedures, making suggestions for improving safety and security rules and procedures, reviewing specifications for bidding risk management services and equipment, and reviewing the analysis of bids
- Develop, implement, and evaluate an annual safety and security audit
- Develop informational materials concerning safety and security on the job, and providing safety and security education and training to employees
- Develop an annual safety and security report for the assistant superintendent for human resources that contains recommendations for improving the school district's safety and security program
- Investigate, assess, and manage safety and security crisis events

Job Qualifications

In terms of education and experience, the director of risk management should possess

- A bachelor's degree (minimum)
- Formal course work in the areas of risk management, human resources administration, and workers' compensation management
- Three years' experience in at least one of the following areas: risk management, safety and security education and training, safety and security assessment, or workers' compensation management

Leadership Theories for Human Resources Administration

Numerous leadership theories are currently in vogue. The most recent are the search for excellence, seven habits of highly effective people, learning organization, new science of leadership, school-based management, cultural leadership, transformational leadership, total quality management, and transcendental leadership. Only two of these theories, transcendental leadership and total quality management, are presented here because they appear to be the most appropriate theories for human resources administration.[9]

Transcendental Leadership

There are three major reasons why transcendental leadership[10] is an appropriate theory for human resources administrators. First, human resources administration operates within a very complex, ambiguous, and stressful milieu. Second, like other educational administrators, human resources administrators are required to perform their responsibilities even though they may not have job security. Finally, boards of education continue to cross the line between governance and administration.

In addition, superintendents, principals, other administrators, and human resources administrators are often criticized or blamed for poor performance of students on standardized tests, substandard teacher performance, outdated curricula, student violence, and a lack of financial stewardship. Although some of these criticisms are legitimate in some schools and school districts, they do not accurately represent the general condition. In spite of such criticism and difficulties, a major influence in the lives of most administrators, including human resources administrators, is the search for meaning that goes beyond the paycheck and prestige that come from being a superintendent, principal, or human resources administrator. This search for meaning may be identified in a concise way as the *transcendent dimension of leadership.*

In this context, *transcendence* means a way of life dedicated to leadership within and on behalf of the academic community and profession, rather than simply finding an administrative position in order to make a living. Obviously, making a living is an important consideration for everyone. However, without a sense of transcendence, administrators may concentrate on performing tasks and neglect to reflect on their overall reasons for being educational leaders.

Accepting the transcendence of leadership requires a person to undertake a lifelong process of discerning how he or she can be of service to the academic community and profession while carrying out the tasks and responsibilities of his or her leadership position within a given school or school district. This sense of service is difficult to sustain unless a person has an agenda to follow. Operating from such a theoretical base ensures that a person will develop and maintain effective job performance. In this context, such an agenda consists of the elements in a transcendental model of leadership.

Because administrators in general—and human resources administrators in particular—are concerned with human growth and development, they are generally more open to the cultural differences that exist between people and institutions. The basic premise of transcendental leadership is that a person acts from the totality of who he or she is as a human. Most administrators are generally aware that their decisions are influenced by more than just the immediately recognizable circumstances, and that the effects of their decisions can go beyond the present situation.

Transcendental leadership has two components: First, there are six elements that pertain to dispositions that individual human resources administrators should possess in order to be centered on human growth and development. Second, there are ten focuses that establish a transcendental culture in a school district. Such a culture is organizationally supportive of human growth and development.

Elements of Transcendental Leadership

Operationalization is a process that includes various elements activated to guarantee that a theory is practiced properly. Many different theories have similar elements, but it is the combination of elements and the disposition of the person using the theory that make it effective. There are six elements that comprise transcendental leadership theory, and these can be applied specifically to human resources administrators.

1. *Utilize reflection on practice.* The first element takes into account the importance of practice as the phenomenon on which theory and foundational values are based. Everything begins with practice. Knowing and understanding what is occurring in human resources administration practice is the only way to evaluate effective leadership. Leadership cannot be a top-down phenomenon, but rather must begin with the processes and practices of human resources administration. This includes knowing and understanding the attitudes, emotions, and opinions of all stakeholders.

2. *Practice the principle of subsidiarity.* This element has a unique history in that it originated in social ethics and social economics. The principle of subsidiarity states that decisions should be made at the lowest possible level in a given school district. There is no question about the relevance of allowing administrators to do their jobs without interference but with monitoring from others. There is also no question about the firsthand knowledge and experience that administrators have, which make them eminently more qualified than others to handle specific issues and problems. Thus, the performance evaluation process must be implemented by first-line supervisors, with support from the human resources department. The human resources function cannot be operationalized without input and assistance from other members of the school district community, as discussed in subsequent chapters.

3. *Act from a political base.* The third element refers to the human phenomenon whereby people try to manage the impact that their actions and decisions will have on the actions and decisions of others and on institutions. In human resources administration, the conceptualization of what constitutes a political base can be understood in a primary tension, the rights of government versus the rights of the individual. The role and function of administrators is to ensure that the rights of individual students, parents, teachers, staff members, and others are not in conflict with the rights of the local, state, and national governments. For example, a certain amount of tension exists between the right of the U.S. Congress to pass the Omnibus Transportation Employee Testing Act of 1991 and the right of employees to due process in the workplace.

4. *Act from a sense of duty and responsibility.* It is not easy to know one's duty and responsibility. For human resources administrators, these obligations can be difficult and, at times, ambiguous. In the most sweeping context, people have responsibilities to themselves and their families, friends, neighbors, and colleagues, in addition to their employing school district, community, state, and nation. Human resources administrators also have a duty and responsibility to their profession. The issue is how to balance all these various duties and responsibilities. At times, these duties and responsibilities come into conflict with each other. Reflection and common sense are the primary tools that help administrators find the necessary balance.

5. *Advocate for social justice.* Pluralism can produce conflict and conflict can lead to injustice. Thus, some basic notions about justice need to be known and understood.

Justice is the guide that regulates how people live their lives as members of a community. In contemporary society, everyone is a member, even if he or she tries to live otherwise. Computer and satellite technology make it possible to locate virtually every person on the planet. A person cannot hide and neglect his or her obligations to society. The choice either to live in society or to retreat from it by living a solitary life no longer exists. The very fact of being brings with it social obligations and the need for effective human relations. Justice is one of the most important aspects of human resources administration because the actions of an administrator can have both an immediate and a long-term effect on people and on that administrator's school district. Unfairness in administering human resources policies and procedures can be masked through the details of management. Thus, a just and fair human resources administrator is critical to social justice.

6. *Formulate professional positions through discourse.* Reasoning is the basis of all discourse in that participants must agree to this rationality if it is to be effective. Participants should be free from external and internal coercion other than the force of the best argument, which supports the cooperative search for truth. Because of the limitations of time and space, it is necessary to institutionalize discourse; the topics to be discussed and the contributions of participants must be organized in terms of opening, adjournment, and resumption of discussion. Discourse can be effective only if it is applied to questions that can be dealt with through impartial judgment. This implies that the process leads to an answer that is equally beneficial to all stakeholders. This means that discourse seeks not to reach consensus, but rather to generate convictions in the participants. Further, the degree to which a society, its institutions, its political culture, its traditions, and its everyday practices permit a noncoercive and nonauthoritarian form of discourse is a hallmark of rationality. Thus, human resources administrators cannot expect to find the best solution to problems or formulate the best policies and procedures if they carry out these tasks without discourse with those who have a stake in the problem or those who will be affected by the policies or procedures.

Focuses That Support Transcendental Culture
The following ten focuses are critical to establishing a transcendental culture[11] in a school district.

1. *Identity focus.* The degree to which administrators, teachers, and staff members identify with the school district as a whole rather than with their job or profession. If individuals identify closely with the school district, then a positive culture operates within that district.

2. *Collaboration focus.* The degree to which administrators, teachers, and staff members organize their work activities around groups rather than individuals. If administrators, teachers, and staff members collaborate in developing the dimensions of the human resources function, rather than relying on a single administrator such as the superintendent, to organize this responsibility, such a school district exemplifies this focus. The obvious advantage of fostering group emphasis is the empowerment experienced by individuals when the human resources function is no longer dependent only on one person who might retire or accept a position in another school district at some time in the future. In like manner, continuity is established even though the superintendent might leave the school district.

3. *Concern for people focus.* The degree to which administrators, teachers, and staff members consider the effects of their decisions on people. Of course, this applies not only to decisions affecting staff but also to decisions affecting students, parents, and members of the community. A high degree of concern is a hallmark of the humanity of the decision makers.

4. *Coordination focus.* The degree to which divisions in the school district are encouraged to operate in a coordinated or interdependent manner. A high degree of coordination and interdependence supports and strengthens the goal attainment of a school district.

5. *Empowerment focus.* The degree to which rules, regulations, and direct supervision are used to control the behavior of administrators, teachers, and staff members. Less control and increased levels of trust and empowerment lead to greater commitment and success.

6. *Risk-supportive focus.* The degree to which administrators, teachers, and staff members are encouraged to be aggressive, innovative, and risk seeking. A high degree of encouragement could lead to higher job satisfaction, an uplifted morale, and cutting-edge programming.

7. *Performance focus.* The degree to which rewards and promotions are allocated according to an administrator's, teacher's, or staff member's performance rather than seniority, favoritism, or other nonperformance factors.

8. *Criticism-tolerance focus.* The degree to which administrators, teachers, and staff members are encouraged to express their criticisms openly. The educational leaders of some school districts mistakenly believe that they can squelch criticism. Heavy-handed techniques used against employees who criticize publicly will result in deep-seated resentment and, in many cases, outright revolt. The mark of an effective school district is an atmosphere of openness within which everyone, including students, is heard without reprisal. This kind of openness sends a signal to all members of the school community that people and their opinions and criticisms are valued and can make a difference in how the school district is administered.

9. *Process focus.* The degree to which administrators, teachers, and staff members focus on the strategies and processes used to achieve outcomes. Particularly in human resources administration, outcomes are not a good measure of progress or success. There are too many variables to control when dealing with people to measure outcomes accurately. Thus, a school district with a positive culture will be constantly engaged in developing, implementing, evaluating, and modifying strategies and processes.

10. *Change focus.* The degree to which a school district monitors and responds to changes in the external environment. Technology, corporate downsizing, shifts in population, violence, health issues, and other phenomena that constantly bombard institutions require a response from administrators, teachers, and staff members in relation to what needs to change in their school district cultures.

Total Quality Management

In post–World War II Japan, an American named W. Edwards Deming introduced the theory and application of *total quality management (TQM)* to the Japanese, with outstanding results. Today, Japan occupies a prominent position among the leading industrial/business nations. It is true that the economy in Japan now suffers from the same pitfalls that plague the economies of the United States and the other industrial/business nations, but this country's rapid rise from devastation is worthy of note and study. Deming's approach was the catalyst for this success.

During the late 1970s, the quality management concept of *quality circles* was introduced in private business and industry. This concept called for groups of employees to meet and discuss how improvements could be made within their areas of responsibility. Supervisors and managers were unprepared for this innovation in most companies, and the technique quickly vanished. However, the TQM approach found support in business and industry during the 1980s and is still gaining momentum.

In education, the TQM approach is just beginning to take hold in some school districts and is certain to continue. This phenomenon is appearing not only in the management aspect of school districts but also in the instructional sphere.

This section discusses how Deming's fourteen principles can be applied to the management of human resources. These principles were elucidated in Deming's 1986 book, *Out of the Crisis.*

1. *Create constancy of purpose toward improvement of product and service.* Too often, human resources administrators are so entangled in the problems of daily operations that they lose sight of the overall vision that should drive the human resources function.

2. *Adopt the new philosophy.* The new philosophy is a belief that all staff members can and should contribute not only to the development of a strategic plan but also to the implementation of the plan. The assistant superintendent for human resources, along with the directors of employee relations, staff development, and affirmative action, should assume the leadership in developing the processes, procedures, and techniques for implementing the eight dimensions of the human resources function; however, interviewers, direct compensation specialists, and administrative assistants, along with all other staff members, should also be intricately involved in this development.

3. *Cease dependence on inspection to achieve quality.* Employees must perceive that they are valued members of the school district community and, in particular, that they are appreciated as providers of service to that dimension of the human resources function for which they are responsible.

4. *End the practice of awarding business on the basis of price tag.* The application of this principle for school district employees is better understood in relation to compensation. Public recognition of and compensation for outstanding performance are good ways to demonstrate that employees are valued and that their contributions to the human resources function are appreciated.

5. *Improve constantly and forever the system of production and service in order to improve quality and productivity.* Improvement must be built into the design of the processes, procedures, and techniques used in the human resources function. Thus, evaluation must be a component in every dimension of human resources management.

6. *Institute training on the job.* With the advances in technology and the research that is being conducted in the behavioral sciences, an employee can never state that he or she knows all there is to know about human resources management in general or about his or her area of responsibility in particular.

7. *Institute leadership.* This principle applies not only to the assistant superintendent for human resources and the other human resources administrators but also to staff members who have human resources responsibilities.

8. *Drive out fear.* Quality performance occurs when staff members take a stand about ideas that they believe enhance the human resources function. Security allows staff members to make mistakes that in turn become learning experiences, helping employees acquire new insight and more effective skills.

9. *Break down barriers between departments.* Collaboration between administrators and other staff members produces a higher quality of service.

10. *Eliminate slogans, exhortations, and targets.* The human resources function should be driven by goals rather than slogans, exhortations, and job targets.

11. *Eliminate management by numerical quotas.* There is nothing more dehumanizing to staff members than reducing their performance to statistics.

12. *Remove barriers that prevent job managers and workers from taking pride in their workmanship.* Generally speaking, everyone wants to do a good job. Human resources administrators should strive to remove obstacles that prevent other human resources staff members from achieving quality performance.

13. *Institute a vigorous program of education and self-improvement.* The human resources function is in danger of becoming mediocre if staff members are not given the opportunity to develop their skills, learn new skills, and receive updated information.

14. *Motivate everyone in the company to work toward the transformation.* The type of change described herein requires not only the commitment of the assistant superintendent for human resources but also the commitment of every human resources staff member. All levels within the organization must support this change because top-level human resources administrators cannot effect it by themselves.

Application of Technology in Human Resources Administration

The impact of technology on the daily lives of people cannot be overestimated. It is a phenomenon that has changed the way people think and act, not only in their homes but also in their workplaces. Virtually every school district in the United States is dealing with the use of technology in relation to the instructional program and in central office administration.

When applied to the school district human resources function, technology has many benefits, including the following:

- *Cost effectiveness.* Fewer people are required to perform certain human resources responsibilities.
- *Efficiency.* Processes and procedures can be computerized.
- *Engagement.* Employees themselves can access services more quickly.
- *Job enhancement.* Human resources department staff members can concentrate on planning and development rather than on routine tasks.
- *Assessment.* Information available in databases can be organized into management reports quickly and easily.

Computer technology has progressed through three phases that began in the 1950s and 1960s with large mainframe computers. With accelerated momentum, minicomputers and personal computers were developed and interconnected through privately owned networks. The period from the 1990s to the present has experienced the emergence of the Internet and the World Wide Web (Web). Excitingly, the future will most likely see the merging of information databases with communication that uses nanotechnology, biotechnology, and genomics. Thus, it is imperative for educational administrators to continue their study and dialogue about the potential of technology for the human resources function. In fact, being proactive in envisioning both the benefits and the cautions of emerging technology should constitute a segment of every educational administrator's responsibility. It would be a professional failing for human resources administrators to neglect becoming the designers of the future when that is exactly what we are meant to do as educators.[12]

Routine Human Resources Procedures

Initial Entry and Change of Personnel Information

Most school district employees would like to have more control over routine human resources procedures, something accomplished easily through technology. Human resources departments have enhanced the level of service to employees by eliminating paper-intensive work through technology, which also tends to reduce errors. Self-service workflow technology also gives employees access to their ongoing status and allows them to verify and/or update their status and benefits. Employees can thus have easy and reliable access to pay stub information: gross pay, deductions, year-to-date accumulations, and tax withholding data.

One of the easiest services to upgrade by using technology in school districts is benefits enrollment. Medical, dental, and life insurance plan enrollment can be accomplished through an interactive voice response telephone system. This technology uses a text-to-speech approach, whereby the system voices the caller's current status and then prompts him or her to make a selection from a series of options. This type of self-service application is commonly referred to as a *kiosk system*, which is a stand-alone center that prompts users when data are entered. There are basically two types of kiosks: those that require the typing of keywords and those that use touchscreen technology.

This can also be accomplished through the Internet or through an intranet system, which is the application of Web technology to the administrative computer network of a school district. Of course, changes in status can also be accomplished through this same technology. Common applications of self-service technology include a change of primary care physician, the listing of a new dependent, and a change of beneficiary.

Interactive voice response and Internet technology also provide convenient ways for retirees who continue to participate in district programs to make changes in their status without visiting the school district's central office or without sending in paperwork that is susceptible to keying error.

In using these technologies, an employee of a school district can initiate a change in his or her home address, notify the human resources department about a newly earned degree, or initiate a change in marital status. In an automated workflow system, these types of changes can be programmed to activate other processes. Thus, a change in marital status might activate a request for additional information concerning a name change or beneficiary election. Another example of this type of event-based processing is as follows: When a new teacher is hired and his or her human resources data file is created, event-based processing triggers the system to create a payroll file and enroll him or her in all standard employee benefits programs. The system then sends a message to the staff development department, which in turn enrolls the new employee in the school district's orientation program. In the case of a newly hired administrator, the system also sends a message to the information systems department to set up a system security identification number. The workflow capabilities of technology are limited only by the imagination and design of human resources administrators.

The potential of workflow systems are particularly promising in relation to carrying out teacher and staff member performance evaluations online. A workflow analytical system could activate a series of considerations that a supervisor should keep in mind, given the evaluation of an employee. For example, if an elementary school teacher is having difficulty teaching a newly adopted mathematics curriculum, a prompt might suggest a series of actions that the principal could consider, including asking the teacher to enroll in a workshop on the new mathematics curriculum being conducted by the publisher of the mathematics materials. The prompt could even include the time and date that the professional development department of the school district has scheduled the workshop. Further, it is possible to design the performance evaluation online system in order to analyze the pattern that emerges in how the principal has evaluated the teachers in his or her school.

Of course, it is possible to incorporate security features into self-service programs. For example, an employee can be required to use a personal email address with a password to transact business, and Internet security features can be used to establish a secure connection to the Website and to encrypt the information that employees enters. Carrying out most, if not all, human resources activities online through an interactive voice response system, the Internet, or an intranet saves valuable time for human resources personnel.

Task Performance

As stated previously, the most important way to save time and energy is to perform most human resources activities through an interactive voice response system, the Internet, or an intranet. It is important for all employees to understand that an email address and a password constitute the same authority and responsibility as a signature. Thus, the safeguarding of passwords is a serious professional responsibility.

Performance evaluation is another example of how the Internet or an intranet can be used to save time and energy and to reduce paperwork. Filling out a form online and storing it in the school district's database is much more efficient than completing a form and keeping it in a file cabinet. Depending on the level of security, the performance evaluation information can be more confidential and secure in the school district's database. It is just as effective, possibly more efficient, and ultimately more cost effective to download the performance evaluation to a disk that can be given to the employee and used as an ongoing record of his or her performance. The principal or department supervisor and the employee can sign the identification sticker placed on the disk as an indication that the contents have been explained to the employee. An employee response can be recorded on the disk, downloaded, and a copy given to the principal, who in turn can follow the ordinary procedure of response and appeal. The difference is that the district's database and a disk become the record, rather than traditional paper forms.

Posting Job Opportunities

Interactive voice response, the Internet, and an intranet are excellent avenues for providing both employees and other people interested in working for the school district with information about available positions. These types of postings can provide the school district with more effective linkage to the best qualified people. Further, these technologies not only provide easily accessed information about job requirements and timely notification of job vacancies but also can become the avenues for potential employees to apply for positions.

The use of these technologies can enhance the affirmative action efforts of a given school district by reaching people who do not live in the school district community or who do not have access to the daily newspapers where job vacancies are posted. This helps recruit people with disabilities, minorities, older workers, and women.

Online Recruitment and Selection

A computerized application process allows principals and department administrators to enter the competencies for a vacant position. The system then searches the database for a match between the competencies and available applicants' skills. Creating the applicant pool can take place through the Internet. For example, a person interested in working for a certain school district could consult the Webpage for that school district, which in turn could direct the person to an online application.

Once a resume is mailed by a potential candidate to a school district, it can be entered into a database and reformatted so that it is available to principals and department directors. Background screening results can be entered online along with other candidate information, providing an ongoing status check for principals and department directors seeking to fill vacancies. Initial screening of qualifications for a position can be handled through a front-end interactive voice response system that sets forth qualifications for vacant positions.

After the board of education votes to hire a candidate, a human resources data file can be created to prompt the delivery of a job description that includes expected competencies and performance criteria on which the newly hired person's performance will be evaluated.

Online Staff Development and Training Programs

Staff development and training programs can be produced and provided to employees through videos and online technology. Further, such programs can be interactive; an employee can be led through a series of exercises with immediate feedback concerning his or her mastery of the information or skill. Although this does not replace other methods of delivering staff development and training programs, most are suited to this approach.[13]

Relational Database Reporting

Human resources staff members once had to expend an enormous number of work hours reformatting data into usable information for the superintendent of schools, assistant superintendents, department heads, and principals. Software is now available that can produce reports immediately from data that have been entered into a database. For example, superintendents and other administrators can now view on-screen data in graphical formats that show turnover statistics in special education. They can also click and drag fields of information into reports or use software to create reports. In addition, reports can be extracted into word-processing documents and spreadsheets. With the advent of email in most school districts, reports can be transferred easily to the offices of numerous administrators. Exhibit 1.2 is an example of a monthly summary report that sets forth the status of those making claims as members of a self-insured school district medical insurance program. When employees, their dependent children, their spouses, or their physicians send in a claim for medical services, the claim is entered into a database from which summary reports can be generated. In an actual report, the designation of employee, spouse, or dependent would be accompanied by the employee's social security number or the name of the person who made the claim.[14]

With the new technologies, human resources administrators and staff members can assume the role of internal consultants who are engaged in critical planning in order to meet the goals and objectives of a given school district. They can now be more involved in solving problems and addressing human resources issues.

EXHIBIT 1.2   Medical Claims Report

Claimant	Paid Year-to-Date	Diagnosis	Current Treatment
1. Dependent	$24,602.38	Broken Arm	Physical Therapy
2. Employee	$33,442.21	Heart Disease	Office Visits & Medication
3. Spouse	$28,179.17	Osteoarthritis	Lab Work, X-ray, Medication
4. Employee	$27,563.02	Breast Cancer	Radiation
5. Employee	$84,253.90	Renal Failure	Dialysis—Waiting for Kidney Transplant
6. Dependent	$47,375.16	Leukemia	Office Visits
7. Dependent	$19,601.43	Acute Anxiety	Office Visits & Medication
8. Spouse	$93,610.34	Lymphomas	Chemotherapy
9. Employee	$110,592.62	AIDS	Office Visits & Medication
10. Employee	$21,237.61	Heart Disease	Lab Work & Medication
11. Dependent	$15,732.72	Intestinal Obstruction	X-ray, Office Visits

Human Resources Administration Computer Hardware and Software

Hardware and Software Selection Process

Technology accelerates processes and procedures, but it does not necessarily correct problems within a dysfunctional human resources department. Thus, the following four steps will help human resources administrators appropriately select computer hardware and software.

1. *Analyze the human resources needs of the school district.* If possible, this should be accomplished through a district-wide strategic-planning process that develops a vision for the entire school district and establishes goals and objectives for each division and department of the district. The human resources function is a vital part of the operation of the entire school district, and significant changes and enhancements to the processes and procedures of the human resources department must be made in consort with the district's overall strategic plan.

   In addition to establishing goals and objectives for the human resources department, conducting an audit of the school district's existing technology is extremely important in determining what hardware and software are being used in the payroll department, the information management department, the school principals' offices, and all other departments because, if possible, new hardware and software should interface with existing hardware and software. This is especially important because principals and department directors use their computer terminals to access human resources information and reports.

   Surveying principals and department directors to ascertain their human resources needs and ideas not only helps in selecting the most appropriate hardware and software but also gives human resources administrators important feedback concerning issues and problems that may be present in human resources processes and procedures. Future needs could also be identified that will be important in purchasing hardware and software that will meet the school's needs for more than just a few years.

   The growth or decline in the school district's enrollment is a key factor because this determines the number of teachers' and staff members' records to be processed by the human resources department. The larger the school district, the greater the need for technology in order to contain costs and maintain effectiveness and efficiency.

2. *Research the types of hardware and software that are available from vendors.* Of course, the first place to search for hardware and software is in computer trade publications, which have extensive advertising. A complementary task in the identification of appropriate hardware and software is asking colleagues in other school districts about the advantages and disadvantages of the products that they are using.

3. *Establish a budget for the purchase of hardware and software, and initiate the bidding process.* The needs assessment and research into available products help in the establishment of a budget. The cost of new technology can be prohibitive, and thus, it is judicious to establish a firm cost limit for the purchase of hardware and software. At this point, it is important to consider hidden costs that might be related to supporting the installation and maintenance of the products.

   The development of specifications for taking bids might require the expertise of a computer consultant if a school district does not have staff members with this type of experience. The specifications must clearly set forth the needs of the school district in such a way that bidders will be able to develop a complete hardware and software package. However, some vendors might be able to submit a bid for the hardware but not for the software, or vice versa. Thus, separating the bid package into these two categories is desirable. After advertising, receiving bids, and eliminating bids that exceed the budget, the human resources department administrators and staff members should begin their analysis. There are ten areas to consider in the analysis phase of the bidding process:

a. Capability of the hardware and software to be integrated with existing systems
b. Degree of difficulty in entering data
c. Degree of difficulty in learning the new equipment and software
d. Scope of program functions that can be carried out
e. Type and depth of reporting possibilities
f. Expandability and upgrading capability of the programs
g. Time line for the conversion process
h. Level and scope of technical support that the vendor will provide in the conversion process and beyond
i. Performance of the demonstration hardware and software
j. Quality of the references given by staff members from other school districts where the products are being used

The level and scope of technical support are most critical because it is possible to purchase excellent hardware and software that cannot be used to its full potential due to inadequate technical support. It is desirable to have onsite support for extensive conversions, whereby staff members can be trained in small groups and coached at their workstations. The establishment of a high-quality working relationship between a school district's staff and the technical support people is critical to the conversion process. The potential for such a relationship can be explored by interviewing the bidding companies and by checking their references carefully.

Of course, it is typical practice to receive demonstration hardware and software from various vendors. Human resources staff can test the products for factors that could impinge upon the decision-making process. The testing should not be rushed but rather extended over a significant period to give staff members the time needed to make an accurate appraisal of the products' performance.

4. *Make a decision based on a cost-to-benefit ranking.* This ranking is established by identifying the lowest-priced hardware and software that meet the human resources department's present and future requirements. In a multiproduct bidding situation, each product can be evaluated using a rating scale, and then the overall package of each vendor can be compared to identify the strengths and weaknesses. A rating may be assigned by each member of the bid evaluation committee, which should be composed of administrators and staff members from the human resources department and include principals and other administrators if they will be using a given type of hardware or software. A weight assigned to the ten areas considered in the analysis phase is then matched to the cost of the products. Table 1.1 provides an example of a weighted evaluation form.

TABLE 1.1 Analysis Rating

On a scale of 1 to 5, with 5 being the highest rating, rate each vendor's product against the following criteria:

————— Integration with Existing Systems

————— Degree of Difficulty in Entering Data

————— Scope of Program Functions

————— Type and Depth of Reporting

————— Expandability and Upgrading Capability of the Programs

————— Time line for the Conversion Process

————— Level and Scope of Technical Support

————— Performance of the Demonstration Product

————— Quality of References

————— **Total Rating (50 is the highest possible rating)**

TABLE 1.2 Bid Comparisons

Vendor	Rating	Cost
Vendor One	41	$132,000
Vendor Two	23	$105,000
Vendor Three	32	$86,000

For example, if three companies are bidding on a payroll program that has an upgraded employee position control component and the evaluation rating system cited here is used, the bid comparisons may look like those set forth in Table 1.2. In this situation, Vendor One has the highest rating but the highest cost, Vendor Two has the lowest rating and the second highest cost, and Vendor Three has the second highest rating and the lowest cost. The decision should be between Vendor One and Vendor Three. According to the cost-to-benefit rating approach, if the bids come in at or below budget, Vendor One should be awarded the contract.

Categories of Software Applications

The amount of software available to human resources departments in school districts increases constantly, especially because the human resources function can be easily adapted to technology. More important, the effective use of technology can free up significant financial resources that can then be allocated to the instructional program. The following nine areas within human resources administration were identified through a review of the "Supplement" section found in every issue of the journal *Workforce* during 2008, and software is available for each application:

1. *Attendance systems.* For support positions such as bus driver, cafeteria worker, and custodian, these systems use software for telephones, magnetic strip cards, and personal computers to record the number of hours worked by employees, which can be generated and sent to the payroll department electronically.

2. *Compensation planning systems.* These systems provide a structured, data-based approach to planning teacher and staff member salary and benefits programs. They can provide the kind of analysis that enhances the collective negotiations process, especially because a planning system makes it possible to identify compensation trends in large school districts.

3. *Competency management systems.* Superintendents and human resources administrators can use these systems to identify teacher and staff member educational levels, certifications, and special skills. Based on the human resources needs of the school district, such software also can help human resources staff members identify staff development needs.

4. *Decision support systems.* When an administrator needs or wants to generate data summaries and reports, these systems provide the analytical capability to reframe information in such a way that decision making becomes more data driven.

5. *Human resources management systems.* These systems constitute the central storage for maintaining records and processing transactions—such as workflow—that can be initiated through self-service events.

6. *Payroll management systems.* These systems manage the entire payroll process, including salary/benefits requirements and governmental regulations such as tax deductions.

7. *Recruitment and selection management systems.* Using these systems, the superintendent of schools, principals, other administrators, and human resources staff members can search databases to find applicants who have specific education, certifications, and skills. These systems also allow administrators to monitor the status of applicants and even to mine the Internet for potential job applicants.

8. *Retirement management systems.* Using the Internet, intranet, or interactive voice response software, retirees can transact business with the human resources department and can receive information or have their questions answered.

9. *Staff development management systems.* These systems retain information about the specific staff development programs and activities that employees attend, and also identify the special skills acquired by the teachers and staff members who attended them. Further, software is available that allows individuals to access learning and training through personal computers and distance learning, which is important in providing staff development in schools so that teachers and staff members do not need to travel to a central office. Also, employees have access to expert knowledge that would not be available to large groups of teachers and staff members on a given occasion. Providing staff development via the Internet and intranet allows people to acquire new knowledge and learn new skills independent of time and location.

Ethics Issues

There are many approaches to the study of ethics that ultimately try to deal with human self-determination and all the issues in our society that militate against human freedom. Because this treatment deals specifically with human resources administration, the approach used here is focused on professional ethics, which is initiated through *best practice* in developing policies and establishing procedures that protect the self-determination of the employees of a school district, while ensuring the quality of educational services to students. It is a balance between the rights and responsibilities of teachers, administrators, and staff members and the rights and responsibilities of children, parents, and the local, state, and national communities.

Best practice ethics attempt to analyze the obligations that educational administrators have in relation to the human resources function. In small- to medium-size school districts, the superintendent of schools, an assistant superintendent, or a building principal may have some or all of the responsibility for the human resources function. In virtually every school district, all administrators, from time to time, have some human resources responsibility, even if it is just involvement in the interviewing process for new teachers. Consequently, cyberethics is an essential dimension of every administrator's professional responsibility.

Cyberethics focuses on those functions of human resources administration that are operationalized through the use of technology. The larger societal issues, such as the effect that technology has had on human communication, are not within the scope of professional cyberethics. Those charged with the human resources function in schools and school districts have a vested interest in the manner in which other human resources professionals are dealing with cyberethics issues. There is a *community of interest* that should be viewed as a responsibility of the professions of human resources administration. Conventions and conferences for human resources professionals in education should address the commonly experienced cyberethics concerns and issues. In this context, issues are analyzed through a form of professional ethics referred to here as *best practice ethics*, which incorporates the notion that best practice evolves and develops as a consequence of the culture within which a school or school district is located. Colleagues, parents, students, board members, state and national elected officials, and government agencies contribute to the idea that there is a best practice in human resources administration.

However, detecting what constitutes a community of interest is open to continual discussion. For example, the Missouri Legislature passed a state law against harassment. The event that precipitated the action was the suicide of thirteen-year-old Megan Meier, who took her life in October 2006, after receiving mean-spirited messages over the Internet. Those who sent the messages were another young girl, a parent of that girl, and an employee of the parent.

The Missouri state law previously required the abusive communication to be in writing or over the telephone. The change in the law included acts of harassment through social media. The amendment also obligated school officials to notify police about harassment and credible threats against the victim, his or her family, his or her household members, and his or her animals.

In this case, there was carryover into human resources administration in the area of education. Every school district must develop policies that comply with the provisions of such state laws, and that set forth how the laws will be implemented in the school district. Further, the superintendent of schools and other central office and building-level administrators must develop those implementation plans, which should include procedures.

Certainly, those administrators responsible for the staff development function must create programs that help teachers and administrators recognize when a student might be experiencing harassment over the Internet. Further, teachers, administrators, and staff members can easily become victims of technological harassment. Finally, teachers, administrators, and staff members can also be perpetrators of such harassment. Procedures must be developed for the notification of law enforcement authorities when harassment is identified.

This one issue can have an effect not only on policy development and staff development but also on the selection process and the manner in which background checks are carried out. The performance evaluation process is also affected, especially in the area of progressive discipline, which requires a clear definition of what constitutes technological harassment.

Neutral Nature of Technology

Can a technological device have unethical design features that would make it detrimental to certain people? The answer to this question begs the answer that it is humans who are capable of using technology for good or bad purposes; the technology itself is only an instrument. Certainly, there are examples in many other areas that are faced with this same question. The incident that resulted in the passage of an amendment to a Missouri law on harassment speaks to this point in the sense that the Internet was used in such a manner that it had a detrimental effect on a student. The Internet itself was not the problem.

The use of closed-circuit video surveillance cameras in school corridors to deter students from engaging in inappropriate behavior and to protect them from unlawful intruders has caused some concern on the part of teachers and staff members who believe that it is a violation of privacy. Also, others have concerns about how surveillance cameras could be used by principals in the teacher and employee performance evaluation process.

Designing technological devices to carry out functions that they would not otherwise be capable of performing has an impact on the issue of technology neutrality. For example, a school district may have employee social security numbers in a database that is easily accessed by other employees. Those employees could download the data through data-mining techniques and subsequently use them to steal the identity of others for financial gain. Thus, design is of concern even if it is viewed as neutral in terms of cyberethics issues.

Of course, the same is true with all administrative design functions. The creation of a fictitious employee, allowed by a lack of checks and balances in the employee selection process and the payroll function, is a design issue commonly referred to as an *internal auditing failure*. This process is then monitored by designated central office staff in order to avoid fraud and should also be audited by an external auditing firm.

A related but major component of the neutrality issue deals with the apparent and unapparent potential uses of technology. Many school district personnel are unaware of the potential uses of the technology they purchase, such as the networking of computers. Search engines and data mining are two of the features that can be accessed through program design once data are entered into the system network. This raises issues of accessibility and how employees are granted accessibility. Do certain employees have a *need to know* those data?[15]

Unfortunately, it is painfully obvious that security issues dominate the technological revolution, particularly in relation to both the Internet and the intranet.[16] Email is the primary indicator that communications are neither completely private nor completely secure. Because human resources administrators use technology to implement the various dimensions of the human resources function, it is critical to understand not only the benefits but also the liabilities of this technology.

Social Media

First and foremost, there have been attempts by the U.S. Congress to prohibit certain uses of the Internet, including the Communications Decency Act of 1996 and the Child Online Protection Act of 1998. These laws have been reviewed by the federal court system, and their implementation is problematic at this time. The same situation is true for the Children's Internet Protection Act of 2000, except that a provision of the law mandates school districts receiving federal funds for Internet access to develop and implement a formal Internet safety policy. The implication for human resources administration is that there should be a policy that restricts the use of school district–owned equipment and access to the Internet for school business purposes only.

Hostile Work Environment

Title VII of the Civil Rights Act of 1964 prohibits verbal and written conduct that produces an intimidating, hostile, or offensive work environment. Further, the U.S. Supreme Court decision in *Burlington Industries v. Ellerth* (1998) clearly holds supervisors legally responsible in Title VII cases for not preventing a hostile work environment. Technology and the Internet have significantly changed the work environment so that new methods of harassment might be used by employees. Thus, abusive emails and Internet content is certainly a violation of Title VII. It is the responsibility of human resources administrators to develop and implement policies and reporting procedures that help other administrators monitor the teaching environment so it is free from harassment.

Employee Privacy

The U.S. Supreme Court, in *O'Connor v. Ortega* (1987), upheld the standards set forth in *New Jersey v. T.L.O.* (1984) concerning justified and reasonable search. In the former case, the Court held that employees have a constitutionally protected right to privacy in the workplace. However, electronic communications of public employees are considered to be discoverable in court under public records laws. The usual practice is that emails are considered private unless subpoenaed by a court.

There are many other areas giving rise to legal and security concerns in relation to the use of technology and the Internet. These include student use of the Internet, student privacy, assistive technology for children with disabilities, plagiarism, copyright issues, fair use, and intellectual property rights. The issues just discussed, however, deal specifically with human resources administration.[17]

Privacy and Technology

Privacy is the most pervasive concern about the use of technology and particularly the Internet. In schools and school districts, networked computers typically display a security message that, if read in detail, states that the Website is secure because it is protected by a security protocol. Obviously, that means the information received and sent is protected and cannot be read by others because the information is encrypted. This is the least of the concerns about privacy, even though it is sometimes considered to be the most important, particularly by those with little knowledge of privacy issues.

Overall, the issue of privacy centers around the amount, type, and duration of information about people that is available in data warehouses. Further, the ease and speed with which such information is collected, stored, and retrieved exacerbate the privacy issue. Physical limitations that are not present in electronic technology were previously the major deterrents to collecting pervasive amounts of data on people. For example, the teaching certifications held by applicants that were listed on paper application forms by would-be employees could not be accessed unless the applications were physically handled and observed by a designated employee. However, online applications allow school district employees with computer skills to use software programs that permit the development of reports setting forth all the teaching certifications of applicants over any period of time. Such information could be of significant assistance in the recruitment of teachers with specific certifications. This is the upside of data mining.

The concern about data mining involves dishonest employees with access to data. Employees who are capable of accessing the social security numbers of other employees could use those numbers to access the financial information of those other employees through external databases.

Privacy has a number of considerations that are within the purview of society in general and that are usually discussed in the media and the political arena, often leading to legal and legislature involvement. Issues such as freedom from interference and unwanted intrusion are the topics of concern in the technological era. The focus here is, of course, on the privacy issues that are present in human resources administration.[18]

Merging Personal Data

Although the retrieval of data was discussed briefly in the context of data mining, the transferring, exchanging, and combining of personal data raise much more serious and problematic issues. There is no significant privacy issue with the mere recording of data in databases; the real concern occurs when those databases are merged with other, unrelated databases for the purpose of integrating the information into a composite file.

For example, consider a school district or a consortium of school districts that has developed self-insured medical and hospital plans. In the process of developing this venture, a third-party administrator is hired to manage the programs. The Health Insurance Portability and Accountability Act (HIPAA), which protects the health records of individuals from disclosure, was passed by the U.S. Congress and signed into law in 2003. Nevertheless, health records are of concern to employees of school districts. Because of their employment, significant amounts of information about those employees are contained in other databases owned by the districts. Depending on the proper use of security measures, there could be little difficulty in merging those health records with other databases.

Ethical issues that could arise from the accessing of information by others are intrusion and interference, both of which come to light and converge in the technological age in the context of surveillance. An example of surveillance is the use of *cookies*, which are files from Websites visited by a Web user that are then stored on the user's hard drive; the cookie for a specific Website can be retrieved from the individual's system and submitted to that Website the next time the person accesses it; this information is then accessed by Website owners and stored in databases.[19] Of course, no company or individual gathers information and stores it in a database without a purpose. This is exactly what happens in credit and medical information bureaus. Such bureaus merge and match databases.

The ethical issues become apparent when certain data-gathering institutions such as lending institutions and political parties engage in this practice.

Future Issues

The future of technology in human resources administration will probably be centered on certain issues that are still evolving. However, the overriding issue that every school district is concerned about is security of the data that are stored and accessed in intranet databases.[20] Thus, the future of human resources administration will be inexorably tied not only to advances in the technology itself but also to ethical issues.

Human resources administrators are constantly challenged to keep up with technological advances and the ethical issues that are certain to follow. Changes in technology appear to have no limits. However, the emergence of ethical issues is certain because people are the focus of human resources administration. Of course, the issue of human dignity is melded into all human resources issues, particularly in the areas of privacy and self-determination. At this juncture in the development of the disciplines of both technology and ethics, a new term, *cyberethics*, has been coined to focus the attention of professionals on emerging legal and ethical disputes. Cyberethics studies how technology has affected public policy. This term connotes the use of computing and communicating technology specifically through handheld devices, desktop and laptop computers, and mainframe computers that are connected directly to the Internet or through privately owned computer networks. More important is the mind-set that this term evokes—one that views all advances and mutations as a condition of technological advances.[21]

Implications for Small- and Medium-Size School Districts

The implications for small- and medium-size school districts are explained easily in relation to Figure 1.3 and Exhibit 1.1. Clearly, the central office positions in Figure 1.3 ultimately report to the superintendent of schools, including five assistant superintendents responsible for human resources, administrative services, elementary education, secondary education, and instructional services. Directors, principals, and coordinators also report to those assistant superintendents. Staff members and teachers report to some directors and to the principals. This is an organizational structure for a school district of approximately 25,000 students. All these positions can be collapsed into the responsibilities of the superintendent of schools in small- and medium-size school districts. The superintendent can then delegate some of his or her responsibilities to an assistant superintendent or director. For example, an assistant superintendent may be responsible for transportation, food services, facilities, and budgeting. Further, building principals may assume the human resources responsibilities of advertising for and selecting the staff members and teachers who will be working in their schools. A coordinator can be given the responsibilities of administering staff development programs, directing special education, and developing curriculum. All these responsibilities can be rather fluid from year to year, depending on such issues as upcoming bond issue elections. In this situation, the assistant superintendent may assist the superintendent in working with architects, construction managers, or bonding attorneys in preparing for a bond issue election. The bottom line is that the superintendent is ultimately responsible for all these functions, and it may be necessary to delegate some of them to central office or building-level administrators.

A further implication for small- and medium-size school districts can be gleaned from the job descriptions of the six major human resources specialists, which include responsibilities for overall human resources administration, employee relations, staff development, affirmative action, employee benefits, and risk management. Once again, all these human resources functions are ultimately the responsibility of the superintendent of schools. He or she may not have other central office administrators to whom he or she can delegate some the human resources responsibilities. This is particularly true in relation to overall human resources administration, employee relations, affirmative action, employee benefits, and risk management. Staff development may be delegated to a building principal, but the others are usually not within the competency of building administrators. An insurance consultant or agent can assist with risk management, and the health insurance provider can assist with benefits management. An attorney can help with affirmative action to a certain degree, but the superintendent is probably the only person in a small- or medium-size school district who can assume the responsibilities of employee relations and certain dimensions of affirmative action. It is the superintendent who has the ultimate responsibility.

Impact of Generation Y Teachers and Administrators on Human Resources Administration

Each generation has a unique set of characteristics, and this is true of the generation of new teachers and administrators that most school districts are attempting to recruit, hire, and retain. The purpose of including a section on Generation Y is to establish a perspective that is helpful to superintendents, human resources administrators, and principals as they initiate the human resources functions. What follows are generalizations, and thus, they may not apply to a given person. All the chapters in this text, except for Chapter 10, contain a section on the impact of Generation Y on the specific content in those chapters.

For example, one of the most important characteristics of Generation Y is the desire to trust in authority. Baby boomers, as a generalization, had little admiration for authority and government. What Generation Y employees want from their leaders is behavior that can be admired, which leads to trust. It is difficult to ask people to trust in principals and superintendents based only on blind faith supported by the titles of their leadership positions. Admired behavior is a powerful force that can transform a school or school district into a true learning community, where all employees feel appreciated and know they can count on the good intentions of administrators when they make decisions that affect the employees' careers.

Another characteristic of Generation Y is the value that they place on education. This characteristic has even been reflected in the popular media, particularly in tandem with the economic crisis facing the United States and, indeed, all world markets. For some time, people have based a significant amount of their social and economic self-worth on what they owned in terms of property and investment portfolios. However, now there is a shift to what economists refer to as *human capital*, defined as the value that a person has based on his or her work ethic, skills, and education. How these human assets are used in getting a job constitutes a kind of capital that is not diminished easily. Of course, there are fewer jobs, but the competition for the remaining jobs will be fierce, and the winners will probably be those with the most human capital. This is how those in Generation Y look on their future economic stability. They value salary and fringe benefits along with wanting to get ahead in a shorter period of time as they seek out purposeful employment.[22]

Summary

Our system of free and universal public education is unique to U.S. society. The school as an institution receives its mandate from the society it serves, and change is an integral part of this society. The content of our educational programs must not only address the fundamental principles of individual freedom, individual responsibility, and democratic government but must also retain the flexibility to meet new developments and conditions.

Implementing society's educational objectives is the responsibility of the individual states. The state's authority to create and govern the public schools is embodied in the state constitution, and it exercises this authority through the state legislature. The administrative arm of the state legislature is the department of education, which is usually governed by a board and administered by a commissioner or state superintendent. The legislature also delegates authority to local units—boards of education. However, the state maintains some control over the local boards by establishing minimum educational program requirements and teacher certification requirements, and by providing funds to help finance education.

The federal government has increased its influence on education through congressional acts that provide funds for special programs, through the regulations of the U.S. Department of Education, and through Supreme Court decisions. However, the federal government's power and influence are still considerably adjunct to state authority in education.

President George W. Bush signed the No Child Left Behind (NCLB) Act into law in January 2002. NCLB ushered in the most extensive changes in federal law concerning public school education in forty years. It is the first time that federal legislation mandated student success; all other federal legislation mandated opportunity rather than success.

The law requires that all children be proficient in reading and mathematics by 2014. Further, schools are required to make adequate yearly progress (AYP) toward the 2014 goal. Thus, each state must develop student testing programs that demonstrate satisfactory student improvement each year. The consequences of not achieving AYP vary from being designated as a school needing improvement to being designated as one facing severe repercussions, such as replacing school personnel or extending the school year, after five years of not achieving AYP.

For human resources administration, the NCLB provisions require serious attention. First, there is the requirement to hire highly qualified teachers who are capable of helping students meet the proficiency requirements. Second, the provision that students must demonstrate AYP has serious implications for teacher performance evaluation and staff development. Finally, noncompliance with AYP for five years might result in the replacement of administrators, teachers, or staff members.

NCLB is a particular manifestation of school reform. The reform movement is always before us in education because change and improvement are embedded in the education profession. The formulas for successful reform have some common elements: a vision that uses a learning community approach leading to organizational reform, the establishment of a leadership team that uses teacher leadership in consort with principals' responsibilities, the importance of making decisions based on evidence, and the benefits of using technology in management and instructional strategies.

School districts are perhaps the most democratically controlled agencies of government. Citizens of a local community elect school board members, who in turn adopt policies for the governance and administration of the schools. The implementation of board policies is the responsibility of the administrative staff.

Administration is the process of managing human, financial, and material resources to accomplish an educational mission formulated as policies by the board of education. Therefore, administration is an executive rather than a policy-making activity. Its various functions include human resources administration, instructional programs administration, and support services administration. Each of these functions has objectives that are implemented through administrative processes, procedures, and techniques.

Functions are performed by administrators within a given organizational structure. The superintendent, as the chief executive officer of the school board, has full control of all school operations. These operations are so complex that his or her efforts must be amplified by an administrative team. This team is usually composed of assistant superintendents who administer the major functions of the school system. These assistant superintendents form a cabinet that helps the superintendent formulate strategies and shares in the decision-making process. Directors and coordinators perform administrative tasks that support the major functions of the district. They report directly to assistant superintendents.

Every school system performs a human resources function, whether accomplished by a central office unit or assigned to various administrators within the system. The goals of the human resources function are to achieve the objectives of the school district and to help individual staff members maximize their potential and develop their professional careers. These goals are implemented through human resources planning, recruitment, selection, placement and induction, staff development, performance evaluation, compensation, and collective negotiations.

All but the very smallest school districts should delegate the human resources function to an assistant superintendent. The complexity of this function in our schools and the great impact it has on total school operations necessitate the hiring of this personnel specialist.

Collective negotiations have also created a need in most school districts for another specialist, the director of employee relations, who reports to the assistant superintendent for human resources and is charged with managing the negotiations process.

The knowledge explosion; increased federal legislation and litigation; and the changing attitudes of parents, students, and educators have necessitated an ongoing staff development program for administrators and teachers. As with collective negotiations, this area is so specialized that most districts should consider establishing the position of director of staff development, who also reports to the assistant superintendent for human resources.

The avalanche of federal legislation and litigation has also necessitated the creation of another central office administrative position, director of affirmative action. Federal legislation requires that a detailed compliance program be established under the direction of an administrator who is free from the influence of other administrators. Thus, the director of affirmative action should report directly to the superintendent of schools.

The escalating costs of healthcare and workers' compensation and the need to implement managed care have reinforced the need for school districts to establish the position of director of employee benefits. This administrator reports to the assistant superintendent for human resources.

As in the rest of society, schools are places of potential risk to students and employees. The risks range from personal violence to accidents to loss of confidentiality. Safety and security audits, rules, and procedures must be developed in order to ensure an environment that is as risk-free as possible for both students and employees. Because of this need, school districts have created the position of director of risk management.

There are two leadership theories that appear most appropriate for the practice of human resources administration: transcendental leadership and total quality management (TQM).

The basic premise of transcendental leadership is that a person acts from the totality of who he or she is as a human. Most administrators are generally aware that their decisions are influenced by more than just the immediate circumstances and that the effects of their decisions can go beyond the present situation.

Transcendental leadership has two components. First, six elements pertain to dispositions that individual human resources administrators should possess in order to be centered on human growth and development: use reflection on practice, practice the principle of subsidiarity, act from a political base, act from a sense of duty and responsibility, advocate for social justice, and formulate professional positions through discourse. Second, ten focuses establish a transcendental culture in a school district that is organizationally supportive of human growth and development: identity, collaboration, concern for people, coordination, empowerment, risk supportive, performance, criticism tolerance, process, and change.

In post–World War II Japan, W. Edwards Deming introduced the theory and application of total quality management (TQM) to the Japanese with outstanding positive results. Aspects of Deming's fourteen principles are being implemented in some school districts throughout the United States. These principles can be applied effectively to the human resources function in school districts.

The impact of computer technology cannot be overestimated in all aspects of educational administration. When this technology is applied to the human resources function, it produces many benefits, including cost effectiveness, efficiency, assessment of school district operations, and engagement of employees. In human resources administration, computer technology is being used for initial entry and changes in personnel information, the request and use of forms, task performance, the posting of job opportunities, online recruitment and selection of personnel, online staff development and training, and relational database reporting. When selecting computer hardware and software, it is important to consider the human resources needs of the district, to research the types of hardware and software available from vendors, to establish a realistic budget for the bidding process, and to make decisions based on a cost-to-benefit ranking. Computer software applications are available for every dimension of the human resources function.

Security issues dominate the technological revolution, particularly in relation to both the Internet and the intranet. The implication for human resources administration is that there should be a policy that restricts the use of school district–owned equipment and access to the Internet for school business purposes only. In addition, abusive emails and Internet content are certainly a violation of the law. It is the responsibility of human resources administrators to develop and implement policies and reporting procedures that help other administrators monitor the teaching environment so that it is free from harassment.

Although electronic communications of public employees are considered to be discoverable in court under public records laws, the usual practice is that emails are considered private unless subpoenaed by a court.

✓ **Self-Check Quiz** Click here to take an automatically-graded self-check quiz.

Discussion Questions and Statements

1. Describe the role of the board of education in relation to the human resources function.
2. What is the human resources responsibility of the superintendent of schools?
3. Describe how the dimensions of the human resources function are interrelated.
4. How does the use of technology in human resources administration support data-driven decision making?
5. If you were a newly appointed assistant superintendent for human resources, how would you initiate the concept of TQM for the human resources function in a department that has had autocratic leadership?
6. Describe the link between the human resources function and both the business and the instructional functions of a school district.
7. Without identifying the school district, which Interstate School Leaders Licensure Consortium (ISLLC) criteria in the chapter appendix are the most difficult to initiate in a school district with which you are familiar? Why?
8. What is transcendental leadership, and how is it related to effective human resources administration?
9. What are the essential elements and focuses of transcendental leadership?
10. What impact does the NCLB Act have on human resources administration?

Suggested Activities

1. Interview an assistant superintendent or director of human resources in a small-size school district with one to three elementary schools, a middle school, and a high school. Engage the assistant superintendent or director in a discussion about the organizational structure of the school district and how it influences the human resources function. Inquire about the way other administrators, teachers, and staff members have been involved in carrying out the human resources function.
2. Develop, in writing, a job description for the director of human resources for a school district with approximately 100 professional personnel.
3. Develop, in writing, a rationale and plan for enhancing the human resources function through the use of technology in a school district with 2000 students and minimal financial resources.

Focus Scenario Activity

Given that you have read and studied this chapter, how would you organize the human resources function in your new position, and how would you use other administrators, teachers, and staff members in carrying out human resources responsibilities and procedures?

Endnotes

1. Mark Penn and E. Kinney Zalesne, *Microtrends: The Small Forces Behind Tomorrow's Big Changes* (New York: Grand Central, 2007).
2. Charles J. Russo, *The Law of Public Education,* 6th ed. (New York: Foundation Press, 2006), 1–13, 157–184.
3. Missouri Department of Elementary and Secondary Education, *Questions & Answers About No Child Left Behind—And What It Means for Missouri* (Springfield: Author, August 2003).
4. David J. Ferrero, "How Key Provisions of New Education Law May Affect Your District," *School Superintendent's Insider,* April (2002): 1–3.
5. David J. Ferrero, "Pathways to Reform: Start with Values," *Educational Leadership,* 62, no. 5 (2005): 8, 10.
6. Barnett Berry, Dylan Johnson, and Diana Montgomery, "The Power of Teacher Leadership," *Educational Leadership,* 62, no. 5 (2005): 56–60.
7. Donald R. Gallagher, Don Bagin, and Edward H. Moore, *The School and Community Relations*, 8th ed. (Boston: Allyn & Bacon, 2005), 41–42.
8. Iowa Association of School Boards, *School Board Member Handbook* (Des Moines: Author, 2009), 37–40.
9. William C. Cunningham and Paula A. Cordeiro, *Educational Administration: A Problem-Based Approach* (Boston: Allyn & Bacon, 2000), 174–187.
10. Ronald W. Rebore, *A Human Relations Approach to the Practice of Educational Leadership* (Boston: Allyn & Bacon, 2004), 75–85, 153–155.
11. Ibid., 153–155.
12. Herman T. Tavani, *Ethics and Technology: Ethical Issues in an Age of Information and Communication Technology* (Hoboken, NJ: 2007), 5–7.
13. William G. Cunningham and Paula A. Cordeiro, *Educational Leadership: A Bridge to Improved Practice,* 4th ed. (Boston: Allyn & Bacon, 2009), 81–88.
14. Vern Brimley, Jr., and Rulon R. Garfield, *Financing Education in a Climate of Change* (Boston: Allyn & Bacon, 2008), 358–359.
15. Tavani, *Ethics and Technology*, 23–26.
16. David M. Quinn, "Legal Issues in Educational Technology: Implications for School Leaders," *Educational Administration Quarterly* 39, no. 2 (2003): 187–207.
17. Tavani, *Ethics and Technology*, 127–141.
18. Ibid., 129–131.
19. Ibid., 132, 136.
20. Florence Olsen, "Security: Threats Will Get Worse," *The Chronicle of Higher Education,* (January 30, 2004), B12.
21. Tavani, *Ethics and Technology*, 1–3.
22. Barbara Kiviat, "Jobs Are the New Assets," *Time*, 173 (special issue), no. 11 (March 23, 2009), 46–47.

Selected Bibliography

Allameh, S., Naftchali, J., Pool, J., and Davoodi, S. "Human Resources Development Review According to Identity, Integration, Achievement and Adaptation Model." *International Journal of Academic Research in Business & Social Sciences*, 2, no. 2 (2012): 42–57.
American Association of School Administrators (AASA). (2009). www.aasa.org.
American Association of School Personnel Administrators (AASPA). (2009). www.aaspa.org.

Ashbaugh, R. M. "Technology for Human Resources Management: Seven Questions and Answers." *Public Personnel Management,* 31, no. 1 (Spring 2002): 7–20.

Berndt, T. J. (2002). "Friendship Quality and Social Development." *Current Directions in Psychological Science,* 11, no. 1 (Spring 2002): 7–10.

Bhasin, J., and Parrey, H. (2012). "Modeling Human Resource Systems and Organizational Effectiveness: An Empirical Study." *International Journal of Exclusive Management Research,* 2, no. 11 (2012): 1–18.

Boudreau, J. W., and Ramstad, P. M. "Talentship and the New Paradigm for Human Resource Management: From Professional Practices to Strategic Talent Decision Science." *Human Resource Planning,* 28, no. 2 (2005): 17–26.

Boudreau, J. W., and Ramstad, P. M. "Talentship and HR Measurement and Analysis: From ROI to Strategic Organizational Change." *Human Resource Planning,* 29, no. 1 (2006): 25–33.

Camps, J., and Luna-Arocas, R. "A Matter of Learning: How Human Resources Affect Organizational Performance." *British Journal of Management,* 23 no. 1, (2012): 1–21.

Després, B. *Systems Thinkers in Action: A Field Guide for Effective Change Leadership in Education.* Lanham, MD: Rowman & Littlefield, 2008.

English, F. W. *Anatomy of Professional Practice: Promising Research Perspectives on Educational Leadership.* Lanham, MD: Rowman & Littlefield, 2007.

Galbraith, J. R. *Designing the Customer-Centric Organization: A Guide to Strategy, Structure, and Process.* San Francisco: Jossey-Bass, 2005.

Gouveia, W., and Shane, R. "Investing in Our Human Resources." *American Journal of Health-System Pharmacy,* 69, no. 12 (2012): 1077–1078. doi:10.2146/ajhp110660

Hong, F., and Hongmin, Z. "Discussion on Strategies of Development and Application of Human Resources." *Asian Social Science,* 6, no. 3 (2010): 12–16.

Human Resource Planning Society (HRPS). (2009). www.hrps.org.

Huseinovic, A. (2012). "Role of Management in the Process of Managing Human Resources in Electronic Media." *Technics Technologies Education Management,* 7, no. 3 (2012): 849.

Kates, A. "(Re)designing the HR Organization." *Human Resource Planning,* 29, no. 2 (2006): 22–30.

Kowalski, T. J., and Lasley, T. J. (Eds.). *Handbook of Data-Based Decision Making in Education.* New York: Routledge Press (2008).

Kritt, D. W., and Winegar, L. T. (Eds.). *Education and Technology: Critical Perspectives, Possible Futures.* Lanham, MD: Rowman & Littlefield, 2008.

Lawler, F. F., III, Boudreau, J. W., and Mohrman, S. A. *Achieving Strategic Excellence: An Assessment of Human Resource Organizations.* Stanford, CA: Stanford Business Books, 2006.

Martin-Rios, C. "Why Do Firms Seek to Share Human Resource Management Knowledge? The Importance of Inter-Firm Networks." *Journal of Business Research,* (2012). doi:10.1016/j.jbusres.2012.10.004.

National School Boards Association (NSBA). (2009). www.nsba.org.

Norton, M. S. *Outlines and Highlights for Human Resources Administration for Educational Leaders.* Upper Saddle River, NJ: Pearson, 2010.

Palmer, J., and Finney, M. I. *The Human Resource Professional's Career Guide: Building a Position of Strength.* Blaine, Canada: Pfeiffer Press, 2005.

Plass, J. L. "Living-Systems Design Model for Web-Based Knowledge Management Systems." *Educational Technology Research and Development,* 50, no. 1 (2002): 35–57.

Smith, R. E. *Human Resources Administration: A School-Based Perspective,* 2nd ed. Larchmont, NY: Eye on Education, 2001.

Society for Human Resources Management (SHRM). (2009). www.shrm.org.

Sulaiman, W. I. W., Mahbob, M. H., and Abu Hassan, B. R. "An Analysis on the Effectiveness of Team Building: The Impact on Human Resources." *Asian Social Science,* 8, no. 5 (2012): 29–37. doi:10.5539/ass.v8n5p29.

Tomé, E. "Human Resource Development in the Knowledge Based and Services Driven Economy: An Introduction." *Journal of European Industrial Training*, 35, no. 6 (2011): 524. doi:10.1108/03090591111150077.

Vinovskis, M. *From A Nation at Risk to No Child Left Behind.* New York: Teachers College Press, 2008.

Webb, L. D., and Norton, M. S. *Human Resources Administration: Personnel Issues and Needs in Education.* Upper Saddle River, NJ: Pearson, 2012.

Wickramasinghe, V. V. "Influence of Total Quality Management on Human Resource Management Practices: An Exploratory Study." *International Journal of Quality and Reliability Management*, 29, no. 8 (2012): 836–850. doi:10.1108/02656711211270324.

Wilmore, E. L. *Superintendent Leadership: Applying the Educational Leadership Constituent Council Standards for Improved District Performance.* Thousand Oaks, CA: Corwin Press, 2008.

Appendix
Selections from the ISLLC Standards*

The Interstate School Leaders Licensure Consortium (ISLLC) is a program sponsored by The Council of Chief State School Officers. Through this program, professionals from twenty-four state education agencies and representatives from various professional associations crafted a set of model standards for school leaders in 1996. The standards are compatible with the new curriculum guidelines for school administration established by the National Council for the Accreditation of Teacher Education (NCATE). Further, the ISLLC standards are being used by many states in the assessment of candidates for administrator certification and licensure.

There are six standards. Each standard is operationalized through three dimensions: knowledge, dispositions, and performances. The content of this text will help those seeking certification and licensure to understand certain ideas and concepts that are usually part of the assessment procedure. A listing of those standards follows, along with their dimensions and the chapters of this text that contain the information.

Standard 1

A school administrator is an educational leader who promotes the success of all students by facilitating the development, articulation, implementation, and stewardship of a vision of learning that is shared and supported by the school community.

Knowledge
The administrator has knowledge and understanding of

- The principles of developing and implementing strategic plans
- Information sources, data collection, and data analysis strategies

This standard and its accompanying knowledge are treated in Chapters 1 and 2.

Source: Council of Chief State School Officers, Educational Leadership Policy Standards: ISLLC 2008, Washington, DC: Author, 2008, http://www.ccsso.org/Documents/2008/Educational_Leadership_Policy_Standards_2008.pdf.

Standard 2

A school administrator is an educational leader who promotes the success of all students by advocating, nurturing, and sustaining a school culture and instructional program conducive to learning and staff professional growth.

Knowledge
The administrator has knowledge and understanding of

- Applied motivational theories
- Diversity and its meaning for educational programs
- Adult learning and professional development models

Dispositions
The administrator believes in, values, and is committed to

- Life-long learning for self and others
- Professional development as an integral part of school improvement
- A safe and supportive learning environment

Performances
The administrator facilitates processes and engages in activities that ensure

- Professional development promotes a focus on student learning consistent with the school vision and goals
- Life-long learning is encouraged and modeled
- There is a culture of high expectations for self, student, and staff performance
- Technologies are used in teaching and learning
- A variety of supervisory and evaluation models is employed

This standard and its accompanying knowledge, dispositions, and performances are treated in Chapters 2, 6, 7, and 8.

Standard 3

A school administrator is an educational leader who promotes the success of all students by ensuring management of the organization, operations, and resources for a safe, efficient, and effective learning environment.

Knowledge
The administrator has knowledge and understanding of

- Theories and models of organizations and the principles of organizational development
- Operational procedures at the school and district level
- Principles and issues relating to school safety and security
- Human resources management and development
- Legal issues affecting school operations
- Current technologies that support management functions

Dispositions
The administrator believes in, values, and is committed to

- Making management decisions to enhance learning and teaching
- High-quality standards, expectations, and performances

- Involving stakeholders in management processes
- A safe environment

Performances

The administrator facilitates processes and engages in activities ensuring that

- Emerging trends are recognized, studied, and applied as appropriate
- Operational plans and procedures to achieve the vision and goals of the school are in place
- Collective bargaining and other contractual agreements related to the school are managed effectively
- The school plant, equipment, and support systems operate safely, efficiently, and effectively
- Financial, human, and material resources are aligned to the goals of schools
- Organizational systems are monitored regularly and modified as needed
- Responsibility is shared to maximize ownership and accountability
- There is effective use of technology to manage school operations
- Human resources functions support the attainment of school goals

This standard and its accompanying knowledge, dispositions, and performances are treated in all chapters of this book.

Standard 4

A school administrator is an educational leader who promotes the success of all students by collaborating with families and community members, responding to diverse community interests and needs, and mobilizing community resources.

Knowledge

The administrator has knowledge and understanding of

- Emerging issues and trends that potentially affect the school community
- The conditions and dynamics of the diverse school community
- Community resources

Disposition

The administrator believes in, values, and is committed to

- The proposition that diversity enriches the school

Performances

The administrator facilitates processes and engages in activities that ensure

- Available community resources are secured to help the school solve problems and achieve goals
- Diversity is recognized and valued
- Opportunities for staff to develop collaborative skills are provided

This standard and its accompanying knowledge, disposition, and performances are treated in Chapters 2, 3, 5, 6, and 8.

Standard 5

A school administrator is an educational leader who promotes the success of all students by acting with integrity, fairness, and in an ethical manner.

Knowledge
The administrator has knowledge and understanding of

- Professional codes of ethics

Dispositions
The administrator believes in, values, and is committed to

- The principles of the Bill of Rights
- Bringing ethical principles to the decision-making process
- Accepting the consequences for upholding one's principles and actions

Performances
The administrator

- Demonstrates a personal and professional code of ethics
- Protects the rights and confidentiality of students and staff
- Demonstrates appreciation for and sensitivity to the diversity in the school community
- Fulfills legal and contractual obligations
- Applies laws and procedures fairly, wisely, and considerately

This standard and its accompanying knowledge, dispositions, and performances are treated in Chapters 2 and 10.

Standard 6

The school administrator is an educational leader who promotes the success of all students by understanding, responding to, and influencing the larger political, social, economic, legal, and cultural context.

Knowledge
The administrator has knowledge and understanding of

- The importance of diversity and equity in a democratic society

Performances
The administrator facilitates processes and engages in activities that ensure

- Communication occurs among the school community concerning trends, issues, and potential changes in the environment in which schools operate
- The school community works within the framework of policies, laws, and regulations enacted by local, state, and federal authorities

This standard and its accompanying knowledge and performances are treated in Chapters 1, 2, and 10.

CHAPTER 2

Human Resources Planning

Focus Scenario

You are the recently employed director of affirmative action in a suburban school district with approximately 10,000 students. This new position in the district was prompted by a series of complaints, some of which have been made to the Equal Employment Opportunity Commission (EEOC), that the school district has a systemic record of discrimination. Thus, the school district is being investigated by the Justice Department because of a series of complaints by applicants for teaching positions that the school district discriminated in the hiring of African Americans, particularly for teaching positions. Also, a complaint had been filed with the EEOC alleging that the school district discriminates against females in promotion to administrative positions. This complaint has been further exacerbated by another complaint to the EEOC stating that the school district does not protect females from sexual harassment.

The board of education and the school superintendent are concerned about the potential harm that such complaints could bring to the district because the district had been engaged in a voluntary desegregation settlement with neighboring city school districts. The status of the civil rights case had been declared unitary.

The board of education and superintendent are looking to you for direction on how to investigate these charges and plan to make the necessary changes to antidiscrimination policies and procedures based on the findings. Both the board and superintendent were under the impression that such discrimination had been eliminated when the district was involved in the voluntary desegregation program because of the many policies and procedures that were instituted at that time.

Please use both the Discussion Questions and Statements and Suggested Activities at the end of this chapter in order to help you develop a way of proceeding in order to address the issues in this section.

Planning is a process common to all human experience. Before embarking on a journey, an individual must understand where he or she is, know where he or she wants to go, and decide how best to get there. In an elementary form, this exemplifies the essence of the process even as it is applied in educational organizations.

Through the process of human resources planning, a school district ensures that it has the right number of people, with the right skills, in the right place, and at the right time, and that these people are capable of carrying out those tasks that will aid the organization in achieving its objectives. If a school district is to achieve its objectives, it needs financial resources, physical resources, and people. Too often, the people are taken for granted, and yet they are the force that directly affects the main objective of a school district—to educate children. Human resources planning thus translates the organization's objectives into people requirements.

In some school districts, long- and short-range objectives are couched in ambiguous language and often known only by certain central office administrators. This makes it difficult to involve building principals in the hiring process when unexpected vacancies occur, when replacements are needed because of natural attrition, or when new programs must be staffed.

From an organizational perspective, human resources planning is a process that analyzes the strengths, weaknesses, opportunities, and threats that could affect having the best possible teachers, administrators, and staff members educating the students of a given school district.[1]

Assessing Human Resources Needs

The process of assessing human resources needs has four aspects. First, human resources inventories must be developed to analyze the various tasks necessary to meet the school district's objectives; these tasks are then matched against the skills of current employees. Second, enrollment projections must be developed for a five-year period. The extreme mobility of the American population has made this aspect increasingly important over the past twenty-five years. Third, the overall objectives of the school district must be reviewed within the context of changing needs. At a time when school district budgets are tight, all but the wealthiest districts must establish priorities in meeting objectives. Fourth, human resources inventories, enrollment projections, and school district objectives must be organized into a human resources forecast, which becomes the mandate of the human resources department.

Implementing this human resources mandate becomes more complex, however, when viewed in light of compliance with federal legislation and, in some districts, when staff reductions are brought on by decreasing enrollment. Because both issues have had such a tremendous impact on the human resources function, they have been given particular emphasis in this chapter.

Human resources planning is sometimes understood only within the confines of the instructional program. However, for every two teachers, there is usually one classified employee. The contemporary school district employs not only teachers and administrators but also cooks, custodians, maintenance personnel, secretaries, computer programmers, warehouse personnel, distribution truck drivers, and other specialists who are often considered by the average citizen to be employed only in the private business sector.

Human Resources Inventories

Human resources planning begins with the development of a profile indicating the status of current human resources. This profile is generated through forms completed by employees, verified by supervisors, and finally sent to the human resources department. Each form should include the employee's name, age, date employed with the school district, gender, job title, place of employment within the district, education and training along with the dates when completed, special skills, and, for instructional personnel, certification.

A human resources profile for each job classification is then developed from the forms completed by the employees. The profile lists all relevant information for each job classification.

From a planning perspective, this information is valuable not only in determining what skills are available but also in developing new instructional programs and support services. The human resources profile also helps administrators as they carry out other human resources tasks such as recruitment and staff development. For example, the length of time since an individual received his or her training or education helps the director of staff development plan appropriate programs.

The profile also provides crucial information for identifying weaknesses in the school district's ability to meet its objectives. For example, reviewing data under the "Date Employed" section helps the administration analyze such problems as staff turnover and job dissatisfaction. The "Age of Employee" information helps administrators formulate strategies for recruitment by identifying those individuals approaching retirement age. Accurate data are essential to every aspect of the human resources process, and human resources profiles are an effective method of presenting such information.

Enrollment Prediction

Because educational institutions are service organizations, enrollment prediction is an essential aspect of human resources planning. Unless a school system makes an effort to predict declines or increases in the number of students to be served, it may unexpectedly experience half-filled classrooms and a surplus of teachers, or overcrowded classrooms and a shortage of teachers.

The major question to be answered by an enrollment prediction is, "How many children are expected to attend a particular school over the next five to ten years?" Many methods can be used to forecast enrollments; among the most popular is the *percentage of retention* or *cohort-survival* technique. This method is predicated on birth rates and the historical retention of students (Figure 2.1). However, other indicators highlight enrollment trends before the statistical time required by the former technique has elapsed. Such indicators identify social, financial, and residential factors for critical analysis of a school and community. The following discussion, Figure 2.1, and Exhibits 2.1 and 2.2 have been adapted from *AASA Executive Handbook Series, Vol. II: Declining Enrollment: What to Do,* published by the American Association of School Administrators,[2] but now out of print.

The following indicators are qualitative in nature because they are based on observations rather than on statistical analysis:

• *Number of children in elementary school classes.* The use of alternative spaces as classrooms, such as the cafeteria, gymnasium, or auditorium stage, is an obvious indicator that enrollment is increasing. A decline in student numbers in certain grade levels could indicate overall decreasing enrollments. Thus, it is important to analyze a decline of even a few children if it occurs in certain grade levels. For example, a trend may be developing when enrollments in the primary grades drop from thirty to twenty-five students, especially if this drop represents fewer students than are enrolled in grades four and five.

Instructions

I 1. Fill in Birth Rate.
   2. Fill in 1st Grade Enrollment.
   3. Do necessary calculations to find Average Ratio.

II 1. Fill in Birth Rate.
    2. Multiply by Average Ratio.

III 1. Fill in enrollment data.
     2. Do necessary calculations to find Retention Ratio.
     3. Fill in Projected 1st Grade Enrollment from II into appropriate columns of III.
     4. Multiply enrollment for a specific year and class by the Retention Ratio for the *next* class. Result is the predicted enrollment for that year, next class.
     5. Complete the chart.

ENROLLMENT PREDICTION CHARTS
I

Birth Rate		1st Grade Enrollment		Clarify what Enrollment Ratio of Birth Rate means?
2000		2006–07		
2001		2007–08		
2002		2008–09		
2003		2009–10		
2004		2010–11		
		Total of Ratios		
		Divide by 5		
		Average Ratio		

II

Birth Rate	× Average Ratio =	Projected 1st Grade Enrollment	For years
2005			2011–12
2006			2012–13
2007			2013–14
2008			2014–15
2009			2015–16

Continued

FIGURE 2.1   Cohort-Survival Technique

Source: Adapted from *AASA Executive Handbook Series, Vol. II: Declining Enrollment: What to Do,* by American Association of School Administrators, 1974, Arlington, VA: Author, pp. 8–9.

III

Year	Enrollment by Grade											
	1	2	3	4	5	6	7	8	9	10	11	12
2000–01												
2001–02												
2002–03												
2003–04												
2004–05												
Total by Grade												
Divide by 5												
Divide Grades		$\frac{2}{1}$	$\frac{3}{2}$	$\frac{4}{3}$	$\frac{5}{4}$	$\frac{6}{5}$	$\frac{7}{6}$	$\frac{8}{7}$	$\frac{9}{8}$	$\frac{10}{9}$	$\frac{11}{10}$	$\frac{12}{11}$
RETENTION RATIO												
P R O J E C T E D E N R O L L M E N T 2011–12												
2012–13												
2013–14												
2014–15												
2015–16												
2016–17												
2017–18												
2018–19												
2019–20												
2020–21												

FIGURE 2.1   Continued

EXHIBIT 2.1   Enrollment Indicator Survey Questions

1. Is your community close to a metropolitan area, and did your community develop and grow as a result of population expansion in that metropolitan area?

2. Is your community one with expensive houses that continue to escalate in price disproportionately to general real estate values?

3. Does your community contain a high percentage of professionals or older persons whose homes fulfill their lifetime needs and whose children are now in (or have been through) the local schools?

4. Even if your community has a highly reputed school system, will that good reputation draw in young families in spite of high-priced houses?

5. Does your community have a high level of mobility, with families moving in and out? (And who's moving in—families with children or retirees?)

6. Does your community contain pockets of middle-income housing that will attract young couples and families with small children?

7. Is there still land available in your community for future residential development?

8. Have service organizations (for example, YMCA, YWCA, community clubs for children, religious groups) been maintaining an emphasis on programs for children of elementary school age?

Source: Adapted from *AASA Executive Handbook Series, Vol. II: Declining Enrollment: What to Do,* by American Association of School Administrators, 1974, Arlington, VA: Author, pp. 8–9.

EXHIBIT 2.2   Commonly Asked Questions about Demographic Surveys

1. *What is a demographic survey?* A demographic survey of the school district includes a thorough census of the population determining who the people are, their living conditions, how many there are, how they intend to use the land, their length of residency, the number of children per household by ages and grades, and the various kinds of dwelling units found in the district.

2. *What are the advantages of a demographic survey?* By combining the information from a demographic survey with in-and-out migration rates, school attrition rates, and number of live births, it is possible to make enrollment projections beyond the conventional linear model. This type of information gives the forecaster the tools with which to project more accurately by "feeling the pulse" of the district.

3. *What are the disadvantages of a demographic survey?* The two major disadvantages are costs and the time limitation on the utility of the data. The major costs are for the personnel involved in planning, organizing, and administering the survey, processing the data, and analyzing the

results, with additional costs that include computer time and supplies. In regard to the time limitation on the utility of the data, unless supplemental surveys are conducted, the lifetime of demographic data usually does not exceed five years. This time limitation may be considerably less in a rapidly changing community.

4. *What kind of district would benefit most from a demographic survey?* In districts where enrollments are fluctuating significantly or changing in a nonlinear fashion, the benefits gained through a demographic survey will probably offset the cost involved.

5. *What specific outside community factors should be taken into consideration when evaluating enrollment projections?* Following are major outside community factors to be considered: transportation, movement of industry (in–out), change in zoning regulations, change in subdivisions regulations, change in government or military installations (opening or closing), urban renewal, subdivision of large land holdings (farms, estates), and highway systems.

Source: Adapted from *AASA Executive Handbook Series, Vol. II: Declining Enrollment: What to Do,* by American Association of School Administrators, 1974, Arlington, VA: Author, pp. 8–9.

- *Persistent trend in elementary school enrollment over a three-year period.* Of course, there may be minor increases and decreases in enrollment over short periods of time. This may be due to outside factors such as the building of a new home subdivision or the demolition of homes because of a highway expansion project. Discounting such major factors, trends in enrollment increase or decrease must call for a larger-scale investigation.
- *Feedback from realtors.* The true insiders concerning the effects of housing on enrollments are realtors. Establishing ongoing communications with real estate firms in the community is of vital importance to enrollment prediction.

These indicators are enhanced by Exhibit 2.1, which sets forth eight normative questions. The answers to these questions, along with the other indicators, can be used by human resources administrators to determine whether a full-scale enrollment prediction such as the cohort-survival technique exemplified in Figure 2.1 is needed. Exhibit 2.2 provides information about demographic surveys, which incorporate census information into the planning process. In summary, qualitative observations, the answers to indicator questions, cohort-survival analysis, and demographic survey information constitute a multilevel approach to enrollment prediction.

Review of School District Objectives

The future objectives of a school district determine future human resources needs. The number and mix of employees are determined by the types of services called for by organizational objectives. Establishing objectives is the prerogative of the board of education. The board, however, must rely on the advice of the school administration as it establishes objectives that will best meet the educational needs of the community.

The review of current objectives in light of future educational needs is a cooperative task. In a district operating under the organizational structure presented in Chapter 1, the assistant superintendents for secondary education, elementary education, and instructional services have the primary responsibility for determining future objectives. The assistant superintendent for human resources develops a human resources forecast to meet the projected objectives developed by the three other assistant superintendents. The assistant superintendent for administrative services then translates the objectives and human resources needs into a fiscal plan. The superintendent of schools is charged with prioritizing the objectives and recommending them to the school board for approval.

This review of objectives is not a one-time task, but rather a continual process. The objectives, however, should be established for at least a five-year period and, if the need occurs, could be revised into a new five-year plan each year. Thus, a set of objectives is always in effect for a set period of time.

Human Resources Forecasting

When the objectives have been reviewed and an overall human resources forecast has been established, a more explicit projection of future human resources needs must be developed.[3] This responsibility can be initiated through utilizing the expertise of the teachers, administrators, and staff members of the school district. They have a vested interest in the future of the school district and insights that can be developed only by doing their jobs. In a sense, they are the experts.

Of course, a human resources administrator can provide historical comparisons with past trends that serve as benchmarks for future needs. Analyzing the responsibilities of current teachers, administrators, and staff members provides a reality check that can be correlated with benchmark data in order to develop the forecast. The human resources inventories on current employees can also provide important and valuable information concerning the age, gender, education, and certification of employees, and the types of positions within the school district.

Supply of Human Resources

An increase in a school system's supply of human resources can come from two sources—newly hired employees and individuals returning from absences such as maternity, military, and sabbatical leaves. Both types of increases are relatively easy to incorporate into a human resources forecast because hiring is controlled and leaves are usually granted for set periods of time.

Decreases in a school system's supply of human resources, however, are more difficult to predict. Deaths, voluntary resignations, and dismissals are unpredictable except in the broadest sense, as through statistical averaging. Some decreases such as sabbatical leaves can be controlled, whereas others such as retirements are easier to predict.

The available labor force has a significant effect on human resources forecasting. Graduates from high schools, colleges, and universities continually replenish the supply of labor necessary to carry out the mandate of public education. In recent years, however, educational organizations have experienced a decrease in the number of applicants for mathematics and science teaching positions because of the higher wages and advancement opportunities available in private business and industry.

A major source of employees other than recent graduates is older individuals, particularly women reentering the workforce and seeking full- or part-time employment, either to supplement family income or, in many cases, to provide the primary income for the family. Divorce rates and the high cost of living are key factors contributing to the number of women reentering the labor force.

Matching Needs with Supply

A final activity in human resources forecasting is matching the school district's future human resources needs with current supply. This pinpoints shortages, highlights areas of potential overstaffing, and identifies the number of individuals who must be recruited from the labor force to satisfy future needs.

In the final analysis, human resources planning ensures that we have the right number and mix of people to meet the school district's future needs as determined by its future objectives.

Reduction in Force

Declining enrollments have particular significance in the human resources planning process and have caused the initiation in some districts of a procedure commonly referred to as *reduction in force (RIF)*. Excess employees are usually placed on involuntary leave according to a seniority system, which follows the principle of "last in, first out." Retained employees may be transferred within the school system to balance a particular staff or faculty. Such changes are certain to create anxiety among individuals who have become accustomed to the atmosphere and procedures of a particular school. Because many school districts have hired minorities only within the past decade, the use of seniority-based reduction procedures usually means that minority employees are among the first to go. Court-mandated desegregation and the legislative demand for affirmative action call for the introduction of alternatives to RIF whenever possible in such school districts. Exhibit 2.3 uses a question format to identify issues that must be addressed by school districts faced with RIF.[4]

Alternatives to Reduction in Force

Two of the most successful alternatives to RIF have been early-retirement incentive programs and the retention of individuals for positions that will become vacant through attrition or will be created because of program development.

In recent years, teacher negotiations have centered on the job security issue, and many contracts now call for teachers in excess areas to be transferred to other positions, hired as permanent substitutes, or retrained for new assignments at the school district's expense.

EXHIBIT 2.3   Commonly Asked Questions about Reduction in Force

1. *What specific steps should be used by the assistant superintendent for human resources in matters of reduction in force (RIF)?*
   - Rank employees in order of seniority.
   - Consult with legal counsel for specific wording of written notices to ensure that all the legal technicalities and notification deadlines are met.
   - It is usually considerate to include some less formal message within the body of the letter.
   - Hold a preliminary meeting with possibly affected teachers.
   - Issue letters informing teachers that they may be excessed within the coming year (registered mail).
   - Issue letters informing teachers that they will be excessed (registered mail).

2. *What can a district do to help well-qualified, excessed teachers?* Many districts send listings of the teachers they are laying off along with their qualifications and recommendations to neighboring districts.

3. *What are alternatives to administrator RIF?* Some districts have used excessed building administrators in one- or two-year consultant positions. In one district, an excessed administrator was reassigned as a RIF coordinator.

4. *What is the role of the principal in school closings?* Elementary school principals are often the least used but probably most valuable resource of the district. Principals frequently operate on the "outer fringes" of the central office, so most teachers do not regard them as "the administration"; likewise, they are not considered part of the teaching ranks by the central office, so most chief administrators do not regard them as "the teachers." The unique position held is that of middle manager, one that seems acceptable to everybody. Usually, principals know and enjoy good relationships with parents and the community—frequently a much closer contact than any other person in the district. Remember, superintendents may come and go, but the elementary principal usually stays. All these factors make

Continued

EXHIBIT 2.3   *Continued*

the elementary principal of unparalleled value in community–school relations, especially in school closings.

5. *What are suggested actions for planning for RIF?*
   - Institute a moratorium on leave policies to reduce the number of teachers returning to claim positions vacated at higher enrollment levels. Offer only one- or two-year termination contracts to new teachers (some states prohibit this policy).
   - Institute an *early-retirement incentive program (ERIP)*.
   - Institute staffing needs studies before going into contract negotiations that may call for job security items in the new contract.
   - Prepare the community and staff for possible teacher reduction.

   - Request that teachers planning to retire or leave the district file such intention at least a year in advance whenever possible.

6. *How can school districts keep job security from becoming a negotiations issue?* Keeping difficult issues off the negotiations table is the responsibility of the school district negotiator. Whether the negotiator is an outside attorney, a professional negotiator, a school administrator, or a member of the school board, the main function of the negotiator is to determine those items that are considered nonnegotiable. Items dealing with control over the school system operations are essentially the domain of the school board and the administration. Increasingly, however, any and all items related to the operations of schools are becoming negotiable. A firm position in this particular matter of job security, along with community understanding, is necessary.

Source: Adapted from *AASA Executive Handbook Series, Vol. II: Declining Enrollment: What To Do.* by American Association of School Administrators, 1974, Arlington, VA: Author, pp. 8–9.

Role of the Principal

A key person in human resources planning is the building principal. He or she is usually the first to spot dwindling enrollments. The principal, of course, can provide the central office staff with up-to-date and projected enrollment figures, with projected maintenance and capital improvement costs, and with projected staffing needs.

The principal also has frontline contact with staff members, students, and parents. Therefore, he or she should be responsible for preparing teachers for possible job loss and for easing the concerns of parents and students. To perform these tasks effectively, the principal must become an integral part of the human resources planning process—being relied on for data and input. In like manner, he or she must be constantly kept informed of central office decisions before they are announced to the staff and public.

The planning process can be enhanced through computer software programs that convert population and student data into an enrollment projection. Likewise, simple statistical programs can be helpful in developing a human resources forecast. Further, software programs commonly referred to as *human resources management system (HRMS) programs* provide easy and immediate access to human resources information such as academic degrees, teaching or administrative experience, licensure, and special skills, including athletic coaching and program sponsorship. The newer software is user friendly and can be linked to other school district information systems.

Federal Influences on Human Resources Planning

A hallmark of our contemporary American society is the avalanche of federal legislation and court decisions delineating and more clearly defining civil rights. The term *civil rights* is somewhat misunderstood and is most often applied to the constitutional rights of racial minority groups. However, it correctly refers to those constitutional and legislative rights that are inalienable and applicable to all citizens. The human resources forecast should provide direction for the recruitment and selection processes. In so doing, this forecast must not violate the civil rights of job applicants or lead the school district into an indefensible position.

What follows is an explanation of major federal legislation, executive orders, and court decisions that should provide direction in the implementation phase of a human resources forecast. It is not meant to be exhaustive because the legislative and judicial processes are organic in nature; therefore, modifications and change will undoubtedly occur. The underlying concept of equality, however, has timeless application.

As a prelude to this information, the important concepts of social justice and affirmative action must be clearly understood because these requirements are incorporated or implied in civil rights legislation and executive orders.

Social Justice and Human Resources Administration

The notion of civil rights emanates from the concept of social justice; thus, it is important to explain briefly how social justice is embedded in the practice of human resources administration.[5] Justice is a guide that regulates how people live out their lives as members of various societies. The idea of justice implies that someone or a group of people can be treated fairly or unfairly. The content of justice is often referred to as *entitlement,* and from this perspective, people have claims that are properly due to them.

Because they are humans, all people have an entitlement to be respected. Not only people but also governments and institutions must afford others this respect, which entails personal integrity, liberty, and equality of opportunity. Thus, human resources planning, recruitment, selection, placement and induction, staff development, performance evaluation, compensation, and collective negotiations policies and procedures have a foundation in social justice.

There are also various types of justice. *Distributive justice* refers to the responsibility of society to the individual, *legal justice* refers to the responsibility of each person to society, and *commutative justice* refers to the responsibility that exists among individuals. All three types are found in human resources administration. For example, the school district as a society has a responsibility to be racially and ethnically unbiased in the recruitment and selection of teachers. Teachers have a responsibility to provide truthful information on employment applications, and human resources administrators have a responsibility to process applications for employment in a timely manner.

The notion of justice also has another dimension—*restitution*. It is recognized that unjustly depriving someone of an entitlement does not nullify the responsibility, but rather requires the implementation of the entitlement in addition to restoring what was withheld. This is easily verified by the actions of the EEOC, which has rendered decisions against school districts for being biased against minorities and women. Some of the decisions by the EEOC have required school districts to hire the people filing the complaints.

A Theory of Justice

John Rawls was an American political philosopher who formulated a theory of justice around the notion of fairness.[6] His influence has been extensive, and he is considered to be a major defender of the social contract theory found in the writings of Immanuel Kant, John Locke, and Jean-Jacques Rousseau. Rawls' basic premise is that the best principles of justice for the basic structure of any society are those that would be the object of an original agreement in the establishment of a society, which are derived by free rational persons as an initial position of equality.

In all Western societies, the original agreements were initially derived through many different means, some of which were violent. In fact, the murky remnants of the past are maintained only in a given society's collective consciousness. The original contracts were eventually reduced to writing and have come down to us through time as constitutions. Nevertheless, in subsocieties, it is possible to observe and even participate in formulating an agreement. The human resources policy formulation process used by boards of education and the administrative formulation of human resources procedures are examples of how original agreements live on in contemporary society. They should be the agreements of equality. Of course, it is true that state and federal laws and governmental agency regulations have established the boundaries within which policies and procedures are formulated. However, the manner in which boards of education, superintendents, and human resources administrators establish and interpret policies and procedures can violate the principle of fairness. This is seen in the human resources function, particularly in regard to affirmative action and equal employment opportunity.

Further, like all other institutions, school districts go through periods of time when it is necessary to reevaluate policies and procedures for the purposes of renewal and reform. As this reevaluation is carried out, the opportunity arises to examine the policies and procedures of a given school district using the notion of fairness as a criterion.

Rawls set forth two principles that he believes people should choose as a means of implementing the notion of fairness. His first principle states that each person should have an equal right to a system of liberties that is compatible with a similar system of liberties available to all people. The concept of *system,* of course, is an essential component of this principle because it establishes that the exercise of one liberty may be, and probably is, dependent on other liberties. Further, Rawls states that the principles of justice are to be ranked and gives the example that liberty can be restricted only for the sake of liberty. Thus, administrative internship programs that are limited to minorities and women because of their underrepresentation in the administrative ranks of a given school district are justifiable based on this principle.

Rawls' second principle asserts that social and economic inequalities must benefit everyone, not just the least advantaged, and that equal opportunity to secure offices and positions must be open to all. This principle of justice must also be ranked so that the principle of efficiency does not occupy the position of first priority. Affirmative action and equal opportunity in employment legislation and court decisions help secure this principle, along with legislation and case law that ensure equal opportunity to seek election to the board of education. The following federal laws, discussed later in this chapter, are examples of how this second principle has been operationalized in American society:

- The Civil Rights Act of 1964, as amended
- Title V of the Rehabilitation Act of 1973
- The Americans with Disabilities Act of 1990

The principle of just savings must be invoked when considering how inequities can benefit the least advantaged. Therefore, a board of education that needs to raise the level of teachers' salaries because the assistant superintendent for human resources is finding it difficult to recruit and hire quality teachers may place before the voters a tax levy referendum that will increase the amount of property taxes each property owner will pay in future years. Such an increase in taxation benefits not only the present generation of students but also future generations.

The application of the second principle through this example demonstrates that the present generation of taxpayers will bear the burden of higher taxes in order to enhance the opportunities of other generations. If there is a lack of quality teachers, then the educational programs will continue to deteriorate, and ultimately the cost will be much higher to bring the programs back to the appropriate level. In addition, competitive salaries will have increased to the point where it will be necessary to significantly increase the amount of taxes in order to attract the caliber of teachers required by the educational needs of the students. Consequently, future generations are saved from becoming the least advantaged through the present and immediate future generations of taxpayers.

In the United States, these principles of justice are embodied in certain documents that were the cornerstones on which the nation was founded. In addition to the Constitution of the United States, the Bill of Rights and the Declaration of Independence contain the principles concerning justice that are set forth in this chapter.[7]

Affirmative Action

Definition

"There can be justice for none if there is not justice for all." This statement captures the intent of civil rights legislation. Affirmative action programs are detailed, result-oriented programs that, when carried out in good faith, result in compliance with the equal opportunity clauses found in most legislation and executive orders.[8] Affirmative action, therefore, is not a law within itself, but rather an objective reached by following a set of guidelines that ensure compliance with legislation and executive orders. Thus, an organization does not violate affirmative action, it violates the law.

Brief History of Affirmative Action

Although the term *affirmative action* is of recent origin, the concept of an employer taking specific steps to treat equally minority groups can be traced to President Franklin D. Roosevelt's Executive Order 8802, issued in June 1941. This executive order, which had the force of law, established a policy of equal employment opportunity in regard to defense contracts. President Roosevelt issued a new order in 1943, extending the order to all government contractors and, for the first time, mandating that all contracts contain a clause specifically forbidding discrimination.

In 1953, President Dwight D. Eisenhower issued Executive Order 10479, which established the Government Contract Compliance Committee. This committee received complaints of discrimination against government contractors but had no power to enforce its guidelines.

The period of voluntary compliance ended in 1961, when President John F. Kennedy issued Executive Order 10925, establishing the President's Committee on Equal Employment Opportunity and giving it the authority to make and enforce its own rules by imposing sanctions and penalties against noncomplying contractors. Government contractors were required to have nondiscrimination clauses covering race, color, creed, and national origin.

In September 1965, President Lyndon B. Johnson issued the very important Executive Order 11246, which gave the secretary of labor jurisdiction over contract compliance and created the Office of Federal Contract Compliance (OFCC), which replaced the Committee on Equal Employment Opportunity. Every federal contract was required to have a seven-point equal opportunity clause, by which a contractor agreed not to discriminate against anyone in hiring and during employment on the basis of race, color, creed, or national origin. Further, the contractor had to agree in writing to take affirmative action measures in hiring. President Johnson's Executive Order 11375, issued in 1967, amended Executive Order 11246 by adding sex and religion to the list of protected categories.

The secretary of labor issued Chapter 60 of Title 41 of the Code of Federal Regulations for the purpose of implementing Executive Order 11375. The secretary delegated enforcement authority to the OFCC, which reports to the assistant secretary of the Employment Standards Administration.

Later renamed the Office of Federal Contract Compliance Programs, this agency provides leadership in the area of nondiscrimination by government contractors and also coordinates matters relating to Title VII of the 1964 Civil Rights Act, as amended, with the EEOC and the U.S. Department of Justice.

The EEOC was established by Title VII of the 1964 Civil Rights Act to investigate alleged discrimination based on race, color, religion, sex, or national origin. The EEOC was greatly strengthened in 1972 by the passage of the Equal Employment Opportunity Act. It extended coverage to private employers of fifteen or more persons, educational institutions, state and local governments, public and private employment agencies, labor unions with fifteen or more members, and joint labor management committees for apprenticeships and training. This act also gave the EEOC the power to bring litigation against an organization that engages in discriminatory practices.

Equal Employment Opportunity Commission

A major failing of many school administrators is their lack of understanding about the EEOC and its influence on human resources administration. From time to time, this five-member commission has established affirmative action guidelines that, if adopted by school districts, can minimize liability when claims of discrimination occur. To further aid employers, on December 11, 1978, the EEOC adopted additional guidelines that can be used to avoid liability for claims of *reverse discrimination* that result from affirmative action that provides employment opportunities for women and racial and ethnic minorities. The following compilation from several sources provides a framework for affirmative action compliance.

Eight steps emerged from federal guidelines[9]: First, each board of education should issue a written policy covering equal employment opportunity and affirmative action to be enforced by its chief executive officer, the superintendent. Commitments that should be included in the policy are a determination to recruit, hire, and promote for all job classifications without regard to race, creed, national origin, gender, age, color, or disability (except where gender or age is a bona fide occupational qualification); a determination to base decisions concerning employment solely on individual qualifications as related to the requirements of the position; and a determination to ensure that all human resources matters—such as compensation, benefits, transfers, layoffs, returns from layoffs, and continuing education—will be administered without regard to race, creed, national origin, gender, age, color, or disability.

Second, the superintendent should appoint a top-level official to be directly responsible for implementing the program. This official usually has the title *director of affirmative action*. He or she should be responsible for developing policy statements and affirmative action programs. In addition, the director of affirmative action should initiate internal and external communications, assist other administrators in the identification of problem areas, design and implement auditing and reporting systems, serve as a liaison between the district and enforcement agencies, and keep the superintendent informed of the latest developments in the area of equal opportunities.

Third, a school district should disseminate information about its affirmative action program both internally and externally. The board policy should be publicized through internal channels such as at meetings and on bulletin boards. External dissemination might take the form of brochures advertising the district; written notification to recruitment sources; clauses in purchase orders, leases, and contracts; and written notification to minority organizations, community agencies, and community leaders.

Step four begins with a survey and analysis of minority and female employees by school and job classification. The percentage and number of minority and female employees currently employed in each major job classification should be compared to their presence in the relevant labor market—that is, the area in which you can reasonably expect to recruit. This determines *underutilization*, defined as having fewer minorities or women in a particular job category or school than could be reasonably expected, and *concentration*, defined as more of a particular group in a job category or school than would reasonably be expected. A survey should also be conducted to identify those females and minorities who have the credentials to handle other jobs. Such employees can be transferred to these positions, if necessary.

With this information, the school district's administration should proceed to step five, developing measurable and remedial goals on a timetable. Once long-range goals have been established, specific and numerical targets can be developed for the hiring, training, transferring, and promoting of personnel to reach goals within the established time frame. During this step, the causes of underutilization should be identified.

Step six calls for developing and implementing specific programs to eliminate discriminatory barriers. This is the heart of an affirmative action program and is discussed. Everyone involved in the hiring process must be trained to use objective standards that support affirmative action goals. Recruitment procedures for each job category must be analyzed and reviewed to identify and eliminate discriminatory barriers. Recruitment procedures should include contacting educational institutions and community action organizations that represent minorities. Reviewing the selection process to ensure that job requirements and hiring practices contribute to the attainment of affirmative action goals is a vital part of step six. This includes making certain that job qualifications and selection standards do not screen out minorities unless the qualifications can be significantly related to job performance and no alternate nondiscriminatory standards can be developed. Upward-mobility systems such as promotions, transfers, and continuing education play an important role in fulfilling step six. Through careful record keeping, existing barriers may be identified and specific remedial programs initiated. These programs may include providing training for targeted minorities and women who are currently qualified for upward mobility, and more extensive training for those who are not yet qualified.

Wage and salary structures, benefits, and conditions of employment are other areas of investigation. Title VII of the 1964 Civil Rights Act and the Equal Pay Act require fiscal parity for jobs of equal skill and responsibility. All fringe benefits such as medical, hospital, and life insurance must be applied equally to personnel performing similar functions. Even in instances where states had "protective laws" barring women from hard or dangerous work, the courts generally found that the equal employment requirements of Title VII superseded these state laws. Courts have also barred compulsory maternity leave and the discharge of pregnant teachers.

Under affirmative action guidelines, the criteria for deciding when a person will be terminated, demoted, disciplined, laid off, or recalled should be the same for all employees. Seemingly neutral practices should be reexamined to see if they have a disparate effect on minority groups. Special considerations, such as job transfers and career counseling, should be given to minorities who have been laid off because of legitimate seniority systems.

Step seven is to establish internal auditing and reporting systems to monitor and evaluate progress in meeting the goals of the affirmative action program. Quarterly reports based on the data already outlined should be available to all administrators, enabling them to see how the program is working and where improvement is needed. The issue of keeping records on current employees and applicants by gender, race, or national origin is a sensitive issue. Such record keeping has been used in the past as a discriminatory device, and some states have outlawed the practice. However, in certain litigation, these records have been used as evidence of discriminatory practices. The data could even be demanded by enforcement agencies, and they are necessary for affirmative action record keeping. The EEOC suggests that such information be coded and kept separate from personnel files.[10]

Developing supportive district and community programs is the final step in an affirmative action program. It may include developing support services for recruiting minority and female employees, as well as encouraging current employees to further their education in order to qualify for promotions.

EEOC Administrative Process

Alleged discrimination charges can be filed with any of the EEOC's district offices. The following outlines the administrative process involved with an allegation of employment discrimination.[11]

Charge of Discrimination   A charge can be filed by any person, by others on behalf of that person, or by any of the EEOC commissioners. This charge must be filed within 180 days from when the alleged discriminatory act occurred. In those states with an employment discrimination law, the time may be extended to 300 days. The EEOC must first refer the charge to the appropriate state agency. The EEOC begins its investigation after the state agency concludes its procedures or sixty days after the date of the referral by the EEOC to the state agency, whichever occurs first.

When an individual is denied employment because of discrimination, this constitutes a specific violation that occurred on a particular date. However, some discriminatory practices are considered to be *continuing violations*. A failure to promote because of a discriminatory system of promotions is an example of a continuing violation because it occurs each day the practice is followed. A continuing violation arises over a lengthy period of time. The time limit for filing a charge involving a continuing violation is 180 days after the cessation of the discriminatory practice. Therefore, as long as a practice continues, there is no time limit for filing a charge.

If an individual is subject to a collective bargaining agreement and believes that he or she has been discriminated against, he or she may follow the grievance procedures set out in the master contract. However, doing so does not alter the time period during which a charge must be filed with the EEOC.

Investigation of the Discrimination Charge   It usually takes eighteen months after a charge is filed for an investigation to begin. The EEOC demands broad access to an employer's records. An employer may object to the subpoena of records on the following grounds: the information is privileged, the compilation of information would be excessively burdensome, or the information sought is irrelevant to the charges.

Determination   When the investigation has been completed, the EEOC makes a determination concerning the discrimination charges. This determination takes one of two forms: *reasonable cause,* which means that the charge is meritorious and that both parties (employer and charging party) will be invited to conciliate the case; or *no cause,* which means that the charge has no merit. If the charging party who receives a *no cause* determination continues to believe that discrimination occurred, the court system is the next avenue of recourse.

Process of Conciliation   The process of conciliation begins when the employer or his or her authorized representative meets with the staff of the EEOC at one of its district offices to explore methods of conciliation. The usual methods employed are as follows:

1. The employer and charging party may agree to a *conciliation agreement.* The terms of this agreement are designed to eliminate the discriminatory practice and may include provisions such as back pay, reinstatement of the charging party if he or she was terminated, and establishment of goals and a timetable for hiring and promoting minorities. The EEOC negotiates thousands of conciliation agreements each year, recovering millions of dollars for employees who have experienced discrimination.

2. With the concurrence of the EEOC, the employer may extend an offer to the charging party. If the charging party rejects the offer, the EEOC issues a *notice of right to sue,* which gives the charging party ninety days to bring legal action against the employer.

3. The employer and the charging party may agree to a settlement for a single individual. However, if the investigation by the EEOC reveals a discriminatory practice against a class of persons such as females or persons with disabilities, and if the employer and the

EEOC are unable to reach an agreement on a class determination, it is considered a *failure of conciliation*, and the case is referred to the litigation division of the EEOC.

4. If the employer, charging party, and EEOC are unable to reach an agreement, this is considered a *failure of conciliation*, and referral is made to the litigation division.

Litigation Division   When conciliation fails, the litigation division evaluates the case to determine if there is a significant legal issue involved or if the case could have a significant impact on systematic patterns of discrimination. If one or both of these conditions exist, the EEOC will most likely bring a lawsuit against the alleged discriminating employer.

The vast majority of employment discrimination lawsuits filed in federal courts, however, are instigated by private individuals or are class action suits filed by a group of citizens. The prerequisites to filing an individual claim of employment discrimination in federal court are as follows: The charge must be filed with the EEOC within the required time, the EEOC must issue a notice of right to sue, and the charging party must file suit within ninety days from receipt of the notice.

A *notice of right to sue,* which allows the charging party to pursue his or her claim through the courts, is usually issued by the EEOC under three circumstances: (1) when a charge of discrimination is determined by the EEOC to have a *no cause* status, (2) when the litigation division of the EEOC rejects a case for legal action, and (3) when the EEOC enters into a conciliation agreement with an employer that does not include the charging party's claim.

If a federal court rules in favor of the charging party, it may grant any award it deems equitable. An injunctive remedy requires an employer to do something such as modify a promotional policy that does not follow affirmative action guidelines and discriminates against minorities. In an individual case of discrimination when back pay is involved, the court may award back pay for a period of up to two years prior to the date when the charge was filed with the EEOC.

Bona Fide Occupational Qualification

Discrimination by gender, religion, or national origin is allowed by the Equal Employment Opportunity Act under one condition, stated in the law as follows:

> Notwithstanding any other provision of this subchapter, (1) it shall not be an unlawful employment practice for an employer to hire and employ employees, for an employment agency to classify, or refer for employment any individual, for a labor organization to classify its membership or to classify or refer for employment any individual, or for an employer, labor organization, or joint labor management committee controlling apprenticeship or other training or retraining programs to admit or employ any individual in any such program, on the basis of his religion, sex, or national origin in those certain instances where religion, sex, or national origin is a bona fide occupational qualification reasonably necessary to the normal operation of that particular business or enterprise, and (2) it shall not be an unlawful employment practice for a school, college, university, or other educational institution or institution of learning to hire and employ employees of a particular religion if such school, college, university, or other educational institution or institution of learning is, in whole or in substantial part, owned, supported, controlled,

or managed by a particular religion or by a particular religious corporation, association, or society, or if the curriculum of such school, college, university, or other educational institution or institution of learning is directed toward the propagation of a particular religion.[12]

Therefore, a school district's personnel administrator has the right to specify a female for the position of swimming instructor when part of the job description includes supervising the locker room used by female students. In like manner, a Lutheran school official may hire only those applicants who profess the Lutheran creed because the mission of the school is to propagate that particular faith.

In certain school districts, the national origin of teachers is extremely important. If, in a particular school district, more than 30 percent of its student population has Spanish surnames, being of Hispanic origin could be a bona fide job qualification for certain teaching positions in that school system.

Judicial Review of Affirmative Action

Court decisions have further modified affirmative action regulations. Although the courts will continue to refine the interpretation of the Civil Rights Act and the Equal Employment Opportunity Act, certain basic conclusions have emerged and provide direction to school districts in their efforts to construct and implement an affirmative action program.[13]

1. Discrimination has been broadly defined, in most cases including a class of individuals rather than a single person. Where discrimination has been found by the courts to exist, remediation must be applied to all members of the class to which the individual complainant belongs.

2. It is not the intent but rather the consequences of employment practices that determine if discrimination exists.

3. Even when an employment practice is neutral in text and impartially administered, it constitutes unlawful discrimination if it has a disparate effect on members of a protected class (those groups covered by a law) or if it perpetuates the effects of prior discriminatory practices.

4. Statistics that show a disproportionate number of minorities or females in a job classification relative to their presence in the workforce constitute evidence of discriminatory practices. When such statistics exist, the employer must show that this is not the result of overt or intentional discrimination.

5. To justify any practice or policy that creates a disparate effect on a protected class, an employer must demonstrate a *compelling business necessity*. The courts have interpreted this in a very narrow sense to mean that no alternative nondiscriminatory practice can achieve the required result.

6. Court-ordered remedies not only open the doors to equal employment opportunity but also require employers to "make whole" and "restore the rightful economic status" of all those in the affected class. In practice, courts have ordered fundamental changes in almost every aspect of employment.

Two U.S. Supreme Court decisions from the late 1970s have had an indirect effect on affirmative action programs in school districts. The first case, *Regents of the University of*

California v. Bakke, was decided in 1978 and dealt with admission quotas to a medical school. The second, *United Steelworkers v. Weber,* was decided in 1979 and dealt with a voluntary race-conscious affirmative action plan in private industry. Both cases could be viewed as establishing precedents in future lawsuits involving school districts. Thus, boards of education might avoid such litigation through policy development that mitigates the possibility of reverse discrimination.

In June 2003, two U.S. Supreme Court rulings addressed a fundamental legal question at the heart of the affirmative action issue—whether the U.S. Constitution permits affirmative action policies. The answer to the question is a resounding "yes". In *Grutter v. Bollinger*, the Court upheld a Michigan law school's admissions policies, stating that the school had a compelling interest in enrolling a racially and ethnically diverse student body because such diversity provides a significant educational benefit. However, although the Court upheld the importance of affirmative action in *Gratz v. Bollinger*, it ruled that Michigan's undergraduate admissions practice placed too much emphasis on race in assessing applicants. The university used a point system that automatically gave substantial bonuses to members of certain minority groups.[14] The implication of these two rulings for human resources administrators is that affirmative action policy is constitutionally permissible, but the practices that implement that policy must be defensible.

Exhibit 2.4 is a sample policy developed to illustrate how school districts can comply with the intent of federal legislation and litigation set forth in this chapter.

EXHIBIT 2.4   Board of Education Policy on Equal Employment Opportunity and Affirmative Action

The board of education recognizes that implementation of its responsibility to provide an effective educational program depends on the full and effective utilization of qualified employees regardless of race, age, sex, color, religion, national origin, creed, ancestry, or disability.

The board directs that its employment and human resources policies guarantee equal opportunity for everyone. Discrimination has no place in any component of this school system. Therefore, all matters relating to recruitment, selection, placement, compensation, benefits, educational opportunities, promotion, termination, and working conditions shall be free from discriminatory practices.

The board of education further initiates an affirmative action program to be in compliance with Title VII of the Civil Rights Act of 1964 and the Equal Employment Opportunity Act of 1972. This program shall ensure that minority and female proportional representation and participation in all employment opportunities; that civil rights will not be violated, abridged, or denied; that recruitment and selection criteria will be unbiased; that information relative to employment and promotional opportunities will be disseminated on an equal basis; and, finally, that every employee has a right to file an internal or external complaint of discrimination and to obtain redress therefrom based on the finding of facts substantiating the complaint.

The following school district administrators are responsible for the effective implementation of the affirmative action program.

Superintendent of Schools. As the chief executive officer of the school system, the superintendent is directly responsible for exercising a leadership role in formulating and implementing procedures that keep with this policy.

Director of Affirmative Action. Under the supervision of the superintendent, the director is responsible for the administration of the affirmative action program.

Civil Rights Act of 1991

The passage of various civil rights legislation during the 1990s set school districts on a new path. This has been particularly true with regard to the Civil Rights Act of 1991.[15] For the first time, the law extends punitive damages and jury trials to employees who have been discriminated against because of their race, national origin, gender, disability, or religion. Thus, school districts must be vigilant in adhering not only to the provisions of this act but also to the spirit of the legislation.

There have been two significant procedural changes. First, the law allows expanded compensatory damages as well as punitive damages. Prior to passage of this law and with few exceptions, plaintiffs' compensatory remedies were limited to lost pay and benefits, reinstatement, and attorney fees. After passage, plaintiffs can also receive compensatory damages for emotional pain, inconvenience, and mental anguish. Further, if the plaintiff can prove that the employer acted with "malice" or with "reckless indifference," the plaintiff may be awarded punitive damages. The major consideration for superintendents, assistant superintendents, and school board members has been that they can be named as codefendants in an action brought against a school district under the Civil Rights Act of 1991. The reason for this is that punitive damages cannot be levied against a school district because it is a governmental agency, but punitive damages can be levied against individuals such as administrators and school board members.

Limits on the amount of compensatory and punitive damages have been established as follows:

- Plaintiffs may be awarded damages up to $50,000 if the school district has between 15 and 100 employees.
- Plaintiffs may be awarded damages up to $100,000 if the school district has between 101 and 200 employees.
- Plaintiffs may be awarded damages up to $200,000 if the school district has between 201 and 500 employees.
- Plaintiffs may be awarded damages up to $300,000 if the school district has more than 500 employees.

There are two exceptions to these limits. For age discrimination, the limit is twice the amount of lost pay and benefits, and for race discrimination, there is no limit. There is another liability for a school district that has not been available in the past in relation to damages. A plaintiff who prevails may also recover the cost of expert witness fees.

The second significant procedural change involves the right of a complainant to receive a jury trial in an employment discrimination case in which compensatory and/or punitive damages are being sought. Jury trials were seldom allowed in employment discrimination cases prior to this law. The major considerations concerning this issue are not only the unpredictability of juries but also the perceived bias of juries against employers.

This law also brought about a significant substantive change in the way in which the school human resources function is managed. The Civil Rights Act of 1991 overruled several U.S. Supreme Court decisions that appeared to be proemployer. School districts are now charged with the burden of proof when a seemingly neutral act results in discrimination against an employee from a protected class.

Equality for People with Disabilities

Title V of the Rehabilitation Act of 1973 contains five sections, four relating to affirmative action for individuals with disabilities, and one dealing with voluntary actions, remedial actions, and evaluation criteria for compliance with the law. The congressional intent of the Rehabilitation Act is identical to the intent of other civil rights legislation, such as the Civil Rights Act of 1964 (covering discrimination based on race, gender, religion, or national origin) and Title IX of the Education Amendments of 1972 (covering discrimination based on gender in educational programs). However, when the then U.S. Department of Health, Education, and Welfare (HEW) published the regulation implementing the Rehabilitation Act in the *Federal Register*, it emphasized a fundamental difference of that act:

> The premise of both Title VII (Civil Rights Act) and Title IX (Education Amend-
> ments) is that there is no inherent difference of equalities between the general
> public and the persons protected by these statutes and, therefore, there should be
> no differential treatment in the administration of federal programs. Section 504
> (Rehabilitation Act), on the other hand, is far more complex. Handicapped per-
> sons may require different treatment in order to be afforded equal access, and
> identical treatment may, in fact, constitute discrimination. The problem of estab-
> lishing general rules as to when different treatment is prohibited or required is
> compounded by the diversity of existing handicaps and the differing degree to
> which particular persons may be affected.[16]

Subpart B of Section 504 of the Rehabilitation Act specifically refers to employment practices. It prohibits recipients of federal financial assistance from discriminating against qualified individuals with disabilities in recruitment, hiring, compensation, job assignment/classification, and fringe benefits. Employers are further required to provide reasonable work environment accommodations for qualified applicants or employees with disabilities unless they can demonstrate that such accommodations would impose an undue hardship. The law applies to all state, intermediate, and local educational agencies. Finally, any agency that receives assistance under the Individuals with Disabilities Education Act must take positive steps to employ and promote qualified persons with disabilities into programs assisted under this act.

Reasonable Accommodation

The requirement that employers make "reasonable accommodations" in the work environment for applicants and employees with disabilities has created a great deal of confusion. *Reasonable accommodations* include providing employee facilities that are readily
accessible to and usable by persons with disabilities and taking actions such as restructuring jobs, adjusting work schedules, modifying and/or acquiring special equipment or
devices, and providing readers.

To determine whether an accommodation imposes an undue hardship on an
employer, the following factors should be considered: (1) the size of the agency or
company with respect to the number of employees, (2) the number and type of facilities
available, (3) the size of the employer's budget, (4) the composition of the workforce,
and (5) the nature and type of accommodation needed. If an employer believes that

reasonable accommodations would impose a hardship, the burden of proof rests with the employer.

Employment Criteria

The Section 504 regulation in concert with the guidelines on selection procedures developed by the EEOC prohibits the use of any employment test or other criteria that screen out or discriminate against persons with disabilities unless the test or selection criteria are proven to be job related. Therefore, in selecting and administering tests to an applicant or employee with a disability, the test results must accurately reflect the individual's job skills or other factors the test purports to measure, rather than the person's impaired sensory, manual, or speaking skills, except when these skills are required for successful job performance.

The term *test* includes measures of general intelligence, mental ability, learning ability, specific intellectual ability, mechanical and clerical aptitudes, dexterity and coordination, knowledge, proficiency, attitudes, personality, and temperament. Formal techniques of assessing job suitability that yield qualifying criteria include personal history and background data, educational or work history, scored interviews, and scored application forms.

School district administrators must realize that they may be called on to present evidence concerning the validity and reliability of the testing procedures they use in selection and promotion processes. Casual techniques, of course, are difficult to defend.

Preemployment Inquiries

Section 504 of the Rehabilitation Act specifies that recipients of federal financial assistance should take (a) remedial action to correct past discrimination, (b) voluntary action to overcome the limited participation of individuals with disabilities, and (c) affirmative action to employ people with disabilities. An employer may use preemployment inquiries to determine progress in complying with the Rehabilitation Act. Subpart B also contains the following provision: An employer must state on all preemployment written questionnaires or, if no written questionnaire is used, must tell applicants that preemployment information is being requested for the purpose of implementing remedial, voluntary, or affirmative action programs; the employer must state that the information is being requested on a voluntary basis, that it will be kept confidential, and that refusal to provide such information will not subject the applicant or employee to any adverse treatment.

Nothing in Subpart B prohibits an employer from making employment conditional on the results of a medical examination prior to the assumption of duties by a person with disabilities. However, this condition can be applied only if all entering employees are required to have a medical examination, and only if the results of such examinations are used in accordance with appropriate remedial, voluntary, and affirmative action programs.

Such medical information must be maintained on separate forms from other employment data and must be accorded the same confidentiality as medical records. These data may be used by supervisors and managers to determine duty restrictions for employees with disabilities and any necessary accommodations. First aid and safety personnel may also use this medical information when emergencies occur. Finally, government officials may have access to such data when investigating an employer's compliance with the Rehabilitation Act.

Organizational Action Required

Although Section 504 does not require school districts to develop an affirmative action program for those with disabilities, it does require three types of organizational activities: remedial action, voluntary action, and self-evaluation. The Office for Civil Rights in the U.S. Department of Education investigates allegations of discrimination by school districts against people with disabilities. The agency can require remedial action if discrimination is confirmed against persons with disabilities who are currently employed, who are no longer employed in the district but were when the discrimination occurred, or who would have been employed in the district had the discrimination not occurred.

In addition, school districts may take voluntary measures to alleviate discrimination. Such measures usually begin with the construction of a self-evaluation procedure. Paragraph 87.4 of the *Federal Register* outlines the self-evaluation requirements as follows:

> Within one year of the effective date of publishing Section 504 regulations (May 4, 1977), local school districts must: (a) evaluate, with the assistance of handicapped individuals and organizations, current district policies and practices that do not meet Section 504 requirements, (b) modify such district policies and practices, and (c) take appropriate remedial steps to eliminate the effects of any discrimination that resulted from adherence to such policies and practices.

Furthermore,

> a local school district that employs fifteen or more persons must, for at least three years following completion of the self-evaluation, maintain on file and make available for public inspection: (a) a list of the interested individuals consulted, (b) a description of areas examined and any problems identified, and (c) a description of any modifications made and of any remedial steps taken.[17]

Table 2.1 lists the components necessary for planning, conducting, and analyzing a self-evaluation procedure.

TABLE 2.1   Conceptual Components for a School District Evaluation Model

- The board of education develops a policy protecting the rights of individuals with disabilities.
- The superintendent of schools establishes objectives with a timetable for implementing the policy.
- The superintendent of schools appoints an administrator to monitor the progress toward implementation and ongoing compliance.
- The administrator develops an evaluation process to measure the progress toward implementation and compliance with the policy.
- The administrator creates a staff development program to inform teachers, administrators, and staff members concerning the implementation and compliance with the policy.
- The administrator makes a yearly report to the board of education on implementation and compliance with the policy.

The Americans with Disabilities Act of 1990

President George H. W. Bush signed into law the Americans with Disabilities Act (ADA)[18] on July 26, 1990. This is the most comprehensive legislation ever passed to protect the rights of individuals with disabilities. From a practical perspective, ADA is an extension of the Rehabilitation Act of 1973. This extension pertains to the private sector and to local and state governmental agencies regardless of whether they receive federal monies. Because almost every school district in the United States receives some federal financial assistance, either directly or indirectly, which is the threshold for requiring adherence to the Rehabilitation Act, school districts in compliance with the Rehabilitation Act have little difficulty complying with the ADA.

There are five titles in the ADA. All except Title IV, which pertains to telecommunications companies, have some impact on school districts.

Title I

Title I regulates employment practices and took effect on July 26, 1992, for school districts.

Title II

All services, programs, and activities of state and local governmental agencies are subject to Title II, even if they are provided by a contractor. Title II took effect on January 26, 1992, and includes activities involving public contact as part of ongoing operations. Thus, classroom instruction and pupil transportation are affected. Even though Title II includes employment practices, the U.S. Department of Justice decided that the EEOC regulations governing Title I are sufficient for Title II.

Title III

Title III also took effect on January 26, 1992. It pertains to public accommodations and applies only to the private sector. School districts are not covered by Title III as such. However, if a school district contracts with a private company, for example, to provide pupil transportation or food service, the district must ensure that the private company is operating in compliance with Title III. This compliance issue is usually set forth as a section in the contract between the district and the company providing the service.

Title IV

Title IV took effect on July 26, 1993, and requires telecommunication companies to provide telecommunication relay services for people with hearing or speech disabilities.

Title V

Title V contains a number of provisions. The most important for school districts involves the relationship of the ADA to other laws. It states, for example, that the "highest standard" applies whether that standard is the ADA, the Rehabilitation Act, a state law, or even a local ordinance. It also prohibits retaliation against persons seeking redress under the ADA and allows the court to award attorney fees to the prevailing parties.

Jurisdiction and Scope of the ADA

Under the jurisdiction of the EEOC, the ADA covered all school districts with 25 or more employees after July 26, 1992, and all districts with 15 or more employees after

July 26, 1994. However, under the jurisdiction of the U.S. Department of Justice, discrimination is prohibited by school districts regardless of the number of employees after January 26, 1992.

Because the U.S Department of Education, the U.S. Department of Justice, and the EEOC have been given jurisdiction for the enforcement of the ADA, coordination among these three agencies is necessary. Further, because the U.S. Department of Labor has jurisdiction in cases involving discrimination and affirmative action under the Rehabilitation Act of 1973, coordination among this agency, the U.S. Department of Justice, and the EEOC is not only necessary but also critical.

Under the ADA, it is unlawful to discriminate in all human resources functions, including

- Recruitment
- Selection
- Promotion
- Training
- Staff development
- Rewards, including direct and indirect compensation
- Reduction in force
- Termination
- Placement
- Leave
- Voluntary fringe benefits

Those Protected by the ADA

Title I sets forth who is qualified to be protected by the ADA. Essentially, under the ADA, a person has a disability if he or she has a physical or mental impairment that substantially limits a major life activity. The ADA also protects individuals who have a record of a substantially limiting impairment and people who are regarded as having a substantially limiting impairment.

The term *physical or mental impairment* in this definition includes cerebral palsy, muscular dystrophy, multiple sclerosis, AIDS, HIV infection, emotional illness, drug addiction, alcoholism, and dyslexia. However, conditions such as a person's height, weight, or muscle tone, if these are within normal ranges, do not qualify under these terms. Further, having a particular hair or eye color, being pregnant, and having served a sentence in prison are not examples of a physical or mental impairment. When determining whether a person has a protected disability, the decision must be made without regard to mitigating measures such as medication and assistive or prosthetic devices (ADA Amendments Act).

The term *major life activity* means an activity that is of central importance for daily living for an average person. Thus, hearing, seeing, speaking, breathing, performing manual tasks, walking, caring for oneself, learning, and working are major life activities. The EEOC takes into account three factors when determining if a disability substantially limits a major life activity: (1) the nature and severity of the impairment, (2) its duration or expected duration, and (3) the actual or expected permanent long-term impact resulting from it. Thus, a broken limb, influenza, and a tonsillectomy, for example, are not disabilities.[19]

The term *record of impairment* refers to a disability for which an individual no longer receives treatment. Therefore, people who have a history of heart disease, mental illness, drug addiction, or alcoholism are also protected by this law.

The term *regarded as impaired* is meant to indicate those individuals who are not physically or mentally impaired but who are regarded as impaired, and about whom there is concern regarding productivity, safety, liability, attendance, accommodation, workers' compensation, or acceptance by other employees.

In March 1995, the EEOC issued an interpretation of the ADA stating that it protects people from employment discrimination who are healthy but who carry abnormal genes. Increasingly more people are taking advantage of new genetic tests that can identify a person's predisposition to Alzheimer's disease, heart disease, and certain types of cancer. This information allows individuals to access preventive measures and early treatment; it is also helpful in predicting what disease genes can be passed on to their children. If the results of these tests are known by potential employers, some of them might discriminate against those applicants who carry abnormal genes in order to avoid future lost days from work and higher employer-paid healthcare premiums.

Selection Process Under the ADA

An applicant for a position in a school district that is protected by the ADA must be otherwise qualified for the job. The term *otherwise qualified* means that the applicant can perform the essential functions of the job with or without reasonable accommodation. Therefore, the applicant must satisfy job requirements for educational background, employment experience, skills, licenses, and other qualifications that are job related. Further, the person must be able to perform those tasks that are essential to the job either with or without reasonable accommodation.

The school district can still hire the best-qualified applicant, and the ADA does not impose any affirmative action obligations.

Determining what the essential functions of a job are is critical to not discriminating against a qualified candidate who is protected by the ADA. This determination about essential functions must be made before carrying out certain processes of the human resources function. This is certainly true in relation to initiating the selection process, which includes developing a job description and advertising the position. A number of factors should be considered in determining whether the function is essential:

- Actual work experience of present and/or past employees in the job
- Time needed to perform a function
- Terms of a collective bargaining agreement
- Consequences of not requiring that an employee perform a function
- Degree of expertise or skill required to perform the function
- Number of other employees available to perform the function or among whom the performance of the function can be distributed
- Whether the reason the position exists is to perform that function[20]

Reasonable accommodation may be defined as any change or adjustment to the job or the work environment that will permit a qualified person with a disability to participate in the selection process, perform the essential functions of a job, and enjoy benefits and privileges of employment equal to those enjoyed by employees without disabilities. There-fore, reasonable accommodation may include

- Acquiring or modifying equipment or devices
- Restructuring the job
- Allowing part-time or modified work schedules
- Adjusting or modifying examinations, training materials, or policies
- Providing readers and interpreters
- Making the workplace readily accessible to and usable to people with disabilities[21]

The reasonable accommodation requirement also applies to employees who become disabled after employment with the district. All of the above, with the addition of reassignment to another position, must be considered for an employee who becomes disabled.

In determining what accommodations may be necessary, the EEOC recommends the following approach. First, determine the essential functions of the job. Second, consult with the individual who has the disability in order to determine his or her precise limitations and how those limitations may be overcome. Third, also with the his or her assistance, identify potential accommodations and assess their effectiveness. Fourth, after considering the pref-erences of the individual with the disability, implement the accommodations agreed on by the individual and the employer. It is important to understand that the ADA does not require selection of the *best* accommodation, as long as the accommodation selected provides the employee an equal opportunity to perform the job. Examples of equipment that may be considered as reasonable accommodations include telecommunications devices, special computer software to enlarge or convert print documents to spoken words, telephone head-sets, speakerphones, and adaptive light switches.

Undue Hardship

It is not necessary to provide a reasonable accommodation if this would cause an undue hardship on the school district. This means that the accommodation would be unduly costly, extensive, substantial, or disruptive, or would fundamentally alter the nature of the operation of the school district. Factors that can be considered in making this determination of undue hardship are the cost of the accommodation, size of the school district, financial resources of the district, and nature or structure of the dis-trict's operations.

If a particular accommodation would be an undue hardship, the school district staff must try to identify another accommodation that does not pose a hardship. Further, if the hardship is caused by the lack of financial resources, the school district must attempt to find funding from an outside source such as a vocational rehabilitation agency. The appli-cant or employee must also be given the opportunity to provide or pay for a portion of the accommodation that constitutes an undue hardship.[22]

Accessibility

Title II contains the provisions of the ADA related to accessibility.[23] The ADA required school districts to conduct a self-evaluation by January 26, 1993. Most school districts have a self-evaluation on file that complied with Section 504 of the Rehabilitation Act of 1973. Thus, these districts could include in the ADA self-evaluation only those policies and practices that were not covered in the previous self-evaluation. This self-evaluation provided an opportunity for input from interested individuals, from individuals with disabilities, and from organizations representing people with disabilities. Each school district is to maintain a file that is open to inspection by the public that includes the names of the interested persons consulted, a description of the areas examined, the problems identified, and a description of any modifications made.

School districts must also maintain on file a transition plan open to inspection by the public that sets forth the structural changes to facilities that were to be undertaken in order to make their facilities accessible. This should include a time schedule for taking corrective action and the name of the school district official responsible for implementing the plan.

The ADA also required school districts to appoint a staff member responsible for investigating complaints regarding noncompliance, and to develop a procedure for the prompt and equitable resolution of such complaints.

Damages for Noncompliance with the ADA

Hiring, reinstatement, back pay, and injunctive relief are some of the remedies that are possible under the ADA.[24] The list was expanded by the Civil Rights Act of 1991 to include damages for future pecuniary losses, inconvenience, mental anguish, and emotional pain, subject to specific dollar limitations. Punitive damages may not be awarded against a school district under the ADA.

AIDS and Discrimination

No issue has received more attention and concern on the part of so many people over time than has the disease of AIDS (acquired immune deficiency syndrome). Without going into a long discussion of the medical aspects of the disease, it is sufficient here to state that the disease can be transmitted to others and that it is always fatal.

The hysteria over this disease caused Dr. C. Everett Koop, the surgeon general when the syndrome was first publicized, to send an explanatory brochure to every household in the United States. All health officials are in agreement about the manner in which the disease may be transmitted, with the most common manner being sexual contact with an infected person and the sharing of drug needles or syringes.

Health officials are also in agreement that the disease cannot be transmitted by casual contact with an infected person. In fact, ordinary and casual contact among family members where a member had AIDS verified that the disease cannot be transmitted this way.

The hysteria continues to exist, however, causing concern in the workplace that has resulted in discriminatory practices by some individuals, companies, agencies, and organizations.[25] A significant development occurred in 1987 that was helpful in dealing with discrimination against people infected with the AIDS virus. In *School Board of Nassau County v. Arline*, the U.S. Supreme Court ruled that an infectious disease could constitute a disability under Section 504 of the Rehabilitation Act of 1973. In this case, the infectious disease was tuberculosis. However, in that same year, a federal circuit court of appeals in California applied the *Arline* decision to a case involving an Orange County teacher with AIDS. The court ordered the school district to reinstate the teacher to his previous duties.

A further development occurred in 1988, when the U.S. Justice Department reversed its earlier position on AIDS and declared that fear of contagion by itself does not permit federal agencies and federally assisted employers to fire or discriminate against workers infected with the virus. This legal opinion is binding on school boards, federal agencies, government contractors, managers of federally subsidized housing projects, and other organizations receiving federal contracts or financial assistance. The opinion emphasized that each situation must be assessed on a case-by-case basis in order to decide if an infected person poses a direct threat to the health of others in the workplace.

The Rehabilitation Act of 1973 and the ADA require an employer to make reasonable accommodations for people with disabilities, which includes AIDS. The accommodations must be made if the person with AIDS can still perform the essential requirements of his or her job. If an employer can demonstrate that making such accommodations would pose an undue hardship, then the company, agency, or organization can be excused. However, the regulations governing undue hardship are very stringent.

A situation in which the reasonable accommodation regulation probably would not apply is the case of a school bus driver who has advanced symptoms of the disease. The effects of AIDS on the central nervous system would preclude that person from continuing to drive a school bus.

It is extremely important to protect the privacy of individuals who have AIDS. Medical information on employees is confidential. This fact is clearly set forth in *Gammel v. United States* (1984). In this case, the U.S. government wanted to review the medical records of Gammel, a federal employee. The government contended that Gammel was a potential health risk to the general public, and that reviewing his medical records would provide the information necessary to assign him to a position where he would not be a threat to the public. Gammel's attorney argued that the Fourteenth Amendment of the U.S. Constitution protects the privacy rights of citizens, and that the release of medical information would violate this amendment unless there was proof that a clear and present danger to public safety existed. The U.S. government failed to establish such proof, and the federal district court ruled in favor of Gammel.

Therefore, if the personnel records of public school districts contain medical information about employees, these records are confidential. The only reason for revealing the contents of such records would be the existence of a clear and present danger to public health or safety.

There is also an area of concern in relation to the rights of coworkers of AIDS-infected employees. This issue has been addressed in a federal court case, *Whirlpool v. Marshall* (1988), involving a private-sector employer. The case reaffirmed that the best available medical information does not consider casual contact with an AIDS-infected person to be a health risk. The contact among staff members in schools and, in fact, among staff members and students can be classified as casual, and thus there is no risk of contracting AIDS. School district human resources policies and procedures must reflect this position.

In summary, case law clearly upholds the employment and privacy rights of persons with AIDS, with AIDS-related complex (ARC), and with an HIV-positive test. Further, case law upholds these same rights for persons suspected of being infected. It is imperative that the assistant superintendent for human resources ensures that school district practices do not result in discrimination against persons with AIDS or with the previously mentioned AIDS-related conditions. There is potential for serious discrimination with regard to life, medical, and hospitalization insurance programs. Exhibit 2.5 is a sample board of education policy that incorporates both the legal rights and the humane treatment that should be provided to employees with HIV, AIDS, and ARC.

The Vietnam Era Veterans' Readjustment Assistance Act

The Vietnam Era Veterans' Readjustment Assistance Act[26] was passed by Congress in 1974. As a result, school districts receiving $10,000 or more in federal funds must take affirmative action to hire veterans with disabilities of all wars and all veterans of the Vietnam era. This act defines a *veteran with a disability* as a person who has a 30 percent or more disability rating from the Veterans Administration, or who was discharged or released from active duty for a service-connected disability.

EXHIBIT 2.5   Sample AIDS Policy

The board of education is committed to providing a school environment free from health risks for all students and staff members. This policy has been developed using information from the federal Centers for Disease Control and Prevention. In particular, it has been written to protect the rights of school personnel who are infected with the human immunodeficiency virus (HIV) that causes acquired immunodeficiency syndrome (AIDS), which, in turn, can cause AIDS-related complex (ARC).

Further, the development of this policy has been guided by medical information that has documented that the HIV virus cannot be transmitted by casual person-to-person contact.

Thus, the board of education sets forth the following provisions:

- Each case of HIV, AIDS, or ARC will be evaluated on an individual basis.
- The administration will provide an ongoing program of education on the subject of HIV, AIDS, and ARC to students, staff, and the community.
- Employees who have been diagnosed as infected with HIV, AIDS, or ARC are encouraged to report this to the superintendent of schools accompanied by a written statement from a licensed physician that reports on the employee's medical condition and capability of continuing in his or her present position.
- This medical information will be confidential to the superintendent of schools. The superintendent will share this information with other employees only on a "need to know" basis, a determination that will be made in consultation with the infected employee. Those staff members so informed will also be instructed by the superintendent on the legal and policy provisions that require this information to be confidential.
- The employee will continue in his or her position unless deterioration in the employee's health significantly interferes with the performance of his or her job responsibilities. The employee's physician may also determine that the employee's job responsibilities pose a threat to his or her health. In either situation, a reasonable effort will be made to place the employee in another position.
- The employee is guaranteed all the protections and safeguards that other employees have according to law and board of education policy.

Mobilization of Military Reserves and National Guard into Active Duty

On August 22, 1990, President George H. W. Bush ordered the mobilization of U.S. military reserves and National Guard units into active duty. This was the first mobilization in twenty years and activated approximately 40,000 troops. This mobilization, of course, was necessary in order to support the then forthcoming war in the Persian Gulf against Iraq. The war was named Desert Storm.

When an employee enters active military service, he or she is immediately covered by the military healthcare system. Dependents of the employee are eligible to be covered by the Civilian Health and Medical Program of the Uniformed Services (formerly CHAMPUS, now called TRICARE[27]) under certain conditions, the most significant of which is the length of time that the employee will be on active duty. If the mobilization is for less than thirty days, dependents cannot be enrolled in TRICARE. However, if the mobilization is extended, TRICARE coverage begins on the thirty-first day of active duty. If the mobilization is for more than thirty days at the outset, coverage begins from the first day of active duty. Dependents must receive healthcare from military health facilities or receive permission to go to a civilian facility. This provision should help school district administrators understand the limits of their responsibilities.

Reservists and National Guard members are covered under the provisions of the Veterans Reemployment Rights Act of 1940, which was amended in 1986. This act obliges school districts to give reservists and National Guard members time off from their civilian jobs to participate in military training and active duty. Also, the act protects them from termination and discrimination because of their military obligations. Further, the reservist or National Guard member is covered by an *escalator principle*, which means that he or she will continue to accrue seniority, fringe benefits, and salary increases. Thus, if other employees in the same job category as the reservist or National Guard member receive an increase in salary and/or additional fringe benefits, the service member receives the same salary increase and/or fringe benefits when he or she returns to work. In addition, if there is a reduction in fringe benefits or salary for all the members of the job category, the same reductions apply to the reservist or National Guard member on return.

On his or her release from military training or active duty, the reservist or National Guard member has ninety days to apply for reinstatement into his or her previously held position. If the previously held position is not available, he or she must be offered a position of like status or the job that is nearest in duties to the one he or she left.

In regard to healthcare benefits, the employer cannot impose a preexisting exclusion or waiting period before reinsuring the reservist or National Guard member.

The Omnibus Transportation Employee Testing Act of 1991

On October 28, 1991, President George H. W. Bush signed into law the Omnibus Transportation Employee Testing Act,[28] which required the secretary of transportation to promulgate regulations for alcohol and controlled-substance testing for persons in safety-sensitive positions, including motor carriers. For districts with fifty or more employees, regulations were implemented in 1994. For districts with fewer than fifty employees, implementation began in early 1995.

Regulations have been established that require school bus drivers and drivers of private motor carriers that transport passengers to submit to controlled-substance testing.

Other regulations require school districts to conduct preemployment, postaccident, random, reasonable suspicion, and return-to-duty testing. School districts must publish the board of education policy concerning this law and implementation procedures, which should include the action that the school district will take if a bus driver is found to be in violation of this law.

School districts must also develop procedures for the collection, shipment, and accessioning of urine specimens. The U.S. Department of Transportation requires urine samples to be analyzed by laboratories certified by the National Institute on Drug Abuse. Laboratories are required to report the analysis to a medical review officer, who then contacts the bus driver concerning the results of the testing and reports the results to the school district. Of course, these reports are confidential. The school district administrator responsible for determining if a reasonable suspicion exists to require a bus driver to undergo testing must receive at least sixty minutes of training on the physical, behavioral, speech, and performance indicators of probable controlled-substance abuse. Finally, a bus driver who has violated this law must receive information from the school district concerning resources that are available for helping the bus driver with his or her drug abuse problem.

Family and Medical Leave Act of 1993

President Bill Clinton signed the Family and Medical Leave Act (FMLA)[29] into law on February 5, 1993. The fundamental purpose of this act is to provide eligible employees, as defined by Section 3(e) of the Fair Labor Standards Act, with the right to take twelve weeks of unpaid leave per year in connection with certain circumstances.

An employee may invoke this law in conjunction with

- The birth and first-year care of a child, including paternity leave.
- The adoption or foster parent placement of a child. The entitlement ends when the child reaches one year of age or the twelve-week period ends.
- The illness of an employee's spouse, child, or parent, including a stepchild, foster child, child over eighteen years of age incapable of self-care, and stepparent.
- The employee's own illness. This means a serious health condition that may result from not only illness but also injury, impairment, or physical or mental condition. It may involve inpatient care or any incapacity that requires absence from work for more than three days and that involves continuing treatment by a healthcare provider. Also, this refers to any prenatal care.

The law became effective on August 5, 1993. However, in those school districts that had a collective bargaining agreement with one or more bargaining units, the law became effective on the termination of the master contract or on February 5, 1994, whichever occurred earlier. Because this is a labor law, the U.S. Department of Labor is the federal agency responsible for implementing regulations.

All employees of private elementary and secondary schools and all employees of public school districts are covered by this law. In business and industry, a company must employ fifty or more people to be subject to the mandates of the law.

To be eligible for leave under this law, an employee must have worked for the school district for at least twelve months. That employment may have been consecutive or non-consecutive. Also, the employee must have worked at least 1,250 hours during the year preceding the leave. Thus, many part-time employees are not eligible. There is also an exemption that could apply to the superintendent of schools and many other administrators. This exemption allows a board of education to deny the request for leave of an employee whose salary falls within the highest 10 percent of salaries for the district because the absence of such an employee may cause substantial and grievous economic injury to the school district.

A school district may use a number of methods to calculate the twelve-month period during which twelve weeks of leave may be requested. For example, the district policy may use the calendar year, twelve months forward from the date that an employee returned from a leave, or any fixed twelve-month period. When both spouses are employees of the same school district, the combined amount of leave for birth, adoption, and family illness may be limited to twelve weeks. Obviously, this restriction does not apply to personal illness.

There are special regulations pertaining to intermittent leave, reduced schedule leave, and leave near the end of an academic term. This provision applies to teachers and does not include teacher assistants and aides unless their principal job is actual teaching. Counselors, psychologists, curriculum specialists, and support staff such as cafeteria, maintenance, and transportation employees are not covered by the special regulations.

Thus, a teacher may take *intermittent leave,* which means a period of time from one hour to several weeks; for example, a person being treated with chemotherapy. However, if a teacher will be absent more than 20 percent of the total number of working days during the period of the leave, which is considered a reduced schedule leave, a school district may require the teacher to take leave for a particular duration, which must not be longer than the duration of the treatment. An alternative approach for a school district is to transfer the teacher to a different assignment on a temporary basis. The teacher must receive equivalent pay and benefits. For example, a school district could assign the teacher to a full-time substitute teacher position.

In regard to leave near the end of an academic year, a school district may require a teacher to continue on leave until the end of the term if the leave begins more than five weeks but continues into three weeks before the end of the term. Further, the school district may require the teacher to continue leave until the end of the term unless the leave is for the teacher's own serious health condition under two circumstances: (1) if the leave begins with five or fewer weeks before the end of the semester but lasts for more than two weeks and ends during the two-week period before the end of the term, or (2) if the leave begins during the three-week period before the end of the semester and will last for more than five days.

If the employee has prior knowledge about the need for a leave, he or she is required to give thirty days' verbal or written notice. When the employee does not have prior knowledge about the need for a leave, notice must be given as soon as is practicable, which may be interpreted as two working days.

The school district may require the employee to first use accrued paid leave such as sick, personal, or vacation leave. The district must continue to pay health plan premiums for the employee during the period of leave, and this period must be treated as continued service for purposes of vesting and eligibility to participate in retirement plans. However, the employee is not entitled to accrue additional benefits during the period of unpaid leave such as additional paid sick leave.

The school district may require certification from the employee's healthcare provider or the family member's healthcare provider concerning the date when the condition began, its duration, the necessity for leave, and the employee's inability to perform his or her job functions. A second opinion from a healthcare provider can be required by the school district at its own expense; a third opinion can be obtained on the same condition, with this opinion being binding.

On return from leave, an employee is entitled to the same position or to a position equivalent to the one he or she had when leave commenced, with the same salary, benefits, and working conditions. The district may require a certification from the employee's healthcare provider stating that the employee is able to resume work. School districts must inform employees about the provisions of this act. Also, policies and procedures for invoking this act must be in writing and be provided to the employee prior to taking leave in order for the district to enforce the act.

Complaints by employees under the FMLA can be initiated with the U.S. Department of Labor. The department may conduct an administrative investigation or file suit in court. Thus, federal record-keeping requirements and investigations are consistent with the Fair Labor Standards Act. The statute of limitations is two years, except in cases where willful violation is alleged, which carries a three-year limitation. A school district that violates this law may be subject to the following damages: (1) lost wages and benefits, and (2) all other costs other than wages that an employee may have incurred as a result of the violation. The other costs usually include attorney and witness fees, but could also include, for example, reimbursement for professional nursing care up to a sum equal to twelve weeks' worth of wages if the employee's leave was denied.

Equality for Women

The French writer Stendhal believed that granting women equality would be the surest sign of civilization and would double the intellectual power of the human race. Although he wrote more than one hundred years ago, equality for women continues to be a significant issue in our society.

In educational organizations, the question of equal employment opportunity for women[30] traditionally applies to a specific job classification—administration. It is clear to all observers that women are well represented in teaching, custodial, food service, and bus driving positions. Skilled trade positions (carpenters, electricians, and plumbers) in most school districts, however, are dominated by males, as are industrial arts teaching positions. In such situations, the norms of affirmative action previously outlined in this chapter are applicable. The critical issue, however, is the need to have women better represented in administrative ranks.

Why are there so few female administrators? Many researchers have put forth various theories. One such study argues that the causes are increased salary levels for teachers, which attracted more men, who were subsequently promoted to administrative positions;

the entry of male veterans into education after World War II and the Korean War, which also led to their eventual entry into administration; and the executive image projected for administrators in the 1950s and 1960s, which attracted more men.

The legal mandate of equal employment opportunity for women emanates primarily from two federal laws: Title IX of the Education Amendments of 1972, which prohibits gender discrimination in educational programs or activities, including employment, when the school district is receiving federal financial assistance; and, of course, Title VII of the Civil Rights Act of 1964, as amended in 1972, which prohibits discrimination on the basis of gender as well as religion, national origin, race, or color.

In February 1992, the U.S. Supreme Court issued a unanimous opinion in the case of *Franklin v. Gwinnett County Public Schools*, which upheld unlimited punitive and compensatory damages for victims of gender discrimination under Title IX. This is a landmark decision. Prior to this, a female employee who believed that she had been discriminated against could seek only back pay in addition to the injunctive and declaratory relief otherwise available.

In November 2004, the U.S. Supreme Court ruled in *Jackson v. Birmingham Board of Education* that advocates and whistleblowers, along with victims, may sue under Title IX. The case involved a physical education teacher in the Birmingham (Alabama) School District who also coached the high school girls' basketball team. He was fired from his coaching position after he complained that the female basketball players were being discriminated against because of their gender.

The coach sued the board of education in 2001. The trial court threw out the suit, stating that Title IX did not apply in that case. The U.S. Court of Appeals for the Eleventh Circuit upheld that decision, but the U.S. Supreme Court overturned the lower courts' rulings.[31]

This is a significant ruling for human resources administrators because it is an extension of the prevailing attitude that retaliation for reporting violations of legal mandates will not be tolerated by the courts and federal agencies. For example, this ruling is certainly in accord with the guidelines of the EEOC that prohibit retaliation in the administration of Title VII of the Civil Rights Act. The EEOC guidelines prohibit firing, demotion, harassment, and other forms of retaliation against individuals who file a charge of discrimination, participate in a discrimination proceeding, or otherwise oppose discrimination. The Supreme Court ruling, however, forges a new dimension in that it gives the same protection against retaliation to advocates and whistleblowers.[32]

Potential Areas of Employment Discrimination Concerning Women

As a general rule, school districts—and all employers—are prohibited from establishing job qualifications that are derived from female stereotyping. The courts have uniformly required employers to prove that any gender restriction is, indeed, a bona fide occupational qualification.

Some of the most common forms of discrimination against females in the industrial/business community are even less defensible in educational organizations. For example, females have been denied employment because of height and weight limitations. In such situations, a woman who is capable of performing the job-related tasks has clearly established case law precedent to rely on in bringing the employer to court. However, it still occurs that an exceptionally talented woman may not be hired for an administrative position because she is a "nice and petite" person who does not measure up to the image of a strong leader.

The EEOC prohibits discrimination against women because of their marital status, because they are pregnant, because they are not the principal wage earner in a family, or because they have preschool-age children.

The preferences of customers and clientele are not bona fide occupational qualifications. Thus, the preference of parents and even students for male principals and administrators in a given school district does not permit the district to discriminate against females seeking administrative positions.

Maternity as a Particular Form of Discrimination

On October 31, 1978, President Jimmy Carter signed into law a pregnancy disability amendment to Title VII of the Civil Rights Act of 1964.[33] The law had the effect of prohibiting unequal treatment for pregnant women in all employment-related situations. The EEOC issued guidelines for implementing this law, indicating that it is discriminatory for an employer to refuse to hire, train, assign, or promote a woman solely because she is pregnant; to require maternity leave for a predetermined time period; to dismiss a woman because she is pregnant; to deny reemployment to a woman who has been on maternity leave; to deny seniority credit to a woman who has been on maternity leave; and to deny disability or medical benefits to a woman for disability or illness unrelated to but occurring during pregnancy, childbirth, or recovery from childbirth.

Recruitment and Selection

To ensure that discrimination against women does not occur in employment, as a first step, the school district's leadership should review recruitment and selection procedures. The following specific actions minimize the potential for discrimination:

- Use women as recruiters and interviewers.
- Develop a list of women for potential promotion from within the school district.
- Encourage female employees to apply for available administrative positions.
- When recruiting outside the school district, contact for referrals such organizations as the American Association of University Women (AAUW), the National Council of Administrative Women in Education (NCAWE), the National Organization for Women (NOW), and minority employment agencies.
- Include female representatives on selection committees.
- Remove such title designations as Mr., Mrs., Miss, and Ms. from application forms.
- When interviewing female applicants, ask only questions that are related to the abilities needed for job performance.
- Review and evaluate the entire selection process to assure that job descriptions, selection criteria, and data-gathering instruments (e.g., tests, job applications) are job related and do not screen out women.

Promotion and Training

Positive steps must be taken to overcome patterns of inequality that have become traditional in some school districts. Among the most effective procedures are the following:

- Publicize all promotional opportunities.
- Seek out capable women and assign them administrative tasks when possible, giving them the experience to move into administrative positions.
- Examine procedures for promotion to eliminate all facets except those that present a fair assessment of the employee's ability and record.
- Recommend women for administrative internship and in-service programs.

Sexual Harassment

In 1980, the EEOC declared sexual harassment to be a violation of Title VII of the Civil Rights Act of 1964.[34] Basically, there are two types of sexual harassment: quid pro quo discrimination and hostile environment discrimination. The first type is obvious. *Quid pro quo discrimination* occurs when an employment or personnel decision is based on an applicant's or employee's submission to or rejection of unwelcome sexual conduct. Thus, a quid pro quo personnel decision occurs when employment opportunities or fringe benefits are granted because of an employee's submission to the employer's or supervisor's sexual advances.

Hostile environment discrimination occurs when unwelcome sexual conduct interferes with the employee's job performance. The standard for deciding whether hostile environment discrimination exists is whether the sexual conduct would substantially affect the job performance of a reasonable person. Factors to consider in investigating hostile environment discrimination are whether the conduct was physical, verbal, or both; the frequency of the conduct; whether the harasser was a coworker or a supervisor; whether other employees were involved in the conduct; whether the conduct was directed against more than one person; and whether the conduct was hostile or patently hostile.

It is also important to investigate if the sexual conduct was unwelcome. Did the person alleging sexual harassment indicate by his or her conduct that the sexual advances were unwelcome? In making this determination, the timing of the protest and whether a prior consensual relationship existed with the alleged harasser are significant factors.

School districts are liable for the actions of their administrators and supervisors when these individuals act as the "agent" for the school district at the time of the harassment. For quid pro quo discrimination, the administrator or supervisor is always acting as the agent of the school district. For hostile environment discrimination, the school district is liable if the district knew or should have known of the sexual harassment of the supervisor.

For coworkers who sexually harass their colleagues, the school district is liable if the agents, administrators, and supervisors knew or should have known about the harassment. When sexual conduct becomes known, the appropriate administrator or supervisor must act to remedy the situation.

It is also the responsibility of the administrators and supervisors to take appropriate action to protect employees in the workplace against sexual harassment by nonemployees. This responsibility is present when school district agents knew or should have known about the harassment.

For a school district to demonstrate to employees and the general public that sexual harassment will not be tolerated, the board of education should adopt a policy prohibiting such conduct, and administrative procedures should be developed to deal effectively with allegations of such conduct. Further, all employees should be required to participate in a staff development program about the issue of sexual harassment.

The board of education policy should set forth the commitment of the school district to deal with sexual harassment in an expeditious and effective manner. Administrative procedures to implement the policy should set forth the complaint process and should include the filling out of a complaint form, which must be signed by the complainant. The appropriate human resources administrator should inform all the parties of their rights. Both the complaint and the investigation should be kept confidential. The procedures should also contain a time line for completion of the investigation. The policy and procedures must be communicated to all staff members.

A staff development program about sexual harassment for all employees should contain an explanation of the board policy and administrative procedures; specific examples of sexual harassment; myths about sexual harassment; and the distinction among *welcome, consensual,* and *illegal* sexual harassment. Administrator and supervisor staff development should not only include the aforementioned, but also should stress the importance of protecting the complainant against retaliation. Exhibit 2.6 is a sample board of education policy on sexual harassment.

EXHIBIT 2.6   Sample Sexual Harassment Policy

The board of education is committed to providing a work environment free from sexual harassment by administrators, supervisors, coworkers, and nonemployees.

It is a violation of this policy for the above-named categories of employees and nonemployees to engage in sexual harassment by making unwelcome sexual advances, by making unwelcome requests for sexual favors, and by engaging in other unwelcome verbal or physical conduct of a sexual nature.

It is a violation of this policy for an administrator or supervisor to make a decision affecting the employment of an individual on the basis of that person's submission to or rejection of sexual conduct. If an administrator or supervisor offers an opportunity or fringe benefit to an employee on the basis of that person's submission to or rejection of sexual conduct, it also is a violation of this policy.

Conduct of a sexual nature that unreasonably interferes with a person's job performance will be considered sexual harassment.

It is the duty of each administrator and supervisor to monitor his or her area of responsibility for the purpose of maintaining an environment free from sexual harassment. Further, it is the duty of each administrator and supervisor to protect an employee who files a complaint of sexual harassment from retaliation.

An employee or former applicant for employment who believes that he or she has been a victim of sexual harassment should file a complaint with the director of affirmative action as soon as possible after the incident. If the director of affirmative action is the alleged harasser, the complaint should be filed with the superintendent of schools. If the superintendent is the alleged harasser, the board of education should receive the complaint.

When the complaint is received, the director of affirmative action should initiate an investigation as soon as possible. If the complainant requests an investigator of the same sex and if the director of affirmative action is not of the same sex, another person of the same sex as the complainant will be

Continued

EXHIBIT 2.6   *Continued*

appointed by the director to conduct the investigation. After the investigation, a report of the findings will be presented to the complainant, the alleged harasser, and the superintendent of schools. Both the investigation and the report are to be considered confidential. An employee who is found to be in violation of this policy will be subject to disciplinary action up to and including termination of employment with the school district.

It is the responsibility of the superintendent of schools to initiate the development of administrative procedures to implement this policy, and to initiate a staff development program concerning sexual harassment in the workplace, this policy, and administrative procedures. This program must be offered to every employee.

Policy of Nondiscrimination on the Basis of Gender

Good intentions by school administrators to remedy past and prevent future practices of discrimination against women are not sufficient. The only defensible course of action is for the superintendent of schools to recommend that the board of education adopt a nondiscrimination policy that complements the school district's affirmative action policy and that provides the assurance required by law. The American Association of School Administrators has published a sample policy to be used as a guide for local boards of education in formulating policies. The sample policy includes sections dealing with educational programs, facilities, and services; the part reprinted in Exhibit 2.7 deals only with employment activities.[35]

EXHIBIT 2.7   **District Employment Activities**

This policy applies to all aspects of the district's employment programs, including, but not limited to, recruitment, advertising, the process of application for employment, promotion, granting of tenure, termination, layoffs, wages, job assignments, leaves of absence of all types, fringe benefits, training programs, employer-sponsored programs, social or recreational programs, and any other term, condition, or privilege of employment. Specifically, the following personnel employment practices are prohibited:

a. *Tests.* Administration of any test or other criterion that has a disproportionately adverse effect on persons on the basis of gender unless it is a valid predictor of job success and alternative tests or criteria are unavailable.

b. *Recruitment.* Recruitment of employees from entities that furnish as applicants only or predominantly members of one gender, if such action has the effect of discriminating on the basis of gender.

c. *Compensation.* Establishment of rates of pay on the basis of gender.

d. *Job Classification.* Classification of jobs as being for males or females.

e. *Fringe Benefits.* Provision of fringe benefits on the basis of gender; all fringe benefit plans must treat males and females equally.

f. *Marital and Parental Status.* Any action based on marital or parental status; pregnancies are considered temporary disabilities for all job-related purposes and shall be accorded the same treatment by the district as are all other temporary disabilities. No inquiry shall be made by the district in job applications as to the marriage status of an applicant, including whether such applicant is "Miss or Mrs." But inquiry may be made as to the gender of a job applicant for employment if it is made of all applicants and is not a basis for discrimination.

Continued

EXHIBIT 2.7   *Continued*

g. *Employment Advertising.* Any expression of preference, limitation, or specification based on gender, unless gender is a bona fide occupational qualification for the particular job in question.

Policy enforcement   To ensure compliance with this policy, the superintendent shall

1. Designate a member of the administrative staff
   a. to coordinate efforts of the district to comply with this policy;
   b. to develop and ensure the maintenance of a filing system to keep all records required under this policy;
   c. to investigate all complaints under this policy;
   d. to administer the grievance procedure established in this policy; and
   e. to develop affirmative action programs, as appropriate.
2. Provide for the publication of this policy on an ongoing basis to students, parents, employees, prospective employees, and district employee unions or organizations, such publication to include the name, office address, and telephone number of the compliance administrator designated pursuant to this policy.

Grievance procedure   Any employee of this district who believes he or she has been discriminated against, denied a benefit, or excluded from participation in any district activity, on the basis of gender in violation of this policy, may file a written complaint with the compliance administrator designated

by this policy. The compliance administrator shall cause the review of the written complaint to be conducted and the written response mailed to the complainant within ten working days after receipt of the written complaint. A copy of the written complaint and the compliance administrator's response shall be provided each member of the board of education. If the complainant is not satisfied with such response, he or she may submit a written appeal to the board of education, indicating with particularity the nature of disagreement with the response and his or her reasons underlying such disagreement.

The board of education shall consider the appeal at its next regularly scheduled board meeting following receipt of the appeal.

The board of education shall permit the complainant to address the board in public or closed session, as appropriate and lawful, concerning his or her complaint and shall provide the complainant with its written decision in the matter as expeditiously as possible following completion of the meeting.

Evaluation   The superintendent shall present a report to the board of education in a public meeting on or about July 21, 1976, and in a public meeting to be held on or about the anniversary of that date each year thereafter, describing the district's compliance with this policy during the previous year, which report can be the basis of an evaluation of the effectiveness of this policy by the board of education and a determination as to whether or not additional affirmative action is necessary in light of all the facts.

Source: Reprinted from Sample Policy for Sex Equality in Education (Arlington, VA: American Association of School Administrators, 1977).

The Equal Pay Act

In 1963, the U.S. Congress enacted in the Equal Pay Act,[36] which requires employers to pay males and females the same salary or wage for equal work. This act amends the Fair Labor Standards Act and protects employees who work for an employer engaged in an enterprise affected by interstate commerce. Interstate commerce was broadly defined by the U.S. Court of Appeals for the Second Circuit in *Usery v. Columbia University* (1977). In addition, the interpretation of *equal work* has been broadly defined to mean substantially equal; thus, the act does not require strict equality of jobs, but rather equal pay for jobs that demand equal skill, effort, and responsibility, and that are carried out under similar working conditions. However, if salaries or wages are contingent on a seniority system, a merit system, or a system that measures pay by production quantity or quality or by factors other than gender, this act does not apply.

An example of a court case involving the Equal Pay Act is *EEOC v. Madison Community Unit School District No. 12*, decided in 1987 by the U.S. Court of Appeals for the Seventh Circuit. In this case, a female who coached girls' track and tennis was paid substantially less than the males who coached the boys' track and tennis at the same school. In addition, a female assistant coach of the girls' basketball team was paid less than a male assistant coach of the boys' track team, and another female was paid less for coaching girls' basketball, softball, and volleyball than a male was for coaching boys' basketball, baseball, and soccer. Finally, an assistant coach of the girls' track team was paid less than the assistant coach of the boys' track team.

The EEOC filed a lawsuit against the school district, stating that the inequities violated the Equal Pay Act. The U.S. Northern District Court of Indiana ruled in favor of the EEOC, but the school district appealed to the Seventh Circuit. This court affirmed the district court's decision in the following situations: boys' and girls' track, boys' and girls' tennis, and boys' baseball and girls' softball. However, it reversed the district court's decision in comparing boys' soccer to girls' volleyball, boys' soccer to girls' basketball, and boys' track to girls' basketball. The court stated that these situations did not require equal skill, effort, and responsibility.[37]

There is another aspect to the equal pay issue. When a school district has a performance-based evaluation system that is used to determine the salaries and wages of employees, the Equal Pay Act does not apply. However, in all organizations, employees tend to compare their salaries and wages with those of coworkers and how productive these coworkers are in comparison with themselves. The effects of this situation can be serious for school administrators. It is a situation that will only fester if it is ignored. The best approach is to reemphasize the relationship between performance and reward; it is also important to reiterate that the performance-based evaluation process is the vehicle for determining the level of performance and the amount of reward.

Obviously, if a school district does not have an effective evaluation process, a merit-based reward program cannot be initiated. Performance and reward are two aspects of the same process—they go hand in hand.

Equality by Age

The Age Discrimination in Employment Act of 1967,[38] as amended, is taking on ever-increasing importance for human resources administrators. This act was passed by Congress to promote the employment of the older worker based on ability rather than age by prohibiting arbitrary discrimination. Also under this act, the U.S. Department of Labor has consistently sponsored informational and educational programs on the needs and abilities of the older worker. The Statement of Findings and Purpose in the Age Discrimination in Employment Act sets forth a rationale for its passage that is a reflection of the effect of current societal trends on the older worker:

Sec. 2. (a) The Congress hereby finds and declares that

(1) in the face of rising productivity and affluence, older workers find themselves disadvantaged in their efforts to retain employment, and especially to regain employment when displaced from jobs;

(2) the setting of arbitrary age limits regardless of potential for job performance has become a common practice, and certain otherwise desirable practices may work to the disadvantage of older persons;

(3) the incidence of unemployment, especially long-term unemployment with resultant deterioration of skill, morale, and employer acceptability is, relative to the younger ages, high among older workers; their numbers are great and growing; and their employment problems grave;

(4) the existence in industries affecting commerce, of arbitrary discrimination in employment because of age, burdens commerce and the free flow of goods in commerce.

Provisions of the Age Discrimination in Employment Act

The law protects individuals who are at least forty years of age but less than seventy. It applies to private employers of twenty or more persons as well as employment agencies and labor organizations having twenty-five or more members in an industry affecting interstate commerce. The law does not apply to elected officials or their appointees.

In January 2000, the U.S. Supreme Court, in a five-to-four decision, held that Congress did not have the authority under the Fourteenth Amendment to the U.S. Constitution to extend this act to states and their political subdivisions. Thus, at this writing, it appears that public school districts cannot be sued in federal court under the Age Discrimination in Employment Act. However, there are age discrimination statutes in almost every state in the nation that can be invoked by job applicants and employees of school districts who believe that they have been discriminated against because of age. Thus, state compliance agencies and the state courts can provide remedies to age discrimination. In addition, school district job applicants and employees can file age discrimination complaints with the EEOC.

It is against the law for an employer to refuse to hire or to otherwise discriminate against any person as to compensation, terms, conditions, or privileges of employment because of age; or to limit, segregate, or classify employees so as to deprive any individual of employment opportunities or adversely affect that individual's status as an employee because of age. It is against the law for an employment agency to refuse to refer for employment or otherwise to discriminate against an individual because of age or to classify and refer anyone for employment on the basis of age. It is also against the law for a labor union to discriminate against anyone because of age by excluding or expelling that person from membership; to limit, segregate, or classify its members on the basis of age; to refuse to refer anyone for employment so as to result in a deprivation or limitation of employment opportunity or otherwise to adversely affect an individual's status as an employee because of age; or to cause or attempt to cause an employer to discriminate against an individual because of age.

Furthermore, the provisions of the Age Discrimination in Employment Act prohibit an employer, employment agency, or labor union from discriminating against a person for opposing a practice that is unlawful because of this act; from discriminating against a person making a charge or assisting or participating in any investigation, proceeding, or litigation under this act; or from publishing a notice of an employment vacancy that indicates a preference, limitation, or specification based on age.

Exceptions to the Age Discrimination in Employment Act
The prohibitions of this act do not apply if age is a bona fide occupational qualification reasonably necessary for the normal performance of a given task. Therefore, test pilot positions may be filled with individuals no older than forty-five because accurate and quick reflexes are necessary for the safe flying of experimental aircraft. However, it would be difficult to justify age as a bona fide occupational qualification in educational institutions.

The prohibitions of the Age Discrimination in Employment Act do not apply when an individual is discharged or disciplined for good cause and when the terms of a new or existing employee seniority or benefits program differentiate by reason of age. However, no employee benefits plan can be used as an excuse for failing to hire an individual because of age.

Enforcement of the Age Discrimination in Employment Act
The administration of this act passed from the U.S. Department of Labor to the EEOC on July 1, 1979. At that time, the annual average number of complaints had reached five thousand. The EEOC can conduct investigations, issue rules and regulations to administer the law, and enforce the provisions of the law through the courts when voluntary compliance cannot be obtained.

Conclusion

This section deals with four major federal influences on the human resources planning process. Although affirmative action and the legislation on equality for people with disabilities, women, and older individuals represent central trends in human resources administration, these are by no means the only federal considerations that affect human resources processes.

The following laws enacted by Congress constitute a significant part of the national public employment policy that directly and indirectly affects the employment policies of public and private educational institutions. They should be studied by all human resources administrators.

1883	Pendleton Act (Civil Service Commission)
1931	Davis–Bacon Act
1932	Anti-Injunction Act
1935	National Labor Relations Act
1935	Social Security Act
1936	Walsh–Healey Public Contracts Act
1938	Fair Labor Standards Act
1947	Labor Management Relations Act

1959	Labor Management Reporting and Disclosure Act
1967	Reemployment of Veterans Act
1968	Wage Garnishment Provisions, Consumer Credit Protection Act
1974	Employee Retirement Income Security Act
1986	Immigration Reform and Control Act
1990	Immigration Act

In addition, it must be kept in mind that various states and cities have enacted statutes and ordinances that exert significant influence on human resources administration.

Finally, this chapter includes three appendices—Appendix A: Steps in Developing an Affirmative Action Program; Appendix B: Summary Facts Concerning Job Discrimination; and Appendix C: Steps in Filing a Charge of Job Discrimination. These provide summary data that further clarify how federal legislation impinges on human resources management.

From the Endnotes and Selected Bibliography of this chapter, it should be obvious that the Internet is a most valuable resource in providing immediate access to original federal documents such as guidelines from the EEOC on the responsibilities of employers. Further, it is helpful to read certain sections of specific federal laws such as the Family and Medical Leave Act of 1993 or the EEOC declaration on sexual harassment. Nothing substitutes for the original documents, which are now readily available to every administrator who has access to the Internet.

Implications for Small- and Medium-Size School Districts

The obvious implications for small- and medium-size school districts begin with the fact that all federal guidelines and laws are mandatory for every school district. There is no excuse for violations. Thus, it is incumbent on superintendents, principals, and all other administrators to know and understand the guidelines and laws. Size of the school district will not be a reasonable defense for noncompliance.

The real issue revolves around how school districts will promulgate and implement the guidelines and laws. Administrators will not have the time to investigate changes in existing guidelines and laws or to become acquainted with new guidelines and laws. Thus, the usual approach that superintendents take is to hire a human resources consultant or attorney who will be able to keep the school district personnel up to date on federal guidelines and laws. This is one reason why it is important for school administrators to become members of local, state, and national professional associations such as the American Association of School Administrators (AASA), the National Association of Secondary School Principals (NASSP), and the National Association of Elementary School Principals (NAESP). Such organizations act as clearinghouses for the legal responsibilities of educational administrators. Likewise, it is important for school board members to be current in their understanding of federal guidelines and laws, which is also facilitated by membership in the National School Boards Association (NSBA). All these organizations have state affiliates, and there are many local organizations of educational administrators where such issues are discussed.

There is a considerable amount of latitude in how small- and medium-size school districts deal with the planning process and particularly with enrollment projections. Because of size, it is easy to keep basic statistics on teacher, administrator, and staff turnover; likewise, it is easy to know population trends in such districts. Communication from and with teachers, administrators, staff members, parents, business leaders, and public officials is often direct, and touches on issues that affect the planning process and enrollment projections.

Coordinating the planning process, projecting enrollment, and complying with federal guidelines and laws are typically the responsibility of the superintendent, but may also become the responsibility of another central office administrator (e.g., an assistant superintendent) or be divided up among multiple administrators. For example, building principals may be responsible for projecting enrollment in their respective attendance areas. A curriculum coordinator may be responsible for having the right number of teachers with the appropriate state licensure. The superintendent may take the lead in working with the school district's attorney on federal compliance issues. The administrator with staff development responsibilities may be the person who organizes continuing education on federal compliance for teachers, other administrators, and staff members. When such delegation is not possible, the superintendent has these responsibilities.

Impact of Generation Y Teachers and Administrators on Human Resources Planning

It is obvious to most people that Generation Y teachers and principals are seriously and intensely involved in communicating by electronic means such as cell phones, text messaging, email, and Websites. Further, such communication is carried out *asynchronously,* meaning that users are not tied to real time in their endeavor to communicate. The communication is instantaneous, and dialogue can continue to whatever extent that the people desire through chat rooms. Of course, the danger in relying solely on electronic communication is that it is not tied to real time, which tends to isolate those using these types of communication. This may seem difficult to understand because a flurry of communication is taking place; however, if we communicate only electronically and not in person, we may not fully understand the person or persons with whom we are communicating.

Electronic communication does not permit a holistic approach to communication that values verbal and nonverbal cues, which often reveal the true intention of the person with whom we are communicating, as well as the realm of one's emotions and feelings. Teachers and principals certainly need to communicate with children and colleagues in all areas: electronic, writing, verbal, and nonverbal.

In the human resources planning process, it is possible for administrators to communicate important information to all employees using electronic devices. This is especially useful in notifying teachers, administrators, and staff members about legislation and policies that affect certain categories of employees or everyone in general. Thus, a change in school district maternity policies and procedures could be communicated to employees through electronic means. The information will certainly reach Generation Y employees, but perhaps not those from other generations. Thus, it should not be the only means of communication.[39]

Summary

Planning is a process common to all human experience. It encompasses an understanding of the present condition, future objectives, and methods for reaching these objectives.

Human resources planning as a process in human resources management is undertaken to ensure that a school district has the right number of people, with the right skills, in the right place, and at the right time.

The first step in the human resources planning process is to assess human resources needs, which includes developing human resources inventories, a five-year enrollment projection, school district objectives, and a human resources forecast.

Two of the most pressing problems facing school districts are human resources planning and increasing and decreasing pupil enrollments. Two of the most successful alternatives to reduction in workforce have been early retirement incentive programs and the retraining of individuals for positions that become vacant through attrition or are created through program development.

A hallmark of our contemporary American society is the avalanche of federal legislation and court decisions, which in turn has had a definite influence on the human resources planning process. Incorporated or implied in all civil rights legislation are the important concepts of social justice and affirmative action.

Justice is a guide that regulates how people live out their lives as members of a given society. The substance of justice is entitlement that refers to those rights to which individuals and groups of people have a claim. The responsibility of society to the individual is called *distributive justice.* The responsibility of each person to society is termed *legal justice. Commutative justice* involves the responsibility that exists between individuals. Justice also involves *restitution,* which is the right of a person to have an entitlement restored.

John Rawls was a contemporary political philosopher who described his theory of justice in terms of fairness. He believed that the best principles of justice for the basic structure of any society are those that would be the object of an original agreement in the establishment of a society. Rawls indicated why people should choose to implement the notion of fairness: (1) each person must have an equal right to a system of liberties that is compatible with a similar system of liberties available to all people; and (2) social and economic inequalities must benefit the least advantaged, and equal opportunity to secure office and position must be open to all. In explaining how present inequities may benefit the least advantaged, he developed the principle of *just savings.*

Affirmative action is not a law within itself, but rather an objective reached by following a set of guidelines that ensure compliance with legislation and executive orders. The Equal Employment Opportunity Commission (EEOC) was established by Title VII of the Civil Rights Act of 1964 to investigate alleged discrimination in employment practices based on race, color, religion, gender, or national origin. This five-member commission has also established, from time to time, affirmative action guidelines. Alleged discrimination charges can be filed with any of EEOC's district offices. The administrative process includes an individual's filing of a charge, investigation of the charge, determination of the charge, and the process of conciliation.

Limited discrimination is allowed by the Equal Employment Opportunity Act under one condition: when there is a bona fide occupational qualification mandating the employing of an individual of a particular gender, religious affiliation, or national origin.

Therefore, a school district human resources administrator has the right to employ a female rather than a male for the position of swimming instructor when the job description includes supervising the locker room used by female students.

The Civil Rights Act of 1991 is landmark legislation because it extends punitive damages and jury trials for the first time to employees who have been discriminated against because of their race, national origin, gender, disability, or religion.

The Rehabilitation Act of 1973 prohibits recipients of federal financial assistance from discriminating against qualified individuals with disabilities in recruitment, hiring, compensation, job assignment/classification, and the provision of fringe benefits. Employers are further required to provide reasonable accommodations for qualified employees with disabilities. The Vietnam Era Veterans' Readjustment Assistance Act of 1974 requires affirmative action to hire veterans with disabilities of all wars and all veterans of the Vietnam era.

The Americans with Disabilities Act of 1990 (ADA) is also landmark legislation because it is the most comprehensive legislation ever passed protecting the rights of individuals with disabilities. There are five titles to the ADA, and all of them except Title IV have some impact on school districts.

On August 22, 1990, President George W. Bush ordered the mobilization of U.S. military reserves and National Guard units into active duty. This triggered several issues concerning the healthcare of dependents and the reentry of reservists and members of the National Guard into the workplace.

On October 28, 1991, President Bush signed into law the Omnibus Transportation Employee Testing Act, which required the secretary of transportation to promulgate regulations for alcohol and controlled substances testing for persons in safety-sensitive positions, including school bus drivers.

President Clinton signed into law the Family and Medical Leave Act (FMLA) on February 5, 1993. The fundamental purpose of this act is to provide eligible employees with the right to take unpaid leave in connection with certain circumstances.

Equality in employment opportunity for women is a central issue in human resources management. The legal mandate of equal opportunity for women emanates primarily from two federal laws: Title IX of the Education Amendments of 1972, which prohibits gender discrimination in educational programs or activities, including employment, when the school district is receiving federal financial assistance; and Title VII of the Civil Rights Act of 1964, as amended in 1972. In addition, in 1978, President Carter signed into law a pregnancy disability amendment to the Civil Rights Act. This law had the effect of eliminating unequal treatment of pregnant women in all employment-related situations.

Since 1980, the EEOC has considered sexual harassment to be a violation of Title VII of the Civil Rights Act of 1964. The issue of sexual harassment in the workplace has gained national attention and will continue to be a concern in school districts across the nation.

The Equal Pay Act of 1963 requires employers to pay males and females the same salary or wage for equal work.

The Age Discrimination in Employment Act of 1967, as amended, promotes the employment of the older worker by prohibiting arbitrary discrimination based on age.

Because of their importance, only major federal influences on the human resources planning process are presented in this chapter in detail. However, human resources administrators must also become familiar with all legislation that protects employment opportunity rights.

Self-Check Quiz Click here to take an automatically-graded self-check quiz.

Discussion Questions and Statements

1. Why is the assessment of human resources needs so important for a school district?
2. Compare and contrast the various methods of human resources forecasting.
3. Define *affirmative action* and explain its significance in establishing accountability in the human resources department.
4. What is the relationship of John Rawls' principles of social justice to human resources administration?
5. Explain the role and function of the Equal Employment Opportunity Commission.
6. What conclusions can be drawn from the judicial review of affirmative action?

Suggested Activities

1. As the assistant superintendent for human resources in a school district with three central office administrators and eleven building-level administrators, develop, in writing, an outline of a presentation on sexual harassment intended to make administrators more aware of potential violations of the school district's sexual harassment policy. Assume that the district's policy is the same as the one presented in this chapter.
2. To become familiar with the cohort-survival technique, simulate an enrollment projection for your school district.
3. Obtain the board of education policies from a school district concerning equal employment opportunity and affirmative action. Write a comparison of these policies with those in this chapter.
4. Develop, in writing, a quick reference guide setting forth the important aspects of the federal laws explained in this chapter.

Focus Scenario Activity

Given that you have read and studied this chapter, how would you alleviate the concerns of the board of education and the superintendent? In other words, what is your plan of action?

Endnotes

1. David A. DeCenzo and Stephen P. Robbins, *Fundamentals of Human Resource Management*, 9th ed. (Hoboken, NJ: John Wiley, 2007), 124–126.
2. American Association of School Administrators (AASA). *AASA Executive Handbook Series, Vol. II: Declining Enrollment: What to Do.* (Arlington, VA: Author, 1974).
3. DeCenzo and Robbins, *Fundamentals of Human Resources Management*, 126–131, 138.
4. AASA, *AASA Executive Handbook Series, Vol. II: Declining Enrollment: What to Do.*
5. Ronald W. Rebore, *The Ethics of Educational Leadership* (Upper Saddle River, NJ: Merrill/Prentice Hall, 2001), 227–238.
6. John Rawls, *Stanford Encyclopedia of Philosophy*, plato.stanford.edu/entries/rawls/.
7. U.S. Constitution, Bill of Rights, and Declaration of Independence, www.archives.gov.
8. U.S. Department of Labor, Office of Federal Contract Compliance Programs, Labor Law Reports—Employment Practices, *Office of Federal Contract Compliance Manual,* 2nd ed., 1975. Report 86, no. 580.

9.   The eight steps are a composite of those found on the EEOC Website.
10. EEOC, verified.
11. EEOC, *Administrative Process*.
12. EEOC, *Bona Fide Occupational Qualification*, Title VII of the Civil Rights Act of 1964, www
     .eeoc.gov/laws/statutes/titlevii.cfm.
13. EEOC, www.eeoc.gov.
14. Peter Schmidt, "Affirmative Action Survives, and So Does the Debate," *Chronicle of Higher
     Education* (special report), (July 4, 2003): S1–S7.
15. Civil Rights Act of 1991, www.eeoc.gov/laws/statutes/cra-1991.cfm.
16. U.S. Department of Health, Education, and Welfare, "Nondiscrimination on the Basis of
     Handicap," *Federal Register*, 41, no. 96 (May 17, 1976).
17. Ibid., paragraph 87.4.
18. EEOC, *The ADA: Your Responsibilities as an Employer*. August 1, 2008, www.eeoc.gov/facts/
     ada17.html.
19. EEOC, "Final Rule: Equal Employment Opportunity for Individuals with Disabilities," *Federal
     Register*, 56, no. 144.
20. Ibid., 35735.
21. Ibid., 35735–35736.
22. EEOC, www.eeoc.gov.
23. EEOC, *Accessibility*, www.eeoc.gov/facts/fs-disab.html.
24. EEOC, *Noncompliance*.
25. American Civil Liberties Organization, *AIDS and Employment Discrimination*, www.aclu.org;
     U.S. Department of Justice, *AIDS and Employment Discrimination*, www.usdoj.gov/crt.
26. U.S. Department of Labor, The Vietnam Era Veterans' Readjustment Assistance Act
     (VEVRAA), www.dol.gov/compliance/laws/comp-vevraa.htm.
27. TRICARE, www.tricare.mil.
28. Omnibus Transportation Employee Testing Act of 1991, www.dot.gov/odapc/omnibus-
     transportation-employee-testing-act-1991.
29. Family and Medical Leave Act of 1993.
30. EEOC, *Equality for Women*.
31. Sara Lipka, "High Court Expands Protections of Title IX," *Chronicle of Higher Education*, 51,
     no. 31 (April 8, 2005): A1, A36.
32. EEOC, *Retaliation*.
33. EEOC, Pregnancy Discrimination Act, Amendment to Title VII of the Civil Rights Act of 1964,
     eeoc.com/guidance/discrimination/pregnancy-discrimination.
34. EEOC, *Guidelines on Sexual Harassment in the Workplace*.
35. AASA, *AASA Executive Handbook Series, Vol. II: Declining Enrollment: What to Do*.
36. Equal Pay Act of 1963, www.eeoc.gov/laws/statutes/epa.cfm.
37. U.S. Department of Justice, *Equal Pay*, www.usdoj.gov.
38. EEOC, The Age Discrimination in Employment Act of 1967, www.eeoc.gov/laws/statutes/
     adea.cfm.
39. Robert Half Technology, "Attracting and Retaining Millennial Workers," *Information Execu-
     tive*, 10920374, 11, no. 7 (July 2008): 4, 9, 11–13.

Selected Bibliography

The Age Discrimination in Employment Act of 1967. www.eeoc.gov/laws/statutes/adea.cfm.
The Americans with Disabilities Act of 1990. www.eeoc.gov/policy/ada.html.

Boohene, R., and Asuinura, E. "The Effect of Human Resource Management Practices on Corporate Performance: A Study of Graphic Communications Group Limited." *International Business Research*, 4, no. 1 (2011): 226–272.

Buckingham, M., and Vosburgh, R. M. "The 21st Century Human Resources Function: It's the Talent, Stupid!" *Human Resources Planning*, 24, no. 4 (2001): 17–23.

Civil Rights Act of 1991. www.eeoc.gov/laws/statutes/cra-1991.cfm.

Devadas, U., Silong, A., Krauss, S., and Ismail, I. "From Human Resource Development to National Human Resource Development: Resolving Contemporary HRD Challenges." *Pertanika Journal of Social Sciences and Humanities*, 20, no. 2 (2012): 265–279.

Deshmukh, R. D. "Human Resource Development in the Context of Globalisation." *Golden Research Thoughts*, 1, no. 10 (2012): 1.

Education Amendments of 1972, Title IX.

Equal Employment Opportunity Act of 1972.

Equal Employment Opportunity Commission. www.eeoc.gov.

Equal Employment Opportunity Commission. *Sexual harassment.*

Equal Pay Act of 1963. www.eeoc.gov/laws/statutes/epa.cfm.

Family and Medical Leave Act of 1993.

Human Rights Campaign. *Statewide Anti-Discrimination Laws and Policies.* www.hrc.org.

Jain, H. C., Sloane, P.J., Horwitz, F., Taggar, S., and Weiner, N. *Employment Equity and Affirmative Action: In International Comparison.* New York: M. E. Sharpe, 2003.

Kellough, J. E. *Understanding Affirmative Action: Politics, Discrimination, and the Search for Justice.* Washington, DC: Georgetown University Press, 2006.

Lee, Y., Hsieh, Y., and Chen, Y. (2013). "An Investigation of Employees' Use of E-Learning Systems: Applying the Technology Acceptance Model." *Behaviour and Information Technology*, 32, no. 2 (2013): 173–189. doi:10.1080/0144929X.2011.577190.

Leonard, B. "On a Mission: Cari M. Dominquez Discusses Her Plans for EEOC." *HR Magazine,* 47, no. 5 (2002): 38–44.

Marler, J. H. "Strategic Human Resource Management in Context: A Historical and Global Perspective." *Academy of Management Perspectives*, 26, no. 2 (2012): 6–11.

Meisinger, S. "Challenges and Opportunities for HR." *HR Magazine,* 5, no. 5 (2005): 10.

Omnibus Transportation Employee Testing Act of 1991. www.dot.gov/odapc/omnibus-transportation-employee-testing-act-1991.

Pregnancy Discrimination Act, Amendment to Title VII of the Civil Rights Act of 1964. www.eeoc.gov/types/pregnancy.html.

Rawls, John. *Stanford Encyclopedia of Philosophy.* plato.stanford.edu/entries/rawls/.

Rehabilitation Act of 1973, Title V. www.eeoc.gov/laws/statutes/rehab.cfm.

Robinson, R. K., Mero, N.P., and Nichols, D. L. "More than Just Semantics: Court Rulings Clarify Effective Anti-Harassment Policies." *Human Resource Planning*, 24, no. 4 (2001): 36–47.

Rose, H. "The Effects of Affirmative Action Programs: Evidence from the University of California at San Diego." *Educational Evaluation and Policy Analysis,* 27, no. 3 (2005): 263–289.

Russo, C. J. *Reutter's The Law of Public Education,* 6th ed. New York: Foundation Press, 2006.

Society for Human Resource Management. www.shrm.org.

TRICARE. www.tricare.mil.

U.S. Department of Justice. www.usdoj.gov.

U.S. Department of Labor. www.dol.gov.

Vickers, M. R. "Business Ethics and the HR Role: Past, Present, and Future." *Human Resource Planning*, 28, no. 1 (2005): 26–32.

The Vietnam Era Veterans' Readjustment Assistance Act (VEVRAA). www.dol.gov/compliance/laws/comp-vevraa.htm.

Wang, G. G., Gilley, J. W., and Sun, J. Y. "The 'Science of HRD Research': Reshaping HRD Research through Scientometrics." *Human Resource Development Review*, 11, no. 4 (2012): 500. doi:10.1177/1534484312452265.

Appendix A
Steps in Developing an Affirmative Action Program*

- Establish a strong policy and commitment.
- Assign responsibility and authority for the program to a company official.
- Analyze the present workforce to identify jobs, departments, and units where minorities and females are underutilized.
- Set specific, measurable, attainable hiring and promotion goals, with target dates, in each area of underutilization.
- Make every manager and supervisor responsible and accountable for meeting these goals.
- Reevaluate job descriptions and hiring criteria to assure that they reflect actual job needs.
- Find minorities and females who qualify or who can become qualified to fulfill goals.
- Review and revise all employment procedures to assure that they do not have a discriminatory effect and that they help attain the goals.
- Focus on getting minorities and females into upward mobility and relevant training pipelines, especially where they have not had previous access.
- Develop systems to monitor and measure progress on a continued basis. If results are not satisfactory in meeting goals, find out why and make necessary changes.

Appendix B
Summary Facts Concerning Job Discrimination†

Title VII of the 1964 Civil Rights Act, as amended, provides that an individual cannot be denied a job or fair treatment on a job because of

- Race,
- Color,
- Religion,
- Sex, or
- National origin.

The act established the Equal Employment Opportunity Commission (EEOC) to ensure that these rights are protected. If an individual employed by any of the following

---

Source: EEOC, Affirmative Action and Equal Employment.
†*Source: EEOC, Title VII of the Civil Rights Act of 1964, www.eeoc.gov/laws/statutes/titlevii.cfm.*

believes that he or she has been discriminated against in the workplace, he or she may file a charge of discrimination with the EEOC:

- Private employer of fifteen or more persons,
- State and local government,
- Public and private educational institutions,
- Public and private employment agencies,
- Labor unions with fifteen or more members, or
- Joint labor management committees for apprenticeship and training programs.

Also a charge may be filed by another person or by a group if the person allegedly experiencing the discrimination gives his or her permission to these other parties.

The EEOC does not cover discrimination because of

- Citizenship,
- Political affiliation, or
- Sexual orientation.

It also does not cover job discrimination by federal government agencies, government-owned corporations, Native American tribes, disability discrimination jurisdiction, or private employers with fewer than fifteen workers.

If a person want to file a charge of job discrimination, he or she must do so promptly—within 180 days from the time the discrimination took place.

An employer is prohibited by law from harassing or bothering an individual in any unfair manner because he or she filed a charge, assisted in an investigation, or opposed unlawful employment practices.

Appendix C
Steps in Filing a Charge of Job Discrimination[††]

To file a charge of job discrimination, an individual must

- Visit the nearest EEOC district office or mail in a Charge of Discrimination form. If a form cannot be obtained, a written statement may be sent identifying all parties and clearly describing what act(s) of discrimination took place.
- Be interviewed by an EEOC intake officer at the district office or by telephone if an in-person interview is impossible.
- Provide information, including records and names of witnesses to the discrimination.
- Swear to or affirm, under oath, the charge of discrimination or make a declaration under penalty of perjury.

As the charging party, an individual must

- Cooperate with the EEOC;
- Attend fact-finding conferences and other meetings when scheduled;

[††]*Source: EEOC, Filing a Charge of Job Discrimination, www.eeoc.gov/facts/howtofil.html*

- Inform the EEOC of changes in his or her address, telephone number, and other such information; and
- Contact the EEOC if he or she wants to withdraw the charge.

After a charge is filed:

- The employer, union, employment agency, or labor management committee named in the charge will be notified.
- In many states, the charge may be referred for remedy to a state or local fair employment practices agency for 60 days (120 days if the agency is new).
- The EEOC may require the person making the charge to attend a fact-finding conference in order to establish facts, define issues, and determine a basis for negotiating a settlement.
- If settlement efforts are unsuccessful, the EEOC may investigate to determine the merits of the charge.
- After the investigation, the EEOC will issue a letter of determination on the merits of the charge.

CHAPTER 3

Recruitment

Focus Scenario

You are the assistant superintendent for human resources in a school district that is experiencing a shortage of qualified teachers and other support employees. You have scheduled a meeting with the administrative staff, teacher organization leaders, and support staff organization leaders to elicit their assistance in recruiting applicants and to help them understand why recruitment needs to be more productive.

After conducting informal telephone interviews with qualified candidates who did not accept your offer of employment or who dropped out of the selection process, it is clear that the school district has a number of obstacles to overcome. First, the school district has a reputation that militates against hiring the best candidates. Its reputation is one of a district that offers students an outdated curriculum with inadequate support services. Further, the district appears to lack support from the community because a bond issue referendum to build an addition to the middle school failed.

The accountability of the administration was called into question by the local newspaper when a teacher was dismissed from the district for incompetence. This same teacher publicly criticized the administration and the board of education for misuse of school district funds because some classroom teachers were using outdated textbooks and instructional materials. The district was further cited for not having an effective technology instructional program while the superintendent of schools was provided with a district-owned automobile and given an annuity, in addition to board-paid medical and hospital insurance for his wife and children.

Also, several applicants stated that other school districts in the same vicinity had higher salaries and better fringe benefits. These issues seem to be why the school district has been unable to hire the first-choice applicants of the administrators and teachers who were involved in the selection process.

Please use both the "Discussion Questions and Statements" and "Suggested Activities" at the end of this chapter in order to help you develop a way of proceeding in order to address the issues in this section.

After the human resources planning process identifies current and future staffing needs, the next step is to recruit personnel. In the 1970s, many school districts experienced a rather dramatic decrease in pupil enrollment. This phenomenon forced districts to lay off large numbers of teachers, which affected the number of college students entering schools of education. Young people interested in teaching anticipated a rather dismal job market on completion of their education and thus changed their career goals. This situation was compounded by the large number of teachers who retired in the 1980s and who defected to the business community.

The current situation is not radically different in terms of teacher turnover and teacher shortages in areas such as special education, the sciences, mathematics, and foreign languages. This is particularly true in rural school districts. The National Center for Education Statistics has issued three reports that must be analyzed and considered in tandem in order to fully understand the future recruitment demands. The first report, issued in 2005, covered the mobility of the teaching workforce. During the 1999–2000 school year, 580,000 teachers, approximately 17 percent of the workforce, were new hires. The second report, issued in 2008, indicates that the teaching workforce will need to increase by 28 percent in 2017. However, the most significant report for this presentation focuses on teacher career choices. This longitudinal study finds that as of 2003, approximately 87 percent of prior graduates reported that they were no longer teaching.[1] The implication for the recruitment process is that competition will be fierce for the best and brightest candidates for teaching positions in general.

Of particular concern are urban school districts, where African American, Hispanic, and Native American student populations continue to grow yearly. Demographers predict that this trend will continue to gain momentum. However, there is no corresponding increase in the percentage of minority teachers, and in fact, the trend signals a decline in African American and Hispanic teachers and administrators.[2]

However, for human resources administrators, diversity is a much broader issue. The United States continues to be a nation of immigrants, but the immigrants no longer come from Western Europe. Although there is a definite influx of immigrants from Eastern Europe, most immigrants come from Asia and the Americas. Of course, this has changed the composition of the U.S. population, not only ethnically but also religiously. Although the United States is still a nation of Christians and Jews, it is also a nation of Muslims, Hindus, and Confucians.

Obviously, the population is also composed of citizens from the traditional categories of age, disability, gender, illness, and lifestyles. Thus, one of the most important issues facing many human resources administrators is recruiting teachers, staff members, and administrators from underrepresented categories. This is a necessity for two reasons: First, it is crucial to have teachers, staff members, and administrators who are ethnically representative of the community in which the schools are located. Second, all children should be exposed to teachers, staff members, and administrators who are representative of the larger population in the United States. Obviously, this situation makes human resources administrators responsible, immediately and in the long term, for developing strategies for recruiting minority employees.[3]

Therefore, the recruitment process has never been more important to school districts as they search for the best people available to help achieve the mission of each district, educating children and young people. This is the major thrust of every recruitment program— not to hire just to fill a position, but rather to acquire the number and type of people necessary for the present and future success of the school district. Affirmative action requirements, future staffing needs, and dual certification are issues that impinge on recruitment programs. It is a mistake to assume that the correct mix of people will be available to fill vacancies without making a concerted effort to find the most qualified individuals to meet specific human resource needs.

Recruitment also entails discovering potential applicants for anticipated vacancies. This perspective on the recruitment process greatly depends on the size of the school district. Although an urban or metropolitan school district recruits potential applicants more often than do smaller suburban districts, many other variables influence the extent of recruiting activities. First, the employment conditions in the community where the school district is located affect recruitment. For example, having a university with a school of education located near the district often ensures sufficient applicants for entry-level teaching positions.

A second set of variables affecting recruitment includes working conditions, salary levels, and fringe benefits provided by a school district. These affect employee turnover and, therefore, the need to engage in recruitment activities. Districts experiencing a rapid increase in pupil population, and hence a need for increased staff, look on recruitment as a major human resources priority.

Finally, even school districts experiencing decreasing enrollment and reduction in the workforce may need to engage in recruitment activities from time to time because certain vacancies require special skills that current employees lack, such as the sciences, special education, and foreign languages. A school district may find that teachers who are already employed and scheduled to be placed on involuntary leave cannot be transferred to fill a vacancy in, for example, industrial arts because they lack the required certification.

Recruitment, therefore, should be common to all school districts. The idea of "stealing" proven employees from another company has become an acceptable practice, considered perfectly legitimate if no coercion or illegal pressures are brought to bear on a potential employee. Talent and skills are scarce commodities. School districts are ethically bound to find the most talented and skilled people available to achieve their mandate of educating children. In practice, this requires them to develop employment conditions, salary levels, and benefits that will attract the best applicants, while remaining within the fiscal constraints of the school district.

The practice of overtly contacting and recruiting individuals who meet a given set of job requirements and encouraging them to become applicants should be emulated by school districts. It is recruitment in its purest form. Many state departments of elementary and secondary education have recognized the need to assist school districts that are having difficulties finding and hiring qualified teachers. Thus, the phenomenon of alternative certification programs has emerged in many states. Usually, these are programs at colleges and universities that provide individuals who have bachelor's degrees the opportunity to become teacher certified in a relatively short period of time. The curriculum varies at different colleges and universities, but the emphasis is on teaching the essentials of pedagogy and adapting a person's life skills and academic knowledge to the instructional process. For example, such programs would help a retired accountant translate his or her knowledge into lesson plans for teaching high school accounting. Of course, considerable attention is also afforded to understanding adolescent and educational psychology. Obviously, the target populations for these programs are retired people and those seeking a second—or even a third—career.

Both job seekers and human resources departments in school districts have discovered the benefits of Internet recruiting. It has transformed the recruiting process, and it is very possible that in the not too distant future, job advertisements in newspapers and professional journals, recruitment brochures, and all other print media will be replaced by the Internet. Most school districts have designed Websites that provide potential employees access to information about school districts such as salary and fringe benefits, student–teacher ratios, financial solvency, employee turnover, student discipline, a mission statement, and so on. Some school districts have also learned the advantage of designing a Website that includes an online response form, which allows potential candidates to fill out and submit an application. With other school districts, potential employees can access information about the application process and even submit their resumes via email.

School districts offering substandard salaries and poor fringe benefits will not be as successful at recruiting via the Internet. That is, because these school districts will probably not provide salary and benefit information on their Websites, seasoned job seekers will be discouraged from considering them as potential employers.

When a school district has an unexpected vacancy, Internet recruiting could provide a sizeable pool of applicants in a short period of time. Various online recruitment providers allow job seekers to post their resumes and school district recruiters to search the resume bank on a daily or weekly basis in order to find suitable candidates for job vacancies. Although this is a compelling reason to use this type of recruitment tool, the greatest advantage to recruiting via the Internet is the ability to reach as many potential applicants as possible in the most cost-effective manner. If this method gains acceptance among job seekers, it could reduce postage costs and may even result in a reduction in the number of staff members needed to manage the recruitment process in school districts.

Another trend that has taken hold, the *websume,* is used by the most aggressive job seekers. Teachers and administrators develop their own Websites, which can include not only a resume but also supporting documents and, in some cases, even a video. This allows job seekers to introduce themselves in a positive way that could attract the attention of school district administrators and even members of the board of education.

Another newer approach, *social network recruiting,* is a modification of the long-standing networking approach that has always existed in some form or fashion. People have always made social contacts with other people to form a supportive network while searching for a different place to work. This has evolved to the point where some companies even provide networking services. Networking companies provide privacy and usually pledge not to sell personal information to a third party. An individual registers by adding his or her name to an enormous list that can be accessed to find contacts by zip code, job, and even place of employment. The objective is to find other people who live and work in places and organizations that interest you. Some companies allow human resources administrators to place job postings on the network and even to transmit applications and other job-related information through email. People who are networked can also direct employment information to each other. The effectiveness of this type of recruiting and job searching is not conclusive. However, no one disputes the large number of people who are members of Internet-based social networks that function for other purposes such as finding a compatible significant other. It is a trend that all human resources administrators should be cautiously investigating.

Thus, technology has the potential to help school districts find and hire the most qualified and creative candidates in the shortest amount of time and most cost-effective manner.

Issues That Affect Recruitment

Here, we consider four issues that affect recruitment of school district employees: affirmative action, a district's public image and policies, the position to be filled, and salary and fringe benefits.[4]

Affirmative Action

Many school districts make a practice of promoting already hired employees into supervisory or administrative positions. A school bus driver could advance to dispatcher; route supervisor; and, eventually, director of transportation. A classroom teacher might become a department chairperson and, if certificated as an administrator, an assistant principal, with eventual promotion into the principalship. This is, of course, a legitimate practice, with many advantages for building morale within the school district.

Employees who recognize that the district provides them with opportunities to advance their careers through promotions are more likely to make a long-term commitment to the school district. In like manner, employees should also be made aware of the link between job performance and promotion. This places responsibility on the administration to develop procedures that ensure promotion opportunities for those who have demonstrated that they are capable of handling higher-level tasks. The appraisal process is the vehicle for documenting the quality of such performance.

Chapter 2 presents in detail the affirmative action and equal employment opportunity requirements mandated by various civil rights laws. This civil rights legislation basically prohibits discrimination in recruitment because of race, age, disability, military service, color, religion, gender, pregnancy, and national origin. The concept of equality in opportunity, however, must eventuate in a set of recruitment procedures.

Internal promotion as a practice does not nullify affirmative action requirements. The only exceptions to such requirements are those situations in which gender, not being disabled, or the like constitutes a bona fide occupational qualification. Thus, a school district may discriminate against a teacher's aide who has an orthopedic disability by promoting another aide to a gymnastics teaching position when the ability to demonstrate routines is part of the job description.

Except for bona fide occupational qualifications, a district must establish promotion procedures that clearly do not discriminate against minorities and protected groups of employees. A district can demonstrate equal opportunity by advertising promotional opportunities, establishing promotion criteria, and offering equal access to career advancement training programs. No position should be filled without giving qualified employees an opportunity to apply. This may be accomplished by publishing promotion opportunities on bulletin boards or in a district publication such as a newsletter. Whatever the method, it must be clear that qualified employees have been informed of the opening and given an opportunity to apply.

Promotion criteria should include the level of current job performance, qualifications and skills, and job knowledge. Affirmative action does not require the promoting of unqualified employees; however, it does require that qualified individuals be given an equal opportunity. Finally, minority employees and those employees with disabilities should be encouraged to participate in educational and training programs that will enhance their knowledge and skills, thus providing them with the qualifications necessary to apply for promotions.

The size of a school district usually determines not only the extent of internal recruitment for promotion but also the extent of external recruitment. In a small school district, it may be the case that none of its current employees are qualified for an administrative or supervisory opening. Thus, external recruitment is the only avenue available for filling such a vacancy.

Affirmative action and equal employment opportunity must be major considerations in developing and implementing recruitment practices and procedures. The days should be gone when a person can be hired simply because he or she is someone's friend or relative. Physical appearance and the interviewer's "hunch" are also no longer acceptable criteria for hiring or promoting an individual.

Public Image and Policies of the School District

A second possible constraint on recruiting candidates for a position emanates from the school district itself. Prospective candidates may not be interested in pursuing a job opportunity in a particular school district because of that district's image in the community. For example, a district that offers an inferior curriculum, is understaffed, or lacks support services will find it difficult to attract the best people in education.

The policies of the board of education and the administrative processes and procedures of the district are also important considerations to most candidates. These are the criteria by which the quality of the work environment may be measured. If, for example, a school district lacks a well-defined and effective appraisal process, prospective candidates will have little confidence in the district's ability to adequately evaluate their future performance, which in turn may affect their chances for salary increases.

Position To Be Filled

A third constraint in recruiting for a position centers around the attractiveness of the job itself. A position viewed as anxiety laden or that lacks promotion potential may not interest the best people.

The most common situation that falls within this category is the succession problem. Following either a successful person or a person who was a failure is difficult. If the person who previously held the position was exceptionally capable, a successor may find the expectations of the school board, parents, students, and even colleagues to be beyond anyone's capabilities. Following someone who failed in a position will probably be easier; however, the responsibilities of the job may have been neglected to the point where chaos and disorganization reign. A person brought in to restore order may make other employees anxious if they have become accustomed to a lack of supervision.

Salary and Fringe Benefits

The best people for a job become candidates only if the financial compensation is in line with the responsibilities of the position. Education is a service enterprise, and, as such, the main priority must be attracting highly qualified employees. Recruiters may need to negotiate compensation with candidates. This practice helps attract highly qualified individuals for less-desirable positions. In school districts, however, the salary for a position is usually fixed on a salary schedule, and the fringe benefits are universally applied to all employees in a certain category. This makes the recruitment of highly skilled candidates a difficult task, particularly if the job is undesirable or if the district has a poor image.

The exceptions to this rule are the central office administrative positions at the super-intendent and assistant superintendent levels. In recruiting candidates for such positions, both salary and fringe benefits are usually negotiable.

Career Choices and Recruitment

Although the focus of human resources administration is organizational practices, in recruitment, it is important to understand those factors that influence the career choices of prospective candidates.[5] First, people have different interests, abilities, and personalities that, nevertheless, will qualify each person for many different occupations. In fact, experience verifies that an individual will probably change his or her occupational field at least three times during his or her lifetime. When recruiting people for a particular position, the recruiter should understand how ability, interest, and personality interface in various occupations. For example, the successful high school journalism teacher may be a good candidate for the position of public relations director. Both occupations require the ability to communicate ideas, an interest in writing, and a person capable of relating to other people on a professional level. There are also links between guidance counseling and human resources administration, and between the principalship and central office administration. The essence of this observation is that the recruitment of candidates for a particular position must not be limited to individuals who already perform similar tasks.

Second, occupational preferences, competencies, and self-images of people change with time and experience, making personal adjustment a continuous process. It is, therefore, unwise to assume that current employees are probably not interested in changing occupations within the organization. An internal search for potential applicants often reveals that many employees are interested in alternative positions.

Third, satisfaction in both life and work depend on how well an individual can use his or her abilities and find adequate outlets for his or her interests, personality traits, and values. A high turnover in a certain position should cause a human resources administrator to reevaluate the responsibilities of the position to ascertain the accuracy of the job description. This reevaluation should then provide a clearer profile of the type of individual who will be successful in the job. It is obviously important to link the interests, abilities, and personality traits of potential candidates to how such individual characteristics will be challenged in the position. For example, a particular middle school principalship located in an urban ghetto may require a self-motivated individual who feels comfortable in an environment laced with a constant demand to handle students who have chronic behavioral problems, while also supervising a highly unionized teaching staff. Not every applicant has the personal characteristics necessary to be successful in this situation.

Fourth, the process of occupational choice is influenced by employment variables such as salary, fringe benefits, location, opportunity for advancement, and nature of the work to be performed. The importance of these variables differs from one applicant to the next. In recruitment, it is important to present this information to every candidate in an extremely clear format from the very start. Sometimes, people are so intent on finding an alternative to their present employment that they initially overlook these variables. However, when an employment offer is made, these factors become very apparent, and the candidate might refuse the position after a search that has cost the school district considerable time and money.

Finally, career choices are compromises between personal characteristics such as interests and abilities and external factors such as the type of work to be performed. The effectiveness of this compromise is tested out through role-playing, whether in fantasy, simulation, or the actual work environment. The emergence of assessment centers gives testimony to this principle. Assessment centers set up career paths for those who are already employed. At such a center, the capabilities of an employee are matched with the requirements of various positions within the school district. A career path is then planned that allows the employee to experience various levels of responsibility in different locations. As he or she demonstrates success at each level, the employee is advanced to a higher level along the path. Thus, an individual who has been hired as a maintenance supervisor may be promoted, after an assessment, to assistant director of maintenance, and eventually to director.

The implication is that job success is the only true measure of the effectiveness of the recruitment process. However, this implication is often overlooked because many school districts never evaluate their recruitment procedures using a follow-up study of those who were already hired.

Methods of Recruitment

It can be demonstrated from experience that certain recruiting methods produce the best candidates for particular job vacancies.[6] Consequently, before initiating the recruitment process, each job vacancy should be analyzed to ascertain what method will be most effective. For example, an advertisement for a business manager's position appearing in the classified section of *School Business Affairs* will most likely reach individuals with the required qualifications. An advertisement in a local newspaper will probably produce few, if any, qualified candidates. In like manner, a recruiter who visits students at a four-year teacher education college in search of candidates for a high school principal's position requiring a minimum of a master's degree in educational administration is looking in the wrong place.

Internal Search

Some school districts find it advantageous to train their own employees for all positions beyond the lowest level. As mentioned, promotion from within has definite advantages, particularly in creating high morale among employees. Another obvious benefit to promoting from within is that people already on the payroll are known entities. Although the selection process discussed in Chapter 4 helps minimize the danger of making the wrong choice, firsthand information about an employee's performance is the best basis on which that person can be promoted.

Many school districts have not traditionally promoted from within because of the minimal number of job categories found in most school districts. Classroom teachers, principals, cooks, custodians, bus drivers, and a superintendent of schools continue to constitute the breadth of differentiation in staffing in rural and small suburban school districts.

In contrast, school districts located in metropolitan areas offer such a multitude of services that promotion from within is a possibility even for teaching positions. Teacher aides and substitute teachers can be promoted into full-time teaching positions when vacancies occur. Similarly, most large school districts have some classroom teachers who are qualified to become principals. The same situation occurs in support areas such as transportation, food services, and maintenance. Theoretically, a cook can be promoted into a commodities purchasing position and then to director of food services.

There are a few disadvantages to rigidly following a system of promoting from within. First, mediocre personnel in the school district may be promoted, whereas excellent individuals in the community are not considered. Second, affirmative action requirements may dictate searching for personnel outside the organization. Finally, there is the possible danger of "inbreeding." New ideas and methods are not only a welcomed change but also absolutely necessary when the personnel in a school district appear content with the status quo.

The observations and performance evaluations of supervisors and principals are sources of information available to human resources administrators as they analyze a promotion-from-within policy.

It is a standard operating procedure in many school districts to post job vacancies on bulletin boards, in newsletters, or in special publications issued from the human resources office. This allows current employees to apply for positions or to notify friends, relatives, and associates about vacancies. The assumption here is that current employees should not be overlooked, but that a policy limiting all promotions to those presently employed is not the most beneficial approach for a school district.

Large urban school districts are using an approach unique to school districts. Because many of these districts are having difficulty recruiting teachers, particularly in the sciences and mathematics, they are offering to pay a portion of the costs for staff members to acquire a college degree to hire them to fill teacher vacancies. Teacher assistants have been targeted as a group of staff members who are likely to take advantage of this kind of program.

Referrals

Current employees are perhaps the best source of referrals when a vacancy occurs for a number of reasons, the most significant being that an employee does not usually recommend someone unless he or she believes that the referred person will do a good job because his or her reputation is at stake.

A quality control on a referral from a current employee is the job performance of the recommender and his or her satisfaction with the school district as a whole. A recommendation from an employee with inferior performance or from an employee who is constantly complaining about the policies and procedures of the district should be reviewed carefully.

The employee recommending a friend may also confuse friendship with potential job success. It is not uncommon for people to want friends in the workplace, for both social and economic reasons. An employee, for example, may want to share a ride to work with a friend who lives in the same neighborhood.

Referrals from teachers and principals, however, often reflect professional rather than social contact. Membership in professional organizations such as the National Association of Secondary School Principals or the National Education Association is one way in which people become acquainted with the competencies of colleagues. Consequently, such referrals may be more credible than referrals based only on social contact.

A school district should establish a policy and procedures that encourage employees to recommend people for job vacancies. A common practice is for the employee to provide the human resources department with the name or names of potential candidates. The human resources department can then send letters to the referred individuals, stating that they have been recommended to become candidates and inviting them to submit an application for the job. It should be noted that the invitation is extended to become a *candidate*; a human resources administrator must be very careful not to give the referred person the impression that the job is being offered.

Employment Agencies

Employment agencies fall into two categories: public or state agencies and private agencies. For all practical purposes, teachers and administrators have made limited use of employment agencies in their search for professional positions. This is not the case for support personnel such as custodians, bus drivers, and cafeteria workers.

A public employment service was established in 1933 as a federal–state partnership. It was created not only to help individuals find suitable employment but also to help employers find qualified workers. Each of the fifty states has a state employment service agency, with branch offices strategically located throughout the states, supervised by the U.S. Department of Labor's Employment and Training Administration. The state agencies provide services to those receiving unemployment benefits, and unemployment benefits are available only to people who are registered with the state employment agency. Although state employment agencies are happy to list individuals with extensive training and highly developed skills, most people with such qualifications go to private agencies. Nevertheless, it is foolish for a school district not to list all vacancies with the appropriate state employment service agency because of the possibility that the right employee may be registered.

Private employment agencies, of course, charge a fee for their services that may be charged to the employer, the employee, or shared by both. The fee arrangement is usually dictated by the supply-and-demand principle—when applicants are abundant, potential employees are usually required to absorb the fee. When applicants are scarce, the employers pay the fee.

Another major difference between public and private employment agencies lies in the scope of services provided. Private agencies not only advertise and screen applicants for a job but also provide a guarantee against unsatisfactory performance for a specified period of time, usually six to twelve months. If a particular employee does not work out, the agency will place him or her elsewhere, and find the company another employee without charging an additional fee.

Some private employment agencies specialize in helping fill executive positions, a practice commonly referred to as *headhunting*. By establishing nationwide contacts and conducting a thorough investigation of each potential executive's credentials, these agencies are able to recommend candidates for executive management positions, usually in private business and industry. They charge a rather high fee for this service, usually a percentage of the executive's first-year salary.

Although most school districts do not engage the services of private employment agencies in searching for potential candidates to fill school executive positions, a growing trend in this direction can be seen, particularly in relation to the position of superintendent of schools. Consulting services offered by the National School Boards Association and such state organizations as the Illinois Association of School Boards offer basically the same type of services as the private employment agencies in searching for school superintendents. The fee, however, is not as high as that charged by the private agencies, usually ranging between $5,000 and $25,000, depending on the time and expenses incurred during the search.

Further, in recent years, private consulting firms have begun to specialize in the recruitment of potential candidates for vacant superintendencies. As with other private agencies, they have nationwide contacts, advertise these positions, and screen potential candidates. This is certainly a healthy trend in education, but it carries with it a potential danger. Associations and private consulting agencies may develop a list of favored candidates who are continually recommended for positions; in turn, it could become difficult for even qualified individuals to "break into" this inner circle.

Colleges and Universities

Most colleges and universities offer placement services not only to recent graduates but also to former graduates. The most important service that these placement departments offer is maintaining a personal file containing references, transcripts, and other pertinent documents. Thus, each time an individual leaves a position, he or she may request his or her supervisor and other colleagues to send letters of reference to his or her placement service. This, in turn, alleviates the burden of requesting former employers and colleagues to write reference letters each time an application is made for a different job. The placement service simply duplicates the references and sends them to prospective employers on the request of the graduate.

In terms of recruiting, listing vacancies with college and university placement services reaches not only recent graduates but also individuals with extensive experience who still use the service as a receptacle for employment references. Because teachers and administrators seeking jobs in school districts seldom use private or public employment agencies, college and university placement services are the best sources for finding potential candidates for professional positions.

Most college and university placement services also sponsor job fairs at which human resources administrators can meet potential teachers. These fairs give recruiters the opportunity to highlight the positive aspects of their school districts in order to attract quality applicants. Some school districts that are having a difficult time recruiting teachers may be given the authority by their respective boards of education to make job offers to qualified candidates at these events.

Professional Organizations

Many professional organizations and labor unions provide limited placement services for their members. These organizations either publish a roster of job vacancies or notify individual members about potential jobs. They usually list job vacancies in the classified section of their publications. However, having a classified section advertising jobs in a professional publication is common only among those organizations representing a specialty in educational administration. Such organizations include the American Association of School Personnel Administrators (AASPA), Association for Supervision and Curriculum Development (ASCD), Association of School Business Officials (ASBO) International, Council of Educational Facility Planners International (CEFPI), National Association of Elementary School Principals (NAESP), National Association of Student Personnel Administrators (NASPA), National Association of Secondary School Principals (NASSP), National School Boards Association (NSBA), and National School Public Relations Association (NSPRA).

The American Association of School Administrators (AASA) is an exception. It publishes a listing of vacancies nationwide covering the following categories: the superintendency, the assistant superintendency, central office positions, administrative positions in higher education, and professorships of educational administration.

Other Sources for Recruitment

There are two other avenues for obtaining potential job applicants: unsolicited ("walk-in") applicants and minority media resources. Although affirmative action requirements usually dictate advertising most positions, the walk-in applicant can be a good candidate. Most unsolicited applicants contact the school district by email and via online application. It is important to inform such individuals of the potential for employment with the district and to present them with an application. If a vacancy occurs that fits an applicant's qualifications, that individual should then be contacted and invited to activate his or her application.

Every metropolitan area has minority populations serviced by media resources that can be used in recruiting minorities. For example, in the southwestern United States, there are many local radio stations directed to the Mexican-American population. Advertising vacancies on these radio stations can be a valuable method of recruiting.

Advertising Position Vacancies

When a school district wants to notify candidates that it has a vacancy, it usually develops a formal advertisement that can be used to implement the various methods of recruitment.

Content and Style of an Advertisement

The content of an advertisement is determined by the job description and criteria to be used in selecting the most qualified candidate for the position. The procedures used in determining and writing job descriptions, along with the method of developing selection criteria, are addressed in Chapter 4.

To be effective, an advertisement must accurately reflect the major responsibilities of the position and the minimum qualifications to become a candidate. This is no easy task because the advertisement must also be brief if it is to appear in a newspaper, newsletter, or professional publication. Appendix A contains sample advertisements that may be used as models in writing vacancy notices and that reflect some factors that should be considered.

Educational organizations traditionally begin by giving the name of the organization and then the title of the position, along with specific and quantitative requirements.

For example, the first advertisement in Appendix A states:

GOODVILLE SCHOOL DISTRICT
SPECIAL EDUCATION POSITIONS AVAILABLE
Instructor for students with severe disabilities.

Further, it states that the positions require a B.S. degree in special education and certification (licensing) to work with students who have severe disabilities, with preference given to applicants who have teaching experience.

Advertisements for positions in private business and industry usually begin by giving the title of the job and then information about the company, along with factual and personal requirements. Further, almost all business and industry advertisements emphasize personal qualifications. However, it is interesting to note that some advertisements in business and industry are called *blind ads*; that is, they do not identify the company. Interested persons are asked to reply to a post office or newspaper box number. Large corporations with a national reputation seldom use blind advertisements when they are seeking to fill a vacant position.

School districts usually identify their districts and list factual rather than personal requirements. These are desirable practices. Candidates should know the name and location of the educational organization because this may determine the level of interest they have in the position and, in turn, may limit the number of applicants to those who are seriously interested in the job. Personal requirements for a job are better evaluated through the selection process. Individuals are seldom good judges of their personal qualifications, and many could be falsely encouraged or discouraged from applying for a position if personal qualifications are listed in the advertisement. The practice of giving information about the organization and listing the job title first effectively attracts the attention of those individuals who are most qualified for the position.

The two models illustrate a common but sometimes misleading technique. Each ad contains multiple vacancies, which may imply that the school district has a high turnover of employees and, further, may suggest that selection will not be a very discriminating process because of the number of applicants. It might be more appropriate for a school district to place fewer vacancies in any one advertisement and, when possible, to advertise each position by itself.

Recruitment Brochures

Appendix B contains samples of a special type of advertisement, the *recruitment brochure,* which is usually mailed to individuals who have indicated an interest in an advertised position. The brochure provides potential candidates with extensive information, enabling them to better determine whether they possess the minimum requirements for the job and whether they want to apply. The recruitment brochure is obviously much more extensive in content and scope than the normal advertisement.

The format for such brochures varies, but certain information is usually provided. The most important information to communicate includes the announcement of the vacancy; the procedure for applying; a description of the qualifications that the successful candidate must possess; information about the community served by the school or school district; and data about the school and/or school district such as financial, personnel, and curriculum information.

Appendix B contains two models of recruitment brochures for the positions of superintendent of schools and high school principal. Such brochures are normally used when recruiting candidates for school executive positions.

Brochures are certainly a valuable recruitment tool and should be used as much as possible for all vacancies in a school district. A general information brochure containing data about the community and school district could be used when recruiting for teachers and support personnel. The tailored, special-position brochure could be reserved for executive educational positions. This approach helps hold down the cost of printing a special brochure for the more commonly occurring vacancies in a school district.

Implications for Small- and Medium-Size School Districts

Recruitment has become a more necessary function as a result of the shortage of teachers in certain areas such as special education, mathematics, and the sciences. In addition, speech pathologists, physical therapists, school psychologists, and counselors are in short supply in certain locations. Further, superintendents and other administrators are professionally mandated to search for and hire the most qualified candidates regardless of the position vacancy.

In many school districts, there is no designated human resources administrator; rather, a central office administrator is responsible for multiple functions, including the human resources function. Of course, in a small school district, the superintendent of schools performs the human resources function. However, regardless of the size of the school district or the staffing of the human resources function, the following elements of the recruitment function are necessary:

- Each school district should have a Website that sets forth in the most positive manner the benefits of becoming an administrator, teacher, or staff member in the district.
- The application process should be as easy as possible for potential candidates. Applying online is quickly becoming an expectation for job seekers.
- In this context, it is understood that many administrators may not have the expertise to develop a district Website, but hiring a firm to design the Website is worth the advantages of such an approach to recruitment.
- The traditional methods of recruitment set forth in this chapter require time and commitment on the part of the administration of the school district. However, overburdened superintendents and other administrators can be assisted in carrying out this function by teachers and other staff members who can be compensated for the extra workload. School employees have a vested interest in recruiting excellent colleagues because both students and employees are affected by the quality of those who are hired.

Impact of Generation Y Teachers and Administrators on Recruitment

Generation Y teachers and administrators want to be convinced of, rather than informed about, the benefits of becoming an employee in a given school district. Thus, principals, superintendents, and other administrators must use the various techniques employed by marketing firms to convince Generation Y teachers and administrators that employment in a certain school district is a good opportunity. As a consequence of this characteristic, school districts must conceptualize recruitment as marketing rather than advertising.

Research indicates that Generation Y teachers and administrators not only want their work experience to be enjoyable but also accept that it will be demanding and challenging. Further, Generation Y teachers and administrators view their work experience more as a career or vocation, and not just as a job. This perspective is important because they see themselves as doing something worthwhile, with value to themselves, others, and society in general.[7] It is interesting to note that approximately 25 percent of Generation Y consult their parents or others before accepting a position.

Other research points out that Generation Y teachers and administrators are also searching for security and stability in the work experience. Thus, they are looking for a school district that is financially solvent and, if not growing in population, then at least stable.

Another implication for recruiting Generation Y teachers and administrators is the extensive use they make of school districts' Websites in order to determine which one meets their needs and desires. This, in turn, influences their decision to search for a position in that district. In general, approximately 75 percent of Generation Y will study the Website of the company or school district in which they are interested.[8]

Summary

After the human resources planning process identifies current and future staffing needs, the next step is to recruit qualified personnel. However, certain constraints on recruitment must be taken into consideration. Affirmative action requirements, the public image and policies of a school district, the responsibilities of positions in education, and the salary and fringe benefits offered in certain school districts influence how a district implements the recruitment process.

To carry out a recruitment program effectively, human resources administrators must have a good understanding of vocational development theory. The following principles are common to many theories and can be used to formulate recruitment strategies. First, people have different interests, abilities, and personalities that qualify them for a number of occupations. Second, the occupational preferences, competencies, and self-images of people change with time and experience, making personal adjustment a continuous process. Third, both life satisfaction and work satisfaction depend on how well individuals can use their abilities and find outlets for their interests, personality traits, and values. Fourth, the process of occupational choice is influenced by employment variables such as salary, fringe benefits, location, opportunity for advancement, and nature of the work to be performed. Finally, vocational development is essentially a compromise between personal characteristics such as interests and abilities and external factors such as the type of work to be performed.

Experience shows that certain recruiting methods produce the best applicants for particular job vacancies. Therefore, before initiating the recruitment process, administrators should analyze each job vacancy to ascertain what method will be most effective. The most common methods include conducting an internal search, soliciting referrals, contacting employment agencies, advertising vacancies with college and university placement services or job fairs, posting positions on the Internet, placing ads in newspapers and in the publications of professional organizations, following up on unsolicited applications, and contacting community organizations that promote the interests of minority groups.

When a school district wants to notify candidates that it has a vacancy, it usually produces a formal advertisement, the content of which is dictated by the job description and criteria to be used in selecting the most qualified candidate for the position. The advertisement must accurately reflect the major responsibilities of the position and the minimum qualifications an individual must possess to become a candidate for the job.

In terms of content and style, the most effective advertisement includes the title of the position, information on the school district, instructions on how to apply, and desired qualifications for candidates. Listing subjective qualifications and using blind ads are generally not appropriate. It is also more effective for a school district to place only a few vacancies in a given advertisement and, when possible, to advertise each position by itself.

General information brochures containing data about the community and school district could be used when recruiting teachers and support personnel. The recruitment brochure is a special type of advertisement used to provide potential candidates with enough information to determine whether they want to apply for the job and whether they meet the necessary requirements. This type of brochure includes the announcement of the vacancy; the procedure for applying; a description of the qualifications that the successful candidate must possess; information about the community served by the school or school district; and financial, personnel, and curricular data about the school and/or school district. This more extensive brochure is commonly reserved for recruiting school executives because the cost of printing such brochures for each vacancy could be prohibitive.

Self-Check Quiz Click here to take an automatically-graded self-check quiz.

Discussion Questions and Statements

1. Given the teacher shortage, what strategies do you think are the most effective in recruiting teachers?
2. Describe the factors that influence people to become applicants in certain school districts.
3. How do the theories of occupational choice affect the recruitment process?
4. Describe the elements that make up an effective newspaper advertisement for position vacancies.
5. What is the advantage of using recruitment brochures in place of newspaper-type advertisements for certain positions?

Suggested Activities

1. Obtain a copy of the advertisements for administrative, teaching, and support services positions in local newspapers, and write a comparison of them with the advertisements in this chapter.
2. Obtain a copy of a recruitment brochure for an administrative position that has been used in a school district in your geographic area, and write a comparison of it with the brochures in this chapter.

3. Review the recruitment policies of a school district, and write an analysis concerning their potential effectiveness.
4. In person or on the telephone, interview a human resources administrator from a school district that is having difficulty recruiting administrators, teachers, or other employees in order to ascertain his or her opinion as to why the district is not having success.
5. Visit a college or university placement office and talk with career counselors to gain a better understanding of their services. Also, ask them about the effectiveness of job fairs and the emerging pool of future teachers and administrators.

Focus Scenario Activity

Given that you have read and studied this chapter, how would you proceed as the assistant superintendent for human resources in a school district that is experiencing a shortage of qualified applicants for teaching and other positions? You have scheduled a meeting with the administrative staff, teacher organization leaders, and support staff organization leaders to elicit their assistance in recruiting applicants. Outline, in writing, your presentation, and develop five discussion questions that will help you interact with them about this issue.

Endnotes

1. National Center for Education Statistics, Institute of Education Sciences, U.S. Department of Education, *Teacher Career Choices; Timing of Teacher Careers Among 1992–93 Bachelor's Degree Recipients*, Postsecondary Education Descriptive Analysis Report, NCES 2008-153 (Washington, DC: Author, March 2008), http://nces.ed.gov/pubs2008/2008153.pdf; National Center for Education Statistics, Institute of Education Sciences, U.S. Department of Education, *Mobility in the Teacher Workforce; Findings from the Condition of Education 2005,* NCES 2005–114 (Washington, DC: Author, June 2005), http://nces.ed.gov/pubs2005/2005114.pdf; and National Center for Education Statistics, Institute of Education Sciences, U.S. Department of Education, *Projections of Education Statistics to 2017; Thirty-sixth Edition,* NCES 2008-078 (Washington, DC: Author, September 2008), http://nces.ed.gov/pubs2008/2008078.pdf.
2. Rebecca Moran, Bobby D. Rampey, Gloria S. Dion, and Patricia L. Donahue, *National Indian Education Study 2007 Part I; Performance of American Indian and Alaska Native Students at Grades 4 and 8 on NAEP 2007 Reading and Mathematics Assessments,* NCES 2008–45 (Washington, DC: National Center for Education Statistics, Institute of Education Sciences, U.S. Department of Education, May 2008), http://nces.ed.gov/nationsreportcard/pdf/studies/2008457.pdf.
3. Kathryn H. Au and Karen M. Blake, "Cultural Identity and Learning to Teach in a Diverse Community: Findings from a Collective Case Study," *Journal of Teacher Education*, 54, no. 3 (May/June 2003): 192–205.
4. David A. Decenzo and Stephen P. Robbins, *Human Resource Management*, 7th ed. (New York: John Wiley, 2002), 150–153.
5. Sheila J. Henderson, "Follow Your Bliss: A Process for Career Happiness," *Journal of Counseling and Development,* 78, no. 3 (Summer 2000): 305–315; Shelley M. MacDermid and Andrea K. Wittenborn, "Lessons from Work–Life Research for Developing Human Resources," *Advances in Developing Human Resources,* 9, no. 4 (2007): 556–568; Roni Reiter-Palmon, Marcy Young, Jill Strange, Renae Manning, and Joseph James, "Occupationally Specific Skills: Using Skills to Define and Understand Jobs and Their Requirements," *Human Resource Management Review,* 16 (2006): 356–375; and Sherry E. Sullivan and Lisa Mainiero, "Using the Kaleidoscope Career Model to

Understand the Changing Patterns of Women's Careers: Designing HRD Programs That Attract and Retain Women," *Advances in Developing Human Resources*, 10, no. 1 (February 2008): 32–49.

6. Decenzo and Robbins, *Human Resource Management*, 154–162.
7. Michael D. Coomes and Robert DeBard, eds., "Serving the Millennial Generation," *New Directions for Student Services* (San Francisco: Jossey-Bass, 2004), 52–56.
8. Robert Half, "Attracting and Retaining Millennial Workers," *Information Executive,* 11, no. 7 (July 2008): 2, 3, 5.

Selected Bibliography

Au, Kathryn H., and Karen M. Blake. "Cultural Identity and Learning to Teach in a Diverse Community: Findings from a Collective Case Study." *Journal of Teacher Education*, 54, no. 3 (May/June 2003): 192–205.

Darling-Hammond, L. "The Challenge of Staffing Our Schools." *Educational Leadership*, 58, no. 8 (May 2001): 12–17.

Dhamija, P. "E-Recruitment: A Roadmap towards e-Human Resource Management." *Researchers World: Journal of Arts, Science & Commerce*, 3, no. 2 (2012): 33–39.

Equal Employment Opportunity Commission (EEOC). www.eeoc.gov.

Hoerr, Thomas R. "Finding the Right Teachers." *Educational Leadership,* 63, no. 8 (May 2006): 94.

Ingersoll, Richard M. "The Teacher Shortage: A Case of Wrong Diagnosis and Wrong Prescription." *NASSP Bulletin*, 86, no. 631 (June 2002): 16–30.

Lahey, Joanna N. "Age, Women, and Hiring: An Experimental Study." *Journal of Human Resources,* 43, no. 1 (2008): 30–56.

Liu, Edward, Susan Moore Johnson, and Heather G. Peske. "New Teachers and the Massachusetts Signing Bonus: The Limits of Inducements." *Educational Evaluation and Policy Analysis*, 26, no. 3 (Fall 2004): 217–236.

Long, J. E. "Grounded Theory: Its Use in Recruitment and Retention." *Journal of Management & Marketing Research*, 11 (2012): 1–8.

Najafi, A. "Investigation of Factors Influencing the Human Resources Recruitment and Maintenance: A Case Study of Educational Staff of Sistan and Baluchestan Province, Iran." *Interdisciplinary Journal of Contemporary Research in Business*, 3, no. 3 (2011): 174–183.

National Center for Education Statistics, Office of Educational Research and Improvement, U.S. Department of Education. *Digest of Educational Statistics 2001*. (NCES 2002–130). Washington, DC: Author, February 2002. nces.ed.gov/pubs2002/2002130.pdf.

National Education Association. *Meeting the Challenges of Recruitment and Retention: A Guidebook on Promising Strategies to Recruit and Retain Qualified and Diverse Teachers*. Washington, DC: Author, 2003.

Newton, Mary Rose. "Does Recruitment Message Content Normalize the Superintendency as Male?" *Educational Administration Quarterly*, 42, no. 4 (October 2006): 551–577.

Ordanini, Andreas, and Silvestri Giacomo. "Recruitment and Selection Services: Efficiency and Competitive Reasons in the Outsourcing of HR Practices." *International Journal of Human Resource Management*, 19, no. 2 (February 2008): 372–391.

Prince, C. *The Challenge of Attracting Good Teachers and Principals to Struggling Schools*. Arlington, VA: American Association of School Administrators, 2002.

Reeves, Douglas. "New Ways to Hire Educators." *Educational Leadership*, 64, no. 8 (May 2007): 83–84.

Taylor, Scott. "Acquaintance, Meritocracy and Critical Realism: Researching Recruitment and Selection Processes in Smaller and Growth Organizations." *Human Resource Management Review,* 16 (2006): 478–489.

Trăistaru, C. "Strategies in Recruitment of Human Resources in Pre-Universitary Education." *Petroleum–Gas University of Ploiesti Bulletin, Economic Sciences Series*, 62, no. 1 (2010): 121–132.

Winter, Paul A., and Samuel H. Melloy. "Teacher Recruitment in a School Reform State: Factors That Influence Applicant Attraction to Teaching Vacancies." *Educational Administration Quarterly,* 41, no. 2 (April 2005): 349–372.

Winter, Paul A., and Jayne R. Morgenthal. "Principal Recruitment in a Reform Environment: Effects of School Achievement and School Level on Applicant Attraction to the Job." *Educational Administration Quarterly,* 38, no. 3 (August 2002): 319–340.

Appendix A
Model Newspaper Advertisements

GOODVILLE SCHOOL DISTRICT
SPECIAL EDUCATION POSITIONS AVAILABLE

Instructor for students with severe disabilities. Requirements are B.S. degree in Special Education and certification in SD; teaching experience is preferred.

Educational examiner. Requires M.A. degree and certification in one or more special education areas. Knowledge of and/or experience in psychometric administration and interpretation is desirable. Expertise in assessment of functional abilities, social adaptation, and perceptual and language skills is mandatory. Previous experience in either diagnostics or educational programming would be highly beneficial.

Speech/language/hearing pathologists. Openings include Language classroom instructors; Speech/Language pathologists. Requirements are M.A. degree, eligibility for state certification; Certificate of Clinical Competence from the American Speech-Language-Hearing Association. Classroom experience preferred. Part-time positions are also available requiring M.A. degree and state certification in Speech Correction. Hours are 4–6, Monday through Thursday.

Interpreter for the hearing impaired. Requires a minimum of 64 college hours, Expressive Interpreter certificate, knowledge of different sign systems, and experience with students who have disabilities.

Excellent fringe benefits. For application call or write

Goodville School District
Director of Human Resources

An Equal Opportunity and Affirmative Action Employer

GOODVILLE STATE UNIVERSITY

Goodville State University is a regional multipurpose institution enrolling 9,000 students. It is located in Goodville, a community with a population of 37,000 situated 120 miles south of a major metropolitan area.

Educational administration and foundations. Associate or Assistant Professor to coordinate Ed.D. Degree Program, teach graduate and undergraduate courses, including Methods of Research and one or more of the following: Educational Finance, Secondary School Administration, and Foundations of Education. Experience with state financial accounting systems and familiarity with schools in or similar to the Southeast state region desired. Doctorate in educational administration or educational leadership required. Five years' experience including district-level administration required.

continued

Educational administration and foundations. Assistant Professor to teach graduate and undergraduate courses, including Methods of Research and one or more of the following: Educational Finance, Secondary School Administration, Secondary School Supervision, and Foundations of Education. Advise graduate and undergraduate students. Doctorate in educational administration or educational leadership desired; doctorate in directly related field considered. Five years' experience in educational administration required. Experience in urban school administration, multicultural programs, or secondary administration desired.

Reading education. Assistant Professor or Instructor to teach undergraduate and graduate courses including developmental, secondary, and remedial reading, and graduate reading practicum. Competency in assessment techniques required. Advise graduate and undergraduate students. Doctorate in reading preferred; active doctoral candidate in reading considered. Five years' experience including elementary or secondary classroom teaching required. College teaching preferred.

University School faculty positions. The University School is a K–12 instructional program for 340 students that functions as an integral part of the Department of Education and the teacher education program. All positions require strong classroom skills and a special interest in working with teacher education programs.

Applications. Applicants are required to have their placement file forwarded immediately. Completed application, current resume, and transcripts should be mailed by February 1 to

Dean
School of Education
Goodville University

HUMAN RESOURCES DIRECTOR

A large, well-established company that is a leader in its field, with its corporate offices conveniently located in the Midwest, is seeking a Human Resources Director. This individual will have the complete responsibility for directing the human resources function, involving such activities as benefits administration, wage and salary administration, staff development, selection, employee relations, and EEOC.

The ideal candidate will have 4–6 years' experience, be degreed (preferably in human resources administration) with previous supervisory experience. Good planning and organizing skills are essential, as well as the ability to communicate effectively.

This highly visible position on our corporate staff offers an excellent compensation and benefits package in addition to professional and personal growth opportunities.

Apply in complete confidence by sending resume and salary requirements to

Metro Daily Newspaper
Box 325

Equal Opportunity and Affirmative Action Employer

DIRECT COMPENSATION SPECIALIST

We're Chemomax, the pace-setting, $4-billion, energy-based company that's increasing America's energy options. Our activities are diverse—natural gas, LNG, propane, coal, and petrochemicals. Our operations extend from Alaska to the Gulf of Mexico, in Canada and in the continental United States, onshore and offshore. Our operations range from transmission and exploration to managing large petro-chemical complexes. Rapid expansion of our alternative energy programs has generated superlative career opportunities.

As our Direct Compensation Specialist, you will be responsible for developing annual proposals for structure increases in the corporation's basic exempt salary schedule and the schedule covering corporate executives. You will be working with our operating companies regarding the design of base salary and incentive plans, as well as recommending new and/or innovative forms of compensation.

You will need at least two years' experience in salary plan design and admin-istration. Some experience in foreign and executive compensation is desirable. You should possess a good knowledge of job evaluation, salary survey tech-niques, and salary structure design, along with government wage laws and related regulations.

To explore this excellent opportunity, please send your resume, including salary history, in complete confidence to

Director of Human Resources
Chemomax Corporation

An Equal Opportunity and Affirmative Action Employer

HUMAN RESOURCES
PLANNING & RESEARCH
SENIOR SPECIALIST

As part of our company's commitment to effectively selecting and developing its employees, the company has launched an extensive approach to selection, career path planning, and employee development. Due to the success of the initial work in this area, an experienced Human Resources Planning and Research Specialist is needed to join a team of talented professionals to assist in development and imple-mentation of these processes.

The successful candidate will have had significant experience with test valida-tion; design and administration of assessment centers; design, administration, and interpretation of organizational diagnostic instruments; career path planning; and succession planning. Experience in the design and development of courses would be a plus. This is a unique opportunity to design and install selection and develop-ment systems for an industry leader whose senior management fully supports the effort. The successful candidate will have a master's degree in the behavioral sciences, preferably a Ph.D., and experience in the industrial application of selection/development programs.

continued

We offer an excellent salary and complete company-paid fringe benefits, including a dental plan. Interested and qualified applicants should send a resume, including education and income history, in confidence to

Director of Human Resources
Windstorm Industries

An Equal Opportunity and Affirmative Action Employer

LABOR RELATIONS

A Goodville corporation is seeking a Manager of Labor Relations. We are a world leader in the institutional furniture industry, with a major commitment in open office systems furniture, entertainment, and transportation seating.

This is an outstanding opportunity for a human resources generalist who enjoys labor relations and wants to concentrate in that field. Must have minimum five years' experience, including contract interpretation. The successful candidate should be aggressive and yet objective; creative, mature, well organized, and a person of integrity. Communication skills are a must as is some experience in safety and training. We offer a professional atmosphere and a secure future.

This highly valuable position offers an attractive salary, equitable relocation assistance, and excellent benefits. Qualified candidates should submit resume and salary history in confidence to

Metro Daily Newspaper
Box 645

An Equal Opportunity and Affirmative Action Employer

Appendix B
Model Recruitment Brochures

POSITION AVAILABLE

SUPERINTENDENT OF SCHOOLS
GOODVILLE SCHOOL DISTRICT

An Equal Opportunity and
Affirmative Action Employer

ANNOUNCEMENT OF VACANCY

The Board of Education of Goodville School District is seeking a superintendent of schools. The salary of the superintendent selected will be determined by his or her professional preparation and by his or her successful experience in educational administration, as well as by other qualifications.

Professional assistance for the initial screening of applicants has been secured, which is a special consultant committee consisting of

- A superintendent from a neighboring school district and
- The Dean of the School of Education, Goodville University

All letters of application, nominations, inquiries, credentials, and copies of legal proof of administrative qualifications should be mailed to the president of the Goodville School Board.

To receive consideration, applicants must do the following by January 1:

1. Submit a formal letter of application indicating a desire to be a candidate for the position.
2. Send up-to-date confidential credentials from their university, an up-to-date resume, and a listing of educational accomplishments.
3. Provide legal proof or other evidence showing qualification to be a superintendent.

THE PERSON NEEDED

The Board of Education of the Goodville School District and the community it serves are committed to the continuing development of quality schools. They are seeking a person who has had successful administrative experience as a superintendent or in a central office position with comparable responsibilities. The superintendent they are seeking should have a thorough understanding of and interest in public school education; a concern for the welfare and motivation of students is of prime importance. By his or her experience, knowledge, and stature, he or she must reflect credit on him- or herself and the district he or she serves.

The superintendent selected must be skilled in providing educational leadership; he or she must be a goals-oriented educator with proven success in the continuing development of teamwork among the administrative/teaching staff, board of education, and community.

Although no candidate can be expected to meet all qualifications fully, preference will be given to candidates with capabilities and/or potential as follows:

- Successful experience in financial management, budgeting, and fiscal responsibility, with the ability to evaluate the financial status of the district and establish a management plan based on projected revenues and future curriculum programs.
- In the area of human relations, the ability to work with the public, students, and staff, thus leading to good school human resources management; this aspect also includes evaluation of and in-service training for staff.
- Successful experience as an "educational manager" who delegates responsibility, yet maintains accountability through the management team concept.
- The ability to exercise leadership and decision making in selection and implementation of educational priorities—based on a realistic and responsible educational philosophy.

continued

- The ability to objectively select, evaluate, assign, and realign staff.
- A willingness to help formulate, review, and effectively carry out board policies, and to communicate and relate openly and honestly with the board of education, keeping members informed on issues, proposals, and developments within the district.
- The ability to maintain desired student behavioral patterns.
- Successful administrative experience in a comparable district.
- A strong academic background in curriculum planning and an ability to evaluate and plan curriculum and programs, while constantly keeping in mind the present and future financial status of the district.
- Skillful, "management-type" educational leadership in the development of long-and short-range district goals and objectives.

THE COMMUNITY

The Goodville School District is currently serving the educational needs of nearly 20,000 residents in a geographic area of great growth potential. It covers 80 square miles—one of the largest school districts in the state.

The district is highly diverse and is rich in cultural background and lifestyles. Approximately 30 percent of the residents live in a rural setting, with the remaining 70 percent located in suburban communities. Our district is enriched by a broad range of ethnic and racial compositions. As Goodville is located 25 miles south of a major metropolitan area, many of our residents can conveniently commute to work to and from the city. Local employment continues to be enhanced with the growth of many industrial parks. As a microcosm of lifestyles and cultures, the school district encourages unique opportunities in community living and education. It is a district of parks, forest preserves, churches, schools, shopping centers, and excellent recreational facilities. We are served by three local newspapers, in addition to a large daily newspaper and a local radio station. Goodville State University is located in our district, and many other colleges and universities are within an hour's drive.

THE SCHOOLS

The Goodville School District enrolls more than 5,600 pupils in K–12. Additionally, the district offers services in preschool education, special education, and adult education. Currently, there are six K–5 elementary schools, two 6–8 middle schools, and one high school fully accredited and recognized. The school system is supported by approximately 361 certificated staff members and 171 support personnel.

Concern and support for the teaching of basic skills has been equally recognized by the school board and administrative staff. However, many innovative services and programs are provided to teachers, parents, and students. An alternative education program for secondary students is recognized as one of the best in the county. Additionally, significant steps have been taken toward identification of pupils' learning styles and the proper modes of instruction to enhance these styles. Bilingual programs, special education, teacher staff development, and parent workshops have led state trends. Extracurricular activities have always been a vital part of the educational program. The district prides itself on its athletic programs and band/orchestra activities for both boys and girls.

PHILOSOPHY OF THE BOARD OF EDUCATION

Policy-Making Body

The Board of Education is primarily a policy-making body and shall maintain an administration to operate the schools efficiently with the funds available, shall constantly strive to improve all aspects of the school system, and shall keep the public well informed about educational issues.

Education of the Child

The Board believes that the education of each child in the district is the heart of the entire school operation and that administration, business management, building management, and all other services should be appraised in terms of their contributions to the progress of instruction. It shall be the goal of the Board to offer each child the opportunity to develop his or her educational potentialities to the maximum. It shall be the intention of the Board of Education to provide for equality of educational opportunity for all children regardless of gender, race, color, creed, national origin, or disability.

STAFF

Administration:	1	Superintendent
	2	Assistant Superintendents
	5	Directors
	9	Principals
	7	Assistant Principals
	6	Curriculum Coordinators
	1	Business Manager
Staff:	314	Classroom Teachers
	14	Guidance Counselors
	12	Learning Resource Specialists
	16	Special Education Teachers
	8	Nurses
	5	Speech and Language Professionals
	30	Paraprofessionals
	43	Secretarial/Clerical Personnel
	40	Custodial/Maintenance Personnel
	30	Bus Drivers

continued

	20	Cafeteria Workers
Student Composition:	730	African Americans
	152	Hispanic Americans
	32	Asian Americans
	9	Native Americans
	4,677	European Americans
	5,600	Total Enrollment

FINANCIAL DATA

Assessed Value	$280,000,000.00
TAX RATE	4.50
Bonded Indebtedness	10,000,000.00
BUDGET EXPENDITURES	40,000,000.00

Announcing a Vacancy

PRINCIPAL OF THOMAS JEFFERSON HIGH SCHOOL

THE COMMUNITY

Goodville is primarily a suburban residential community with easy access to the metropolitan area and all major shopping centers. Parochial schools, both elementary and secondary, are located within the school district's boundaries. There are many active parent organizations working on behalf of the students, all of which foster a close relationship between the schools and the parents in the community. The Chamber of Commerce functions as a viable catalyst for the business community. Among the school districts in the county, the Goodville School District has one of the highest tax bases.

THE PRINCIPAL

The Goodville School District is seeking qualified applicants for the position of principal for Thomas Jefferson High School. The following qualifications and leadership abilities will be taken into consideration in the selection process:

- Good interpersonal relations skills
- Skill in all types of communications
- Ability to generate support and enthusiasm among students, faculty, and the community for the total educational program, including extracurricular activities
- Proven ability to formulate and implement both short- and long-range objectives
- Experience in the evaluation process of both staff and programs

- Certification as a secondary school administrator
- Classroom teaching experience for five years
- Educational administrative experience for three years

THE SCHOOL DISTRICT

The Goodville School District was organized in 1875. Education in Goodville encompasses the entire community. Starting with the preschooler, aged 3–5, there are tuition-sponsored programs in early childhood education. Evening courses are offered to adults in a continuing education program.

The total district enrollment is about 5,600 students. There are four elementary schools, one middle school, and one high school. The district employs approximately 361 professional educators and 171 support employees.

The Board of Education is composed of six members, each elected for a three-year term. The district's budget is $40 million, and the average per pupil expenditure is approximately $7,000.

THE HIGH SCHOOL

Thomas Jefferson High School has an enrollment of 2,000 students and a staff of 98 full- and part-time certificated professionals. The school is fully accredited by the North Central Association of Colleges and Secondary Schools.

Approximately 68 percent of the graduating class goes on to college. This requires a comprehensive offering of courses, which currently numbers approximately 150.

The high school campus is located on a twenty-four-acre site. Built in several stages, the school was completed in 1972, when a major addition provided much-needed classrooms and expanded physical education and drama facilities.

THE STAFF

"Experienced and highly qualified" is the phrase that best describes the high school faculty. Approximately 65 percent have more than fifteen years' teaching experience; 60 percent have taught fifteen years or more in the high school; 75 percent of the faculty members have a master's degree or higher.

Salaries are paid according to placement on an adopted schedule that recognizes experience and education. Fringe benefits include a unique plan for staff sick leave, personal leave, major medical insurance, dental insurance, term life insurance, and excellent retirement benefits. Administrators with a twelve-month contract receive one month's vacation.

Contact the Human Resources Department of the Goodville School District for an application package.

CHAPTER 4.

Selection

Focus Scenario

Parents and the school district's professional teacher association have complained to the superintendent of the school and the board of education that the human resources department has failed to hire the *best and the brightest* for teaching positions in the district. You are the newly hired assistant superintendent for human resources. The community that is served by the school district is somewhat affluent, and most of the parents are well educated, with the majority having at least a bachelor's degree and many having graduate or professional degrees. However, the downturn in the economy has been personally experienced by some parents who lost a considerable amount of their investment funds and by others who were laid off as a result of corporate downsizing. Those parents who lost their jobs and are searching for positions are painfully aware of the shrinking job market opportunities and the similar issues surrounding the selection process in some dysfunctional companies and firms.

Additional problems also exist in the selection process. For instance, the application process is flawed, and the application forms are outdated and appear to have no effect on the selection of employees. Job descriptions seem to be outdated, and the selection criteria are at the sole discretion of the assistant superintendent for human resources, who has been the primary decision maker concerning who should be hired. In fact, hiring decisions have usually been made using only his professional opinion, with no input from other administrators or teachers. Some administrative positions have been filled without advertising the positions publicly instead, the assistant superintendent selected the candidates.

Finally, two people had been hired for positions without adequate background checks, which resulted in their termination because they lied on their applications. The teacher hired had been terminated from another school district for drinking alcohol at school, and a bus driver had been convicted of child abuse. Thus, the board of education and the superintendent of schools hired you for the position because of your experience in human resources administration, and they expect you to develop defensible and effective human relations selection procedures.

Please use both the "Discussion Questions and Statements" and "Suggested Activities" at the end of this chapter in order to help you develop a way of proceeding in order to address the issues in this section.

The objective of the selection process is to hire individuals who have the potential to be successful on the job as measured by the school district's formal performance evaluation. As self-evident as this purpose may appear, its implementation requires a rather thorough process. The cost of selecting employees is a major expenditure for most school districts. If the process does not produce effective employees, the cost to the district is often incalculable because of inadequate performance, the expense connected with the termination process, and the expense involved in hiring new employees.

The minimum cost of hiring a new employee has been calculated at $1,000, and it can cost more than $25,000 to hire a superintendent of schools. In selecting an individual for most positions in a school district, the costs include the actual expenses incurred for advertising the position and for printing and mailing applications, as well as the personnel time required to review applications, interview candidates, and check references. This presupposes that many routine tasks such as writing job descriptions and establishing proper selection criteria have already been accomplished. The additional cost of training and orienting new employees is directly related to the hiring process but is often overlooked. Therefore, selecting individuals who have the potential to meet the performance evaluation criteria and who will remain with the school district for a reasonable period of time is an extremely important human resources process, not only significant in fulfilling the district's mandate to educate children but also affecting the financial condition of the school district.

Chapter 2 established the necessity of human resources planning because it is impossible for school districts—indeed, for any organization—to achieve their goals and objectives without having the right number of people with the right skills in the right place at the right time. Adequate human, financial, and physical resources constitute the three requisites for organizational success. However, organizational success is synonymous with organizational change. School districts must meet the ever-changing educational needs and expectations of parents and students in order to be successful. In Chapter 6, the concept of organizational change is molded into the notion of the professional learning community.

It is important for human resources administrators to understand the current research on organizational change that has proved to be helpful not only to schools and school districts but also to many business enterprises. School districts have much in common with other organizations, and many of the principles concerning change are applicable across all organizations. For example, two fundamental principles apply to all organizations, including school districts—stakeholders and vision.

First, internal stakeholders constitute the organization. Thus, the board of education, superintendent, central office administrators, principals, teachers, and other employees are, in the aggregate, the school district; buildings and financial and other material resources are not the school district. Rather, the board, administrators, teachers, and staff members use these resources to fulfill their responsibilities and the mission of education.

Second, organizations are driven by a vision. The board of education, superintendent, other administrators, teachers, and staff members usually operationalize the vision through the establishment of goals and objectives. The vision of a school district revolves around the intellectual, emotional, physical, and ethical development of students. Of course, stakeholders should be engaged in the establishment of a school district's vision, which means that parents, students, and other members of the community, along with the board and staff, must be engaged in public discourse.

The implications for human resources administration are obvious. The planning process, as set forth in Chapter 2, requires the school district to focus on a vision that addresses the signs of the times, along with operational goals and objectives. The steps in the selection process that follow must support these directives. This is particularly important in relation to the selection criteria, which must incorporate indicators that reflect the vision, goals, and objectives of the school district. Such an approach ensures the hiring of administrators, teachers, and staff members who are not only capable of implementing but also willing to implement the directives. Appendix B contains selection criteria indicators that model such directives.

A selection process may result in four possible decisions: two are correct and two are errors. The correct decisions occur when the individual hired proves to be successful on the job and when a rejected applicant would have performed inadequately if hired. In both instances, the selection process has met the objective of hiring the more appropriate candidate. The process has failed when a rejected candidate could have performed the job successfully or when the individual hired performs inadequately. Thus, embedded in the selection process must be predictors of success, which are usually identified through the performance evaluation process set forth in Chapter 5. The steps discussed here have the reliability and validity that result from experience, making them invaluable in reaching reasoned employment decisions. With this in mind, it behooves human resources administrators—and in small- and medium-size school districts, the superintendent of schools—to analyze the effects of the performance evaluation process in light of the selection process.[1]

Implementation of the steps in the selection process can be enhanced significantly through the use of technology, particularly in the small- and medium-size school districts. For example, the school district's Website can contain a link to an online application that can be electronically transmitted directly to the school district and even to the person who has been designated to receive the applications, such as the principal of the building in which a teaching vacancy exists. Communications with candidates can occur through email, and because the applications are in electronic form, they can be sent to members of the search committee. The references and credentials checks and background review can, in part or in whole, be carried out electronically. Further, credentials such as transcripts and teaching certifications can be scanned into a database and electronically stored for review by the search committee. Ultimately, they can form the beginning of a permanent file for the successful candidate. In fact, written documents that are needed for every aspect of the selection process—including the job description, selection criteria, advertisement for the position, and those items mentioned previously—can be developed and stored electronically and accessed when necessary in the present or future.

The selection process should be implemented through a series of activities that minimizes the chances of hiring individuals who are inadequate performers. Exhibit 4.1 sets forth these activities in a sequence that will serve as a model throughout this chapter.

EXHIBIT 4.1   Steps in the Selection Process

1. Write the job description.
2. Establish the selection criteria.
3. Write the vacancy announcement and advertise the position.
4. Receive applications.
5. Select the candidates to be interviewed.
6. Interview candidates.
7. Check credentials and references.
8. Select the best candidate.
9. Implement the job offer and acceptance.
10. Notify unsuccessful candidates.

Steps in the Selection Process

Write the Job Description

A written job description is the product of a process commonly referred to as *job analysis*. This process gathers information about the position: what an employee does; why he performs certain tasks; how he does the job; what skills, education, or training are required to perform the job; what relationship the job has to other jobs; and what physical demands and environmental conditions affect the job. A number of recognized techniques can be used in job analysis. These include the following:

1. *Observation.* For example, a human resources administrator or building principal directly observes a teacher, secretary, or other employee as he is performing his job.
2. *Individual interview.* In like manner, a human resources administrator or director of maintenance engages a custodian in an interview and perhaps analyzes the results from a number of such interviews in order to create a job description.
3. *Group interview.* When a school district uses a search committee approach, the committee might interview a building principal before developing a job description for the principalship.
4. *Job questionnaire.* Some school districts have developed job questionnaires that substitute for the interview technique in developing job descriptions.
5. *Consulting.* In very large school districts, it might be more efficient to hire a human resources consulting firm to develop categorical job descriptions for teacher, administrator, and staff member positions.
6. *Supervisor analysis.* Of course, it is always helpful to consult with the supervisors of the employees—the assistant superintendent for secondary education, building principal, director of transportation, or superintendent of schools—before writing job descriptions.
7. *Diary method.* For central office positions, it is probably more effective for those holding the positions to keep a diary of their daily activities for a given period of time.[2]

The methods described here are not meant to be used in isolation. Rather, they are complementary techniques that result in a superior job analysis if used in combination. Of course, the techniques listed here are appropriate for conducting a job analysis that leads to the development of a job description. However, certain techniques are more appropriate to particular classifications of jobs. Techniques 1 through 3 are probably more effective for analyzing the jobs of classified employees. Techniques 4, 5, and 7 are beneficial in analyzing the tasks common to professional positions. Technique 6 is always helpful in analyzing professional jobs.

The job analysis is, as mentioned previously, the vehicle for obtaining the data necessary to write the job description. The job description is an outline providing specific details about the job and the minimum qualifications necessary to perform it successfully.

No one format for writing a job description can be universally acclaimed as the most effective in every circumstance; however, certain elements should be common to most job descriptions, including the title of the job, the duties that must be performed, the authority and responsibilities accompanying the job, and the specific qualifications necessary to successful performance of the job.

The two sample job descriptions in Appendix A use a style that is particularly appropriate for school district positions. Note that the titles for these two positions are specific:

The first is a job description for a middle school principal, and the second is one for a high school biology teacher.

Each description begins with a summary of the job, outlining the overall responsibilities of the position, and is followed by a detailed explanation of specific job tasks and the relationship of the job to other positions in the organizational structure of the school district. At a time when legal rights and responsibilities are being emphasized by parents and employees, organizational relationships are extremely important and must be clearly explained to prospective employees. Finally, minimum job qualifications are listed as an integral part of the job description.

Job descriptions should be updated periodically because working conditions change with advances in technology and education. Further, it is absolutely critical to perform a job analysis and revise the job description for a position each time it becomes vacant. This affects the establishment of the selection criteria and ensures that the individual being hired properly understands the responsibilities and duties of the job.

There is another important reason to be diligent in developing an accurate and complete job description. If the person hired ultimately does not fulfill the job requirements of the position in a satisfactory manner, ultimately resulting in his termination, the job description provides the normative criteria used to identify the responsibilities that were not acceptably fulfilled.

Establish the Selection Criteria

The second step in the selection procedure is to establish the criteria against which the candidates are evaluated to determine who is offered the job. *Selection criteria* are different from the *job description* in that the selection criteria delineate those ideal characteristics that, if possessed by an individual to the fullest extent possible, ensure the successful performance of the job. Obviously, no one person possesses all these characteristics to their fullest extent, and not all these characteristics have equal importance in determining who is the best candidate.

The selection criteria can also be used to quantify the expert opinions of those who interview candidates. Without criteria, each interviewer is left to his own discretion in determining if an individual is able to perform the job.

Quantifying the opinions of interviewers also provides data to show that the best candidate was offered the position, thus demonstrating that the school district is an affirmative action and equal opportunity employer. The candidate with the highest score should be offered the position first; if he does not accept, then the candidate receiving the next highest score should be offered the position, and so on.

It is a generally accepted practice for the human resources department to assume responsibility for organizing and conducting job analyses, writing job descriptions, and establishing the selection criteria used in filling a vacancy.

The timing for writing the job description and developing the selection criteria is extremely important. Both tasks should be performed before a job vacancy is advertised and before applications are received, not only because the advertisement should be based on the description but also because it demonstrates that the criteria were not prepared to favor a particular applicant.

Appendix B presents three sets of selection criteria: one for a high school English teacher, a second for a sixth-grade teacher, and a third for an elementary school teacher in a self-contained classroom. Each of these instruments has been constructed in such a way that particular characteristics can be rated to obtain a final score. The significant difference between the first two instruments and the third is the weighting designated on the third instrument. The compatibility of an applicant's educational philosophy with the school district's policies and curriculum is of primary importance, as indicated on this third instrument. Professional preparation is second, personal characteristics are third, and experience is the least important. The assumption underlying this third selection instrument is that an individual best meets the needs of the school district if he has the proper attitude and philosophy. Experience enriches an individual's performance, but philosophy is necessary to direct the benefits obtained from that experience. In like manner, an individual grows in the job if his educational values are in harmony with those of the school district.

Note, too, that this third instrument is less specific in describing desirable characteristics and leaves the interviewer with more discretion in making a judgment about the candidate's qualifications. For example, an individual with a Ph.D. in early childhood education may not be the most desirable candidate for a first-grade, self-contained classroom position. That applicant may be more effective in a laboratory school attached to a university in which aspiring teachers observe instructional techniques. In this latter situation, the candidate with a Ph.D. would likely receive the maximum number of points in the *Professional preparation* category.

The first two instruments, containing selection criteria for a high school English teacher and a sixth-grade teacher, are rather detailed and more traditional in style and content. Each is divided into categories delineating academic, personal, and experiential qualifications. This method of evaluating candidates requires each interviewer to make a discerning judgment concerning the qualifications of each individual. However, the interview itself is not the only source of information used to fill out the selection criteria instrument; the application, placement papers, transcripts, and letters of reference are also used by the interviewers in determining an individual's qualifications for the job.

Each interviewer signs and returns to the human resources department a selection criteria instrument for each person interviewed. The human resources department is then responsible for compiling the results.

Write the Job Vacancy Announcement and Advertise the Position

Chapter 3 describes the nuances of writing a job vacancy advertisement. Writing a job vacancy is a detailed undertaking. The advertisement should be viewed as an integral part of the selection process, based on the job description and providing potential candidates with sufficient information to make a decision on whether to apply for the position. Consequently, an advertisement must clearly identify the job title, the major responsibilities of the job, the name and location of the school district, the procedure for applying for the job, and the minimum qualifications to become a candidate.

It is the responsibility of the human resources department to write the advertisement and publish it according to the recruitment policy of the school district. The advertisement should include a deadline for receiving applications. Common practice allows a two-week period for receiving applications for classified and teaching jobs, whereas a month is usually allotted to receive applications for school executive positions. Of course, each individual situation dictates the length of time allotted for receiving applications and may deviate from these times.

A common mistake made by some school administrators and inexperienced human resources administrators is not providing sufficient time to implement the selection process effectively. A hurried process may place the school district in an indefensible position in terms of affirmative action requirements and, in addition, may result in the hiring of the wrong person. In an average-size school district, with a human resources department or at least one human resources administrator in the central office, two months is a comfortable period in which to carry out the selection process, beginning with the publication of an advertisement and extending to when a job offer is made.

Receive Applications

A central office staff member, usually a secretary, should be assigned to receive all the applications for a given job vacancy. As the applications are received, they should be dated and placed in a designated file folder, thereby providing integrity to the process as well as a method of monitoring the incoming applications for a particular vacancy.

Many applicants request their college or university placement offices to send their transcripts and letters of reference to the school district. These documents must also be dated and attached to the appropriate applications.

After the deadline for receiving applications has been reached, a master list should be compiled with the names, addresses, and telephone numbers of those who have applied. The master list should also include, by title, the documents that have been received in support of each application, such as transcripts and letters of reference. The master list and the entire folder of applications with supporting documents can be given to a human resources administrator, who then performs the initial screening of the applications.

Keeping applicants informed during the selection process helps cut down on the number of enquiries received in the human resources department. One effective method is to send a postcard to each applicant stating that his application has been received and listing a date by which individuals will be selected for interviews.

It is also important to immediately notify those who sent in applications after the deadline that they will not be considered for the position. A common practice is to accept applications postmarked up to and including the day of the deadline.

Some school districts and many colleges and universities have initiated the practice of receiving applications until the position is filled. Under this procedure, individuals who sent their applications to the school district by the deadline are given first consideration. If a suitable candidate is not identified, then those individuals who sent their applications to the district before a later designated date are considered, and so on, until a suitable candidate is offered and accepts the position. This is an acceptable practice that can encourage qualified individuals to apply for a position even though they did not know about the position in a timely manner.

At this point, a procedure can be initiated to help evaluate the effectiveness of the school district's affirmative action program. The master list of applicants should be given to the administrator responsible for monitoring the affirmative action program. He can then send a letter to all those who have made application, asking them to indicate on an enclosed form whether they belong to one or more minority groups and requesting them to mail the form back to the school district. Because the purpose of the selection process is to hire the best candidate, it is important to state in this letter that filling out and returning the form has no bearing on who is hired for the position. Consequently, the form should not be signed by the applicant and should not be sent to the human resources department, but rather to the affirmative action officer.

Select the Candidates To Be Interviewed

Screening the applications is the fifth step in the selection process. It is initiated to identify those applicants who are to be interviewed for the position. The application form should contain a statement requesting the applicant to have his placement papers, transcripts, and letters of reference sent to the human resources department. These documents, along with the application form, provide the human resources administrator with sufficient information to be able to evaluate each person against the selection criteria and against the minimum education and certification requirements.

The number of applicants to be interviewed depends on the number of people who apply and on the nature of the position to be filled. If only five people apply for a vacancy and if each person meets the minimum qualifications, all five can be interviewed. This, of course, is not the norm, except for those few job classifications in which there is a shortage of qualified individuals, such as the field of special education. On average, between three and five applicants are selected to be interviewed for classified and teaching positions. For school executive positions, the average number interviewed is between five and ten applicants.

Interview the Candidates

Interviewing candidates is a responsibility shared between the human resources employees and other school district employees. The individuals who participate in the interviewing process are determined by the position to be filled. It is important to include not only those who will supervise the new employee but also others who have expert knowledge about the duties to be performed by the successful candidate. For example, candidates for a high school biology teaching position should be interviewed by the high school principal, the chairperson of the biology department, a biology teacher, a human resources administrator, and the assistant superintendent for secondary education. In like manner, candidates for an elementary principal position should be interviewed by the superintendent of schools, the assistant superintendent for elementary education, an elementary school principal, and a human resources administrator. This same process is also useful in hiring classified employees. Applicants for a custodial position can be interviewed by the head custodian in a building, the director of maintenance and custodial services, a custodian, and a human resources administrator.

Members of the interviewing committee should participate in a staff development program on the strategies of credentials evaluation and interviewing. Selecting a group of teachers, department chairpersons, classified employees, and building principals who participate in the selection process for a year's time holds down expenses and allows the district to take maximum advantage of the skills they learn through the staff development program. Each year, a different group of employees can be selected and trained to participate in evaluating credentials and interviewing applicants.

How these individuals are selected to participate in the hiring process depends on the size of the school district. Seniority in the school district, of course, is one of the most defensible methods for selecting participants, but it is also imperative to have individuals who represent all job categories and teaching disciplines. Thus, a maintenance staff member, bus driver, cafeteria worker, elementary school art teacher, mathematics teacher, science teacher, social studies teacher, and so on are needed and should be available.

Released time from work is the most effective way to involve staff members. Substitute teachers and temporary classified employees are needed to fill in for individuals who evaluate credentials and interview candidates during the working day. The average turnover rate of employees during a year's time is usually between 5 and 10 percent. This means that a given employee participates in the selection process only on particular occasions, probably no more than ten working days a year.

Some school executives, such as assistant superintendents, are more involved in the process because of their line authority to so many categories of employees. The assistant superintendent for elementary education, for example, interviews candidates for all elementary teaching and administrative vacancies. Of course, the immediate supervisor for the position to be filled is always a member of the committee.

Definition of an Interview

Most interviews are structured around a conversation among individuals who have related objectives. In this situation, the objective of the candidate is to obtain a job, and the objective of the school district officials is to hire the best candidate for the job. The essence of all interviews is communication, which is particularly important for teaching and other professional educator positions.[3] However, there are certain dimensions to every interview that distinguish it from an ordinary conversation. The job interview has a definite purpose and format, with a beginning, a middle, and a conclusion.

Types of Interviews

There are two basic types of interviews: the standardized interview and the open-ended interview. The *standardized interview* is conducted by asking a set of questions established to help ensure that the responses of the candidates can be readily compared. It is most effective in the initial interviewing of all candidates.

The *open-ended interview* encourages the candidate to talk freely and at length about topics introduced by the interviewer. This type of interview is helpful in the selection of administrators. The interviewer is attempting to learn as much as possible about the candidate's professional opinions and attitudes.

Some school districts have moved away from conducting in-person interviews because of the cost and time commitment. In those districts, the candidate pool is interviewed by telephone, after which the finalists for the position are selected and then interviewed in person. The opinion of many interviewers is that telephone interviews are just as effective as in-person interviews.[4]

Role of the Interviewer

The interviewer has extremely important responsibilities. Not only does he direct the interview by asking questions but he must also record the respondent's answers and present the respondent with a favorable image of the school district. Through the interview process, the interviewer must evaluate and come to a conclusion about the suitability of each candidate. A selection criteria instrument is used to quantify the observations of the interviewer, but ultimately these observations are subjective interpretations.

Interviews are usually more effective if they are conducted in a pleasant environment. This helps put the candidates at ease and facilitates the kind of verbal exchange that gives the interviewer the most information about each candidate. Interviews should be conducted in a location that gives the candidates the best information about where they will work. Thus, a classroom is an excellent place to interview candidates for a teaching position.[5] In like manner, the bus garage is the best place to interview bus driver candidates, and a school building is the best place to interview housekeeping candidates.

Of course, the interviewer must be careful to present a demeanor that is accepting to such a degree that candidates feel free to answer questions without hesitation and with the understanding that there are no wrong answers.[6] The interviewer must also avoid the pitfall that occurs when he unintentionally identifies with the candidate; for example, when both the interviewer and the candidate are certificated mathematics teachers, are from the same city, or have the same hobby.[7]

Legal Implications of Interviewing

Federal legislation and court decisions have had a significant impact on the types of questions that can be legally asked in an interview.[8] For example, it was once common practice to ask a candidate if he had ever been arrested or spent time in jail. Because of the U.S. Court of Appeals for the Ninth Circuit case, *Gregory v. Litton Systems, Inc.*, school districts are now permitted to ask only about a candidate's record of criminal conviction. The following are common topics of inquiry that have legal implications: age, race, ethnicity, disability, religion, lifestyle, and marital and family status.

The Art of Questioning

The success of the interviewing process rests on the interviewer's skill in asking questions, a skill acquired through experience. However, a well-planned interview with a pre-established set of questions can be extremely useful to even the most experienced interviewer and is a necessity in the standardized interview.

Group Interviewing

Some school districts prefer *group interviewing,* in which a number of staff members interview a candidate jointly. Group interviewing can be effective, and it certainly cuts down on the amount of time spent on this process. The dynamics described in this chapter are also applicable to the group interviewing method. However, to be effective, one staff member must serve as the group leader and take responsibility for directing the interview.

Check Credentials and References

Checking credentials and references, step 7 in the selection process, has profound implications for employee selection.

Credentials

A candidate's credentials include such items as a college or university transcript, an administrator or teacher certification document, and a physician's verification of health. Transcripts and health verifications should not be accepted from the applicant; rather, they should be mailed directly to the school district by the respective college or university and physician. It is important to inform a candidate that his file is not complete until these documents are received.

It is common and accepted practice to request a health verification from a candidate only if he is chosen for the position. However, a contract of formal employment should not be initiated until the health verification has been received by the human resources department. It is best to state on the application form that a health examination is required as a condition of employment if a job offer is made.

An administrator or teacher certification document is usually issued by the state department of education and given directly to the individual. Although the candidate presents the certification document to the human resources department, it is still necessary to contact the issuing state in order to ascertain if the certification is valid. When a certification is revoked, the individual does not always return the actual document to the state department of education.

If a person is applying for a teaching or administrative position in a state where he not currently certificated, he is responsible for obtaining written verification from the state department of education that he has the qualifications to receive certification. For such positions, a contract should never be offered to a candidate in the absence of a certification document or verification letter.

Letters of Reference

Letters of reference are the most vulnerable part of this process. A human resources administrator must write, telephone, or contact in person those individuals who have sent reference letters supporting an applicant. The application form should state that a minimum of three reference letters is required; these letters should be mailed directly to the human resources department, and must include a reference letter from the applicant's current or last immediate supervisor.

Evaluating reference letters is a difficult task. There are three basic types of references. First is the glowing letter, affirming in detail that the candidate is an excellent employee with tremendous potential. Second is the letter indicating that the applicant's performance has been inferior and that he would be the wrong person for the job. Third is the reference letter telling little about the applicant and couched in vague language. In fact, reference letters often have hidden messages, and understanding the significance of these references requires the talent of a human resources administrator who is skilled in detecting discrepancies among the candidate's credentials, his interview performance, and the reference letters. Consider, for example, the candidate who performs rather poorly in the interview and has unimpressive credentials but who has an excellent letter of reference from his immediate supervisor. It could be that this individual is not performing satisfactorily in his present position, and that his supervisor would be happy to see him find another job.

Obviously, it is the responsibility of a human resources administrator to verify the reference letters of the candidates who have been interviewed. It is impossible and unnecessary to check every reference for each candidate. However, it would be difficult to choose the best candidate from those interviewed without reference verification.

Another issue with significant effect on the reference verification process in our litigious society is the fear of being sued for giving a truthful but negative reference. Of course, this is an important consideration for the hiring school district and the districts in which candidates were employed. Some states have passed legislation that protects employers from being sued for providing a negative reference if it was truthful and given in good faith. Also, if an employee gives his former employer written permission to provide a reference to potential employers, the former employer has protection in potential litigation, even if such information is negative, if it is held to be privileged and confidential.[9]

Criminal Background Investigation

The risk of hiring a person who has a criminal record has created much concern for human resources administrators. School districts have been sensitized to this possibility because of the news media notoriety given to educators who have been convicted of child molestation, probably the ultimate nightmare of every school administrator.

Criminal background investigations are time consuming and expensive, in addition to being controversial. The National Education Association has taken a position in opposition to fingerprinting as a condition of employment. The often-heard criticism is that fingerprinting is an insult to teachers and their profession. However, many school districts require the fingerprinting of potential employees as part of a background investigation conducted through law enforcement agencies.

Whether to conduct criminal background investigations and the extent of such investigations should not be dependent on the discretion of the interviewing human resources administrator and should be initiated regardless of state statutes. In most school district, the extent of the investigation is usually limited to checking with the local and state police to ascertain if the potential employee has been convicted of a crime. If he is a teacher, it is also possible to check with the Teacher Identification Clearinghouse (TIC), which is maintained by the National Association of State Directors of Teacher Education and Certification. This nationwide clearinghouse has a database of all teachers who have been denied certification and whose certification has been revoked or suspended for moral reasons. Only states can join the TIC, and the data are available only to those states. Individual school districts can neither join TIC nor directly obtain information from it.

Those states that are members of TIC agree to list—by name, any known alias, date of birth, and social security number—those persons for whom certification has been withdrawn or withheld in the past fifteen years. The individual state certification officials are responsible for finding out why the action was taken.

A school district wanting to check the fingerprints of an applicant against the files of the Federal Bureau of Investigation can do this only if the state in which the school district is located has passed legislation authorizing this type of investigation. This legislation must also have the approval of the U.S. Attorney General's Office. Even then, the request must be processed by a law enforcement agency such as the state police. Finally, all states have sex offender registration laws, which make the resulting sex offender registries available to school district administrators. Thus, it is good human resources administration practice to conduct criminal background investigations. In fact, if the wrong person is hired because a criminal background investigation was not conducted, the liability of the school district for the wrongs committed by this person could be staggering.

As a final note on the issue of background checks in general and criminal background checks in particular, small- to medium-size school districts with limited personnel may find it advantageous and cost effective to hire a third-party company that conducts background checks, thus avoiding the situation in which a building principal, an assistant superintendent, or a superintendent must spend an enormous amount of time conducting an investigation that takes him away time from his regular duties. Because small- and medium-size school districts probably do not hiring a large number of teachers and other staff members, the cost of outsourcing the background checking may be relatively insignificant.[10]

Unlawful Employment of Aliens
In 1986, the U.S. Congress passed the Immigration Reform and Control Act, which makes it unlawful to knowingly hire an unauthorized alien, to knowingly continue the

employment of one who becomes an unauthorized alien, or to hire any individual without first verifying his employability and identity.

Select the Best Candidate

The human resources administrator responsible for implementing the selection process for a particular vacancy must organize all relevant data in such a manner that a choice may be made by the superintendent of schools. The data should include the rank ordering by scores obtained using the selection criteria of those candidates who were interviewed, verified credentials and reference letters, and application forms.

The superintendent then selects the candidate who appears best qualified. If this selection process is used, the candidate who scored the highest in terms of the selection criteria is usually chosen.

Implement the Job Offer and Acceptance

Professional Positions

The superintendent of schools may want to interview the candidate he selects for a position or to interview the top two, three, or five candidates before making a final choice. When the final decision has been made, the selected candidate must be offered the job in a formal manner. If this individual accepts the offer, a contract must be approved by the board of education and signed by the finalist. Usually, a board of education requires the superintendent to make a recommendation of employment and requires an explanation of why this particular person was selected.

Classified Positions

The superintendent may want to interview candidates for classified positions, but in most cases, he accepts the recommendation of the human resources department to hire the candidate with the highest score in relation to the selection criteria. The superintendent may make the job offer personally or delegate this to a human resources administrator. Once the candidate accepts the offer, employment may commence at a mutually acceptable time.

Notify Unsuccessful Candidates

The final step in the selection process is to notify all applicants that the position has been filled. This is initiated only after the offer of employment has been accepted by the selected candidate because there may be a need to offer the position to another candidate if the selected candidate refuses the offer. Good public relations also dictate that all applicants be notified when the job has been filled because applicants have expended time and money in applying for the position.

Principles of Constructing Application Forms

The initial step in applying for a position is filling out an application form, an often tedious task enjoyed by few people. There are two major reasons why most people dislike these forms: First, some forms require information that seems irrelevant; and second, some forms allot too little space for filling in the required information.

Application forms are constructed using one of two basic formats. The one style emphasizes detailed and extensive information about the individual, and little or no attention is given to the person's attitudes, opinions, and values. Conversely, the other style emphasizes the applicant's attitudes, opinions, and values, and asks for less factual information.

All application forms must contain an affirmative action and equal employment opportunity statement in order to notify potential applicants and the school district community that the district is and will continue to be in compliance with federal and state laws governing employment. There is also a legal necessity to include a falsification statement that sets forth the fact that a person's employment with the school district can be terminated if he deliberately provides false or incorrect information on the application form.

Appendix C provides examples of both styles, which are composites of the forms used by a variety of school districts. The applications for a teaching position and for a classified position are samples of the factual information style. The third application form, one for a high school principal's position, is a sample of the attitudes/opinions/values style.

These samples also demonstrate the styles commonly used for particular positions. The style is dictated by the kind of information the district must elicit from the applicants. For teaching and classified positions, factual information about the applicants' personal characteristics, their work experience, their professional preparation, and supportive data such as references help the human resources department determine who should be interviewed. For school executive positions, the minimum requirements are highly specialized and thus can be requested on an application in a relatively limited space. Applicants to be interviewed are best selected by evaluating a set of responses that give some indication of each person's attitudes, opinions, and values.

Contents of the Application Form

The basic principle in constructing application forms is to ask only for information you need to know. Most information requested on applications falls under one of the following headings: personal data, education and professional preparation, experience, and references. Exhibit 4.2 lists information that is inappropriate on an application form, either because it is irrelevant or because it is illegal under civil rights and labor legislation.

EXHIBIT 4.2 Information That Is Irrelevant or Inappropriate for Application Forms

- Maiden name
- Marital status
- Name of spouse
- Occupation of spouse
- Number and age of children
- Arrest record ("convictions" is appropriate)
- Height and weight (unless these are bona fide occupational qualifications)
- If applicant owns a home or rents
- If applicant has relatives employed by the school district (a policy against hiring relatives of present employees is questionable)
- If the applicant has an automobile and a driver's license (unless this is a bona fide occupational qualification)
- Where the applicant attended elementary and high school (irrelevant on professional applications)
- Religion
- National origin
- Race

The physical layout of the application form should give an individual sufficient space to answer the questions and provide the requested information. The kinds of information requested should also be grouped under headings to provide continuity. This helps the individual in providing the data and the human resources department in analyzing the applications.

Employment Tests

Intelligence, aptitude, ability, and interest tests can provide valuable data when selecting classified employees. Legal rulings, however, have limited their use significantly because tests must be clearly job related to justify their administration. Aptitude and ability tests are easiest to justify and can be used successfully for most classified jobs. In fact, it would be inappropriate to hire a person to train as a school bus mechanic if he did not possess mechanical aptitude. In like manner, an applicant for a secretarial position could be given a test to measure his computer skills. It should be remembered that testing has definite limitations and that the results must be interpreted in relation to the interview, references, and other employment documents.

Assessment Centers

Assessment centers are places where supervisors have an opportunity to observe candidates for a particular job. They are used primarily for management positions. The candidates are taken through a series of simulations dealing with administrative problems of the type that will probably be encountered on the job. The simulations usually take the form of case evaluations or decision-making exercises. Although the expense of establishing an assessment center makes it prohibitive in most school districts, large metropolitan districts could find the use of an assessment center extremely beneficial in selecting teachers to be promoted into the principalship and other administrative positions.

Implications for Small- and Medium-Size School Districts

There is no doubt that school districts should follow the steps in the selection process because they fulfill two major objectives. First, state and federal equal opportunity and affirmative action laws require a defensible process that clearly demonstrates compliance with those laws. Second, the steps demonstrate that a school district has used a process for hiring the best candidates for teaching and other positions. With a small central office staff that may even be just the superintendent of schools, it is necessary for teachers, principals, and other employees to be responsible for certain dimensions of the process.

Thus, writing the job description and establishing the selection criteria may become the responsibility of faculty members. Advertising the position and receiving the applications may become the responsibility of the principal of the school where the vacancy exists. As an example for a teaching position, a search committee composed of teachers, the principal, and the superintendent may select the candidates to be interviewed, conduct the interviews, and make a recommendation to the board of education. The superintendent should validate the person's credentials, contact the references, and conduct a background review. Of course, the superintendent should make the job offer, and the principal could notify the unsuccessful candidates. This approach also has the secondary effect of solidifying the professional relationship among administrators, teachers, and other staff members.

Impact of Generation Y Teachers and Administrators on Selection

Members of Generation Y are different from the members of other current generations in the degree to which they develop their career paths. At some point in their professional careers, prior generations of teachers and administrators came to a decision about what they wanted to accomplish, usually in a linear fashion, throughout the rest of their careers. For example, a teacher might decide to become an assistant principal and might leave his present teaching position to obtain that desired position in another school district. To prepare for this career, he might decide to obtain a master's degree in school administration. Generation Y teachers and administrators tend to be more focused on balancing the demands of their professional and personal life experiences. If and when that sense of balance diminishes, they search for alternative positions that could provide the personal fulfillment that they have lost. It is an inward search rather than a strict career path that propels Generation Y.[11]

The same inner passion affects Generation Y administrators who might be searching for a superintendent's position. Of course, Generation Y teachers and administrators searching for personal fulfillment will certainly come to realize that, like their counterparts, they must obtain a master's degree and/or a doctorate in school leadership or administration in order to qualify themselves for new opportunities. In this respect, Generation Y wants to achieve the next level of professional responsibilities much quicker than did prior generations. It is fair to state that Generation Y wants to work in a school district that provides opportunities for both professional and personal growth.[12]

Summary

The objective of the selection process is to hire individuals who have the potential to be successful on the job as measured by the performance evaluation process of the school district. Individual success is measured against organizational success, which is synonymous with organizational change. Because of the evolutionary nature of human needs, school districts must continually involve stakeholders in crafting their vision. Further, the selection process results in major expenditures for most school districts, including the monetary costs of advertising the position and printing and mailing applications, as well as the human resources costs of interviewing candidates and checking credentials and references. The selection process should be implemented through the following series of steps that minimize the chances of hiring individuals who are inadequate performers:

1. *Write the job description.* The job description is the product of a process known as the *job analysis,* and gathers information about each job through observations, interviews, questionnaires, consulting, and the diary method. The job description outlines specific details of a position and establishes the minimum qualifications needed to perform the job successfully.

2. *Establish the selection criteria.* Selection criteria instruments delineate those ideal characteristics that, if possessed by an individual to the fullest extent possible, ensure the successful performance of the job. They can also be used to quantify the expert opinions of those who interview candidates.

3. *Write the job vacancy announcement and advertise the position.* The advertisement is based on the job description and provides interested individuals with sufficient information to decide if they want to apply for the position. The advertisement must clearly identify the job title, major responsibilities, name and location of the school district, application procedure, and minimum job qualifications.

4. *Receive applications.* A central office staff member should be assigned to receive all applications for a given vacancy. As the applications are received, they should be dated and filed in a designated folder, thereby providing integrity to the process and establishing a method of monitoring the progress toward filling the vacancy.

5. *Select the candidates to be interviewed.* The application form should contain a statement requesting the applicants to have their placement papers, transcripts, and letters of reference sent to the human resources department. The application should provide sufficient information to evaluate each person against the selection criteria and against the minimum requirements for the job. A selected group of applicants is then interviewed for the position.

6. *Interview the candidates.* Interviewing candidates is a responsibility shared by the human resources employees and other school district employees. It is important to include not only those who will supervise the new employee but also others who have expert knowledge about the duties to be performed by the successful candidate. An interview is essentially a conversation that involves two or more individuals and is conducted to generate information about the candidate. Interviewing is a learned skill; it also has profound legal implications.

7. *Check credentials and references.* *Credentials* refers to such items as a college or university transcript, teaching certification, and physician's verification of health. These credentials, along with letters of reference, whenever possible, should be sent directly to the human resources department by the issuing source.

8. *Select the best candidate.* The human resources administrator who is responsible for implementing the selection process for a particular vacancy must organize all relevant data in such a manner that a choice may be made by the superintendent of schools.

9. *Implement the job offer and acceptance.* For professional positions, a contract must be approved by the board of education and signed by the finalist before this step is completed. For classified positions, once the candidate affirms that he accepts the offer, employment may commence at a mutually acceptable time.

10. *Notify the unsuccessful candidates.* Notification is initiated only after the offer of employment has been accepted by the candidate because there may be a need to offer the position to another individual if the first selected candidate refuses the offer.

The risk of hiring a person who has a criminal record has created much concern for human resources administrators in recent years. Whether to conduct criminal background investigations and the extent of such investigations usually depends on a mix of school district policy, state statutes, and the discretion of the interviewing human resources administrator. The extent of an investigation is usually limited in most school districts to checking with the local and state police in order to ascertain if the potential employee has been convicted of a crime. When the potential employee is a teacher, it is also possible to check with the TIC, if the school district is in a state that is a member of this organization. A school district wanting to check the fingerprints of an applicant against the files of the Federal Bureau of Investigation can do so only if the state in which the district is located has passed legislation authorizing this type of investigation.

The first step in applying for a position is filling out the application form. There are two basic formats used in constructing applications. The first format emphasizes detailed factual information, whereas the second emphasizes the applicant's attitudes, opinions, and values.

The basic principle in constructing application forms is to ask only for information you need to know. The information requested on most applications falls under one of the following headings: personal data, education and professional preparation, experience, and references. The physical layout of the form should allot sufficient space for answering the questions and providing the requested information.

Aptitude and ability testing can be used as part of the selection process for most classified jobs in school districts. In fact, these tests are necessary for some positions. Assessment centers are places where supervisors have an opportunity to observe candidates for a particular job. Candidates are taken through a series of simulations dealing with administrative problems of the kind that will probably be encountered on the job. Large metropolitan school districts could find the use of an assessment center beneficial in selecting teachers to be promoted into the principalship and other administrative positions.

Self-Check Quiz Click here to take an automatically-graded self-check quiz.

Discussion Questions and Statements

1. Identify the steps in the selection process, and explain how they are interrelated.
2. Why is the sequence of steps so important in the selection process?
3. Describe the most common methods of performing a job analysis.
4. How is the job description related to the selection criteria?

Suggested Activities

1. Your school district has been investigated by the Equal Employment Opportunity Commission because of complaints concerning the interview process filed by a number of people who are members of minority groups protected by federal laws. The school district was cited for asking questions that were biased against people of color. In your position as the assistant superintendent for human resources, you are meeting with the administrators, teachers, and support staff members who are involved in the interview process to fill a number of vacancies. Write a brief explanation of the interview process, setting forth its objectives and format. Also, identify the types of questions that are appropriate and those that are not.
2. Obtain the selection policies from a school district, and write a comparison of them with the process set forth in this chapter.
3. Review a school district's job descriptions for both a teaching position and an administrative position. Write a comparison of them with those found in this chapter.
4. Review a school district's application forms, and evaluate them in relation to the principles of application construction found in this chapter.
5. Develop, in writing, a list of interview questions that you believe help identify the most qualified applicant.
6. Interview a human resources administrator in person or on the telephone in order to find out how his school district conducts background checks.

Focus Scenario Activity

Given that you have read and studied this chapter, how would you proceed to rebuild the confidence of the board of education and superintendent that the human resources function will be fair, equitable, and transparent?

Endnotes

1. David A. DeCenzo and Stephen P. Robins, *Human Resources Management*, 7th ed. (New York: John Wiley, 2002), 191.
2. Ibid., 136–143.
3. H. B. Polansky and M. Semmel, "Hiring the Best and Retaining Them," *School Administrator*, 63, no. 8 (2006): 46–47.
4. M. Yate, *Hiring the Best: A Manager's Guide to Effective Interviewing and Recruiting* (Avon, MA: Adams Media, 2006), 109.
5. S. M. Koenigsknecht, "Stacking the Deck During Interviews," *School Administrator*, 63, no. 3 (2006): 55.
6. W. G. Cunningham and P. A. Cordeivo, *Educational Leadership: A Problem-Based Approach* (Boston: Pearson, 2006), 286–287.
7. L. Davila and L. Kursmark, *How to Choose the Right Person for the Right Job Every Time* (New York: McGraw-Hill, 2005), 44.
8. Equal Employment Opportunity Commission (EEOC). www.eeoc.gov.
9. N. L. Essex, "The Legal Toll of Candor in Personnel Recommendations," *School Administrator*, 62, no. 9 (2005): 47.
10. C. Garvey, "Outsourcing Background Checks," *HR Magazine*, 46, no. 3 (2001): 95–104.
11. Robert Half, "Attracting and Retaining Millennial Workers," *Information Executive*, 11, no. 7 (July 2008): 2, 3, 5.
12. Michael D. Coomes and Robert DeBard, eds., *Serving the Millennial Generation: New Directions for Student Services* (San Francisco: Jossey-Bass, 2004), 52–56.

Selected Bibliography

Anderson, N., "Applicant and Recruiter Reactions to New Technology in Selection: A Critical Review and Agenda for Future Research." *International Journal of Selection and Assessment*, 11 (2003): 121–136.

Equal Employment Opportunity Commission (EEOC). www.eeoc.gov.

Gibson, Cathy Lee. *Mission-Driven Interviewing: Moving Beyond Behavior-Based Questions*. Huntington, CT: PTI, 2006.

Katsurayama, M., S. Silva, W. Eufrázio, R. de Souza, and M. Becker. "Computerized Tests as an Aid in the Selection of Human Resources." *Psicologia: Teoria E Prática*, 14, no. 2 (2012): 141–151. ISSN: 15163687

Laurer, Steven D. "A Practitioner-Based Analysis of Interviewer Job Expertise and Scale Format as Contextual Factors in Situational Interviews." *Personnel Psychology*, 55, no. 2 (Summer 2002): 267–306.

Liu, Edward, and Susan Moore Johnson. "New Teachers' Experiences of Hiring: Late, Rushed, and Information-Poor." *Educational Administration Quarterly*, 42, no. 3 (2006): 324–360.

McDermid, Shelley M., and Andrea K. Wittenborn. "Lessons from Work–Life Research for Developing Human Resources." *Advances in Developing Human Resources*, 9, no. 4 (November 2007): 556–568.

Nicholsen, Gilbert. "Screen and Glean: Good Screening and Background Checks Help Make the Right Match for Every Open Position." *Workforce,* 79 (October 2000): 70, 72.

Posthuma, Richard A., Frederick P. Morgeson, and Michael A. Campion. "Beyond Employment Interview Validity: A Comprehensive Narrative Review of Recent Research and Trends Over Time." *Personnel Psychology,* 55, no. 1 (Spring 2002): 1–81.

Reiter-Palmon, Roni, Marcy Young, Jill Strange, Renae Manning, and Joseph James. "Occupationally-Specific Skills: Using Skills to Define and Understand Jobs and Their Requirements." *Human Resource Management Review,* 16 (2006): 356–375.

Rothstein, Mitchell G., and Richard D. Goffin. "The Use of Personality Measures in Personnel Selection: What Does Current Research Support?" *Human Resource Management Review,* 16 (2006): 155–180.

Russo, Charles J. "Teacher Certification, Employment, and Contracts." In *Reutter's The Law of Public Education,* 6th ed., 476–564. New York: Foundation Press, 2006.

Society for Human Resource Management (SHRM). www.shrm.org.

Stone, Dianna L., Kimberly M. Lukaszewski, Eugene F. Stone-Romero, and Teresa L. Johnson, "Factors Affecting the Effectiveness and Acceptance of Electronic Selection Systems." *Human Resource Management Review, 23* (2013): 50–70. (Emerging Issues in Theory and Research on Electronic Human Resource Management (eHRM)). doi:10.1016/j.hrmr.2012.06.006

Sullivan, Sherry E., and Lisa Mainiero, "Using the Kaleidoscope Career Model to Understand the Changing Patterns of Women's Careers: Designing HRD Programs That Attract and Retain Women." *Advances in Developing Human Resources,* 10, no. 1 (February 2008): 32–49.

U.S. Department of Justice. www.usdoj.gov.

U.S. Department of Labor. www.dol.gov.

Wright, E. W., T. A. Domagalski, and R. Collins. (2011). "Improving Employee Selection with a Revised Resume Format." *Business Communication Quarterly,* 74, no. 3 (September 2011): 272–286. doi:10.1177/1080569911413809

Young, I. P., and D. A. Delli. "The Validity of the Teacher Perceiver Interview for Predicting Performance of Classroom Teachers." *Educational Administration Quarterly,* 38 (2002): 586–612.

Young, I. P., and J. A. Fox. "Asian, Hispanic, and Native American Job Candidates: Prescreened or Screened Within the Selection Process." *Educational Administration Quarterly,* 38, no. 4 (2002): 530–554.

Appendix A
Job Descriptions

JOB DESCRIPTION FOR A MIDDLE SCHOOL PRINCIPAL

Job Summary

The middle school principal is responsible for the maintenance and continuation of a sound instructional program within his school building. This includes using leadership and communication skills in dealing with teachers, counselors, and other professional staff members and with classified personnel in order to develop a climate that promotes quality educational practices.

Organizational Relationships

The middle school principal has a line relationship with the assistant superintendent for secondary education. He is directly responsible to the assistant superintendent for secondary education. The middle school principal also has a line relationship with the building staff, which includes the assistant principal, teachers, counselors, librarian, and other certificated and classified personnel within the building complex.

Organizational Tasks

The middle school principal is responsible for establishing administrative processes and procedures in the middle school for the following areas: staff development, curriculum planning, scheduling and grading, budget development, building and grounds maintenance, classroom instruction, and consulting with individual pupils, parents, and staff members. He is also responsible for other duties assigned by the assistant superintendent for secondary education, and is directly responsible for supervising and evaluating the assistant principal, teachers, counselors, librarian, educational specialists, secretaries, and custodians within the building complex.

Job Qualifications

The middle school principal should possess the following educational and professional qualifications:

- A master's degree in educational administration
- A state middle school principal's certificate
- Minimum of 5 years' experience as a classroom teacher
- Minimum of 2 years' experience as an assistant principal

JOB DESCRIPTION FOR A HIGH SCHOOL BIOLOGY TEACHER

Teaching Responsibilities

The high school biology teacher is responsible for teaching five periods of Biology I per school day with one non instructional period for planning, grading papers, and conducting individual conferences with parents and students. Teaching biology includes following the general curricular program established by the science department and approved by the building principal. He is responsible directly to the building principal.

Professional Responsibilities

The high school biology teacher is responsible for promoting an effective instructional program in the classroom. He accepts responsibility for the academic success of students by evaluating the strengths and weaknesses of the curricular program and instructional materials; helping develop, implement, and evaluate new ideas, methods, and techniques for teaching biology; assisting in departmental budget preparation to ensure the appropriateness of instructional supplies; recognizing that each student is an individual with different needs and abilities; utilizing a variety of instructional techniques; serving on textbook committees; maintaining effective discipline and high academic standards; accepting constructive criticism; and recognizing the need for continuous self-evaluation. In addition, the teacher is expected to keep up to date on biology research findings by participating in local and state science associations.

Required Qualifications

The high school biology teacher should possess the following minimum educational and professional qualifications:

- A bachelor's degree with a major or minor in biological science
- A state secondary school teaching certificate in high school biology

Appendix B
Selection Criteria

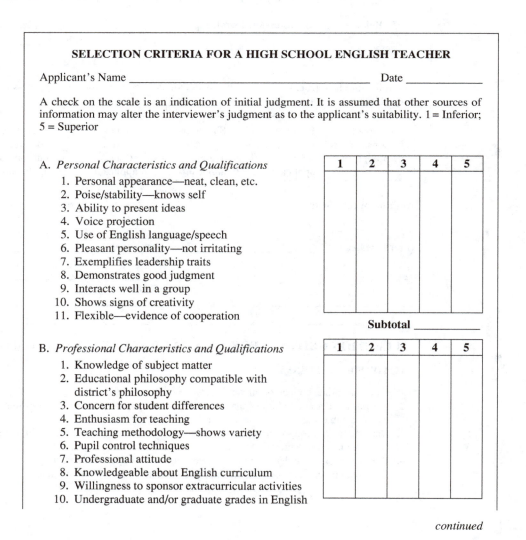

SELECTION CRITERIA FOR A HIGH SCHOOL ENGLISH TEACHER

Applicant's Name _____ Date _____

A check on the scale is an indication of initial judgment. It is assumed that other sources of information may alter the interviewer's judgment as to the applicant's suitability. 1 = Inferior; 5 = Superior

A. *Personal Characteristics and Qualifications*

	1	2	3	4	5
1. Personal appearance—neat, clean, etc.					
2. Poise/stability—knows self					
3. Ability to present ideas					
4. Voice projection					
5. Use of English language/speech					
6. Pleasant personality—not irritating					
7. Exemplifies leadership traits					
8. Demonstrates good judgment					
9. Interacts well in a group					
10. Shows signs of creativity					
11. Flexible—evidence of cooperation					

Subtotal _____

B. *Professional Characteristics and Qualifications*

	1	2	3	4	5
1. Knowledge of subject matter					
2. Educational philosophy compatible with district's philosophy					
3. Concern for student differences					
4. Enthusiasm for teaching					
5. Teaching methodology—shows variety					
6. Pupil control techniques					
7. Professional attitude					
8. Knowledgeable about English curriculum					
9. Willingness to sponsor extracurricular activities					
10. Undergraduate and/or graduate grades in English					

continued

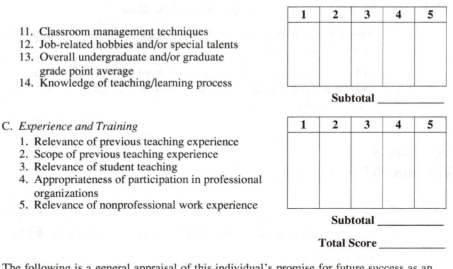

11. Classroom management techniques
12. Job-related hobbies and/or special talents
13. Overall undergraduate and/or graduate
    grade point average
14. Knowledge of teaching/learning process

	1	2	3	4	5

Subtotal _____

C. *Experience and Training*
1. Relevance of previous teaching experience
2. Scope of previous teaching experience
3. Relevance of student teaching
4. Appropriateness of participation in professional
   organizations
5. Relevance of nonprofessional work experience

	1	2	3	4	5

Subtotal _____

Total Score _____

The following is a general appraisal of this individual's promise for future success as an English teacher in our school district.

Should not be considered; poor applicant	Endorse with reservations; inferior applicant	Should be considered; average applicant	Good first impression; strong applicant	Exceptional potential; outstanding applicant

Additional comments:

Interview began _____   **Interview ended** _____

_____
Interviewer

SELECTION CRITERIA FOR A SIXTH-GRADE TEACHING POSITION

ACADEMIC CRITERIA

1. Has appropriate college or university course work and degree(s)
2. Has earned a grade point average in undergraduate and/or graduate courses that meets the acceptable standards of the district
3. Demonstrates through an appropriate interview a working knowledge of the English language in verbal and written context
4. Demonstrates an understanding and working knowledge of elementary mathematics skills that are compatible with the district's mathematics curriculum guide

continued

5. Demonstrates the skills necessary to teach reading in a manner compatible with the district's reading curriculum guide
6. Has had some formal or informal education in music and has developed the skill to perform with a musical instrument
7. Has completed courses in drama or participated in extracurricular dramatic performances, plays, or musical presentations during high school or college

PERSONAL CRITERIA

8. Indicates a willingness to interact and communicate in a constructive fashion with district staff and community constituents
9. Exhibits healthy, considerate, mature attitudes that would promote positive intrastaff and community relationships
10. Dresses in a manner meeting the expectations of the school district and meets socially acceptable standards of hygiene and health care
11. Is capable of actively participating with minimum proficiency in a sixth-grade outdoor experience that includes rappelling, canoeing, spelunking, and ropes course participation
12. Expresses a willingness to abide by and implement the district's policies as prescribed by the board of education

EXPERIENTIAL CRITERIA

13. Has relevant past teaching experience
14. Has relevant student teaching experience
15. Has a record of participating in extracurricular activities during high school and/or college (extracurricular being defined as any organized school-approved activity)
16. If applicant has had teaching experience, has demonstrated an interest in ongoing self-improvement by participating in professional workshops, seminars, college/university courses, or other professional programs

SELECTION CRITERIA GRID FOR A SIXTH-GRADE TEACHING POSITION

Name of Applicant _____ Date of Interview _____

	Academic Criteria							Personal Criteria					Experiential Criteria				Total Points
	1	2	3	4	5	6	7	8	9	10	11	12	13	14	15	16	
3																	

continued

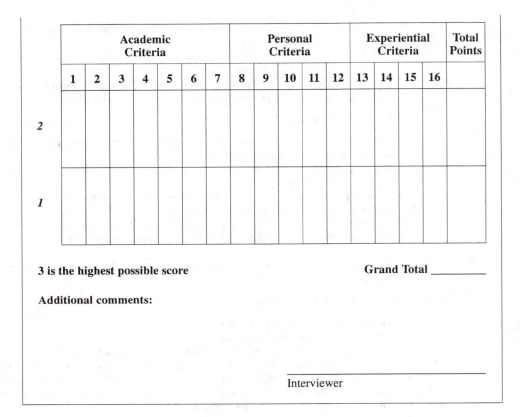

	Academic Criteria							Personal Criteria					Experiential Criteria				Total Points
	1	2	3	4	5	6	7	8	9	10	11	12	13	14	15	16	
2																	
1																	

3 is the highest possible score   Grand Total _____

Additional comments:

_____
Interviewer

SELECTION CRITERIA FOR AN ELEMENTARY SCHOOL TEACHER, SELF-CONTAINED CLASSROOM

Applicant _____ Date of Interview _____ Interviewer _____

	Possible Points	Designated Points
1. *Professional preparation.* Does the applicant hold the necessary and desired college preparation and state certification?	25	
2. *Experience.* Was the applicant's past teaching experience or student teaching experience successful?	10	

continued

3. *Personal characteristics.* Are the applicant's mannerism and dress appropriate to the standards of the school district?	15	
4. *Educational philosophy.* Are the educational ideas and values of the applicant compatible with the school district's policies and curriculum?	50	

Comments:

Appendix C
Job Applications

TEACHER'S APPLICATION
Goodville School District

For Office Use Only

Interview Date _____

Interviewer _____   Date _____

Position _____   Soc. Sec. No. _____

I. Personal Information:

Name _____
      Last   First   Middle

Date of birth _____ Age _____

Present Address _____ Phone _____
                  Street   City   State   Zip

Permanent Address _____ Phone _____
                  Street   City   State   Zip

General conditions of health _____

Are you willing to take a physical exam? _____

II. Professional Information:

List in order of preference the subjects or grades you are prepared to teach:

1. _____ 2. _____ 3. _____

List Teaching Certificates held: State Retirement No. _____

_____

List Teaching Certificates held (other States):

_____

continued

Membership in professional organizations: _____

What co-curricular activities are you prepared to sponsor (secondary level)? _____

_____

III. List the Teaching . . .

List experience in chronological order (starting with first position held), and account for each school year since you began teaching.

No. Yrs Exp.	Inclusive Dates		Name of School	Location City or County, State	Grades, Sub. or Position	Annual Salary	Name of Prin.	Present Address of Principal
	From	To						

Kindergarten _____ Years   Middle School _____ Years

Elementary _____ Years   High School _____ Years   Other _____ Years

Total Teaching Exp. _____ Years

Name of superintendent under whom you last taught _____

IV. Educational and Professional Education:

Total Number of Hours to Date _____ Undergraduate _____ Graduate _____

Major _____ Number of Major Hrs. _____ Minor _____ Number of Minor Hrs. _____

	Name of Instit. Attended	State	Dates Attended		Time in Yrs. and Fractions of Yrs.	Graduation		Subjects	
			From	To		Date	Degree	Major	Minor
A. Undergraduate Work									
B. Graduate Work									
C. Additional Education									

D. For both secondary and elementary majors

continued

Hours of Student Teaching	
Place of Student Teaching	
Name of Coop. Teacher	
Subject or Grade Level of Student Teaching	

V. Professional References:

Location of confidential placement file _____

It is the responsibility of the applicant to have his/her placement file and college/university transcripts sent to the school district.

Please list three people who have firsthand knowledge of your work performance. Have these individuals send letters of reference to the human resources department if references are not included in your placement file. One of the three reference letters must be from your current or last immediate supervisor.

Name	Official Position	Present Address

Signature: _____

Goodville School District

For Office Use Only

Date Received _____

Interview Date _____

Starting Date _____

Position _____

School _____

Salary _____

Termination Date _____

continued

CLASSIFIED APPLICATION FOR EMPLOYMENT

Position _____

PLEASE PRINT OR TYPE

Today's Date _____

PERSONAL INFORMATION

Name _____
      Last   First   Middle

Present address _____
      Street   City   State   Zip code

Phone _____ **Social security no.** _____

Date of birth _____ **Place** _____

General condition of health _____

Are you willing to take a physical exam? _____

EDUCATION INFORMATION

**Circle Highest Grade
Completed:**   1 2 3 4 5 6 7 8 9 10 11 12 13 14 15 16

Name of school and location:	Dates of Attendance	Day or Night	Full- or Part-Time	Type of Course(s)
Elem.	from _____ to _____	_____	_____	_____
Jr. High	from _____ to _____	_____	_____	_____
Sr. High	from _____ to _____	_____	_____	_____
College	from _____ to _____	_____	_____	_____

MILITARY SERVICE

Branch _____ From _____ To _____ Present Status _____

Highest rank _____ Duties _____

List any special training received in service _____

Type of discharge _____

EMPLOYMENT RECORD

List the most recent employment first and work back consecutively.

From	To	Firm Name & Supervisor	Firm Address	Salary Beg.	Last	Position, Duties, and Reason for Termination

continued

List any experience, skills, or qualifications that you feel would especially fit you for work in our district: _____

Are you a member of the Non-Teacher Retirement System? _____

If Yes, give Retirement No. _____

GENERAL INFORMATION

When can you start work? _____ What wage or salary do you expect? _____

List civic organizations to which you belong and office(s) held within past three years:

_____

Have you ever been convicted of any violation of law other than a traffic violation? _____

If yes, give particulars of each conviction and state what disposition was made of each:

_____

Have three people with firsthand knowledge of your work performance send letters of reference to the human resources department. One of the three reference letters must be from your current or last immediate supervisor.

_____
Signature

APPLICATION FOR HIGH SCHOOL PRINCIPAL

PERSONAL INFORMATION

Date _____

_____

Last Name _____ First _____ Middle _____

Business Address _____ Telephone _____

City _____ State _____ Zip Code _____

Home Address _____ Telephone _____

City _____ State _____ Zip Code _____

PRESENT POSITION _____

School's student enrollment _____ School's annual budget _____

Salary during current school year _____

PROFESSIONAL PREPARATION: Highest degree earned _____

Institution and Location	Major/Minor	Degree	Date Received
_____	_____	_____	_____
_____	_____	_____	_____

My confidential file can be acquired from:

Name of Institution: _____

Address: _____

_____

continued

SUMMARY OF EXPERIENCE: List all experience in reverse chronological order. Please include both school and nonschool experience.

Institution and Location	Position	From/To	Years	Size/Unit	Highest Salary
_____	_____	_____	_____	_____	_____
_____	_____	_____	_____	_____	_____
_____	_____	_____	_____	_____	_____
_____	_____	_____	_____	_____	_____

Type of administrator certificate held _____

In which state(s) _____

QUESTIONS

The following questions are designed to help the interviewers know you as a person and as a professional. Your concise and candid responses are very important.

1. Why do you or did you want to become a high school principal?

2. What do you or would you consider to be your major strengths as an administrator?

3. In your previous experience, in what ways have you most influenced a school?

4. What basic problem-solving approaches do you or would you use to deal with school issues?

5. What methods or approaches do you or would you use to bring about change in a school?

6. How do you or would you delegate responsibilities to others?

7. As a principal, what communication approaches are or would be most effective for you?

8. How do you or will you, as a principal, work most effectively with central office administrators?

9. What about being a high school principal has been or will be most rewarding to you?

_____
Signature

CHAPTER 5

Placement and Induction

Focus Scenario

One of your responsibilities as the director of human resources is the placement and induction of administrators, teachers, and staff members. The school district, located in a rural area with a changing population, has approximately 400 teachers and 150 support personnel. For years, the European American population has been decreasing, but as a result of the recent opening of a manufacturing factory, a significant number of Mexican immigrants now live in the school district. The culture of the community has changed, and the new residents are voicing significant concern about the lack of understanding of the Mexican culture by administrators, teachers, and support personnel. In fact, no Mexican Americans are working as administrators or teachers in the district.

Also, because of the downturn in the economy, the state has experienced a decrease in revenue from business and industry. Thus, the amount of state aid that the school district can expect for the next fiscal year has been reduced by 20 percent.

Further, parents generally believe that first-year teachers lack the professional training to instruct children from diverse backgrounds because their university pre-teaching experiences were with children from European American families. Also, there is a lack of curricular materials for children who have English as their second language. The parents of children in the district have voiced their concerns for their children to the superintendent and the board of education on numerous occasions; however, the parents still believe that the board of education does not fully understand the cultural issues they have raised because all the board members are of European American decent.

As director of human resources, you have decided to develop a strategic plan that addresses the processes and procedures for assigning staff, inducting staff, and, particularly, mentoring first-year teachers.

Please use both the "Discussion Questions and Statements" and "Suggested Activities" at the end of this chapter to help you develop a way of proceeding in order to address the issues in this section.

After a person has been hired, the next two processes involve placing the individual in an assignment and orienting him or her to the school community. Both processes are covered in this chapter because they are interrelated; both are also continual processes because some staff members will be reassigned each year and, thus, will require a certain amount of induction. Placement and induction are not one-time tasks but ongoing concerns of the human resources department.

Placement

In all but the smallest districts, a new employee should not be told that he or she has been hired for a particular job in a specific school building. The selection process explicated in Chapter 4 results in the employment of an individual for a certain position. However, the employee must understand from the outset that the assignment may be changed if the administration deems such to be in the best interest of the school district.

Placement Policy

The following sample board of education placement policy specifies how placement could be handled by a school district:

The placement of employees within the school system is the responsibility of the superintendent of schools. The superintendent may delegate the implementation of the placement process to other administrators as appropriate, but he or she ultimately retains the responsibility for placement. In determining assignments, the preferences of the employee are taken into consideration if they do not conflict with the requirements of the district's programming, staff balancing, and the welfare of students. Other factors such as educational preparation and training, certification, experience, working relationships, and seniority with the school system are also taken into consideration in making assignments.

An annual staffing survey form will be secured from each employee in January to assist in making assignment plans for the forthcoming school year.

Professional staffing assignments will be announced by April 1. Administrators affected by an assignment change will be notified of the change by the superintendent of schools. Teachers affected by a change in grade, subject assignment, or school building will be notified of the change by their respective building principals.

Classified staffing assignments will be announced by May 1 and will become effective on July 1. Supervisors and managers affected by an assignment change will be notified of the change by the superintendent of schools or his or her designated representative. Other employees affected by a change in assignment will be notified by their immediate supervisors.

This sample placement policy clearly specifies the role of the superintendent in assigning all staff members to particular positions within the school system. The planning required in making assignments is complicated, demanding the full-time attention of at least one human resources administrator in most metropolitan school districts. The human resources planning inventories described in Chapter 2 could provide the human resources department with valuable information for making assignments. Of course, it is to the advantage of the school district to make assignments that are in harmony with the desires of employees. A significant cause of low morale, particularly among teachers, is the assigning of individuals to schools, grade levels, and subject areas that they find undesirable. Using a staffing survey is one method of minimizing discontent over reassignments. The survey instrument can be simple in construction and easy to fill out. Exhibit 5.1 is an example of an instrument that could provide the human resources department with information concerning the placement preferences of staff members.

The human resources department must also consider a number of circumstances—including maternity leave, resignations, retirements, deaths, and terminations—in trying to fulfill the desires of employees in making reassignments, as well as balancing staff, affirmative action requirements, certification of professional employees, experience in an assignment, and working relationships.

For example, a teacher who is having difficulty accepting a certain principal's philosophy about how to handle children with behavioral problems might request reassignment to another school. The human resources department then would determine if another position is or will become available that requires the certification qualifications that teacher holds. Further, an analysis must be made to determine if such a reassignment would upset the balance in either school in terms of experienced and inexperienced teachers, male and female teachers, and minority representation.

The welfare of students and the implementation of the school district's instructional program are other important considerations. A biology teacher who is also certificated as a physical education teacher might be denied reassignment to the physical education department because applicants for biology positions are scarce or because that teacher has taught only biology throughout his or her fifteen-year teaching career.

When there are a number of requests for reassignment, seniority is a defensible criterion in making decisions only after the needs of the school district have been considered.

EXHIBIT 5.1   Staffing Survey

Name _____

Present Job Position Assignment _____

_____

Present Building Assignment _____

_____

I want to be considered for reassignment as follows:

Requested Job Position Assignment _____

_____

Requested Building Assignment _____

_____

   I understand that reassignment requests will be reviewed but are not guaranteed, and that all decisions will be based on seniority and availability, and will be made in accordance with the best interests of the school district.

_____

Signature

Those employees with the most seniority in the school district should be given the first choice of assignments; involuntary reassignments, sometimes necessary as a result of unexpected vacancies, should be given to those employees with the least seniority.

Placement Grievance Procedure

The following sample grievance procedure explains how to contest a change in assignment:

> If an employee has a concern regarding a permanent or temporary change in assignment, the following procedure must be observed: (1) The employee should initiate an interview with the administrator who processed the assignment change. (2) If agreement is not reached at this point, the employee may initiate an interview with the superintendent of schools and formally request a review of the reassignment; should the employee continue to be dissatisfied, he or she may resign his or her position with the school district.

This grievance procedure identifies the superintendent of schools as the ultimate authority in reviewing assignments within the school district. A grievance procedure is necessary to operate the district effectively; it highlights the fact that an individual is employed in the district and not in a particular school or position. Exhibit 5.2 is an example of a form that can be used when reviewing an assignment that an employee finds undesirable.

EXHIBIT 5.2   Request for Assignment Review

Name _____

Present Job Position Assignment _____

_____

Present Building Assignment _____

_____

Job Reassignment _____

_____

_____

Please state in detail why you want to have your assignment reviewed:

_____

_____

_____

_____

_____

_____

_____

_____

_____

_____

Signature

Induction

Induction is the process designed to acquaint newly employed individuals with the community, the school district, and their colleagues. Reassigned employees need to be acquainted with their new school, program, and colleagues; this is equally applicable to both newly employed and reassigned individuals. Induction is an administrative responsibility that is often neglected or loosely organized in many school districts. The industrial and business communities place a high priority on induction; they have recognized for many years the cause-and-effect relationship of this process to employee retention and job performance.

An effective induction program must have well-defined objectives that reflect the needs of new employees and the specific philosophy of the school system. Although the objectives of an induction program will vary among individual school districts, some universal objectives should be common to all programs:

1. To make the employee feel welcome and secure
2. To help the employee become a member of the "team"
3. To inspire the employee toward excellence in performance
4. To help the employee adjust to the work environment
5. To provide information about the community, school system, school building, faculty, and students
6. To acquaint the individual with other employees with whom he or she will be associated
7. To facilitate the opening of school each year

These objectives support the ultimate purpose of an induction program: to promote quality education for children. The employee who is able to adjust in a reasonable period of time to a new position helps accomplish this purpose.

Once the overall purpose and specific objectives are defined, the subsequent steps include deciding on the most effective method of implementation and on the content of the program. Some school districts consider a one- or two-day orientation at the beginning of each school year to be sufficient, whereas other districts provide an ongoing induction program to orient new employees and reassigned employees. Certainly, an ongoing program is better able to meet the concerns of reassigned individuals in large school districts who need information about their new school building, the faculty, the students, and the community it serves. The fallacy, as previously mentioned, is assuming that induction is a one-time task, only for new employees.

Induction programs fall into one of two major categories: informational and personal adjustment programs. *Informational programs* are concerned with either presenting initial material or updating information. Initial material consists primarily of information about the school system, the community it serves, and the particular school in which the employee will work. New employees, of course, are targeted for this type of program. Programs to update information are geared to employees who have been reassigned; these programs concentrate on the particular school and community to which those employees will now serve.

Personal adjustment programs aim at helping newly hired or reassigned employees interact with the principal, faculty, students, and parents of a particular school. With classified employees, the emphasis should be on helping them interact with their supervisors and coworkers as well as those administrators, faculty members, students, and parents with whom they will come into contact.

The following four sections deal with the content and methods of four induction programs. The first is most effective in orienting employees to their new school systems; the second helps orient employees to the communities served by the school systems or particular schools; the third is designed to orient employees to the schools to which they are assigned; and the fourth is geared to orienting employees to the people with whom they must establish relationships.

School District

The human resources department is responsible for implementing this part of the induction process. The main thrust is to convey an understanding of the school system's policies and services, and to identify system-wide personnel such as assistant superintendents, program directors, and coordinators.

All employees should receive a copy of the school board policies and the employee manual that pertains to their specific job. They should be allowed time during the orientation sessions to become familiar with these policies and manuals. To be truly effective, the program should also give the employees the opportunity to ask clarifying questions about policies and procedures.

Of course, the policies of the school district should set forth the vision and mission of the district. It is always a good idea to begin an orientation session with the vision and mission statements. Because schools are service-rendering institutions, the vision and mission are people driven; thus, most statements are focused on providing the children with an opportunity to develop all dimensions of their potentiality to the fullest extent possible, including the intellectual, emotional, physical, ethical, and cultural aspects of education. Teachers, staff members, and administrators are usually interested in this type of presentation; it is why they chose education as their career. Such an approach adds significance to the more mundane aspects of employment orientation.

The employee benefits provided by the school district must be explained carefully to new employees. Major medical and hospitalization insurance applications, retirement forms, government payroll withholding forms, and other enrollment documents are generally explained to new employees at the earliest possible time during the orientation process. Most insurance programs require a new employee to enroll a spouse and/or dependents within thirty days of commencing employment. If a spouse and/or dependents are enrolled after that time, they are usually required to get physical examinations. For example, a newly employed female teacher who does not enroll her husband in a medical insurance program within the thirty-day grace period may be denied coverage for him because he has a heart condition. The most effective vehicle for conveying an understanding of policies, procedures, and services is the small-group seminar, where five to ten employees are assigned to a human resources administrator who presents the material and instructs them on how to fill out all necessary forms, usually within the first few days of employment. A meeting, breakfast, or luncheon could be held each year, during which the superintendent of schools, board members, and other central office administrators and staff members are introduced to new employees. Such a special event is effective in conveying to new employees their importance to the district.

Community

Orientation to the community is also the responsibility of the human resources department. Employees should be presented with information about the economic, social, racial, cultural, ethnic, and religious makeup of the community. Orientation should also include specific coverage of occupations, customs, clubs and organizations, church denominations, museums, libraries, colleges or universities, and social services.

This orientation usually begins during the selection process, particularly during the interview. Candidates are told about the community and questioned about how they would respond to its various publics if they were employed with the district.

An effective way to begin the orientation process after selection is with a tour of the community conducted by the human resources department or, perhaps, the Chamber of Commerce. Other methods include introducing new employees at club or organization meetings and inviting representatives from community resource services such as libraries or museums to inform the new employees about their programs.

Orientation to the community does not end with the initial program; rather, the human resources department should provide continuous updating. For example, information about improvements or changes to community service resources should be brought to the attention of school staff members.

School Building and Program

The building principal is responsibile for orienting new teachers to a particular school. The first and most important step is introducing new teachers to all other employees, both professional and classified, who work in the building. Classified employees should be introduced by their immediate supervisors to both professional and other classified employees.

New employees must know, in detail, the layout of the building in which they will work. This is best accomplished by giving new employees a tour of the facility and, if it is a large school, presenting them with maps. Explaining administrative procedures is also the responsibility of the building principal. It is essential for new teachers to know how to complete attendance forms, where to obtain supplies and materials, how to requisition audiovisual equipment, and how the school schedule operates. An initial conference with the building principal, an assistant principal, or a department chairperson is one method of explaining these procedures.

Orienting the new teacher to the instructional program is the responsibility of the building principal. As with orientation to administrative procedures, this may be delegated to an assistant principal or a department chairperson. At times, explaining the instructional program might be a central office task, especially when the school district has subject-matter coordinators and a uniform curriculum in all the schools.

In some school districts, a new teacher is assigned to an experienced teacher during the first year of employment. The new teacher then has a specific person to call on when questions arise about the curriculum or building procedures. This has proved to be a successful technique because the experienced teacher does not pose a threat to the new teacher, whereas an administrator might.

Personal Adjustment

In line with the current research on the effectiveness of participatory decision making, establishing good working relationships among colleagues is viewed as most important if an organization is to achieve its objectives. In a service-rendering organization, such as a school district, it is even more crucial because good human relations provide the basis for the effective delivery of services. Forming relationships with other staff members helps an employee achieve satisfaction in his or her work. Nothing is less satisfying than being alienated from colleagues in an organization. The responsibility for helping a new employee do this rests with the individual's immediate supervisor or, if the new employee is a teacher, with the building principal.

A highly effective orientation method for new employees is to organize activities that give them the opportunity to socialize with other staff members. Many schools make a practice of serving refreshments and allotting a certain amount of time for personal interaction either before or after meetings. Holiday parties or dinners are also an effective means of enabling employees to meet each other on a social level, which can provide staff members with new insights about each other.

Service on faculty, school, and district committees is another way for employees to become acquainted with each other, while providing the district with valuable assistance in carrying out projects. Textbook selection, energy conservation, and principals' advisory committees are common in many school districts and have proved to be very successful in the orientation process.

Finally, it is important for professional staff members to become affiliated with local, state, and national teacher and administrator organizations. These organizations not only provide an avenue for exchanging ideas but are also a source of current professional information. Their social activities certainly help the individual form relationships with professionals in other school districts.

A Final Note

Many new employees come from other nations or states or, at least, have lived beyond the immediate vicinity of the school district. Although not a part of the formal induction program, helping the new employee relocate is a valuable service that can be provided by the human resources department; this can be facilitated by making initial contacts with real estate agents for new employees and by chauffeuring them around the area, pointing out aspects of neighborhoods reasonably close to their school and the district.

Evaluating the effectiveness of induction programs is an extremely important part of the induction process, and is best accomplished by establishing an induction committee chaired by a human resources administrator and composed of teachers, principals, and supervisors. This committee should gather input from new teachers that can be used to make changes in the programs. This same procedure can be initiated to evaluate programs for classified employees—that is, by establishing a committee comprising classified staff members and supervisors to react to the suggestions and insights of new employees after their first year with the district.

Induction of First-Year Teachers

Although other professions provide transitional assistance for new members (e.g., residents in medicine, interns in architecture, associates in law), historically, the education profession has ignored the support needs of its new recruits.[1]

Statistical information on the plight of new teachers indicates that nearly one-fourth of them leave the profession after two years of service, and a staggering one-third leave after three years. These data clearly indicate that the needs of new teachers are not being met by school districts. Possible remedies for this situation fall within the following categories:

- A school-level systemic approach to mentoring
- Assistance in knowing and understanding the teacher's role and function
- Assistance in knowing and understanding school and school district policies and procedures
- Collegial encouragement and support[2]

School district and school building administrative policies can have a significant effect on the induction of beginning teachers. The scope and sequence of such policies are most effective if they call for a multiple-year approach to the mentoring of new teachers. From this perspective, the administrators of the school district and the individual schools assume the role of teacher educators.[3]

To study the induction of first-year teachers, the National Association of Secondary School Principals created a committee that developed a four-phase time period during which induction should occur. Phase I begins during the summer months and concentrates on orienting the new teachers to the school, school district, and community. Phase II, scheduled for the week before school opens, emphasizes procedures and identifies support personnel. Phase III, during the first semester, includes daily meetings between a beginning teacher and a cooperating master teacher in which they review practical aspects of teaching such as lesson planning, testing, grading, and disciplinary techniques. During the second semester, the fourth and final phase emphasizes a more theoretical approach to teaching. The new teacher is encouraged to begin evaluating his or her performance and verbalizing his or her philosophy of education.

Mentoring as an Induction Strategy for Beginning Teachers

As a result of the education reform movement, which formally began with the publication of *A Nation at Risk*, twenty-seven states (as of this writing) have enacted legislation calling for the inclusion of mentoring programs as an induction strategy for newly hired teachers. These programs differ from one another to some degree; however, the basic concept is the same: the pairing of an experienced teacher with a beginning teacher to provide the beginning teacher with support and encouragement.

The experienced teacher can act as a role model and, through coaching, can help the beginning teacher develop his or her competencies, self-esteem, and sense of professionalism. In some school districts, beginning teachers attend traditional orientation and induction programs. A mentor is assigned to each beginning teacher and then provides support for that teacher throughout the entire year. In other school districts, beginning teachers are assigned to a group composed of other beginning teachers, the interaction of which is facilitated by a mentor.

It is important to clarify the role of the mentor to building principals and to beginning teachers. This is especially true in relation to teacher evaluation. The mentor should not be an evaluator, but rather someone who assists the beginning teacher in his or her first year; teacher evaluation should only be the responsibility of administrators.

The criteria for selecting mentors and the process for matching such mentors with beginning teachers are also important considerations. Research indicates that mentoring is successful when it functions through in-class coaching by experienced teachers from the same subject areas or grade levels as the beginning teachers.[4]

Other research sets forth issues that confront beginning teachers and, therefore, reveals the kinds of competencies that mentors must possess, extremely helpful information in the mentor selection process. Beginning teachers not only need assistance from mentors primarily in the areas of pedagogical methods and lesson planning, but also need help with learning how to handle time pressures, the ever-growing amount of paperwork, and non-instructional meetings.[5]

Newly selected mentors usually require some type of staff development in order to acquire or enhance certain skills. For example, programs to enhance mentors' supervision and coaching techniques or to update them on instructional strategies can be most helpful.

Mentoring as an Induction Strategy for Beginning Administrators

Whereas mentoring programs for beginning teachers are commonplace, this is not the situation for beginning administrators. Usually, a beginning principal or superintendent may seek the opinions of more seasoned administrators that he or she encounters through membership in administrator professional associations or at regional and state administrator meetings.

However, mentoring is typically recognized as an indispensable tool in professional development, and some school districts do assign experienced principals or other educational administrators as mentors to beginning and less experienced administrators. Also, it is not uncommon for administrators to move freely along a line that runs from being a protégé at one end to being a mentor at the opposite end. The same person may even find him- or herself in both roles. This phenomenon is not surprising because change is a constant in leadership positions. Social, political, and economic factors constantly impinge on the responsibilities of superintendents, principals, and all other educational administrators. The private business sector has experienced this phenomenon for many years and views the mentoring relationship as having the most influence on the practices of less experienced administrators. Further, the emotional involvement of protégés and mentors can be intense.[6]

Research on the relationship between protégés and mentors seem to indicate that those leaders who were protégés were also the most effective mentors. Mentors were also more enthusiastic about their role when they recognized positive leadership traits in protégés and considered themselves to be role models in the mentoring process. Finally, mentors learned their role as mentors from their mentors. Thus, mentoring was viewed as passing on the wisdom of leadership.[7]

There are ethical considerations in the mentoring process that revolve around three issues: cultural replication, access, and power. Mentoring can have a negative effect when the mentor is so influential that the protégé unquestionably accepts the mentor's opinions and practices. A key objective in the mentoring process is for the mentor to encourage and direct the protégé to analyze situations critically, and to use evidence and data when making decisions. In this context, the mentor is a support person, not the primary decision maker.[8]

Access to mentorship is a concern in school districts where there are few experienced women and minority administrators who can act as mentors for beginning women and minority administrators. Cross-gender and cross-ethnicity mentoring is usually very effective. However, in some situations, same-gender or same-ethnicity mentoring might be more effective if that is the desire of the protégé or mentor.[9]

Of course, sometimes power issues occur, and it is not always on the side of the mentor. The underlying concern is the motive behind a power play. Strong differences of opinion on how a beginning administrator should address an issue or make a decision are not the problem. Rather, power issues demand the attention of the superintendent when a protégé uses deception or exploits the mentor relationship. For example, an unscrupulous protégé may damage the reputation of an experienced administrator through lying about the counsel of his or her mentor.[10]

An Induction Model

The model discussed in the Appendix, Orientation Checklist for Newly Assigned Teachers, deals with the major problems associated with induction through a series of one-on-one interviews, explanations, observations, and evaluative discussions, and constitutes an expansion of the mentoring approach.

The new teacher encounters key staff members who can offer assistance in becoming acclimated to the total school community. The approach set out in the Appendix applies the team concept to the induction process. Several people have roles to play in the induction process based on their position and professional expertise. The most appropriate team to work with a new high school teacher includes the principal, an assistant principal, the new teacher's department chairperson, a guidance counselor, a technology coordinator, and a mentor, each of whom meets with the new teacher throughout the academic year. The principal or assistant principal and department chairperson observe classroom activities individually. The mentor observes classroom activities upon an invitation by the teacher.

Mentoring Support

Although beginning teachers and administrators may have the assistance of mentors and others who orient them to the nuances of the school and school district, they are still on their own to a certain degree and could surely benefit from online support. In a sense, it breaks the isolation that sometimes occurs when beginning teachers and administrators are overwhelmed with the requirements of teaching and administering.

Some of the most valuable help can come from www.teachers.net, a Website that serves approximately 50,000 teachers. It provides a forum where teachers can communicate about their pedagogy and other education topics, as well as job listings. Photos of classrooms and shared lesson plans augment the chat rooms. The teachers subscribing to this Website are from around the world. The Teachers Network, www.teachersnetwork.org, besides providing assistance similar to that of the previous Website, boasts a hotline for new teachers that enables them to obtain expert advice on education issues within seventy-two hours.

The New Teacher Center at the University of California at Santa Cruz, newteachercenter.org, is a valuable resource for those administrators and staff members who are responsible for managing induction programs. This Website supports the development of innovative methods to induct beginning teachers and administrators. It also seeks to strengthen the relationship between school districts and the university. Specifically, the quality of mentoring is a focal point for the center's Network of Researchers on Teacher Induction, which makes available papers and presentations addressing topics related to induction. A school district can also share information, documents, and other materials that the administrators of the district use for the induction process.

California initiated Beginning Teacher Support and Assessment (BTSA) Induction, www.btsa.ca.gov, a program geared to first- and second-year teachers. It helps teachers learn about effective methods of teaching and includes program standards for the teaching profession.

School districts that are having a difficult time hiring teachers can get help from the National Teacher Recruitment Clearinghouse, www.Teachers-Teachers.com, which provides advice about job search strategies, job banks, links to state education departments, and information about financial aid.

There are also international Websites that provide information about effective induction programs in foreign countries that can have transference to education here in the United States. For example, WestEd, www.wested.org, includes articles about effective programs in foreign countries. The National College for Teaching and Leadership, www.ncsl.org.uk, is a Website that supports beginning and experienced principals in the UK. There is also a research and development link on that Website that lists publications on issues of interest to U.S. administrators.[11]

Implications for Small- and Medium-Size School Districts

The process for placement of principals, other administrators, teachers, and staff members is the same in all school districts. It is the prerogative of the superintendent in consultation with the board of education. In the uncertain financial times that school districts are currently experiencing, teachers and administrators with dual or multiple certifications and experience will continue to be in demand. The process cannot be other than it is, regardless of the size of the school district.

However, induction is a different process altogether and is certainly affected by the size of the school district and the number of new hires it experiences on a yearly basis. Some large school districts hire hundreds of teachers and other employees annually, whereas in some districts the overall number may be small. Turnover in a school district is an important factor, more so even than the actual number of teachers and others who are employed. In small- to medium-size school districts, the number of new hires each year may be less than ten. For such a small number, the induction process may not require the assistance of a human resources administrator and may become the responsibility of building principals and the superintendent of schools. Of course, managing the payroll forms and enrolling new employees in such benefits as medical and hospitalization insurance can be handled by a business manager or the superintendent.

Induction takes on two main thrusts in small- and medium-size districts: the culture of the school community and the nuances of teaching or administering. The school community is composed of the school and school district in addition to the community in which the students live. A school bus ride around the district can help the beginning teacher or administrator learn from observation the economic status of the community. Personal contact with students and their parents at a "Meet the Parents" event can help a new teacher or administrator understand the social and educational concerns and issues of the parents.

The more difficult challenge resides in the instructional or administering process, which is learned more effectively in a mentoring relationship with an experienced teacher or administrator. Sometimes, it might be difficult to find a person who is capable of being or willing to be a mentor due to a lack of experience or just being overworked. A possible solution to such a situation is for a number of small school districts to come together and support newly hired teachers and administrators as a group. Mentors can be effective even if they are not from the same districts as the beginning teachers or administrators. Because every school district will need to hire new teachers and administrators at some time in the future, being of assistance to another school district ensures that assistance will be provided when it is needed by the helping school district.

Mentoring can also be effective if a group of new teachers or administrators meets to discuss responsibilities and issues. Thus, a group of three to five new teachers or administrators can learn from each other, and can invite an experienced teacher or administrator to join in the discussions when possible.

Impact of Generation Y Teachers and Administrators on Placement and Induction

Generation Y teachers, administrators, and staff members have a definite impact on the culture of school districts and individual schools. It is important for human resources administrators to recognize the importance of this fact in placing and inducting Generation Y employees. The effect, of course, is reciprocal. The culture of a given school and school district has an effect on how Generation Y employees must adjust their behavior in working with teachers, administrators, and staff members from other generations.

Members of Generation Y are certainly adventuresome, but in a manner that is somewhat different from members of other generations. They definitely enjoy collaboration to the degree that it involves continual involvement with other teachers and administrators. They want to know what other professionals know and think about the issues that arise during the performance of their responsibilities. In a sense, they prefer to have a work area that they share with other teachers rather than being isolated from them.[12]

Generation Y teachers and administrators also tend to look at the phenomenon of change in a different way. Rather than dealing with the consequences of change, they seek ways to precipitate change and often embrace change as something not only expected but also exciting—as long as they see the value and worth in the change. Thus, new models for developing curricula and new curricular materials are often welcomed and present desired challenges to Generation Y teachers and principals. More fundamental to embracing change, Generation Y employees view themselves as being altered by the change and even enriched. To a degree, they conceptualize themselves as being reinvented rather than bothered by change.[13]

In placing Generation Y employees, it is important to capitalize on these strengths while helping them engage others from different generations in mutual learning experiences. An awareness of these characteristics can also be valuable to those who need to plan and implement induction programs that use the perspectives of Generation Y employees.

Summary

After a person has been hired, the next two processes involve placing that individual in an assignment and orienting him or her to the school community. The placement of employees within the school system is the responsibility of the superintendent of schools. The planning required in making assignments is a complicated task, demanding the full-time attention of at least one human resources administrator in most metropolitan area school districts. It is to the advantage of the school district to make assignments that are in harmony with the desires of the employees. A staffing survey is one method of gathering information systematically on the placement preferences of employees, as well as balancing staff, certification requirements, experience, and working relationships. However, the welfare of students and the implementation of the school district's instructional program are the most important considerations. When there are a number of requests for reassignment, seniority is a defensible criterion after these other variables are considered. A procedure should be established to give employees the opportunity to have an assignment reviewed by the appropriate administrator.

The process designed to acquaint newly employed individuals with the school system and with other staff members is called *induction*. It is also the process for acquainting reassigned employees with their new school, program, and colleagues. An effective induction program must have well-defined objectives that help the employee feel welcome and secure, become a member of the "team," be inspired toward excellence in performance, adjust to the work environment, and become familiar with the school community.

Induction programs fall into one of two major categories: informational and personal adjustment programs. *Informational programs* are concerned with providing either initial material or updated information. Initial material consists primarily of information about the school system, the community it serves, and the school where the new employee will work. Updated informational programs are geared to employees who have been reassigned and concentrate on particular schools and communities. *Personal adjustment programs* are designed to help newly hired or reassigned employees interact with the other people for whom and with whom they will work.

To effectively orient new employees to the school district, policies and services must be explained thoroughly and system-wide personnel identified. Orientation to the community must convey to employees knowledge of the economic, social, cultural, ethnic, racial, and religious makeup of the community. Its occupations, customs, clubs and organizations, church denominations, museums, libraries, colleges and universities, and social services are also topics that should be covered in this program.

Orienting a new employee to a particular school begins with an introduction to the other staff members. A tour of the facility and an explanation of administrative procedures, as well as an orientation to the instructional program, are also important aspects of this induction.

Personal adjustment orientation centers on encouraging new employees to establish working relationships with their colleagues. Organized activities such as faculty meetings, holiday parties or dinners, faculty and district committees, and professional organizations provide new employees with the opportunity to establish desired relationships with other professionals.

Evaluating the effectiveness of the induction process is extremely important and provides the necessary data for improving the process. An area of special concern is the induction of first-year teachers. Many potentially excellent teachers may have been lost to the education profession because they were not inducted properly. A number of suggestions and models have been developed, all of which recognize the importance of giving first-year teachers time to consult with colleagues and providing them with feedback concerning their performance. Many school districts have developed mentoring programs not only for beginning teachers but also for entry-year administrators.

Self-Check Quiz Click here to take an automatically-graded self-check quiz.

Discussion Questions and Statements

1. When placing employees in certain job positions, what variable should be taken into consideration?
2. What is the rationale for having an assignment grievance procedure?
3. What are the most common objectives of an induction program?
4. Identify reasons why the induction of first-year teachers is so important.
5. Describe *mentoring,* and explain why it is such an effective method of induction.
6. What are the elements of mentoring programs for both first-year teachers and new administrators? Who (by job position) does what and at what time in the programs?

Suggested Activities

1. As the director of staff development, you have prepared an induction program for newly hired employees. Identify, in writing, the elements of the program that you have created, and further describe how the program differs for teachers and support personnel.
2. Obtain a copy of a school district's placement policies, and write a comparison of them with the placement policy and grievance procedures in this chapter.
3. Obtain a copy of a school district's induction policies, and write a comparison of them with the principles of induction set forth in this chapter.

4. Interview a human resources administrator in person or on the telephone to elicit his or her opinion about the difficulties and positive aspects of the induction process.

Focus Scenario Activity

Given that you have read and studied this chapter, how would you proceed to develop a strategic plan? Explain in detail who would be responsible for what.

Endnotes

1. Linda Molner Kelley, "Why Induction Matters," *Journal of Teacher Education*, 55, no. 5 (November/December 2004): 438.
2. Synthia Simon Millinger, "Helping New Teachers Cope," *Educational Leadership*, 61, no. 8 (May 2004): 66–69.
3. Pamela Grossman and Clarissa Thompson, "District Policy and Beginning Teachers: A Lens on Teacher Learning," *Educational Evaluation and Policy Analysis*, 26, no. 4 (Winter 2004): 298.
4. Elizabeth Useem and Ruth Curran Neild, "Supporting New Teachers in the City," *Educational Leadership*, (May 2005): 46.
5. Linda Gilbert, "What Helps Beginning Teachers?" *Educational Leadership*, 62, no. 8 (May 2005): 38.
6. Connie R. Wanberg, Elizabeth T. Welsh, and Sarah A Hezlett, "Mentoring Research: A Review and Dynamic Process Model," in *Research in Personnel and Human Resources Management, Volume 22*, eds. Joseph J. Martocchio and Gerald R. Ferris (Oxford, UK: Elsevier Science, 2003), 39–124.
7. Manda H. Rosser, "Mentoring from the Top: CEO Perspectives," *Advances in Developing Human Resources*, 7, no. 4 (November 2005): 527, 530–537.
8. A. Darwin, "Critical Reflection on Mentoring in Work Settings," *Adult Education Quarterly*, 50 (2000): 197–211.
9. Kimberly S. McDonald and Linda M. Hite, "Ethical Issues in Mentoring: The Role of HRD," *Advances in Developing Human Resources*, 7, no. 4 (November 2005): 571–572.
10. Lillian T. Eby, Stacy E. McManus, Shana A. Simon, and Joyce E. A. Russell, "The Protégé's Perspective Regarding Negative Mentoring Experiences: The Development of a Taxonomy," *Journal of Vocational Behavior*, 57, no. 1 (August 2000): 1–21.
11. Rick Allen, "Web Wonders/Supporting New Educators," *Educational Leadership*, 62, no. 8 (May 2005): 96.
12. Robert Half, "Attracting and Retaining Millennial Workers," *Information Executive*, 11, no. 7 (July 2008): 4–5.
13. Michael D. Coomes and Robert DeBard, eds., *Serving the Millennial Generation: New Directions for Student Services* (San Francisco: Jossey-Bass, 2004), 34–43.

Selected Bibliography

Achinstein, B., and A. Barrett. "(Re)Framing Classroom Contexts: How New Teachers and Mentors View Diverse Learners and Challenges of Practice." *Teachers College Record*, 106, no. 4 (2004): 716–745.

Allen, Rick. "Web Wonders/Supporting New Educators." *Educational Leadership*, 62, no. 8 (May 2005): 96.

Athanases, S. Z., and B. Achinstein. "Focusing New Teachers on Individual and Low Performing Students: The Centrality of Formative Assessment in the Mentor's Repertoire of Practice." *Teachers College Record*, 105, no. 8 (2003): 1486–1520.

Barry, Carol Kuhl, and Jan Kaneko. "Mentoring Matters!" *Leadership*, 31, no. 3 (January/February 2002): 26–29.

Carver, Cynthia L., and Daniel S. Katz. "Teaching at the Boundary of Acceptable Practice: What Is a New Teacher Mentor To Do?" *Journal of Teacher Education*, 55, no. 5 (November/December 2004): 449–462.

Cochran-Smith, M., and K. Fries. "Researching Teacher Education in Changing Times: Politics and Paradigms," in *Studying Teacher Education*, eds. M. Cochran-Smith and K. Fries, 69–109. Mahwah, NJ: Lawrence Erlbaum, 2005.

Fadia Nasser-Abu, A., and Barbara, F. "Socialization of New Teachers: Does Induction Matter?" *Teaching and Teacher Education*, 26 (n.d.): 1592–1597. doi:10.1016/j.tate.2010.06.010

Fox, Suzy, and Paul E. Spector. "Emotions in the Workplace: The Neglected Side of Organizational Life Introduction." *Human Resource Management Review*, 12, no. 2 (2002): 167–172.

Gilbert, Linda. "What Helps Beginning Teachers?" *Educational Leadership*, 62, no. 8 (May 2005): 36–39.

Grossman, Pamela, and Clarissa Thompson. "District Policy and Beginning Teachers: A Lens on Teacher Learning." *Educational Evaluation and Policy Analysis*, 26, no. 4 (Winter 2004): 281–301.

Hezlett, Sarah A., and Sharon K. Gibson. "Mentoring and Human Resource Development: Where We Are and Where We Need To Go." *Advances in Developing Human Resources*, 7, no. 4 (November 2005): 446–469.

Hezlett, Sarah A., and Sharon K. Gibson. "Linking Mentoring and Social Capital: Implications for Career and Organization Development." *Advances in Developing Human Resources*, 9, no. 3 (August 2007): 384–412.

Hoerr, Thomas R. "Meeting New Teachers' Personal Needs." *Educational Leadership*, 62, no. 8 (May 2005): 82, 84.

Ingersoll, R. M., and M. T. Smith. "Do Teacher Induction and Mentoring Matter?" *NASSP Bulletin*, 88 (2004): 28–40.

Johnson, S. M. *Finders and Keepers: Helping New Teachers Survive and Thrive in Our Schools.*, San Francisco: Jossey-Bass, 2004.

Kardow, S. M., S. M. Johnson, H. G. Peske, D. Kauffman, and E. Liu. "Counting on Colleagues: New Teachers Encounter the Professional Cultures of Their Schools." *Education Administration Quarterly*, 37, no. 2 (2004): 250–290.

Kelley, Linda Molner. "Why Induction Matters." *Journal of Teacher Education*, 55, no. 5 (November/December 2004): 438–448.

Laiho, M., and Brandt, T. "Views of HR Specialists on Formal Mentoring: Current Situation and Prospects for the Future." *Career Development International*, 1, no. 5 (2012): 435–457. doi:10.1108/13620431211269694

Maloch, B., and A. S. Flint. "Understandings, Beliefs, and Reported Decision Making of First-Year Teachers from Different Reading Teacher Preparation Programs." *Elementary School Journal*, 103, no. 5 (2003): 431–457.

McCauley, Cynthia D. "The Mentoring Tool." *Advances in Developing Human Resources*, 7, no. 4 (November 2005): 443–445.

McDonald, Kimberly S., and Linda M. Hite. "Ethical Issues in Mentoring: The Role of HRD." *Advances in Developing Human Resources*, 7, no. 4 (November 2005): 569–582.

Millinger, Synthia Simon. "Helping New Teachers Cope." *Educational Leadership*, 61, no. 8 (May 2004): 66–69.

Rosser, Manda H. "Mentoring from the Top: CEO Perspectives." *Advances in Developing Human Resources*, 7, no. 4 (November 2005): 527–539.

Strong, M., and W. Baron. "An Analysis of Mentoring Conversations with Beginning Teachers: Suggestions and Responses." *Teaching and Teacher Education*, 20, no. 1 (2004): 47–57.

Tillman, Linda C. "Mentoring New Teachers: Implications for Leadership Practice in an Urban School." *Educational Administration Quarterly*, 41, no. 4 (October 2005): 609–629.

Useem, Elizabeth, and Ruth Curran Neild. "Supporting New Teachers in the City." *Educational Leadership*, 62, no. 8 (May 2005): 44–47.

Wanberg, Connie R., Elizabeth T. Welsh, and Sarah A. Hezlett. "Mentoring Research: A Review and Dynamic Process Model," in *Research in Personnel and Human Resources Management, Volume 22*, eds. Joseph J. Martocchio and Gerald R. Ferris, 39–124. Oxford, UK: Elsevier Science, 2003.

Wang, Jian, and Sandra J. Odell. "An Alternative Conception of Mentor/Novice Relationships: Learning to Teach Reform-Minded Teaching as a Context." *Teaching and Teacher Education,* 23, no. 2 (May 2007): 473–489.

Wang, Jian, Sandra J. Odell, and Sharon A. Schwille. "Effects of Teacher Induction on Beginning Teachers' Teaching: A Critical Review of the Literature." *Journal of Teacher Education*, 59, no. 2 (March/April 2008): 132–152.

Wayne, Andrew J., Peter Youngs, and Steve Fleischman. "Improving Teacher Induction." *Educational Leadership*, 62, no. 8 (May 2005): 76–78.

Appendix
Orientation Checklist for Newly Assigned Teachers

Newly assigned teachers are typically in need of assistance from colleagues who can provide information about the curriculum, instructional technology, materials, and policies and procedures of the school building and school district. This information is essential to the performance of instructional responsibilities and personal adjustment of newly hired teachers. The following are the minimal requirements for accomplishing professional and personal orientation and induction, along with an indication of who, within a school and school district, has what responsibilities. This checklist indicates the timeframe within which the orientation should take place.

Who	Action To Be Taken
Superintendent of schools	• Welcomes the teacher to the school district • Discusses the district's policies concerning teachers and the learning-instructional process • Provides the teacher with a district handbook • Provides information about fringe benefits, retirement, and payroll deductions • Presents the teacher with a countersigned copy of his or her contract or the master agreement with the teachers' association
Principal	• Welcomes the teacher to the school • Provides the teacher with information about the curriculum and other instructional materials and supplies • Provides the teacher with information about student services, including the guidelines for student rights and responsibilities • Provides the teacher with information about the substitute teacher process when a teacher is absent from school

Who	Action To Be Taken
Assistant principal or principal	• Discusses the special education policies and procedures in the school and school district • Discusses the procedures for reporting student absenteeism • Discusses the school district policies on sick leave, leave of absence, and attendance at professional conference and meetings
Department chairperson or assistant principal or principal	• Introduces the teacher to other members of the department or grade level • Discusses the department objectives, pedagogy, instructional technology, and materials • Reviews the school and school district policies on guest speakers and field trips • Discusses the assessment of student progress and grading • Explains the various types of activities available to students and the role of faculty advisors • Explains state athletic association policies and guidelines • Explains how student activities can be financed and the role of the faculty in fundraising • Discusses the regulations and guidelines for use of school facilities outside the regular school day • Discusses the library services that are available to students and teachers
Mentor	• Meets with the teacher and explains the mentoring process • Stresses the confidentiality of the mentoring process • Stresses the scope of the mentoring process, including the instructional-learning process, school and school district policies and procedures, professionalism, and personal adjustment
Guidance counselor	• Discusses the general characteristics of the student body • Discusses the procedure for referring students to the counselor • Provides the teacher with the building guidelines on student discipline • Discusses the role of the teacher in dealing with student discipline issues
Technology coordinator or chairperson or assistant principal or principal	• Explains the procedures for acquiring technology hardware and software • Explains how technology can be utilized in the instructional-learning process, including common problems and how to obtain assistance

The department chairperson evaluates the performance of the teacher after the first two months of the first semester. The principal or assistant principal evaluates the performance of the teacher at the end of the first semester.

Department chairperson	• Discusses the performance observations and emphasizes the positive aspects of the observations, especially those that the teacher may not be aware of • Discusses those aspects of the performance observations that are negative, especially those that the teacher may not be aware of • Suggests ways that the teacher can improve his or her performance • Discusses the staff development programs in the school district that can help the teacher improve his or her performance • Agrees with the teacher on an action plan that will help the teacher improve • Writes a summary report for the principal, setting forth observations about the teacher's performance • Gives the teacher a copy of the report • Points out others in the school or school district who may be able to assist the teacher, such as the guidance counselor, the librarian, or a special education teacher

Continued

Who	Action To Be Taken
Mentor	• Meets with the teacher to discuss the teacher's reaction to the performance evaluation of the department chairperson • Stresses the confidentiality of the mentor relationship • If the teacher shares the action plan, discusses how the plan can be implemented • If the teacher shares the report with the principal, discusses the aspects of the report in relation to the action plan • Asks if the teacher needs more information about instructional technology, special education procedures, student rights and responsibilities procedures, equipment, or faculty responsibilities
Principal or assistant principal	• Discusses the action plan that was agreed on by the teacher and the department chairperson • Discusses performance observations • Discusses the success or failure of the action plan • Establishes a revised action plan for the second semester • Ensures that the plan addresses not only deficiencies but also positive results that should be continued • Reviews the technology resources of the school district • Reviews the staff development opportunities provided by the school district
Mentor	• Meets with the teacher to discuss the teacher's reaction to the performance evaluation of the principal • Reemphasizes the confidentiality of the mentor relationship • If the teacher shares the evaluation of the action plan, discusses how he or she implemented the plan • If the teacher shares the principal's revised action plan, suggests how it can be implemented • Again, asks the teacher if he or she needs information or assistance with the policies and procedures of the school and school district

The department chairperson and the mentor meet with the teacher during the second semester to assist the teacher with his or her action plan and to provide support and guidance.

Department chairperson	• Discusses the teacher's success in implementing the revised action plan • Asks the teacher if he or she needs information or assistance with the policies and procedures of the school and school district • Meets with the teacher in order to encourage and support the teacher professionally and in his or her personal adjustment to the school and school district • If the reviewed action plan is shared with the mentor, discusses with the teacher successes and those areas that need improvement

In April, the principal meets with the teacher about his or her performance.

Who	Action To Be Taken
Principal	• Meets with the department chairperson in order to get feedback about the teacher's success in implementing the revised action plan • Meets with the teacher about the teacher's implementation of the action plan • Discusses the teacher's implementation of the revised action plan • Discusses extension of the teacher's contract for the next academic year • Discusses the teacher's first-year experience and how he or she feels about teaching as a career, the school and school district, the faculty, and the students • Discusses the teacher's strengths and weaknesses in relation to the instructional-learning process, student rights and responsibilities, school and school district policies and procedures, and assistance offered to the teacher • Discusses the effectiveness of the induction process and, particularly, the mentoring process

The principal or assistant principal evaluates the performance of the teacher at the end of the academic year.

CHAPTER 6

Staff Development

Focus Scenario

You are the director of staff development for a school district with approximately 300 teachers and 125 support personnel. Because of pressure from parent organizations, the state legislature has just mandated that 1 percent of the state aid that a school district receives must be used for teacher staff development. Thus, you have approximately $250,000 to spend on staff development.

The school district is somewhat unstable. Parents and other citizens have not been supportive of the district in terms of passing tax levy and bond issue referendums. The school district experienced significant growth in the 1950s and 1960s, but experienced a decrease in student population in the 1970s and 1980s. The houses in the school district declined in value to the point that younger families with children wanted to purchase homes in other school districts, and empty nesters were not able to sell their homes in order to move to better housing even though their mortgages were paid off. This situation caused the school district to lose enrollment, and thus, the district was forced to lay off younger teachers. The administrators, teachers, and support personnel have become rather set in their ways; they are in need of staff development programs to help them renew their enthusiasm, and bring them up to date on current best practices in administering and teaching children. The local teachers' association has endorsed the need of the district to rethink its staff development commitment and programming. Further, the administrators and teachers have a positive attitude toward this end, and are ready and willing to participate in staff development.

Please use both the "Discussion Questions and Statements" and "Suggested Activities" at the end of this chapter in order to help you develop a way of proceeding in order to address the issues in this section.

Change is a constant occurrence in contemporary society. Instant communication channels, the result of technological advances, present students and educators with changes in politics, economics, science, and social status from every corner of the world. The mandate of public schools, of course, is to educate the children, adolescents, and young adults of the United States to help them meet the challenges that tomorrow will bring as a result of these changes.

As an organization, a school district needs well-qualified administrators, teachers, and support personnel to fulfill this mandate. As the positions and job requirements within a school district become more complex, the importance of staff development programs increases.

Staff development practices have undergone considerable change since the early 1990s. Three trends that have contributed to this metamorphosis are results-driven education, the systems approach to school and school district organization, and constructivism. As a practice, *results-driven staff development* is concerned with changing the behavior and attitudes of teachers, administrators, and staff members, not with counting the number of participants in such programs. The *systems approach to administration* recognizes the interrelatedness of all components in a given school and, ultimately, in a school district. Thus, an innovation in elementary school instructional techniques could have ramifications for the counseling program and for the curriculum committee in a school. Across the district, an innovation in an elementary school could affect the instructional program in that district's middle school and, eventually, in its high school. Finally, *constructivism* is based on the premise that learners build knowledge structures in their minds. The implication for educators is that they can benefit from nontraditional methods of delivering professional development activities such as workshops and presentations when these activities arise from their daily professional responsibilities. Action research is a good example of how focusing on a coherent purpose can build on the constructivist approach to staff development.[1]

It is literally impossible today for any individual to take on a job or enter a profession and remain in it for forty or so years with his or her skills basically unchanged. Therefore, staff development is not only a desirable activity but also one to which each school system must commit human and fiscal resources if it is to maintain a skilled and knowledgeable staff.

Professional Learning Communities

As a dimension of the human resources function, staff development can be organized according to various structures. Currently, the most effective structure is the professional learning community, which has four major focuses:

1. Learning rather than teaching
2. Collaborating
3. Viewing all members of the community as learners
4. Practicing self-accountability

The first focus is a departure from the traditional approach to educating students, which centers on the responsibility of schools and school districts to ensure effective teaching. When the focus is placed on learning, teachers, administrators, teachers, and staff members tend to see their responsibilities in a different light. They begin to analyze the cultures of the school and school district in order to ascertain whether they support student learning. Further, teachers, administrators, teachers and staff members begin to understand that effective school and school district cultures are founded on a commitment to learning that must be articulated to all stakeholders, which includes students and parents. It is important to keep in mind that the term *staff members* refers to guidance counselors, media specialists, special education teachers, assistant superintendents for instruction, human resources administrators, and all other professional and support members of the school and school district community.

Of course, this focus on learning, which can be investigated through cultural analyses and commitment, leads to the second focus, which is collaborating. Teachers, administrators, and staff members must collaboratively discourse and investigate what students need to learn, how to assess what students have learned, and how to help students who are having difficulty learning. Collaborating also means that teachers, administrators, and staff members recognize that every aspect of the learning process is subject to team efforts. For example, if a certain student is having difficulty learning, assisting the student is not the responsibility only of his or her classroom teacher. All members of the community who have related expertise should formulate a timely and required intervention plan to help the student. The usual format for collaborating is *teaming,* whereby a number of different teams of teachers, administrators, and staff members come together based on the expertise of the individual members in order to address common professional issues. Once formed, a given team may meet on a continuing basis or only when necessary.

The third focus of professional learning communities empowers all members of the school and school district communities, not just students, to become learners. Of course, the most fundamental reality of this focus is the phenomenon of change. Thus, it is impossible for anyone to know all that he or she needs to know in relation to his or her job. Consequently, parents, teachers, administrators, and staff members are constantly in need of new information, knowledge, skills, and attitudes. It is impossible to remain static in the dynamic environments of schools and school districts. This, of course, is the domain of staff development.

The final focus centers on self-accountability. The notion of professional learning communities rests on the ability of all members to self-actualize in a manner that contributes to the mission of their respective schools and school district. For the human resources function, this means not only that professional staff development programs must be organized and carried out in relation to the four focuses of the professional learning community but also that the other human resources functions must be geared toward these same focuses. The recruitment, selection, and performance evaluation functions are the most affected by the professional learning community approach. Thus, the concepts and processes set forth in this chapter constitute a professional learning community approach to human resources administration and, in particular, to professional staff development.[2]

Dimensions of the Learning Process

Because of the focus on professional learning communities, staff development activities for newly hired teachers, administrators, and staff members sometimes result in misunderstandings about programming. Typically, certain educators think of staff development activities as something that others bring to them in the form of presentations and information. However, in keeping with adult learning theory and effective programming experiences with professionals, development activities build on the existing knowledge base and skills of educators; the participants must enhance the professional development activities through personal reflection and discussion with other colleagues. Further, the learning community model requires collaboration and dialogue between the human resources administrator responsible for staff development and those educators who are the target of staff development. Planning, delivery, and assessment of staff development programs are integral elements of this kind of collaboration.[3]

Staff development usually consists of learning through training and education. Training is the process of learning a sequence of programmed tasks that constitute the job responsibilities of employees such as custodians, cooks, and maintenance personnel; employees usually learn these tasks on the job and are required to know best practice in performing them. *Education* is the process of helping teachers, administrators, and staff members acquire knowledge that will help them make discretionary decisions based on the evidence that confronts them in carrying out their job responsibilities. Education emphasizes acquiring sound reasoning processes rather than learning a body of serial facts. Education helps an employee develop a rational approach toward analyzing the relationship between variables and consequently understanding phenomena.

Teachers and administrators have job responsibilities that, in most respects, require education rather than training. Teachers and administrators usually do not perform programmed work. For example, an administrator can be trained in management techniques and procedures. However, an administrator cannot be trained to manage. Speaking about managers in the private sector, David A. DeCenzo and Stephen P. Robbins summarize the differences between training and education:

> Successful employees prepared for positions of greater responsibility have analytical, human, conceptual, and specialized skills. They think and understand. Training per se cannot overcome an individual's inability to understand cause-and-effect relationships, to synthesize from experience, to visualize relationships, or to think logically. As a result, we suggest that employee development be predominantly an education process rather than a training process.[4]

In discussing the distinction between training and education, care must be taken not to assume that all job-related activities of a particular position are either trainable or educable. Teachers and administrators perform some activities that can be enhanced by training because these activities are capable of being programmed. Both teachers and administrators need good listening skills and interviewing skills; in today's technological society, they also need skills in using various types of computer software. However, understanding the instructional learning process and being able to create a learning environment conducive to teaching goes beyond the scope of training and requires education.

This same distinction must also be applied to support personnel. An administrative assistant must develop and upgrade skills in using word-processing programs and in carrying out routine office procedures; these are trainable skills. However, this person is often called on to make decisions about setting up and prioritizing appointments for an administrator; this requires an understanding of the importance of each appointment relative to the responsibilities of that administrator. An effective administrative assistant should also be able to analyze enquiries and refer them to the appropriate staff member. Acquiring such abilities goes beyond the scope of training and requires education.

To some, this distinction between *training* and *education* may seem to be only an academic exercise; however, it has very practical application. As demonstrated later in this chapter, it is extremely important to categorize and analyze the needs of employees to establish objectives for the various components of a staff development program. Understanding the type of learning required to meet these needs is essential to an effective program.

A staff development program centers on instructional learning situations. Consequently, those charged with creating such a program must know and understand the psychological dimensions of learning. Numerous theories have been proposed about how learning occurs. This chapter touches on only a few principles of learning related to staff development.

Learning is a change in human capability that can be retained and is not ascribable simply to the process of growth. The change described in this definition is manifested in the behavior of the learner. The extent to which learning has occurred is measured by comparing those behaviors that were present before the individual was placed in the instructional learning situation to those behaviors that can be demonstrated after the experience. The desired change is usually an increased skill or capability of more than momentary significance. That change is brought about by certain aspects of the learning process. A *stimulus* is someone or something that initiates an action. An instructor stimulates a learner by asking a question. The learner answering the question makes a *response*. If the instructor responds to the learner with "That is a correct and appropriate answer," the learner is receiving *reinforcement*. Finally, if the learner perceives completion of the course of instruction as a means of obtaining a job, promotion, raise in salary, or some other desired goal, the learner is said to have *motivation*. Although this explanation of the four basic components of learning is rather simplistic, it does present the necessary conditions for learning to take place.

Considerations that impinge on these aspects of the learning process are mentioned here because they are related to staff development planning. First, a certain amount of planning must precede the instructional learning situation to determine the most appropriate learning structure for the subject matter to be taught. In learning, every new capability builds on a foundation established by previously learned capabilities. Planning specifies and orders these prerequisite capabilities so that a learning objective can be reached. For example, a staff development workshop designed to help teachers construct metric system materials for classroom use should be preceded by a seminar explaining the metric system to teachers who are not proficient with the system.

Second, the environment of learning must be managed effectively. Those responsible for planning should ask themselves what the most appropriate time and setting are to carry out instruction. A comfortable and stimulating environment certainly enhances learning, and especially for adult learners, the instruction should take place at a time of day when they are not fatigued. This suggests that certain staff development seminars, workshops, or courses for teachers should be scheduled on days when school is not in session; alternatively, employees should be provided with released time from their regular duties so they can attend during the working day.

Third, instruction must have some practical application for the adult learner. Adults generally can learn more material in less time when they understand that the material can help them in their work. A school bus driver who attends a workshop on managing student behavior must be shown techniques that he or she can actually use with disruptive students.

Fourth, learning rarely takes place at a constant rate; rather, it fluctuates according to the difficulty of the subject matter or skill to be learned and the ability of the learner. Developing computer skills is a good example. During the first three months of instruction, the learner becomes familiar with the basic techniques. During the next three months, the individual develops speed, and learning accelerates. After six months of instruction, learning usually slows because the individual has progressed to the point of technique refinement.[5]

Creating a Staff Development Program

Experience has taught human resources administrators the folly of approaching staff development using the "Let's have a workshop" model. This traditional concept of what was and still is referred to in some school districts as *in-service training* has severe limitations, not only in scope but also in effectiveness. Rather, the concept of *staff development* addresses the real needs of educational organizations.[6] The evolution of this approach is mirrored in all of our societal institutions. In the past, changes were thrust on the schools without giving teachers and administrators an opportunity to prepare for them. With the decline in pupil enrollments, there was a greater need to develop existing personnel resources to assume different positions created by this change. Also, both the Elementary and Secondary Education Act of 1965 and the Education Professions Development Act of 1968 provided funding for staff development projects. These funds helped encourage the current interest in staff development.

Since the early 2000s, there has been a myriad of research on staff development. Most of this research centers on identifying those variables that produce effective staff development programs. As a consequence of this research, many models have been created. Some of the most often proposed in staff development literature are PET (Program for Effective Teaching), RPTIM (Readiness, Planning, Training, Implementation, Maintenance), CBAM (Concern-Based Adoption Model), and SDSI (Staff Development for School Improvement). A common thread connecting all these models is the goal of producing effective instruction through clinical supervision. As principals evaluate and supervise teachers to improve instruction, staff development programs become a vehicle through which teachers can enhance skills and remedy deficiencies.

Some employees perceive staff development activities as ineffective because they receive little support for implementing newly acquired skills and ideas. The lack of appropriate program organization and lack of supervision during implementation also affect the success of the program. Clearly, these conditions are symptomatic of a more fundamental problem—lack of commitment. In any organization, this commitment must emanate from the highest level of responsibility down through the various levels of administration to the employees. To be effective, the staff development program must be supported by the board of education, organized and supervised by the administration, and planned—at least in part—by the employees.

In delineating the tasks to be performed by the various components of a school district, the board of education must set the stage by creating a positive climate for the staff development program and by providing the necessary fiscal funding and appropriate policies for its implementation. The central office administration, through the director of staff development, is responsible for creating a master plan and for providing overall management and supervision of the program. Building principals and supervisors are responsible for identifying the knowledge, skills, and abilities needed to carry out the goals and objectives of the school district. Teachers and staff members are responsible for participating not only in program planning but also in the programs. Consequently, the success of a staff development program depends on the commitment of each individual within each level of the school district. Firestone, Mangin, Martinez, and Polovsky confirm the importance of commitment:

> The top leader in this district made improved literacy, and later mathematics, his top priority. After hiring and removing staff to get a team that shared his commitment, he began a long-term process of helping teachers develop a deeper understanding of subject areas and how to teach them. . . . The professional development effort was part of a broader change program that became central to all decision making in the district, and it required constant protection from threats to resources and its coherence.[7]

Firestone and his colleagues also promote the concepts of local initiative and internal accountability, particularly when a school district is using professional development to initiate and sustain reform efforts.[8]

The steps necessary for designing an effective program are summarized in Figure 6.1 and elucidated in the following pages.

School District Goals and Objectives

Educational goals and objectives, taken in the broadest sense, are similar across the United States. Schools are concerned about educating our children in the basic skills and developing in them the cultural values that perpetuate our American heritage.

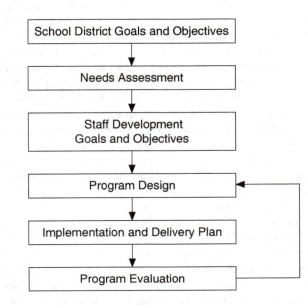

FIGURE 6.1   Model for a Staff Development Program

A school district's educational goals and objectives form the basis for its staff development program. When they are formulated into written policies of the board of education, these goals and objectives provide the staff development program with the guidance necessary for integrating the individual goals of employees with those of the school district.

Needs Assessment

The primary purpose of a staff development program is to increase the knowledge and skills of employees, and thereby increase the potential of the school district to attain its goals and objectives. The process of assessing employee needs is essentially one of determining the discrepancy between existing and needed staff competencies.[9] This analysis must also consider projected human resources needs. Thus, a staff development program must be concerned not only with the abilities individuals currently occupying positions need but also with the abilities individuals need to qualify for promotion to positions of more responsibility. The data obtained from the human resources inventories used in the human resources planning process, along with the data obtained from needs assessment techniques, provide the framework within which program goals and objectives can be established.

Staff Development Goals and Objectives

Staff development goals and objectives change continually to meet the changing needs of individual staff members and the school district. A predominately European American suburban school district that begins to get an influx of Mexican American families might consider creating a program for the administrative, teaching, and support staffs on the impact that the mingling of these two distinctive cultures will have on the functioning of the school district. As another example, the purchase of new computer equipment creates a need to instruct the office staff on its most effective use.

These examples of changes that affect the operations of a school district should be formulated more broadly into goals and objectives. For example, a staff development goal involving integration might be stated as follows: To prepare the administration, teachers, and staff to address the integration of Mexican American students into the school community. Objectives supporting this goal could be formulated as follows:

- To develop a sense of appreciation for cultural differences on the part of teachers, administrators, and staff members
- To develop strategies that help students acquire an understanding of different cultural heritages

Such a goal, with its accompanying objectives, provides direction to the next phase in creating a staff development program—designing the program.

Program Design

Designing a program involves more than simply finding a university professor who is interested in giving a workshop on a particular topic. Broadly conceived, *program design* is the process of matching needs with available resources through an effective delivery method.[10] Therefore, it is obviously unproductive to assign or endorse an activity without considering how this activity helps meet goals and objectives.

Also, it is unproductive to consider only one method of delivering a staff development program. The National Education Association's Research Division lists nineteen methods used in program delivery:

1. Courses	**11.** Camping
2. Institutes	**12.** Work experience
3. Conferences	**13.** Teacher exchanges
4. Workshops	**14.** Research
5. Staff meetings	**15.** Professional writing
6. Committee work	**16.** Professional association work
7. Professional reading	**17.** Cultural experiences
8. Individual conferences	**18.** Visits and demonstrations
9. Field trips	**19.** Community organization work
10. Travel	

This is certainly not an exhaustive list of all the possibilities for designing a staff development program, and it is important to recognize that no one design will satisfy all. A variety of resource people—the most available and knowledgeable of whom are teachers, senior staff members, college and university professors, professional consultants, journal authors, teacher organization representatives, and administrators—enhance a staff development program.

Group-oriented design has proved to be an effective method for delivering staff development programs. Some of these group-oriented programs are centered around behavior modification techniques in the instructional learning environment. Individualized programs are another alternative to the traditional program design model and allow the individual maximum creativity in matching personal interests and needs to the goals and objectives of the school district. Teachers who engage in personalized activities usually improve their teaching skills; such activities include writing for professional journals, serving on school district curriculum research committees, attending conferences, making presentations at conferences, engaging in professional reading, participating in professional development traveling, developing curriculum materials, becoming active in community relations events, and sponsoring student activities. Program design is an organic process that will continually change to meet the needs of individual staff members and the needs of the school district.

Implementation and Delivery Plan

A critical aspect in all staff development programs is the implementation and delivery phase.[11] The best intentions and planning may fail unless attention is paid to providing employees with appropriate incentives to participate, satisfactory time arrangements are made, and ordinary organizational problems are handled properly.

A common practice is to reimburse employees for tuition and fees incurred in attending workshops or taking courses. Many school districts also pay for substitutes to facilitate program arrangements. The research on staff development programs generally agrees that incentives should be provided. Reimbursement for attending professional conferences and for taking university courses, as well as advanced placement on the salary schedule, are also incentives. Although direct payment in the form of salary increments is a proved incentive, this study indicates that indirect financial aid is more influential in promoting participation in staff development programs.

Time is a valuable commodity to all employees, and, thus, it is a key factor in organizing and encouraging employee participation in development programs. There is a growing trend to incorporate staff development programs as part—or at least as an extension of—the working day. Some school districts set aside a number of afternoons each month for development programs; others bring courses and lectures directly to the schools. A variation of this approach is to release students by subject area so that the teachers in a given discipline can meet for an entire day.

Whatever the arrangement for delivering a staff development program, experience indicates that the least effective time is after a full day of teaching or work. No teacher, administrator, or employee is able to assimilate new ideas when fatigued.

A final consideration in administering a staff development program is providing the administrative mechanism to handle the ordinary problems that occur in all human interaction. For example, some teachers may not be certain of the objectives of the staff development program. Likewise, if a program is not structured in such a way that teachers readily recognize its relevance to their particular situation, they may see the program as a waste of time and energy. Staff development programs for large groups of teachers tend to hinder participation, and not having the best possible presenters creates a negative impression of the program. Finally, all teachers understand the need to evaluate all programs, which is even more important if they are staff development programs. When administrators do their best to deal with such problems effectively, employees more readily participate and are more satisfied with the development programs.

Program Evaluation

Effective evaluation is the final phase in a staff development program.[12] Some school districts see this as a rather complicated task involving multiple applications of statistics; others neglect it entirely. For most programs, a perception-based approach is both appropriate and effective. Participants are asked to rate the instructor or individual conducting the program, content of the program, organization of the program, and time and place of the program presentation.

When a particular program centers on skill or technique acquisition, it is appropriate to conduct a follow-up evaluation after the participants have had the opportunity to implement the technique or use their new skill. The evaluations are then used in future program planning and also should provide the data necessary to improve the entire staff development program. Significant dimensions of program evaluation are as follows:

- The evaluation of staff development programs should attempt to ascertain whether the participants acquired the intended knowledge and skills.
- The evaluation should attempt to ascertain whether the participants use their newly acquired knowledge and skills in fulfilling their responsibilities.
- The evaluation should address the impact that the new knowledge and skills have had on student learning outcomes.[13]

Also, the director of staff development should evaluate the program to ascertain whether the program is helping achieve the mandate of the school district as outlined in its goals and objectives. This is a much more complicated process than evaluating a specific course or workshop, and must involve the perceptions of the board of education, superintendent of schools, other central office administrators, and building administrators.

Staff Development Support Resources

Educational administrators searching for information and opportunities to enhance their school districts' staff development programs can find no better online resources than what are available from the National Staff Development Council (NSDC; www. LearningForward.org) and the Association for Supervision and Curriculum Development (ACSD; www.ascd.org).

The NSDC provides learning opportunities for individuals and custom-designed services for school districts, newsletters, and blogs. The learning opportunities include the annual conference, specialized conferences, and institutes. However, the cybertechnological services are centered around the custom design of opportunities that support the job responsibilities of staff development administrators and other administrators charged with staff development responsibilities. The NSDC will conduct online staff development audits in order to assist school districts as they establish professional development goals and institute programming. Staff development[14] administrators can avail themselves of online coaching, and can make use of the Standards Assessment Inventory, an effective research tool that helps districts assess their present effectiveness in meeting well-established staff development standards and then set appropriate goals. In addition, books and staff development materials are available for purchase online. Thus, the staff development opportunities are a mixture of resources that support staff development administrators, superintendents of schools, principals, teachers, and staff members as they fulfill their professional responsibilities.

The ASCD is an equally important cybertechnological resource for administrators of staff development programs and for administrators, teachers, and staff members interested in individual development. In addition to providing conferences and workshops for educators, the ASCD sponsors the LEAP Institute, which brings together staff development administrators to present their educational needs, concerns, and suggestions to Congress and various national agencies. Information is available on the Website about national initiatives such as Healthy School Communities and Outstanding Young Educators. The ASCD store contains books, videos, newsletters, and other materials that can be purchased online. There are a number of related Website links that are helpful in specific ways. For example, www.ascd.org/professional-development. aspx contains information about onsite staff development consulting and online courses in such areas as classroom management and various dimensions of learning. Also, www.ascd.org/research-a-topic allows professional development administrators and other educators the opportunity to research specific topics such as neuroscience and what it can teach educators about learning.

Staff Development for the Instructional Staff

During the first few decades of the twentieth century, boards of education were concerned about encouraging teachers to earn a baccalaureate degree. In the 1970s, the emphasis changed to the remediation of teacher deficiencies. The current thrust is to provide teachers with the opportunities to maintain a favorable outlook on teaching and to improve their effectiveness in the classroom.[15] At times, it is necessary for principals to recommend certain staff development programs to teachers who are not performing at the level established by the board of education. Therefore, performance appraisal and staff development are complementary aspects of effective supervision. A staff development program can offer the teacher opportunities to

1. *Update skills and knowledge in a subject area.* The knowledge explosion has created the need to reinterpret and restructure former knowledge. A teacher can no longer assume on the basis of past learning that he or she understands the nuances of a subject area.

2. *Keep abreast of societal demands.* Our society is continually changing. This has presented the teacher with a need to understand and interpret the new demands society is placing on all its institutions and on the school in particular. Teachers must become acquainted with research on the instructional process and on new methods of teaching. Like other professionals, teachers generally have good intentions about keeping up with the advances being made in their field. However, a shortage of available time often prevents them from carrying out these intentions, and a staff development program can meet this need.

3. *Become acquainted with the advances in instructional materials and equipment.* The Internet and computer-assisted instruction are only a few of the many innovations that have potential for improving the quality of classroom instruction.

The following sources of information can be of considerable help when assessing teacher needs and designing a responsive staff development program. First, the teacher needs assessment survey has been an effective technique. Most surveys take the form of a checklist containing many areas of possible needs and interests (see the Appendix).

Second, the community survey, which is administered to parents usually through a school-based organization such as the Parent–Teacher Association, may reveal parental concerns about a wide range of issues such as grading, student groupings, discipline, and drug use by students.

Third, certification requirements vary from state to state and occasionally change. The director of staff development must keep all teachers and other certificated employees informed about requirements and plan appropriate credit courses on both an off-campus and an on-campus basis. The human resources master plan also provides the director with information about the future needs of the district in relation to certain categories of certificated employees.

The final source of information is curricular research. Staff development programs can be planned to correlate with future curriculum changes. Research points to future skills and competencies that can be acquired and gradually introduced to ensure an even transition.

The historic report *A Nation at Risk*, published by the National Commission on Excellence in Education, was the impetus for many states to pass legislation centered on improving the quality of education. Much of this legislation calls for the establishment of professional development committees composed of teachers and other staff members who are responsible for assisting the administration in identifying the staff development needs of teachers. Along with the administration, these committees are involved in the creation of staff development delivery systems.

Staff Development for School Principals

All administrators wonder occasionally about how they will be able to continue meeting the multiple challenges of their jobs, but school principals are particularly vulnerable because they are on the front line.[16] James L. Olivero, a member of the Association of California School Administrators, wrote a significant article for the *Bulletin of the American Association of School Administrators* entitled "Reducing Battle Fatigue—Or: Staff Development for School Principals," which addresses this problem. Much of the material in this section was gleaned from this article.

Types of Staff Development Programs

Many studies concerning the ever-changing role of the school principal have been conducted since the early 1990s and have identified the following major areas as appropriate for development programs:

- *Instructional skills.*
  - To effectively evaluate and supervise the instructional process, which includes providing curriculum leadership and securing instructional resources.
- *Management skills.*
  - To establish job objectives and assess the needs of the staff.
  - To identify problem areas and plan toward an effective solution.
  - To perform unit budgeting and review priorities in the efficient use of scarce resources.
- *Human relations abilities.*
  - To establish an open system of communication among students, parents, teachers, and other members of the community.
  - To develop a method of involving parents, students, and teachers in school-based decision making.
  - To create an atmosphere of trust in the school that encourages the staff and students to perform to the best of their abilities.
- *Political and cultural awareness.*
  - To identify the leaders within the community and involve them in school-level decision making.
  - To address with positive techniques the resolution of conflicts between the school and community.
  - To work toward meeting the needs of all clients of the school through school programs.

- *Leadership skills.*
  - To keep current with advances in the field of education through a plan of self-development.
  - To share leadership skills with other professionals and with parents and other publics.
- *Self-understanding.*
  - To develop a plan of self-improvement through evaluation by school-based publics.

Programming for Principals

Two types of programming can meet the development needs of principals. The first is the more traditional vehicle, including workshops, conferences, and seminars that usually focus on a single topic and attempt to transmit a given body of information on such issues as new legislation and drug abuse.

A growing number of school districts are taking a more personalized approach to staff development for principals by emphasizing the acquisition of skills that either help principals with their jobs or enhance their personal development. The first includes preparing budgets, developing performance objectives, and initiating procedures to improve building maintenance, whereas the second approach emphasizes personal growth, and might address techniques for working with advisory groups, methods of communicating verbally and in writing, stress management, and time management.

Whatever an individual principal identifies as the area of personal need, a prerequisite for success is commitment. Therefore, it is advantageous to write down such personalized programs in a document that includes a personal needs assessment and a plan of action.

Future Directions for Principal and Staff Development

Dramatic changes have occurred in our society since the beginning of the twenty-first century, and they, in turn, have created a new set of competencies that principals must acquire. Many principals were educated before the emergence of such current trends as cultural pluralism, community involvement, program assessment, technology-assisted instruction, and the inclusion of students with disabilities. These trends, of course, are by no means the end but rather just the beginning of even more dramatic changes taking place at an accelerated pace. We must be prepared to meet this ongoing challenge in staff development. Effective staff development for principals can be enhanced if the development programs are systematic, concrete, and relevant to the principal's job, including not only what the job is but also what the job should be. Thus, staff development opportunities should be

- Ongoing and personalized
- Flexible and adaptable to change as the need arises
- Carried out when the participant is not fatigued because of work
- An integral part of the school district's policies and supported by adequate funds

Staff Development for Classified Employees

Employee development programs in some school districts are limited to teachers and administrators. Development programs for classified employees have just recently taken hold on a large scale throughout the United States.

Three methods of development are commonly used for classified employees: on-the-job, off-the-job, and apprenticeship training. Because of the nature of their job responsibilities, classified employees' development programs are aimed more at training than education. Nevertheless, there is a growing awareness that administrative assistants, custodians, bus drivers, and cafeteria workers perform more efficiently if they are given the opportunity to participate in personal growth activities. Time management and human relations skills are important abilities for all school district employees, particularly with the current emphasis on community involvement in the schools.

Staff development has a definite orientation for classified employees. It is used not only to update skills but also to introduce new employees to the requirements and tasks they will be responsible for performing. In most cases, classified employees who are promoted to supervisory positions learn how to handle their new responsibilities through a staff development program. This is also a nuance of development programs for classified employees.

On-the-Job Training

Most training takes place on the job, and in all probability, this method is an effective means of training.[17] Besides being the easiest form of training to organize, it is also the least costly to implement. Employees are placed in the actual work situation, which immediately makes them feel productive. They learn by doing, which is the most suitable training method for jobs that are difficult to simulate or that can be learned quickly by performance. A significant drawback to on-the-job training is the possibility of future low productivity because in this setting an individual may never fully develop the necessary work-related skills when left to work alone.

A modification of on-the-job training is job instruction training, a more systematic approach to training. This highly effective method consists of the following steps: (1) preparing trainees by telling them about the job, (2) presenting information essential to performing the job, (3) having trainees demonstrate their understanding of the job, and (4) placing trainees in the job on their own and assigning a resource person to assist the trainees if they need help.

Off-the-Job Training

The term *off-the-job training* refers to various kinds of programs, such as lectures, seminars, workshops, case studies, programmed instruction, and simulations.[18] The lecture method is best suited to conveying information such as procedures, methods, and rules. Contrary to common assumptions, lectures can be either highly structured or fairly informal, allowing for a considerable amount of two-way communication.

Since the early 1990s, the use of case studies, programmed instruction, and simulation exercises in training programs has increased. The *case study* allows the employee to study a particular problem in depth. After analyzing the problem, the individual evaluates alternative courses of action and finally selects one that appears to provide the best potential for solving the problem.

Programmed instruction is a method that can be carried out through manuals and textbooks as well as teaching equipment. This approach condenses the material to be learned into a highly organized and logical sequence. The trainee responds to a question or set of circumstances and is provided with immediate feedback, telling the trainee if the response was right or wrong.

Simulations are not only the most expensive but also the most effective method of training. The trainee is placed in an environment that nearly duplicates the actual work situation. This method has been widely used by airlines to train pilots and by schools to train students in driver education classes. By using computer-enhanced instruction, it is possible to simulate a wide variety of job dimensions without risking mistakes in a real-life situation, which might be dangerous or very costly.

Assistant-to Training

The oldest form of training is the apprenticeship, which is commonly referred to as an *assistant-to* position.[19] With this method, a trainee studies under a master worker for a given period of time or until the trainee acquires the necessary skills. Assistant-to positions are common in the skilled trades but have seldom been used in staff development programs. However, the concept is applicable and gaining in popularity.

Teacher Centers and Staff Development

The U.S. Congress, in the Education Amendments of 1976, funded the establishment of local teacher centers that operated in-service programs aimed at improving the classroom skills and techniques of teachers. This legislation was a direct outgrowth of the strategy used by the National Education Association in its efforts to help teachers gain more control over curricular innovations. Teacher centers existed throughout the world long before their appearance in the United States; however, by the early 1980s, there were ninety teacher centers operating under the U.S. Department of Education's Teacher Center Program. Although the orientations of such centers varied considerably, many had evolved as a mechanism to help teachers deal with change. With the proliferation of teacher center literature, many different center models emerged in the United States. Many were cooperative endeavors that included centers established by local school districts and universities. Some state-funded teacher centers also appeared, along with federally funded centers established under Title III of the Elementary and Secondary Education Act.

Essentially, a teacher center program is concerned with curriculum development and/or in-service education for elementary and secondary teachers in one or more local education agencies. The teacher center's policy board should be composed primarily of practicing elementary and secondary teachers from the area served, although administrators, board members of school districts, or representatives from institutions of higher education could also serve.

Teacher centers were founded on the premise that teachers are self-motivating professionals who are capable of determining their own needs and who, through the policies of the governing board, can best deliver a staff development program to meet these needs.

Although the premise is undeniably true, there remain a number of concerns that must be outlined. First, federal funding for teacher centers no longer exists. Second, staff development is a need not only for teachers but also for all employees of a school district. Therefore, a board of education should assume the initial responsibility in providing fiscal resources to develop and administer such staff development programs. Third, teacher centers are essentially delivery systems and should be funded with local and state funds if this is determined to be the most effective way to conduct a staff development program. Teachers, like all employees, must be involved in the entire staff development planning process if such programs are going to meet their needs. This is a normal procedure in all effective staff development programs.

Teacher centers have been a worthwhile innovation for those school districts that lacked an effective staff development program, but they should not be considered a panacea for all school districts. With commitment and proper local and state funding, most school districts are capable of providing adequate programs using a more traditional model administered by a director of staff development.

Implications for Small- and Medium-Size School Districts

Because many school districts do not have a human resources department or even a human resources administrator, the responsibility for promoting, organizing, and implementing staff development programs falls to the superintendent of schools, building principals, or both. Also, because the number of teachers, administrators, and staff members is relatively small in many school districts, the programming for staff development is targeted to individuals rather than to groups of individuals. Consequently, the most effective programming is offered in tandem with the notion of the *learning community*. Thus, self-accountability and collaboration are usually characteristics of staff development programs in such school districts. Of course, the methods of delivery are enhanced through technology. Further, the model used by other professions, tailor-made programming, particularly accommodates teachers and administrators. Attendance at professional conferences and meetings is also an important staff development activity. In some areas, a number of school districts may come together for programs that address common concerns. Mentoring is also appropriate to small- and medium-size school districts. The needs are generally the same throughout all schools and school districts; it is only the delivery models that are different, shifting from group to individual design. Thus, the staff development opportunities set forth in the previous section on technology and staff development are very supportive of small- and medium-size school districts.

Impact of Generation Y Teachers and Administrators on Staff Development

Much of the research concerning members of Generation Y seems to indicate that they are keenly interested in staff development that centers on personal development. This is easily applicable to Generation Y teachers and administrators who are in the business of holistically educating all children. It is a resurgence based on the premise that the core of a person's individual life is constantly in a state of flux, but purposefully tending toward becoming rather than regressing. This self-awareness of Generation Y teachers and administrators is evident in their lifestyles, which appear to be geared toward becoming well-balanced persons capable of controlling their life aspirations. Thus, they are keenly aware of the need for staff development, not only for their professional lives but also for their personal lives.

In pursuing their professional careers, they also value the principal or superintendent who is both capable of coaching and willing to coach them in their professional careers. They want a principal or superintendent whom they can trust and who is an empathetic and genuine professional. They like continual feedback and are appreciative of the value that professional development can have in their professional careers.

Generation Y teachers and administrators are capable of *multitasking,* which means that they can do a good job teaching and mentoring students and engaging colleagues on committees, and they enjoy being members of the learning community. They want to have an impact on their students and colleagues. Thus, Generation Y teachers and administrators not only are appreciative, but also have expectations that a school district will provide them with development opportunities.[20]

Summary

Change is a constant condition of our American way of life. Because of improved electronic communications, changes in all segments of society are placed before students and educators as soon as they occur.

School districts have a mandate to educate the youth of our country. To do so successfully, schools need well-qualified teachers, administrators, and support personnel. No employee will remain qualified in the face of accelerating change without some form of ongoing education and training. This is the impetus behind the recent emphasis on staff development programs.

As a dimension of the human resources function, staff development can be organized according to various structures. Currently, the most effective structure is probably the professional learning community. Such a structure has four major focuses: learning rather than teaching, collaborating, viewing all members of the community as learners, and practicing self-accountability.

Adult learning usually consists of two processes: training and education. *Training* is designed to teach a sequence of programmed behaviors; *education* seeks to impart understanding and an ability to interpret knowledge. Depending on the objectives to be reached, both types of learning can occur in a staff development program.

In all learning environments, four basic components must be present to ensure success: stimulus, response, reinforcement, and motivation.

Creating a staff development program consists of six separate but sequential processes: (1) establishing school district goals and objectives, which become the foundation of the program; (2) assessing the needs of the school district employees to determine whether there is a discrepancy between the competencies of the staff and the requirements of the organization; (3) establishing staff development goals and objectives; (4) designing a program that meets staff development requirements; (5) implementing the designed plan in such a way that effective learning may occur; and (6) evaluating the program to ascertain whether it is meeting its objectives, which, in turn, affect future program designs.

A staff development program for the instructional staff focuses on updating subject area skills and knowledge to improve instruction, outlining societal demands and changes, presenting the findings of research on teaching methods and practices, and updating teachers on the advances in instructional materials and equipment.

In assessing the needs of teachers, four sources of information may be helpful: (1) the teacher needs assessment survey, (2) community surveys, (3) certification information coupled with the human resources master plan, and (4) research and curricular studies.

Since the early 2000s, school principalship has experienced multiple challenges brought on by such trends as cultural pluralism, community involvement, program assessment, technology-assisted instruction, and the inclusion of students with disabilities. A study conducted in California identified the following areas as appropriate for development programs for principals: instructional skills, management skills, human relations abilities, political and cultural awareness, leadership skills, and self-understanding.

In addition to the traditional models of staff development for principals, which include workshops and seminars, many school districts are taking a more personalized approach, directed at helping principals acquire skills that relate simultaneously to their job and to their personal development.

Staff development programs have been limited to the professional staff in many school districts. However, all employees can profit from development programs, and classified employees should have the opportunity to increase their skills and participate in personal growth activities. Newly hired and promoted classified employees can be inducted into the responsibilities of their positions through a staff development program. The three most commonly used methods are on-the-job, off-the-job, and apprenticeship training.

An innovation in staff development programming was the emergence of teacher centers, a direct result of the Education Amendments of 1976. These federally funded centers were locally governed and operated. They aimed at continually trying to improve the instructional techniques of teachers.

Self-Check Quiz Click here to take an automatically-graded self-check quiz.

Discussion Questions and Statements

1. Explain how staff development is related to the performance evaluation of employees.
2. Discuss the benefits of effective staff development programs.
3. What are some strategies that can be used to motivate employees to participate in staff development programs?
4. How might the principles of adult learning influence the creation of staff development programs?
5. What types of staff development programs are best suited for employees in classified positions?
6. Identify and describe staff development programs that are most beneficial for building administrators.

Suggested Activities

1. You are the director of staff development for a school district with 250 teachers and 9 administrators. The state legislature has just mandated that 1 percent of the state aid that a school district receives must be used for teacher staff development. Thus, you have approximately $150,000 to spend on staff development. Describe, in writing, the staff development program that you would develop with the money. Begin by stating the program goals and objectives.
2. Obtain the staff development policies of a school district. Write a comparison of the policies with the principles set forth in this chapter.
3. Obtain needs assessment surveys that are being used in a school district to create staff development programs for administrators, teachers, and classified employees. Using the principles in this chapter, write an analysis of the surveys.
4. Interview a director of staff development concerning the strategies that can be used to create and deliver effective staff development programs.

Focus Scenario Activity

Given that you have read and studied this chapter, set forth a detailed plan on how you would use state funds the district received to enhance staff development opportunities for teachers and administrators.

Endnotes

1. William A. Firestone, Melinda M. Mangin, M. Cecilia Martinez, and Terrie Polovsky, "Leading Coherent Professional Development: A Comparison of Three Districts," *Educational Administration Quarterly,* 41, no. 3 (August 2005): 415–416.
2. Richard DuFour, "What Is a 'Professional Learning Community'?" *Educational Leadership,* 61, no. 8 (May 2004): 6–11.
3. Vicki R. Husby, *Individualizing Professional Development: A Framework for Meeting School and District Goals* (Thousand Oaks, CA: Corwin Press, 2005), 3–4.
4. David A. DeCenzo and Stephen P. Robbins, *Fundamentals of Human Resource Management,* 9th ed. (Hoboken, NJ: John Wiley, 2007), 211.
5. Husby, *Individualizing Professional Development,* 6–7.
6. Peter Earley and Sara Bubb, *Leading and Managing Continuing Professional Development: Developing People, Developing Schools,* (London: Paul Chapman, 2004), 39–46.
7. Firestone et al., "Leading Coherent Professional Development," 417.
8. Ibid.
9. Early and Bubb, *Leading and Managing Continuing Professional Development,* 47–52.
10. William G. Cunningham and Paula A. Cordeiro, *Educational Leadership: A Bridge to Improved Practice,* 4th ed. (Boston: Allyn & Bacon, 2009), 315–319.
11. William Penuel, R. Barry, J. Fishman, Ryoko Yamaguchi, and Lawrence P. Gallagher, "What Makes Professional Development Effective? Strategies That Foster Curriculum Implementation," *American Educational Research Journal,* 44, no. 4 (December 2007): 928–932, 949–952.
12. Earley and Bubb, *Leading and Managing Continuing Professional Development,* 77–84.

13. Thomas R. Guskey, "Does It Make a Difference? Evaluating Professional Development," *Educational Leadership,* 59, no. 6 (March 2002): 45–51.
14. Stephen P. Gordon, *Professional Development for School Improvement: Empowering Learning Communities,* (Boston: Pearson Education, 2004), 129–130.
15. Gabriel Diaz-Maggioli, *Teacher-Centered Professional Development* (Alexandria, VA: Association for Supervision and Curriculum Development, 2004), 1–18.
16. Gordon, *Professional Development for School Improvement,* 138–140, 145–153.
17. DeCenzo and Robbins, *Fundamentals of Human Resource Management,* 211–212.
18. Ibid., 211–213.
19. Ibid., 212.
20. Suzette Lovely and Austin G. Buffum, *Generations at School: Building an Age-Friendly Learning Community,* (Thousand Oaks, CA: Corwin Press, 2007), 75–88.

Selected Bibliography

Association for Supervision and Curriculum Development (ASCD). www.ascd.org.

Berdo, S. Education Factor and Human Resources Development. *Academicus,* 1 (2010): 72–79.

Bereiter, C. *Education and Mind in the Knowledge Age.* Mahwah, NJ: Lawrence Erlbaum, 2002.

Borko, Hilda. "Professional Development and Teacher Learning: Mapping the Terrain." *Educational Researcher,* 33, no. 8 (November 2004): 3–15.

Brewer, P. D., and K. L. Brewer. "Knowledge Management, Human Resource Management, and Higher Education: A Theoretical Model." *Journal of Education for Business,* 85, no. 6 (2010): 330–335.

Bullock, A. A., and P. P. Hawk. *Professional Teaching Portfolios for Practicing Teachers.* Bloomington, IN: Phi Delta Kappa Educational Foundation, 2001.

Cohen, S. *Teachers' Professional Development and the Elementary Mathematics Classroom: Bringing Understanding to Light,* Mahwah, NJ: Lawrence Erlbaum, 2004.

Cordingley, P. "Bringing Research Resources to School Based Users." *Professional Development Today,* 4, no. 2 (2003): 13–18.

Dall'Alba, Gloria, and Jörgen Sandberg. "Unveiling Professional Development: A Critical Review of Stage Models." *Review of Educational Research,* 76, no. 3 (Fall 2006): 383–412.

Davis, E. A., and J. S. Krajcik. "Designing Educative Curriculum Materials to Promote Teacher Learning." *Educational Researcher,* 34, no. 3 (2005): 2–14.

Diaz-Maggioli, Gabriel. *Teacher-Centered Professional Development.* Alexandria, VA: Association for Supervision and Curriculum Development, 2004.

DuFour, Richard. "What Is a Professional Learning Community?" *Educational Leadership,* 61, no. 8 (May 2004): 6–11.

Earley, Peter, and Sara Bubb. *Leading and Managing Continuing Professional Development: Developing People, Developing Schools.* London: Paul Chapman, 2004.

Firestone, William A., Melinda M. Mangin, M. Cecilia Martinez, and Terrie Polovsky. "Leading Coherent Professional Development: A Comparison of Three Districts." *Educational Administration Quarterly,* 41, no. 3 (August 2005): 413–448.

Fishman, B. J., R. W. Marx, S. Best, and R. Tal. "Linking Teacher and Student Learning to Improve Professional Development in Systemic Reform." *Teaching and Teacher Education,* 19, no. 6 (2003): 643–658.

Florea, N. "New Forms of Human Resources Development: e-Learning in Education." *Petroleum-Gas University of Ploiesti Bulletin, Educational Sciences Series,* 62, no. 1A (2010): 249–257.

Gordon, Stephen P. *Professional Development for School Improvement: Empowering Learning Communities,* Boston: Pearson Education, 2004.

Huang, W. H., W. Y. Huang , and C. C. Chui. "The Impact of Specified Professional Development Programme Information as a Marketing Tool for Effective Recruitment." *Human Resource Development International,* 14, no. 1 (2011): 57–73. doi:10.1080/13678868.2011.542898

Husby, Vicki R. *Individualizing Professional Development: A Framework for Meeting School and District Goals,* Thousand Oaks, CA: Corwin Press, 2005.

Jaffry, Q., F. Rahman, M. Ajmal, and N. Jumani. "Education as an Indicator for Human Resource Development." *Language in India,* 10, no. 10 (2010): 378–389.

Kirkpatrick, Donald L., and James D. Kirkpatrick. *Evaluating Training Programs: The Four Levels*, 3rd ed. San Francisco: Berrett-Koehler, 2006.

Knapp, M. S., M. A. Copland, B. Ford, A. Markholt, M. W. McLaughlin, and M. Milliken. *Leading for Learning Sourcebook: Concepts and Examples.* Seattle: Center for Teaching Policy, 2003.

Kuchinke, K. "Human Development as a Central Goal for Human Resource Development." *Human Resource Development International,* 13, no. 5 (2010): 575–585. doi:10.1080/13678868.2010. 520482

Lama, S., and M. Kashyap. "Empowering the Human Resources and the Role of Distance Learning." *Turkish Online Journal of Distance Education (TOJDE),* 13, no. 3 (2012): 239.

Lawless, Kimberly A., and James W. Pellegrino. "Professional Development in Integrating Technology into Teaching and Learning: Knowns, Unknowns, and Ways to Pursue Better Questions and Answers." *Review of Educational Research,* 77, no. 4 (2007): 575–614.

Martin, Vivien, and Joyce Barlow. "Staff Development for a More Inclusive Curriculum." *Learning and Teaching in Higher Education,* 3 (2007–2008): 3–19.

Miron, L. F., and E. P. St. John, eds. *Reinterpreting Urban School Reforms: Have Urban Schools Failed or Has the Reform Movement Failed Urban Schools?* Albany: State University of New York Press, 2003.

National Staff Development Council (NSDC). www.nsdc.org.

National Staff Development Council (NSDC). *Standards for Staff Development, Revised and Edited,* Oxford, OH: Author, 2001.

Nen, M., R. Stoika, and C. Radulescu. "Lifelong Learning of Human Resources for Sustainable Development." *Environmental Engineering & Management Journal (EEMJ),* 10, no. 9 (2011): 1305.

Penuel, William R., Barry J. Fishman, Ryoko Yamaguchi, and Lawrence P. Gallagher. "What Makes Professional Development Effective? Strategies That Foster Curriculum Implementation." *American Educational Research Journal,* 44, no. 4 (December 2007): 921–958.

Peterson, Kent. "The Professional Development of Principals: Innovations and Opportunities." *Educational Administration Quarterly,* 38, no. 2 (April 2002): 213–232.

Sambrook, S. "Finding Connections in Human Resource Development (HRD): Factors, Actors and Activities." *Human Resource Development International,* 14, no. 3 (2011): 249–251. doi:10.10 80/13678868.2011.585059

Scherer, Marge, ed. *Keeping Good Teachers,* Alexandria, VA: Association for Supervision and Curriculum Development, 2003.

Senge, Peter M. *The Fifth Discipline: The Art and Practice of the Learning Organization.* New York: Currency, 2006.

Senge, Peter, Nelda Cambron-McCabe, Timothy Lucas, Bryan Smith, Janis Dutton, and Art Kleiner. *Schools That Learn: A Fifth Discipline Fieldbook for Educators, Parents, and Everyone Who Cares about Education,* New York: Doubleday, 2000.

St. John, Edward P., Genevieve Manset-Williamson, Choong-Geun Chung, and Robert S. Michael. "Assessing the Rationales for Educational Reforms: An Examination of Policy Claims about Professional Development, Comprehensive Reform, and Direct Instruction." *Educational Leadership,* 41, no. 3 (August 2005): 480–519.

The Teaching Commission. *Teaching at Risk: A Call to Action,* New York: Author, 2004.

Tripon, A., and P. Blaga. "Stimulation of the Innovative Potential in Online Life Long Training of Human Resources." *Scientific Bulletin of the Petru Maior University of Targu Mures,* 8, no. 2 (2011): 262.

Appendix
Needs Assessment Survey for the Instructional Staff

Directions: Please check all items according to your degree of interest.

	Degree of Interest		
	None	**Some**	**Much**
Motivating Students to Study	_____	_____	_____
Behavior Modification	_____	_____	_____
Dealing with Individual Differences	_____	_____	_____
Learning Community	_____	_____	_____
Teaching Critical Thinking Skills	_____	_____	_____
Designing Independent Projects	_____	_____	_____
Work-Study Programs	_____	_____	_____
Career Education	_____	_____	_____
Using Performance Objectives	_____	_____	_____
Advanced Placement	_____	_____	_____
Teacher-Made Tests and Electronic Scoring	_____	_____	_____
Demystifying Math Workshop	_____	_____	_____
Elementary School Science Experiments	_____	_____	_____
Online Programming	_____	_____	_____
Oral Communication	_____	_____	_____
Education for Economic Competencies	_____	_____	_____
Developmental Reading	_____	_____	_____
Using Cybertechnology Workshop	_____	_____	_____
African American History Workshop	_____	_____	_____
Consumer Education in the Secondary Curriculum	_____	_____	_____
Ecology Workshop	_____	_____	_____
Seasonal Art Projects for Elementary Classrooms	_____	_____	_____
Spanish for Teachers	_____	_____	_____
Learning Disabilities Identification and Remediation	_____	_____	_____
Art Workshop	_____	_____	_____
Field Trips	_____	_____	_____
Physical Therapy	_____	_____	_____
Pupil Personnel Services	_____	_____	_____
Speech Therapy	_____	_____	_____
Teaching English Composition	_____	_____	_____
Economics	_____	_____	_____

	Degree of Interest		
	None	**Some**	**Much**
School Law Update	_____	_____	_____
Math Enrichment	_____	_____	_____
Retirement and Social Security for Teachers	_____	_____	_____
Early Childhood Curriculum	_____	_____	_____
Teachers' Legal Liabilities	_____	_____	_____
Learning and Behavior	_____	_____	_____
Learning Resource Center	_____	_____	_____
Parent–Teacher Relations	_____	_____	_____
Music for Secondary School Teachers	_____	_____	_____
Psychology of the Exceptional Child	_____	_____	_____
Classroom Management	_____	_____	_____
Parliamentary Procedure	_____	_____	_____
Guidance Workshop	_____	_____	_____
Adolescent Psychology	_____	_____	_____
Newspapers in the Classroom	_____	_____	_____
Creative Classroom Displays and Bulletin Boards	_____	_____	_____
Creating Instructional Materials	_____	_____	_____
Creating Instructional Games	_____	_____	_____
Community Resources	_____	_____	_____
Effective Questioning	_____	_____	_____
Interaction Analysis	_____	_____	_____
Drug Abuse Seminar	_____	_____	_____
Other Suggestions	_____	_____	_____

CHAPTER 7

Performance Evaluation

Focus Scenario

You are the assistant superintendent for human resources in a school district with approximately 500 teachers and 250 support personnel. Until now, the school district was very stable. Parents and other citizens supported the district in terms of passing tax levy and bond issue referendums. The school district experienced significant growth in the 1970s and 1980s, but experienced a decrease in student population in the 1990s and 2000s because many home mortgages in the district were higher than their market values. Thus, the current home owners were unable to sell their houses, and younger families with school-age children could not afford to buy homes in the district. The empty nesters had no interest in leaving the district because of the lower market value of their homes.

This situation caused the school district to lose enrollment, and thus the district was forced to lay off younger teachers. The administrators, teachers, and support personnel have become rather set in their ways and are in need of staff development programs to help them renew their enthusiasm and bring them up to date on current best practice in administering and teaching children. The local teachers' association endorses the need of the district to rethink its staff development commitment and programming. Further, the administrators and teachers have a positive attitude toward this end, and are ready and willing to participate in staff development.

However, it has become obvious to the board of education and the superintendent of schools that some teachers are not interested in improving their instructional methodologies or learning best practices for updating the curriculum. Therefore, the board of education mandated the development of a new performance evaluation process that focuses more directly on the learning instructional process from a learning community perspective. Also, the board of education mandated the review and updating of the employee termination process to focus on the accountability of administrators to initiate more effective procedural due process procedures. The superintendent of schools has asked you to create a new staff development program and review the termination process.

Please use both the "Discussion Questions and Statements" and "Suggested Activities" at the end of this chapter in order to help you develop a way of proceeding in order to address the issues in this section.

The evaluation of teachers' performance is as old as the education profession. However, for the most part, American education was concerned with the formal evaluation of teachers during only three periods of the twentieth century. In the 1920s, these efforts were primarily centered on analyzing whether a given teaching style correlated with the philosophy and psychology of William James or John Dewey. The second stage was more concerned with ascribing certain personality traits as being related to excellence in teaching. The final stage, which appeared in the 1960s and persisted through the 1970s, emphasized generic teaching behaviors that would be effective in all instructional settings. The research in this area coined such catchwords as *structured* and *task oriented* when speaking about the types of teacher behavior that produced effective student outcomes.

In 1976, the National Institute of Education, in a request for proposals, called for a new approach to the definition of effective teacher training. This signaled the growth of a movement to license teachers based on their competencies and performance, rather than on their completion of a teacher education program at an accredited college or university. Obviously, such an approach is predicated on a preconceived notion of what constitutes effective teaching.

Advent of Value-Added Performance Evaluation

The past decade has ushered in a dramatic change in the concept of quality teaching centered on the relationship among teacher qualifications, teacher preparation, teaching performance, and educational outcomes.[1] In addition, an ongoing trend requires more accountability at all levels of performance. School board members are also subject to this trend toward accountability, which has developed to the point that school employees, parents, and even organizations support specific candidates in school board elections because of their dissatisfaction with the policies of particular board members.

The *systems approach* to management, which has been used extensively by industry and received a big boost in the early 1960s, when Robert S. McNamara advocated its use in the U.S. Department of Defense, shifted the emphasis away from the traditional concept of evaluation to the broader concept of employee performance. *Performance by objectives* has become a touchstone, implying that an employee can be evaluated effectively only within the context of attaining certain pre-established objectives. Setting up these objectives is part of the overall process of determining the learning instructional objectives of the school district.

Because of the integral organizational relationship among all employees and because one employee's performance can affect the performance of other employees, all personnel should be evaluated. This begins with the evaluation of the superintendent of schools by the board of education and proceeds down through the chain of command, with each administrator evaluating those employees reporting to him or her. This process applies not only to the professional staff but also to classified employees, whose performance should be evaluated by their immediate supervisors.

It is important for all employees to recognize the positive nature of value-added performance evaluation.

- Evaluation fosters the self-development of each employee.
- Evaluation helps identify a variety of tasks that an employee is capable of performing.
- Evaluation helps identify staff development needs.

- Evaluation helps improve performance.
- Evaluation helps determine whether an employee should be retained in the school district and, if so, how large a salary increase he or she should be given.
- Evaluation helps determine the placement, transfer, or promotion of an employee.

Of the six reasons for evaluation given here, only the fifth could be interpreted as being negative. However, it is a positive reason because students are entitled to the best services possible. Thus, it is not the reasons for performance evaluation that make it a negative experience; rather, in some school districts, it is the manner in which it is carried out.

Procedural due process is an important element in value-added performance because it ensures fairness and the positive effects of evaluation. This is the role played by teacher and labor unions; it is also the role of negotiated master contracts. Value-added performance evaluation is always considered a management prerogative process; however, a master contract negotiated by a teacher or labor union will certainly include a clause on procedural due process that helps protect employees' rights to fairness.

Parents and taxpayers are demanding increased accountability in employee performance, whereas employees are demanding accountability in the evaluation methods and techniques used in their evaluations. Administrators and supervisors are being asked to defend their evaluations and the procedures they used in making them. Consequently, it is extremely important to develop a consistent benchmark in establishing a value-added performance evaluation process.

The benchmark is the *job description* under which an individual was employed. Thus, employees are evaluated in relation to their job descriptions, which is the only defensible criterion against which performance should be measured.[2] Although this does not mean that a given job position will remain unchanged, it does imply that a revised job description may be needed if a job has undergone considerable modification.

A significant distinction must be made at this point to avoid confusion. This chapter addresses the evaluation process from a central office perspective, with emphasis on the development of procedures, use of instruments and methods, and legal considerations of the process. However, value-added performance evaluation is also concerned with supervision as a task of the principal and other administrators. Supervision addresses the human interaction between teachers and administrators, an interaction required of the principal in fulfilling his or her role as the instructional leader within a particular school.

Developing a Performance Evaluation Process

The ultimate goal of all school districts is to educate children and adolescents. How this is accomplished depends on a multitude of subordinate goals and objectives. It is not only organizationally appropriate but also legally wise for a school board to establish a policy statement on employee appraisal that serves as one of these supportive goals. Such a policy gives direction to the various administrative divisions of the school district in their development of organizational objectives. A policy statement might read:

Recognizing that quality education for the children and adolescents of this school district depends on the level of teacher, administrator, and staff member performance, the board of education directs the superintendent of schools to develop and implement a process for employee evaluation.

This process must address as its first priority the impartial and objective evaluation of individual employees in relation to the requirements of their positions within the school district. A second priority is to analyze how these positions help actualize and support the instructional goals and objectives of this school board.

Thus, organizational context is critical to the development and attainment of school and school district goals.[3] The three major divisions in most school districts are human resources, instruction, and support services. Following the organizational structure outlined in Chapter 1, the assistant superintendents for human resources, administrative services, elementary and middle school education, secondary education, and instructional services must develop divisional objectives. In the human resources division, objectives might center on improving recruitment techniques, human resource planning methods, or interviewing procedures. The administrative services division could establish objectives in business management aimed at constructing a more effective investment schedule. The transportation component of this division might work on fuel-efficient bus routing, which could free up funds to improve other areas in the organization.

It is certainly obvious that this procedure of developing objectives may reach a level of refinement within a division that would reach down to component objectives developed by directors (director of federal programs, director of special education, director of pupil personnel services, etc.). However, individual school districts may not need this level of refinement, and divisional objectives could be sufficient—the assumption being used in this chapter.

After divisional objectives have been established by the appropriate assistant superintendents, all employees in these divisions are responsible for developing personal objectives that support the divisional objectives. An assistant superintendent for secondary education may see a need to be present more often in the schools to observe operations firsthand. This constitutes a personal objective to be accomplished over a given period of time. A high school teacher of U.S. history might develop an objective aimed at using more audiovisual techniques in lesson presentations. A custodian might attempt to reorganize the floor-waxing schedule to make better use of work time when students are not in school. This constitutes an objective for the custodian.

The next step in the evaluation development process is to decide on formal evaluation procedures that should be in written form and made available to the entire staff. A concern often voiced by employees is that they were not adequately informed about the evaluation process. Because evaluation procedures are applicable to all school district employees, a common practice is to incorporate them into the board of education policy manual that is distributed to all employees when they are hired. Other school districts have employee handbooks that outline working conditions and specify the procedures and forms used in the evaluation process.

Developing the actual procedures is a task that is best performed by employee representatives who both perform evaluations and are evaluated. This committee approach produces a sense of involvement and accountability that helps defend evaluation procedures in the face of possible criticism.

The employees of the school district should be divided into two groups, professional and classified, when organizing the evaluation development committees. The work situations of these two groups are significantly different and, consequently, may necessitate different evaluation procedures. It is more defensible to have committee members elected by the employees they represent than to have them appointed. If a school district's employees belong to unions or professional associations, these organizations should appoint representatives to serve on the committees.

The number of committee members varies depending on the size of the school district, number of employees represented, and number of unions and associations active in the district. However, the most important consideration is that the committee have an odd number of members, such as three, five, seven, or nine, to avoid the possibility of deadlocked decisions.

In addition to being tailored to the needs of the individual school district, each set of procedures should address the following questions:

- Who, by position, has the primary responsibility for making evaluations? (*Examples:* assistant superintendent for elementary education, principals, director of transportation, director of food service)
- Who is evaluated by these designated positions? (*Examples:* assistant superintendent for secondary education evaluates secondary school principals; building principals evaluate teachers; director of maintenance evaluates carpenters)
- In what settings will formal evaluations take place? (*Examples:* a teacher will be evaluated in the classroom when he or she is teaching a lesson; a principal will be evaluated on how he or she conducts a staff meeting)
- On how many occasions will formal evaluations occur? (*Examples:* tenured teachers will be evaluated on one formal occasion each year; probationary teachers will be evaluated at a minimum on two formal occasions)
- In what setting will the results of formal evaluations be communicated to the person evaluated? (*Examples:* in a conference held immediately after the evaluation in the teacher's classroom; in a conference held in the principal's office at the end of each semester)
- If an employee disagrees with his or her evaluation, what grievance procedure should be available? (*Examples:* written rebuttal may be attached to the evaluation form; appeal may be made to the superintendent)
- What effect will evaluation have on salary increase? (*Examples:* a teacher with an excellent rating may receive a double step on the salary schedule; an employee may receive a merit increase in addition to a step increase on the salary schedule)

Appendix A presents a typical set of such forms and indicators for most of the questions. In analyzing these forms and indicators, it is important to realize that evaluation of all employees is a continual and ongoing process. However, it is just as important to have "formal" evaluations when an employee can demonstrate his or her performance capabilities. Formal evaluation is applicable to situations that involve interaction between an individual and a defined group. Teachers are subject to this process because of their interaction with students. Principals can be evaluated in this manner on how effectively they handle administration activities (see Appendix B). In addition, all employees perform jobs that are more appropriately evaluated on a continuing basis. However, some employees are not evaluated on formal occasions such as custodians, groundskeepers, and the maintenance staff. They are evaluated on results obtained bases. But, their evaluations are usually communicated to them in a formal setting, (see Appendix C). All three appendices present forms and indicators that were originally developed in 1985 and that have undergone modification in subsequent years (www.lindbergh.k12.mo.us).

The final step in the evaluation process is analysis of the results obtained through employee evaluations to determine whether division objectives are being met. If objectives have not been reached, this suggests that the employee objectives apparently did not support the divisional objectives. If the divisional objectives are still relevant to implementing the objectives and goals of the school board, the divisional objectives should be realigned to support them. If both the divisional and the employee objectives have been realized, new objectives can be identified that further the goals of the organization and the development of individual employees. Figure 7.1 is a schematic representation of the development and implementation of an evaluation process.

Numerous popular evaluation techniques such as self-evaluation, peer evaluation, and student evaluation are not addressed in this section. These techniques are aimed more at personal growth, and do not directly affect the evaluation process from a central office perspective. They are more properly referred to as *supervisory techniques.*

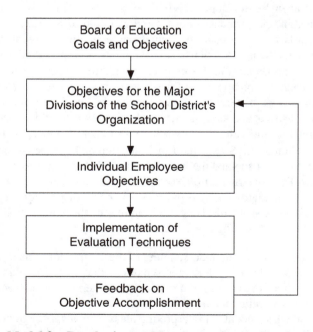

FIGURE 7.1   Model for Developing and Implementing an Employee Evaluation Process

Construction of Performance Evaluation Instruments

As with the development of evaluation procedures, evaluation instruments should be constructed using the committee process. Many management consulting firms have developed evaluation forms that are easily adapted to the requirements of a given school district. However, the construction of evaluation forms is not difficult, particularly with the many prototypes available from neighboring school districts.

The basic format of an evaluation instrument has certain theoretical overtones. Most authors recognize two basic categories: trait forms and results forms. The trait approach rates the employee against a predetermined list of indicators to ascertain his or her level of performance, whereas the results method compares the employee's performance to goals and objectives that were developed by the employee and agreed to by his or her supervisor. Using instructional assessment, teachers and supervisors can document how the goals and objectives were reached.[4]

Many school districts are using standards developed by several professional associations as guides in constructing performance-based evaluation instruments. The Interstate Teacher Assessment and Support Consortium (InTASC) standards, formed under the auspices of the Council of Chief State School Officers, are currently considered to be best practice for licensure requirements in many states. The InTASC standards are also compatible with the advanced certification standards of the new National Board for Professional Teaching standards and can be transformed into performance criteria.

Representatives from the teaching profession, colleges and universities, and state education agencies developed the InTASC standards. InTASC also set out knowledge, dispositions, and performances considered essential to meeting each standard. There are also standards for art education, elementary education, English language arts, foreign languages, mathematics, science, social studies, and special education.[5]

The appendices to this chapter provide trait instruments that have roots in standards, knowledge, dispositions, and performances similar to those developed by InTASC. The focus may be different, however, given the specific issues and concerns of individual school districts and state agencies. This is how it should be because standards and indicators must be individualized by school districts and state agencies.

Although the State Board of Education and the Department of Public Instruction of North Carolina adopted the InTASC standards for licensure, they developed their own indicators. The construction of North Carolina's indicators has been guided not only by the InTASC standards but also by the knowledge, dispositions, and performances indicators found in these standards. Here, for example, are the North Carolina key indicators for the first InTASC standard. The candidate

- Demonstrates an understanding of the central concepts of his or her discipline
- Uses explanations and representations that link curriculum to prior learning
- Evaluates resources and curriculum materials for appropriateness to the curriculum and instructional delivery
- Engages students in interpreting ideas from a variety of perspectives
- Uses interdisciplinary approaches to teaching and learning
- Uses methods of inquiry that are central to the discipline[6]

This author believes that the most appropriate method of evaluating performance combines the use of a trait instrument to ascertain overall performance and the use of a results approach to develop performance improvement objectives. The results method also helps ascertain whether employee objectives are supporting divisional and school board objectives. Employee objectives can be easily developed if overall performance has been measured. Although the simultaneous use of trait instruments and objectives is not a common practice, the exclusive use of one or the other has never proved in experience to be superior. Appendices A, B, and C represent various trait formats that have wide use in educational organizations.

Job descriptions play an important role in constructing appraisal instruments and developing objectives. The job requirements of a position are the legal parameters within which evaluation can be conducted. An employee performs job requirements at a superior, acceptable, or unacceptable level. To require an employee to assume responsibilities that are not within his or her job description and to evaluate how he or she carries out these responsibilities constitutes poor management. The dismissal of an employee because he or she did not perform responsibilities that were omitted from the job description may not hold up in court.

Employee Discipline

The term *discipline* often has a negative connotation. However, the term itself refers to a condition in an organization created by employees conducting themselves according to the rules and regulations of the organization and in a socially accepted manner. Most individuals are self-disciplined and have little difficulty in following rules and regulations. Also, fellow employees can exert significant pressure on people who violate socially accepted norms. A typical example of conduct offensive to most people is using inappropriate language.

There are two areas of misconduct that call for some action on the part of management: excessive absence from work and inappropriate on-the-job behavior. Absenteeism has become a major issue, costing literally millions of dollars. Many theories have been proposed for this change in work ethic, but the cause is usually rooted in the person, who must take responsibility for his or her actions. Inappropriate on-the-job behavior is composed of a variety of offenses such as carelessness, failure to use safety devices, fighting, and alcohol and drug abuse.

Numerous variables affect the seriousness of absenteeism and inappropriate on-the-job behavior. The administration must consider the nature duration, and frequency of the problem; the employee's work history; and other extenuating factors. However, practicing administrators know that a response must be made in order to correct the problem.

The response of the administration to such problems must be corrective rather than punitive, and the action taken must be progressive if it is to withstand the test of due process. For example, if a custodian is tardy for work two times within a given week, the custodial supervisor should give that custodian a verbal warning. If the custodian is late the following week, the supervisor should then present the custodian with a written warning. If the tardiness continues for a third week, the custodian should be suspended from work for a week without pay. If the inappropriate behavior continues after the suspension period, the supervisor must continue with progressive discipline involving demotion, a pay cut, and, finally, dismissal.

When terminating an employee, it is critical for the supervisor and a designated staff member from the human resources department to carefully review the reasons for termination with the school district's attorney to ensure that defensible and appropriate procedures are being followed. In preparing for the meeting at which the employee will be informed of his or her termination, the individual's supervisor and a human resources staff member should complete all the necessary reports and documents and obtain the individual's final paycheck. It is important to have two representatives of the school district, usually the person's supervisor and a staff member from the human resources department, at the meeting. This provides a witness to the proceedings, which may be important in the event of a lawsuit filed against the school district by the fired employee. It may be helpful to role-play what will take place at the meeting, including the anticipated reaction of the person to be fired.

The time and place of the meeting are important because the objectives are to conduct the meeting in a professional manner for the person being fired and in the least disruptive way possible for other employees. For example, Monday afternoon may be the most appropriate time to have the meeting because the fired person will be able to use the rest of the week to search for another job, whereas Friday afternoon might result in the person's anger intensifying over the weekend. At the meeting, it is important to tell the person why he or she is being dismissed. Of course, the person is entitled to ask questions for clarification, but it is not the time to defend the decision. However, during the meeting, it is important to explain the school district's appeal process. This is also the time to discuss such issues as severance pay and legal benefits available to dismissed employees.[7] Immediately after the meeting, the dismissed person should return any district property, and, after collecting any personal property, he or she should be escorted out of the building by either the supervisor or the human resources staff member.

In a school district with a negotiated collective master agreement, the progressive disciplinary process should be clearly outlined in the agreement. Although this type of disciplinary process is quite effective with classified personnel such as custodians, cooks, and bus drivers, it is not overly useful with teachers and administrators. The following section deals with the due process applied more appropriately to certificated staff members. Both processes, however, may lead to the same outcome—termination of employment. It is important to keep in mind that a progressive discipline process does not supersede the evaluation process; rather, it is a method of dealing with problems that cannot wait to be dealt with through the normal evaluation process.

Developing Termination Procedures

A universally accepted purpose for evaluating an individual's performance is to make a determination concerning the desirability of retaining that person as an employee of the school district. The decision to dismiss an employee is, of course, extremely difficult to make due to the importance of employment to the welfare of the employee and his or her dependents.

Employment counselors have seen the devastating financial and psychological effects that being fired has on a person's life. In fact, the trauma usually centers on an individual's self-concept. Common emotions are feelings of inadequacy, failure, self-contempt, and anger.

Although most people are able to cope with such situations, others never fully recover. Consequently, it is not only good human resources management but also a humane responsibility for school district administrators to develop termination procedures that are objective and fair, and that incorporate a due process procedure that gives employees the opportunity to modify or defend their behavior. The Missouri State Statutes Governing Revocation of License, Contract Management, and Termination Procedures present a model used here to explicate the nuances of due process and the grounds for terminating employment. Although the statutes pertain specifically to teachers, the concepts explained are applicable to other categories of employees.

Grounds for Terminating a Tenured Teacher

A tenured teacher may have his or her employment terminated for one or more of the following causes: physical or mental condition making him or her unfit to instruct or associate with children; immoral conduct; insubordination, inefficiency, or incompetency in the line of duty; willful or persistent violation of, or failure to obey, the state laws pertaining to schools; willful or persistent violation of the published policies and procedures of the school board; excessive or unreasonable absence from work; or conviction of a felony or a crime involving moral turpitude.

The first cause listed, physical or mental condition making him or her unfit to instruct or associate with children, must be understood within the context of the Rehabilitation Act of 1973. A disability does not constitute a physical condition that may in any way be construed as making an individual unfit to associate with or instruct children or students. In fact, the prevalent interpretation of the law is that an aide must be hired to assist an employee with a disability in carrying out instructional responsibilities. The only possible physical condition that would prevent an employee from associating with children is a contagious disease, which is a potential cause for dismissal only if the individual refuses to get medical treatment and insists on working while he or she is contagious. Emotional illness that produces dangerous or bizarre behavior is also a potential cause for dismissal if the employee refuses to receive medical treatment and insists on working while ill. In both cases, documentation from a physician is necessary to proceed with the termination process. Of course, the school district is responsible for all expenses incurred in securing the expert opinion of the physician.

Immoral conduct must be judged within the context of local standards, but this judgment also must be reasonable and consistent with recent court decisions. A number of significant court cases have been reviewed and form the foundation for the recommendation that the following principles be used in judging employee conduct: First, the health of the pupil–teacher relationship is the criterion for judging employee behavior. A teacher or other employee who establishes a relationship with a student that goes beyond friendship and is exhibited in some form of "dating" is unacceptable. Second, illegal sexual acts are cause for immediate suspension. If an employee is convicted of performing such an act, his or her employment with the district must be terminated. Suspension is a justifiable practice while investigating allegations of sexual misconduct if the employee receives his or her salary during this period. Third, a private nonconventional sexual lifestyle is not a cause for employee dismissal. For example, homosexuality or cohabitation outside matrimony may be unacceptable to some people in the community, but these lifestyles do not inherently affect an individual's performance in the workplace. These and other practices are displayed publicly on television and in other media, which to an extent has nullified their impact on students. Fourth, if an employee advocates a nonconventional sexual lifestyle at school, the employee has placed him- or herself in a position where termination is possible when such a lifestyle are in direct conflict with local standards.

Insubordination in the line of duty is always a cause for dismissal. Although the interpretation of what constitutes insubordination may appear to be self-evident, it has a restricted application. Employees can be insubordinate only if they refuse to comply with a directive of their supervisor that is clearly within their job expertise. If a principal asks a teacher to supervise the children on the playground during the teacher's preparation time and the teacher refuses, the teacher is insubordinate because teachers have the job-related responsibility of supervising children. However, if the principal were to direct a custodian to supervise the children on the playground and the custodian refused, he or she would not be guilty of insubordination because this is not within his or her occupational expertise. Nor would it be insubordination if a teacher refused to fill in for the principal's secretary who was absent from work due to illness. The teacher was not hired to perform secretarial functions and may refuse this directive. The manner in which an employee responds to a directive does not usually constitute insubordination if the employee performs the task. Thus, if a teacher responds in a sharp tone to the principal when assigned to playground duty, but obeys the directive, he or she is not guilty of insubordination.

Inefficiency is relatively easy to document, and usually refers to the inability of an individual to manage those tasks that are integral to a job responsibility. A teacher who never takes class attendance or who cannot account for the equipment, books, or materials assigned to his or her class is obviously inefficient. A principal who is always late in turning in building budgets or other reports also falls into this category.

Incompetency is perhaps the most difficult cause to document in terminating an employee. It is also directly related to the formal evaluation process. If a tenured teacher is performing in an incompetent manner, it means that he or she is hindering the instructional learning process. The evaluations made by the principal must clearly indicate that major deficiencies have been identified and that objectives to remedy those deficiencies have not been met.

Claiming willful or persistent violation of state school laws or board of education policies and procedures as a cause for termination presupposes that school district employees have been informed of these. An effective method of notifying employees about these laws, policies, and procedures is through the publication and distribution of a handbook or manual that clearly outlines the employee's responsibilities.

Excessive or unreasonable absence from work is a relative circumstance that can be substantiated only through a policy defining what is meant by *excessive* or *unreasonable*. Local school boards may rely on patterns of absences in making their determinations. Five consecutive days per month over a year's span, for example, could be considered excessive if the employee is not suffering from a chronic physical condition that interferes with attendance at work.

Conviction of a felony is obviously a reason to terminate the employment of an individual. However, conviction for a crime involving moral turpitude requires some explanation. Prostitution is usually classified as a misdemeanor, but because it involves morally offensive conduct according to most community standards, it is a reason to terminate a tenured teacher. The selling of pornography or a conviction for the use or sale of drugs also falls within the definition of moral turpitude.

In 1988, Congress passed the Drug-Free Workplace Act, which gives employers the choice of rehabilitating or dismissing staff members working in federal grant programs who are convicted of drug abuse offenses in the workplace. This law and federal administrative regulations require school districts to maintain a drug-free work environment by explicitly prohibiting employees from manufacturing, distributing, dispensing, possessing, or using unlawful drugs in the workplace. In addition, schools must provide a drug-free awareness program, which must include a description of the dangers of drug abuse, notification of the new requirements and penalties for violations, and information on available employee assistance programs. Employees must inform their supervisor within five days of a criminal conviction for a workplace drug crime. Job applicants must inform a potential employer of prior workplace drug convictions. The 1988 law also gives school district administrators the right to require persons to be tested for drugs when there is reason to suspect that these individuals are using or are under the influence of drugs on school premises or at school functions.[8]

It is becoming common practice for school districts to give a second chance to persons convicted of a workplace drug offense by offering them the services of a drug rehabilitation program. This also points out the growing necessity of employee assistance programs as a voluntary fringe benefit for all employees.

Notification of Charges against a Tenured Teacher

After a behavior has been identified that could result in the termination of an employee, the next step in a due process procedure is *notification,* a formal procedure of serving the employee with written charges specifying the alleged grounds that, if not corrected, will result in dismissal. It must be kept in mind that notification with an opportunity to correct behavior is applicable only to charges arising out of incompetency, inefficiency, or insubordination in the line of duty. Physical or mental conditions as described previously, immoral conduct, violation of school laws or board of education policies and procedures, excessive absences, and conviction of a felony or crime involving moral turpitude require a hearing before termination of employment, but they obviously do not require a period of time to correct the behavior. The behavior has already gone beyond what is rectifiable in an educational setting. A hearing is required, however, to determine if the facts substantiate the allegation.

Notification of charges, an extremely formal process, must not be confused with evaluation procedures that permit an employee the right to disagree with a written evaluation. As a normal course of action, employees may attach a written rebuttal to the evaluation instrument, setting forth points of disagreement and including any documentation to support their position.

Time periods are an essential component of the notification process. Three time periods are specified in the Missouri statutes: a thirty-day period during which time the employee has an opportunity to modify his or her behavior; a twenty-day period before a hearing is held, which allows the employee time to gather evidence supporting his or her position; and a ten-day period after an employee is served an opportunity for hearing notice, during which time he or she must respond to the notification that he or she wants to have the hearing. If the employee does not want to have a hearing on the charges, the board of education may terminate his or her employment with the school district by a majority vote of the board members.

These statutes also set forth another common practice in termination proceedings: The teacher may be suspended with pay until the board of education makes a determination concerning his or her employment.

Termination Hearing on Charges against a Tenured Teacher

The Missouri statutes outline a procedure that must be followed in conducting a hearing that may result in the dismissal of a tenured teacher. Once again, these statutes present a model that is applicable to all termination proceedings.

1. The hearing shall be held in a public forum. There is a distinction between a *public hearing* and a *hearing held in public*. At a public hearing, those in attendance are usually allowed to address those conducting the hearing according to pre-established procedures; at a hearing held in a public forum, only those representing the party making the allegation and those representing the party against whom the allegation is made are allowed to speak and participate in the hearing.

2. Both parties may be represented by an attorney, who may cross-examine witnesses.

3. The testimony given at the hearing shall be under oath. Government agencies such as school districts are usually allowed the privilege of administering oaths in official proceedings. Usually, the president or secretary of the board of education is the official so empowered.

4. The board of education may subpoena witnesses and documentary evidence requested by the teacher. As with the power to administer oaths, school districts usually have subpoena rights and may limit the number of witnesses called on behalf of the teacher or school district administrators.

5. The proceedings at the hearing should be recorded by a stenographer employed by the school district. A tape recording of the hearing is usually acceptable in lieu of a stenographer. A transcript of the proceedings must be made available not only to the school board but also to the teacher. The transcript of a hearing held in public should be open to public inspection.

6. Except for the fee paid to the attorney representing the teacher, all expenses for conducting the hearing should be paid by the school district.

7. The decision by the board of education should be reached within a pre-established time period to ensure fair treatment to the employee.

The board of education is exercising judicial authority in conducting the hearing and reaching a decision on the possible dismissal of a tenured teacher. This is a unique circumstance because the school board acts in two capacities: prosecution, in the sense that the charges are brought against the employee in the name of the school board; and judiciary, because the school board renders the decision. In this respect, the board of education is reviewing its own action. Consequently, it is extremely important to demonstrate, as much as possible, impartiality in the hearing structure. The evidence should be presented by an attorney representing the building principal and other line administrators because these administrators have the responsibility for evaluating and reviewing employee performance.

The room should be arranged to delineate clearly the functions exercised at the hearing. The board of education will be seated at a table in a central place in the room. A second table with a chair, where witnesses will give testimony, could be set up perhaps ten to fifteen feet in front of and facing the board members. To either side of the board table and facing each other should be two tables: seated at one, the teacher and his or her attorney, and seated at the other, the appropriate administrator with the school district's attorney. Those in attendance should be seated in a manner that clearly indicates that they are observers and not participants in the proceedings.

Another mechanism, sometimes used in lieu of a formal hearing when discussing the possible termination of an employee, is an executive session board meeting. Most states have statutes permitting government bodies to hold such private meetings at which public attendance is excluded. If a teacher or any employee is confronted with documentary evidence that could possibly result in his or her termination, and if that employee has been given notice that his or her behavior must be modified, it may be possible to invite the employee to discuss his or her lack of improvement at an executive session of the school board. If the employee resigns in the face of the documentation, the expense and potential embarrassment of a public hearing are avoided.

Figure 7.2 shows a schematic representation of the process for the termination of a tenured teacher as provided for by the statutes discussed in this section.

Appeal by a Tenured Teacher to a Termination Decision Issued by the Board of Education

Because school districts are state government agencies, an appeal to the decision of a school board is made to the state circuit court, which is the court of original jurisdiction in state civil and criminal matters. In most states, this appeal must be made within a set period of time. All evidence, documentation, records, and the transcript of the hearing will probably be requested by the court. Of course, the employee has the right to appeal the decision of the circuit court, as in all civil cases, to a court of appeals and to the supreme court if there is a justifiable reason.

Termination Procedures for Probationary Teachers

A distinction must be made from the beginning of this section between terminating the employment of a probationary teacher and not renewing a probationary teacher's contract. In the latter situation, no formal due process is necessary; the employer–employee relationship simply ceases to exist with the expiration of the contract. This may occur if a probationary teacher is not performing at a level acceptable to the administration. A probationary teacher may have difficulty interacting with the students, staff, or parents in the school district, or may be teaching at a minimal level. It is not only to the district's benefit but also to the teacher's benefit not to renew the contract because the teacher may be more successful in another school district. Not renewing a contract presupposes that evaluations have been made by the teacher's principal, deficiencies have been pointed out, and advice and help have been offered on how to improve performance or correct the stated deficiencies. If such a process has occurred without sufficient improvement, nonrenewal of the teacher's contract is justified.

The Missouri statutes refer to terminating the employment of a probationary teacher before his or her contract expires. As with all other school district employees, the probationary teacher must be given a written statement setting forth the deficiencies, as well as a reasonable time to correct them and improve performance. If such corrections or improvements are not made within the specified time, the employee may be dismissed by action of the board of education.

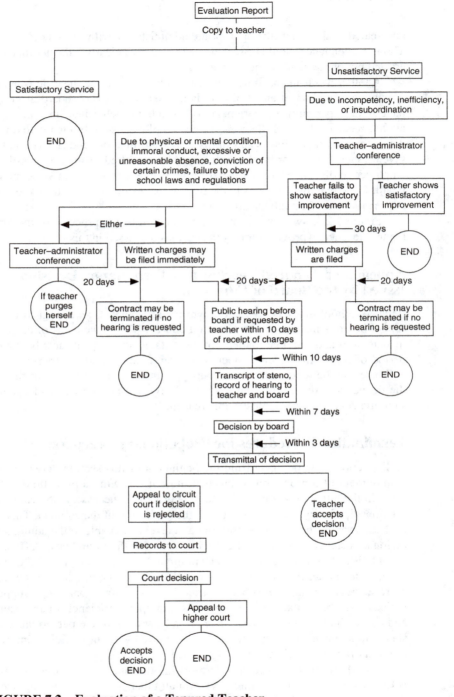

FIGURE 7.2 Evaluation of a Tenured Teacher

Source: "Evaluation of a Permanent Teacher," handout, Missouri State Department of Elementary and Secondary Education, 1970.

Grounds and Procedure for Revocation of a Teacher's License to Teach

A final formal procedure must be alluded to briefly when discussing termination procedures. A teacher's license to teach may be revoked if it can be proved that he or she has exhibited incompetency, cruelty, immorality, drunkenness, neglect of duty, or the annulling of a written contract with the board of education. As in the statutes dealing with the termination of a tenured teacher, the reasons for revocation of a teacher's license have a narrow interpretation.

Incompetency means that the teacher seriously hinders the instructional learning process. A chronic mental illness or sociopathic behavior that has been diagnosed by a psychiatrist is an example of incompetency that could result in revocation of a teacher's license.

Cruelty refers not only to physical but also to mental or emotional abuse of children. The conditions that constitute cruelty may be summarized as follows: Any act that is meant to injure or bring serious ridicule and embarrassment to a child is abusive and cruel.

Of course, *immorality* is an extremely sensitive accusation. For practical reasons, this cause is commonly interpreted to mean that an individual has been convicted of a serious sexual offense or a crime involving moral turpitude. The examples provided previously in this chapter are applicable to immorality as a cause for revocation of a teacher's license.

Drunkenness as a cause for revocation of an individual's license is usually interpreted to mean that the employee either is intoxicated or drinks alcoholic beverages while working. This cause is further strengthened by the fact that drinking alcoholic beverages in a government building such as a school is a misdemeanor in most states. A complicating factor is how drunkenness relates to the issue of alcoholism. Because alcoholism is considered a disease by the medical profession, the same considerations should be afforded the alcoholic as are granted to other employees with a medical problem. These considerations usually involve granting sick leave to an employee receiving medical treatment or reassigning the employee to a position with limited responsibilities during treatment. If an employee is not a diagnosed alcoholic and if he or she persists in drinking alcoholic beverages at work or continuously arrives at school intoxicated, license revocation is in the best interest of a school district clientele, the children.

Neglect of duty presupposes that an employee has been informed about the responsibilities that are integral to his or her position with the school district. This is usually accomplished through written job descriptions or in policy manuals and handbooks specifying these responsibilities. Neglect of duty as a cause for revoking a teacher's license requires that the teacher be given an opportunity to rectify his or her behavior. Thus, evaluations that set forth the employee's deficiencies are necessary to such a situation. It must also be remembered that revocation of a teaching license is extremely serious, and the neglect of duty, in like manner, must be extremely serious and chronic. A teacher who leaves young children unattended on a field trip—behavior that could result in injury to a child—and who continues such irresponsible behavior after being informed of the danger by the principal has exhibited a lack of understanding that seriously affects his or her ability to supervise children. This is a reason not only to terminate the employment of the individual but also to safeguard against this teacher's potential employment with another school district by proceeding to have his or her license revoked.

The provision on the annulling of a written contract with the board of education is improperly worded in the Missouri statutes. *Annulment* means that both parties have agreed to the dissolution of the contract and that the governing board has formally approved the dissolution. As cause for revocation of the teaching license, however, this aspect of the statutes refers to the breaking of a contract by a teacher. Sometimes a teacher or other employee is offered a position with another school district or in private business and industry. If that teacher neglects to request a contract annulment from the school board and assumes another position, the board of education may proceed to have his or her license revoked. Most school boards are not resistant to annulling a contract except in those cases in which the education of the students would be seriously affected. A teacher who tenders a resignation the day before the opening of school in September may not receive a contract annulment until a suitable replacement is obtained.

It should be clearly understood that the board of education does not have the authority to revoke a license; rather, the board may follow a statutory procedure that could eventuate in the revocation of a teacher's license. The state board of education, which issues teaching licenses, has the sole authority to revoke them.

Finally, revocation of a teacher's license is usually irreversible unless the statutory procedures were neglected or the evidence was faulty. It is, therefore, a serious matter that should be initiated only if the education or health and safety of children will be significantly jeopardized now or in the future. Terminating the employment of an individual obviously removes him or her from injuring the children presently in his or her care. Revocation of his or her license prevents the teacher from bringing such injury to children in another school district where he or she could be employed. A classic example involves the teacher who is convicted of child molestation and is fired from his or her position, but who manages to get hired in another school district and commits a similar crime because his or her license was not revoked.

Humane Considerations in the Termination Process

The procedures described in this section may appear to overemphasize the legal and negative side of the evaluation process. It is, however, an extremely important and seldom addressed aspect of evaluation. Confusion over appropriate and fair termination procedures could result in a school district being saddled with an employee who hinders the instructional learning process or who, in fact, may place children in an unsafe situation.

The educational welfare of children is the primary responsibility of a school district. The hiring, retaining, developing, and terminating of personnel should be guided by this mandate. However, employees also have rights that must be taken into consideration when developing procedures and dealing with employee evaluations. Due process is one right that has long been a fundamental principle in English common law and is basic to the legal procedures of American democracy.[9]

Chapter 6 makes the point that a legitimate objective of a staff development program is helping teachers and other employees overcome deficiencies that affect their job performance. In like manner, Chapter 5 provides guidelines for the transfer and placement of personnel to improve their performance. Humane human resources management presupposes that all alternatives have been exhausted in helping employees improve their performance or remove deficiencies before the process of termination is initiated.

Other humane considerations concerning performance evaluations can be divided into two different aspects: First, the performance evaluation of salaried and hourly waged employees tends toward using a trait approach. The school district human resources department or the superintendent develops a set of indicators that are associated with the effective and efficient performance of certain tasks. For example, a school bus driver could be evaluated by a supervisor while he or she is driving the bus. A safety protocol could be devised that the driver follows by extending the stop sign when picking up children and by checking the bus at the end of the route for children who may not have departed the bus at their stops.

Using criteria and recording the performance of the employee after an observation allows for consistency and ease of performance evaluation. The same approach can be used with cafeteria workers, custodians, clerical/secretarial people, and maintenance workers. As another example, compliance with student safety and health standards is a crucial issue in the evaluation of cafeteria workers and custodians. Other electronic devices and computers are efficient and effective tools for maintaining accurate and timely performance evaluation records. Such records are easy to access and analyze in terms of performance, which could indicate successful or unsuccessful staff development programming. If there is a serious breach in protocol in terms of safety in the way cafeteria food is stored and prepared, the training program for cafeteria workers must be reviewed. This approach is analogous to the approach being used not only in businesses and corporations but also in healthcare administration.

Second, the performance evaluation of contracted personnel such as teachers and principals tends to function on a somewhat different level. The performance of tasks is not the main responsibility of the professionals; rather, the decision-making process, which involves taking into consideration a significant number of factors in making those decisions, is the focus. Thus, decisions about teaching methodology, student behavior management, curricular materials, and parental issues are not subject to the exclusive use of the trait-and-factor approach for teacher performance evaluation. Further, principals make ongoing decisions about problems and issues that have more than one or a few possible solutions. Finding a solution sometimes requires a trial-and-error approach that may ultimately be considered *best practice* in a given set of circumstances.

However, it is important to keep accurate records of how teachers and principals address the various situations that occur in the human dynamics of working with students, parents, and colleagues. For example, the human relations skills of a teacher may be effective, sometimes effective, or ineffective; perhaps his or her skills are effective with students but not with parents, or perhaps his or her skills are effective with students and parents but not with colleagues. Indicating the type of situation in which the human relations skills were observed could be helpful in the future.

Accurate and timely record keeping could be important in the dismissal of a teacher or principal who was not able, through procedural due process, to learn new ways of handling human relations situations in an effective manner. Accurate and timely kept records could make the difference in the dismissal of ineffective teachers and administrators.

In conjunction with this approach, having performance evaluation policies and procedures on the school district's website provides the type of transparency that is often needed in the termination process. Through this approach, there would be no question that the teacher or principal knew what was expected of him or her. Finally, it is important for parents and citizens in general to know how all staff members will be evaluated in terms of policies and procedures.

Implications for Small- and Medium-Size School Districts

The size of the school district has no bearing on why performance evaluation of employees is vitally important. Most of the literature deals with the performance evaluation of teachers and somewhat with the evaluation of administrators. However, there is a serious lack of information about the performance evaluation of secretaries, cooks, custodians, bus drivers, and maintenance personnel. The reasons are the same. Performance evaluation is necessary to foster self-development, improve performance, identify staff development needs, create performance incentives, decide on employee promotion and placement, and develop termination processes and procedures. All these dimensions of school and school district leadership are dependent on the quality of performance evaluation.

Regardless of the size of the district, the organizational issues are the same, including board of education policies that deal with performance evaluation and the melding of personal and school or school district performance objectives. Thus, the processes and procedures are essentially the same in all school districts. It is also important to remember that the size of a school district does not necessarily translate into more or fewer performance evaluations. For example, a small school district may have so few administrators that the number of teachers to be evaluated by an individual could be more than in a larger school district.

The process of performance evaluation, the development of standards, and the creation of evaluation instruments, of course, should be initiated in conjunction with representatives of the various employee classifications. The issue that some small- or medium-size school districts might encounter is the time necessary to implement these elements of performance evaluation. Larger school districts undoubtedly have central office administrators who can assist the superintendent of schools and building principals with these necessary tasks. Also, numerous evaluation prototypes can be adapted to a given school or school district. Neighboring schools and school districts are usually willing to share their performance materials and procedures, which could be of help to school districts with a limited number of administrators.

Termination procedures take a considerable amount of time to initiate properly. However, attorneys are available who can guide superintendents and principals through the difficulties of terminating employees who are not fulfilling their responsibilities and who have been given the necessary due process. State departments of education can also be consulted about legislation and guidelines for implementing the termination procedures. Once again, the major difference between smaller and larger school districts is fewer central office administrators who can provide support to the superintendent and principals.

Impact of Generation Y Teachers and Administrators on Performance Evaluation

Generation Y teachers and administrators tend to be very proactive. For example, a teacher must require a certain amount of order in his or her classroom. Students who are constantly being disruptive to the instructional learning process or teachers who are performing at a less than adequate level require a response that may lead to an adjustment in behavior that is acceptable in terms of best practice. Rather than just teaching, Generation Y teachers and principals seem to want to search for ways not only to address the situation that requires the reaction but also to alter it. In other words, they appear to be proactive in addressing issues in a policy manner.

In searching for the answers to problems and issues, Generation Y teachers and administrators appear to be ready and willing to take a multidisciplinary approach. They do not limit themselves to a search of education theory and practice, but are willing to find solutions wherever they can be found.

Generation Y teachers and administrators are capable of *multitasking,* meaning that they can do a good job teaching and mentoring students and engaging colleagues on committees and enjoy being a member of the learning community. They want to have an impact on their students and colleagues. In all these endeavors, they are supportive of the merit pay concept because they believe that such a system motivates and rewards those who want to go beyond just the requirements of being a teacher or an administrator.

Thus, in establishing performance evaluation policies and procedures, these characteristics of Generation Y teachers and administrators should be taken into account by superintendents and human resources administrators. The same criteria for performance are much more effective if they are culturally sensitive in terms of the expectations and values of the multiple generations of employees that are found in most school districts.[10]

Summary

During the twentieth century, U.S. education was concerned with the evaluation of teachers during three historical stages. In the 1920s, efforts were primarily centered on analyzing if a given teaching style correlated with the philosophy and psychology of William James or John Dewey. The second stage was concerned with ascribing certain personality traits as being related to excellence in teaching. In the 1960s, the final stage emphasized generic teaching behaviors.

The past twenty years have ushered in a dramatic change in evaluation procedures. The traditional concept of teacher evaluation has been replaced by the broader concept of evaluation management. Using this approach, an employee is evaluated in terms of whether he or she attains certain preestablished objectives.

The establishment and implementation of an evaluation process for all school district employees is justified in order to foster self-development, identify a variety of tasks that an employee is capable of performing, determine staff development needs, improve employee performance, decide whether an employee should be retained and what his or her salary increase should be, and help in the proper placement or promotion of an employee.

A significant aspect of an employee appraisal process is measuring his or her performance against his or her job responsibilities as outlined in the job description. In developing an evaluation process, the board of education should establish a policy on employee evaluation that gives direction to the various divisions within a school district. These divisions are responsible for developing objectives aimed at implementing the goals of the school board. Each employee is then responsible for developing personal objectives that further the divisional objectives. Consequently, employee performance is measured against the degree to which each individual has attained his or her objectives. Feedback data are then available for use in determining whether divisional objectives have been reached. The actual evaluation procedures for implementing this process are best developed with the involvement of representatives of the employees who will be evaluated.

Some school districts are using the standards developed by the Interstate Teacher Assessment and Support Consortium (InTASC) as a guide in constructing performance-based evaluation instruments. In essence, the standards then become performance criteria. The ten InTASC core standards are considered necessary for all teachers.

As with the development of evaluation procedures, evaluation instruments are more appropriately constructed by the committee process. There are two basic categories of evaluation instruments: trait forms and results forms. The trait approach rates an employee against a predetermined list of traits to ascertain overall performance. The results approach compares an employee's performance to objectives that were developed by the employee and agreed to by his or her supervisor. Using both types of instruments helps identify areas in which improvements are needed.

Termination procedures, an aspect of the evaluation process that is seldom addressed, are extremely important. Because being fired has such a devastating effect on the financial and emotional welfare of an individual, termination procedures must be fair and objective. Most states have statutory provisions outlining the due process that must be afforded teachers before termination. Such legislation, although applying to the professional staff, also provides a model for boards of education in establishing similar procedures for all employees. The educational welfare of students is the primary concern of a school district, but employees also have rights that must be taken into consideration when developing appraisal procedures and dealing with employee dismissal.

Self-Check Quiz Click here to take an automatically-graded self-check quiz.

Discussion Questions and Statements

1. What is the rationale for the performance evaluation of employees?
2. How does performance evaluation benefit both the employee and the school district?
3. Explain how performance evaluation can be an integral component of effective supervision.
4. What type of evaluation report forms do you think are the most effective, and why?
5. Explain the relationship between the performance goals and objectives of the school district and those of individual employees.

Suggested Activities

1. You are the assistant superintendent for human resources in a school district with approximately 500 employees. Develop a due process procedure for the termination of an employee that you believe is humane and also meets the responsibility of the board of education. Write a comparison of your procedure with the statutes that govern the termination process in the state where you live.
2. In writing, compare and contrast these same state statutes and your procedure with the principles for teacher termination in this chapter.
3. Obtain a copy of the evaluation report forms in a school district, and write a comparison of them with the model forms in this chapter.
4. Construct what you think is an ideal administrator evaluation form.

5. Interview a human resources administrator in person or on the telephone about how the performance evaluation and termination processes are interrelated, and further discuss the practical implications of both processes.

Focus Scenario Activity

Given that you have read and studied this chapter, how would you proceed to create a new staff development plan? Also, describe the essential elements in an employee termination process.

Endnotes

1. Marilyn Cochran-Smith, "Teaching Quality Matters," *Journal of Policy, Practice, and Research in Teacher Education*, 54, no. 2 (March/April 2003): 95.
2. David A. DeCenzo and Stephen P. Robins, *Fundamentals of Human Resource Management*, 9th ed. (Hoboken, N J: John Wiley, 2007), 291–293.
3. Carolyn J. Kelley and Kara Finnigan, "The Effects of Organizational Context on Teacher Expectancy," *Educational Administration Quarterly*, 39, no. 5 (December 2003): 618–620.
4. Charlotte Danielson and Thomas L. McGreal, *Teacher Evaluation: To Enhance Professional Practice*, (Princeton, NJ: Educational Testing Service, 2000), 110–114.
5. Council of Chief State School Officers, *New Teacher Assessment and Support Consortium*, (May 2005), www.ccsso.org.
6. North Carolina State Board of Education and Department of Public Instruction, *The InTASC Standards* (May 2005), www.dpi.state.nc.us/pbl/pblintasc.htm.
7. DeCenzo and Robins, *Fundamentals of Human Resource Management*, 100–106.
8. Drug-Free Workplace Act of 1988, www.dol.gov/asp/programs/drugs/workingpartners/regs/dfwp1988asp.
9. Equal Employment Opportunity Commission, www.eeoc.gov.
10. Suzette Lovely and Austin G. Buffum, *Generations at School: Building an Age-Friendly Learning Community*, (Thousand Oaks, CA: Corwin Press, 2007), 75–88.

Selected Bibliography

Barkert, Cornelius I., and Claudette J. Searchwell. *Writing Meaningful Teacher Evaluations—Right Now!! The Principal's Quick-Start Reference Guide.* Thousand Oaks, CA: Corwin Press, 2004.

Barkert, Cornelius I., and Claudette J. Searchwell. *Writing Year-End Teacher Improvement Plans—Right Now!! The Principal's Time-Saving Reference Guide*, 2nd ed. Thousand Oaks, CA: Corwin Press, 2008.

Cederblom, Doug, and Dan E. Pemerl. "From Performance Appraisal to Performance Management: One Agency's Experience." *Public Personnel Management*, 31, no. 2 (Summer 2002): 131–140.

Coppola, Albert J., Diane B. Scricca, and Gerard E. Connors. *Supportive Supervision: Becoming a Teacher of Teachers.* Thousand Oaks, CA: Corwin Press and the National Association of Secondary School Principals, 2004.

Dana, Nancy Fichtman, and Diane Yendol-Hoppey. *The Reflective Educator's Guide to Classroom Research: Learning to Teach and Teaching to Learn through Practitioner Inquiry*, 2nd ed. Thousand Oaks, CA: Corwin Press, 2009.

Danielson, Charlotte, and Thomas L. McGreal. *Teacher Evaluation: To Enhance Professional Practice.* Princeton, NJ: Educational Testing Service, 2000.

Daresh, John C. *Leading and Supervising Instruction.* Thousand Oaks, CA: Corwin Press, 2006.

Downey, Carolyn J., Betty E. Steffy, Fenwick W. English, Larry E. Frase, and William K. Poston, Jr. *The Three-Minute Classroom Walk-Through: Changing School Supervisory Practice One Teacher at a Time.* Thousand Oaks, CA: Corwin Press, 2004.

Glickman, Carl D., Stephen P. Gordon, and Jovita M. Ross-Gordon. *SuperVision and Instructional Leadership: A Developmental Approach*, 6th ed. Boston: Allyn & Bacon, 2004.

Gullickson, Arlen R. *The Personnel Evaluation Standards: How to Assess Systems for Evaluating Educators*, 2nd ed. Thousand Oaks, CA: Corwin Press, 2008.

Hall, Susan L. *Implementing Response to Intervention: A Principal's Guide.* Thousand Oaks, CA: Corwin Press, 2008.

Ho, Andrew Dean. "The Problem with 'Proficiency': Limitations of Statistics and Policy under No Child Left Behind." *Educational Researcher*, 37, no. 6 (August/September 2008): 351–361.

Hursh, David. *High-Stakes Testing and the Decline of Teaching and Learning: The Real Crisis in Education.* Lanham, MD: Rowman & Littlefield, 2008.

Jha, S., & Bhattacharyya, S. "Study of Perceived Recruitment Practices and Their Relationships to Job Satisfaction." *Synergy (0973–8819)*, 10, no. 1 (2012): 63–76.

Kelley, Carolyn, Herbert Heneman III, and Anthony Milanowski. "Teacher Motivation and School-Based Performance Awards." *Educational Administration Quarterly*, 38, no. 3 (August 2002): 372–401.

Kennedy, Mary M. "Contributions of Qualitative Research to Research on Teacher Qualifications." *Educational Evaluation and Policy Analysis*, 30, no. 4 (December 2008): 344–368.

Lawrence, C. Edward. *The Marginal Teacher: A Step-by-Step Guide to Fair Procedures for Identification and Dismissal*, 3rd ed. Thousand Oaks, CA: Corwin Press, 2005.

Love, Nancy, ed. *Using Data to Improve Learning for All: A Collaborative Inquiry Approach.* Thousand Oaks, CA: Corwin Press, 2009.

Margulus, Lisabeth S., and Jacquelyn Ann Melin. *Performance Appraisals Made Easy: Tools for Evaluating Teachers and Support Staff.* Thousand Oaks, CA: Corwin Press, 2004.

McEwan, Elaine K. *Ten Traits of Highly Effective Teachers: How to Hire, Coach, and Mentor Successful Teachers.* Thousand Oaks, CA: Corwin Press, 2002.

McEwan, Elaine K. *How to Deal with Teachers Who Are Angry, Troubled, Exhausted, or Just Plain Confused.* Thousand Oaks, CA: Corwin Press, 2005.

McMillan, James H. *Formative Classroom Assessment.* New York: Teachers College Press, 2007.

Peterson, Kenneth D., and Catherine A. Peterson. *Effective Teacher Evaluation.* Thousand Oaks, CA: Corwin Press, 2006.

Saginor, Nicole. *Diagnostic Classroom Observation: Moving Beyond Best Practice*, Thousand Oaks, CA: Corwin Press, 2008.

Stronge, James H. *Evaluating Teaching: A Guide to Current Thinking and Best Practice*, 2nd ed. Thousand Oaks, CA: Corwin Press, 2006.

Sullivan, Susan, and Jeffrey Glanz. *Supervision That Improves Teaching: Strategies and Techniques*, 2nd ed. Thousand Oaks, CA: Corwin Press, 2004.

Tobias, Sigmund, and Thomas M. Duffy, eds. *Constructivist Theory Applied to Instruction: Success or Failure.* New York: Routledge, 2009.

Wiles, Jon W. *Supervision: A Guide to Practice*, 6th ed. Upper Saddle River, NJ: Merrill/Prentice Hall, 2004.

Wilkerson, Judy R., and William Steve Lang. *Assessing Teacher Competency: Five Standards-Based Steps to Valid Measurement Using the DAATS Model.* Thousand Oaks, CA: Corwin Press, 2007.

Wilkerson, Judy R., and William Steve Lang. *Assessing Teacher Dispositions: Five Standards-Based Steps to Valid Measurement Using the DAATS Model*. Thousand Oaks, CA: Corwin Press, 2007.

Woo, Yen Yen Joyceln. "Combining Qualitative and Quantitative Methodologies in Research on Teachers' Lives, Work, and Effectiveness: From Integration to Synergy." *Educational Researcher* 37, no. 6 (August/September 2008): 321–330.

Appendix A
Teacher Performance Evaluation Report Forms
and Performance Indicators[*]

LINDBERGH SCHOOL DISTRICT

4900 So. Lindbergh Blvd.
St. Louis, MO 63126

TEACHER EVALUATION REPORT

Teacher _____ School _____ Year _____

Subject or grade _____ Years in system _____

Status of Teacher   ( ) Probationary   ( ) Tenure

Philosophy Evaluation is a means of improving the quality of instruction.

Purposes

1. To improve the quality of teaching and service to students
2. To enable the teacher to recognize her/his role in the total school program
3. To assist the teacher in achieving the established goals of the curriculum
4. To help the teacher identify her/his strengths and weaknesses as a personal guide for her/his improvement
5. To provide assistance to the teacher to help correct weaknesses
6. To recognize the teacher's special talents and to encourage and facilitate their utilization
7. To serve as a guide for renewed employment, termination of employment, promotion, assignment, and unrequested leave for tenured teachers
8. To protect the teacher from dismissal without just cause
9. To protect the teaching profession from unethical and incompetent personnel

Implementation

The evaluation is to be made by the building principal, grade principal, assistant principal, or acting principal. If a teacher does not agree with an evaluation, she/he may request an additional evaluation to be made by another administrator of her/his choice.

Evaluation of a probationary (nontenured) teacher's services will be made semiannually during the probationary period, with one of the evaluations completed during the first semester, and both completed before April 1. Each evaluation must be preceded by at least one classroom visit.

Continued

---

[*]*Source:* Adapted from Lindbergh School District, St. Louis, Missouri, 1985.

Evaluation of a permanent (tenured) teacher's services will be made every year with the evaluation completed before April 1. Each evaluation must be preceded by at least one classroom visit.

Definition of terms

1. *Superior:* Consistently exceptional
2. *Strong:* Usually surpasses standards of Lindbergh School District
3. *Average:* Generally meets standards of Lindbergh School District
4. *Improvement needed:* Occasionally does not meet standards of Lindbergh School District
5. *Unsatisfactory:* Does not measure up to standards of Lindbergh School District

NOTE: The space at the end of this form marked "Principal's Comments" may be used to record the observations of the teacher's exceptional performances and/or to record the principal's recommendations for improvement.

The space at the end of this form marked "Teacher's Comments" may be used by the teacher to record any comment or comments that she/he wants to make.

	Superior	Strong	Average	I-N	Unsatis-factory
	1	2	3	4	5

I. TEACHING PERFORMANCE

A. Plans and organizes carefully
1. Develops well-planned lesson
2. Sets definite goals, including student participation
3. Makes clear, specific assignments
4. Is familiar with appropriate guide and adapts to the recommendations therein
5. Provides for individual and group instruction

B. Is skillful in questioning and explaining
1. Asks thought-provoking questions
2. Gives clear explanation of subject matter
3. Exposes students to varying points of view
4. Is aware of both verbal and nonverbal acceptance or rejection of student's ideas, and uses this skill positively

C. Stimulates learning through innovative activities and resources
1. Encourages class discussion, pupil questions, and pupil demonstrations
2. Uses a variety of teaching aids and resources

	Superior	Strong	Average	I-N	Unsatis-factory
D. Displays knowledge of and enthusiasm for subject matter taught					
E. Provides a classroom atmosphere conducive to good learning					
1. Maintains a healthy and flexible environment					
2. Observes the care of instructional material and equipment					
F. Keeps adequate and accurate records					
1. Records sufficient quantitative and qualitative data on which to base pupil progress reports					
G. Has wholesome relationship with pupils					
1. Knows and works with pupils as individuals					
2. Encourages relationships that are mutually respectful and friendly					
3. Uses positive language with students that is devoid of sarcasm					
H. Initiates and preserves classroom and general school management and discipline					
1. Rules of pupil conduct have been developed, and teacher requires observance of these rules					
2. Rules of safety have been developed, and teacher requires observance of these rules					

II. PROFESSIONAL QUALITIES

	Superior	Strong	Average	I-N	Unsatis-factory
A. Recognition and acceptance of out-of-class responsibilities					
1. Participates in the general and necessary school activities					
2. Sometimes volunteers for the "extra" duties					
3. Serves on school committees					
B. Intraschool relationship					
1. Cooperates effectively and pleasantly with colleagues, administration, and nonprofessional personnel					
C. Public relations					
1. Cooperates effectively and pleasantly with parents					
2. Practices good relationships between school and community					

Continued

	Superior	Strong	Average	I-N	Unsatis-factory
D. Professional growth and vision					
1. Accepts constructive criticism					
2. Participates in conferences, workshops, and studies					
3. Tries new methods and materials					
E. Utilization of staff services					
1. Makes proper use of available special services					
F. Understands the growth patterns and behaviors of students at various stages of development and copes satisfactorily with situations as they occur					
G. Ethical behavior					
1. Protects professional use of confidential data					
2. Supports the teaching profession					

Definition of Terms for Personal Qualities

S *Satisfactory:* Meets or surpasses standard for Lindbergh School District teachers

I *Improvement needed:* Does not measure up to standards Lindbergh School District teachers meet

	S	I
III. PERSONAL QUALITIES		
A. Health and vigor		
1. Has a good and reasonable attendance record		
2. Is cheerful		
3. Displays a sense of humor		
B. Speech		
1. Is articulate		
2. Can be heard and understood by all pupils in the room		
3. Speaks on the level of pupils' understanding		
C. Grooming and appropriateness of dress		
1. Practices habits of good grooming		
D. Promptness in meeting obligations		
1. Reports to classes on time		
2. Performs assigned tasks properly		
3. Completes reports on time		

A copy of the written evaluation will be submitted to the teacher at the time of the conference following the observation(s). The final evaluation report form is to be signed and retained by the principal, and a copy is to be retained by the teacher. In the event the teacher believes that the evaluation was incomplete, inaccurate, or unjust, she/he may put the objections in writing for attachment to the evaluation report that will be placed in her/his personal files. The teacher's signature acknowledges that the conference has taken place.

DATE OF OBSERVATION(S) _____

TIME OF OBSERVATION(S) _____

LENGTH OF OBSERVATION(S) _____

DATE OF EVALUATION _____

PRINCIPAL'S SIGNATURE _____

TEACHER'S SIGNATURE _____

PRINCIPAL'S COMMENTS _____

TEACHER COMMENTS _____

Performance Indicators

Indicators for the evaluation items in the Teacher Evaluation Report were developed by the administrators in the Lindbergh School District. The indicators are representative of the kinds of teacher learning techniques the evaluator will be looking for when observing a teacher in a classroom situation. It is expected that each teacher will perform the skill as listed, but that the final evaluation will be based on the degree of performance.

I. TEACHING PERFORMANCE

A. Plans and organizes carefully

1. *Develops well-planned lesson*
   a. Written plans are available and followed by classroom teacher.
   b. Lesson includes preview, statement of objective, and review.
   c. Lesson fits within an allotted time frame.
   d. Lesson follows a logical sequence.
   e. Lesson meets the needs of the student group.
   f. Long- and short-range goals are clearly defined.
   g. Lesson indicates the teacher has used the concept of diagnosis and prescription.
   h. Lesson is flexible to permit spontaneous teaching.
   i. Plans and procedures are provided.
   j. Materials and equipment are readily available.
2. *Sets definite goals, including student participation*
   a. Long- and short-range goals are clearly defined.
   b. Students are involved in the goal-setting process when appropriate.

Continued

3. *Makes clear, specific assignments*
   a. Reasonable and clear assignments are given in written form.
   b. Adequate time is given for clarification and discussion of assignment.
4. *Is familiar with appropriate guide and adapts to the recommendation therein*
   a. Lesson reflects thorough knowledge of curriculum guide.
   b. Long-range planning for coverage of objectives in curriculum guide is indicated.
5. *Provides for individual and group instruction*
   a. Lesson provides for individual instruction.
   b. Lesson provides for group instruction.
   c. Type of instruction is suited to lesson presented.

B. Is skillful in questioning and explaining
1. *Asks thought-provoking questions*
   a. Questions asked require more than a one-word answer.
   b. Questions stimulate critical and divergent thinking.
   c. Written questions are thought provoking.
   d. Questions asked stimulate a response from students.
2. *Gives clear explanation of subject matter*
   a. Obtains response indicating understanding before continuing further explanation.
   b. Presents ideas in a logical sequence.
   c. Consistently uses correct grammar and vocabulary suited to student.
   d. Presents accurate and complete content information.
3. *Exposes students to varying points of view*
   a. Establishes a background of general information on the topic before presenting varying points of view.
   b. Presents varying points of view consistent with curriculum.
   c. Elicits students' points of view.
4. *Is aware of both verbal and nonverbal acceptance or rejection of students' ideas, and uses this skill positively*
   a. Does not show rejection through verbal or physical expression.
   b. Does not allow peer rejection.
   c. Praises, elicits, and responds to student questions and answers before proceeding.

C. Stimulates learning through innovative activities and resources
1. *Encourages class discussion, pupil questions, and pupil demonstrations*
   a. Listens patiently to students' comments, questions, and answers.
   b. Questions are asked according to students' ability to answer correctly.
   c. Gives each student an opportunity to participate.
2. *Uses a variety of teaching aids and resources*
   a. Looks for and uses models, manipulative materials, films, outside speeches, worksheets, records, etc.
   b. Materials and resources are appropriate for the lesson.
   c. Displays materials that are coordinated with the lesson.

D. Displays knowledge of and enthusiasm for subject matter taught
1. *Displays knowledge of subject matter taught*
   a. Displays knowledge of content of textbook(s).
   b. Demonstrates competence and familiarity with subject matter.
   c. Has comprehensive knowledge of related disciplines and uses it when appropriate.
   d. Answers students' questions readily and thoroughly.

      e. Probes for knowledge of content presented (encourages questions and activities that are designed to stimulate critical thinking).

      f. Goes beyond the textbook to enhance the content (may be observed by use of films, resource persons, reference materials, charts, etc.).

  2. *Displays enthusiasm for subject matter taught*

      a. Students respond positively to the teacher (Do the students appear interested? Are they listening to the teacher? Are they awake? Are they talking to other students? Do they appear bored?).

      b. Interest and enthusiasm are evidenced from the teacher's presentation.

      c. Responds positively to the students, both verbally and visually.

      d. Elicits enthusiastic response from the students to the questions and answers.

      e. Uses techniques that engender enthusiasm in students (a change of pace, voice inflections, body movement).

E. Provides a classroom atmosphere conducive to good learning

  1. *Maintains a healthy and flexible environment*

      a. Sets the tone for students to feel free to ask and respond to questions (students are not intimidated).

      b. Classroom atmosphere is controlled but not dominated by the teacher (students interact with the environment).

      c. Differing views and values are discussed.

      d. Positive interpersonal relationships are easily observed.

      e. Uses humor in proper perspective.

      f. Room reflects students' work.

  2. *Observes the care of instructional material and equipment*

      a. Equipment in use is carefully supervised.

      b. Equipment or material not in use is properly stored.

      c. Equipment is properly maintained and/or reported to the office for repair.

      d. Desks are devoid of writing and graffiti.

      e. Promotes respect for instructional materials and equipment.

F. Keeps adequate and accurate records

  1. *Records sufficient quantitative and qualitative data on which to base pupil progress reports*

      a. Records a number of written assignments, test scores, daily grades, and exam grades in the grade book (indicators of each student's performance).

      b. Quality of data recorded shows relationship between the objectives and grades.

      c. Daily attendance is correctly recorded.

G. Has wholesome relationship with pupils

  1. *Knows and works with pupils as individuals*

      a. Individual strengths and weaknesses of each student have been identified.

      b. Knows and calls each student by name.

      c. Listens carefully and politely to each student.

      d. Encourages student ideas and concentrates on sutdent's response.

      e. Students do not hesitate to ask for clarification.

      f. Students appear to be an active part of the class.

      g. Creative responses are encouraged.

Continued

2. *Encourages relationships that are mutually respectful and friendly*
   a. Encourages positive behavior by maintaining complete control of self.
   b. Words and actions are positive.
   c. Exhibits qualities of warmth toward students.
   d. Elicits student responses.
   e. Sets an example of respect.
   f. Is sensitive to students' moods.
   g. Behavior is consistent with all students and situations.
   h. Handling of misconduct centers on the conduct or behavior, not the student.
   i. Requires student attention and gives attention in return.
3. *Uses positive language with students that is devoid of sarcasm*
   a. Praises and elicits responses from students.
   b. Sarcasm is not used.
   c. Is positive in actions, voice tones, and movements.
   d. Tone of voice is moderate and even.

H. Initiates and preserves classroom and general school management and discipline

1. *Rules of pupil conduct have been developed and teacher requires observance of these rules*
   a. Classroom incidents handled so as not to interrupt entire class.
   b. Pupils are aware of rules and regulations.
   c. Students understand and follow room routine readily without teacher's direction.
   d. Demonstrates behavior that is achievement oriented or businesslike.
   e. Is consistent and fair in expectations of behavior.
   f. Students enter room quietly and take seats.
   g. Students ask and receive permission to change patterns.
2. *Rules of safety have been developed and teacher requires observance of these rules*
   a. Classroom behavior shows a concern for safety.
   b. Safety procedures are properly posted and followed.
   c. Horseplay is not tolerated.
   d. Plays an active and positive role in the supervision of halls, restrooms, lunchrooms, and pre/post class time as well as at assemblies.
   e. Classroom is free of hazards.

II. PROFESSIONAL QUALITIES

A. Recognition and acceptance of out-of-class responsibilities

1. *Participates in the general and necessary school activities*
   a. Performs assigned duties consistently.
   b. Follows the school time schedule.
   c. Attends and participates in school-related activities.
   d. Participates in assigned meetings.
2. *Sometimes volunteers for the "extra" duties*
   a. Accepts responsibilities other than those considered general or necessary.
   b. Initiates volunteer services to the overall school program.

3. *Serves on school committees*
   a. Serves on district and/or school committees.
   b. Attends school and/or district committee meetings.
   c. Participates in school and/or district-level committees.

B. Intraschool relationship

1. *Cooperates effectively and pleasantly with colleagues, administration, and non-professional personnel*
   a. Relationships with other professionals indicate acceptance of differing views or values.
   b. Practices relationships that are mutually respectful and friendly.
   c. Shares ideas, materials, and methods.
   d. Informs appropriate personnel of school-related matters.
   e. Cooperates fairly and works well with all school personnel.
   f. Is effective in providing a climate that encourages communication between self and professional colleagues.

C. Public relations

1. *Cooperates effectively and pleasantly with parents*
   a. Maintains good communication with parents.
   b. Keeps best interest of student in mind.
   c. Provides a climate that opens up communication between the teacher and parent.
2. *Practices good relationships between school and community*
   a. Enhances school involvement with communities.
   b. Encourages community involvement and attendance in school situations.

D. Professional growth and vision

1. *Accepts constructive criticism*
   a. Asks positive questions.
   b. Responds pleasantly to criticism.
2. *Participates in conferences, workshops, and studies*
   a. Is engaged in activities that promote professional growth.
   b. Engages in professional activities that are not required.
3. *Tries new methods and materials*
   a. Uses new methods and materials at appropriate times.
   b. Modifies materials when needed.
   c. Understands new techniques before using.

E. Utilization of staff services

1. *Makes proper use of available special services*
   a. Makes use of and cooperates with district service personnel (guidance, library, supervisory, specialists, as well as classified staff members).
   b. Makes student recommendations and referrals to appropriate staff members as needed.

F. Understands the growth patterns and behaviors of students at various stages of development and copes satisfactorily with situations as they occur

a. Uses a variety of techniques to achieve desired work and skills, and adjusts the techniques to the age and maturity of the student.

Continued

    b. Does not expect identical behavior from all students, but allows for individual differences.

    c. Is understanding and sympathetic to students with special learning and behavior problems.

G. Ethical behavior

    1. *Protects professional use of confidential data*

      a. Confidential information concerning students and their parents and staff members is not discussed in the lounge, cafeteria, or classroom.

      b. Respects confidential information.

    2. *Supports the teaching profession*

      a. Has a positive attitude toward teaching.

      b. Uses positive statements regarding teaching, students, school, and profession.

III. PERSONAL QUALITIES

A. Health and vigor

    1. *Has a good and reasonable attendance record*

      a. Absences are infrequent and justifiable.

      b. Places emphasis on assigned duties.

      c. Except in cases of extreme illness, is present at school and is prepared.

    2. *Is cheerful*

      a. Allows occasional humorous interruptions.

      b. Can relax and joke with students.

      c. Laughs with, not at, others.

    3. *Displays a sense of humor*

      a. Smiles easily.

      b. Has a friendly attitude.

B. Speech

    1. *Is articulate*

      a. Consistently uses appropriate grammar.

      b. Communicates clearly.

    2. *Can be heard and understood by all pupils in the room*

      a. Consistently uses appropriate tone of voice.

      b. Is easy to hear and understand.

    3. *Speaks on the level of pupils' understanding*

      a. Uses appropriate vocabulary and examples according to student's level of understanding.

C. Grooming and appropriateness of dress

    1. *Practices habits of good grooming*

      a. Is clean and neat.

      b. Clothes are appropriate for job task.

      c. Dress adds to rather than detracts from classroom performance.

D. Promptness in meeting obligations

    1. *Reports to classes on time*

      a. Arrives at classroom before students.

      b. Classroom is open and in readiness prior to student arrival.

    c. Classroom preparations do not interfere with obligations.
    d. Arrives in the building at the required time.

2. *Performs assigned tasks properly*
    a. Tasks are completed on time.
    b. Tasks are completed to letter and in spirit of the assignment.

3. *Completes reports on time*
    a. Does not have to be reminded of reports that are due.
    b. Completes reports according to expectations of administrator.

LINDBERGH SCHOOL DISTRICT

4900 So. Lindbergh Blvd.
St. Louis, MO 63126

SHORT CLASSROOM VISIT FORM

The purpose of this form is to record data that will be pertinent in the overall evaluation of the teacher. The form will be used in conjunction with the Teacher Evaluation Report.

TEACHER _____ DATE OF VISIT _____
LENGTH OF VISIT _____ PERIOD _____

1. Did the lesson appear to be well planned? _____
   Topic being discussed _____
2. Was enthusiasm evidenced in the teacher's presentation? _____
_____
3. Class reaction to the lesson _____
   Were the students involved? _____ Did they appear to be interested in the lesson?
_____
4. Describe the type of interactions between the teacher and students, and students with students _____
5. Was there any unusual activity taking place? _____
6. Was there anything unusual about the physical appearance of the room? _____
_____
7. Were personal qualities positive? _____
_____

(speech, dress, grooming)

Principal's suggestions, comments _____
_____
_____

_____
Principal's Signature

Appendix B
Administrator Performance Evaluation Report[*]

Administrator Evaluation Report

ADMINISTRATOR _____ YEAR _____

POSITION _____ SCHOOL _____

YEARS IN LINDBERGH ADMINISTRATION _____

Purposes

Evaluation is to ensure that the administrator displays adequate management skills and leadership among the students, staff, and community. The evaluation process will ensure that the administrator has goals appropriate to his or her level of responsibility and in line with overall school system goals. This process will aid the administrator in the improvement of his or her performance and provide a basis for merit pay adjustment.

Implementation

1. The superintendent will evaluate all building principals.
2. Evaluation of grade principals and assistant principals will be made by the building principal. The superintendent will review these evaluations and confer with the principal prior to the formal evaluation.
3. The evaluator will receive appropriate input from all central office administrators prior to completing the evaluation.
4. Administrators will be evaluated on the standards and expectations of Lindbergh School District.
5. The evaluation will be made on a scale of 1 to 9 ranging from improvement needed to consistently outstanding.
6. The overall rating will not be adversely affected by items marked not applicable.
7. The formal evaluation will take place following the close of the school year.

ADMINISTRATIVE SKILLS	Consistently Outstanding							Needs Improvement	NA
1. Has implemented procedures for budget preparation and accounting methods for monitoring the budget									
2. Has implemented a plan for the effective cleaning and maintenance of the facility									
3. Has implemented a process for inventorying, acquiring, and replacing of equipment									
4. Has implemented safety and energy conservation procedures									
5. Has established procedures for the use of student, teacher, and parent feedback									

---

[*]*Source:* Adapted from Lindbergh School District, St. Louis, Missouri, 1985.

ADMINISTRATIVE SKILLS	Consistently Outstanding						Needs Improvement	NA
6. Has developed and follows procedures for administrative scheduling and reporting								
7. Has completed written communications accurately and on schedule								

Total points _____ ÷ _____ number of items marked = _____ average marking.

INSTRUCTIONAL LEADERSHIP	Consistently Outstanding						Needs Improvement	NA
1. Has demonstrated knowledge of curricular issues in various subject areas								
2. Has assisted classroom teacher in the implementation of the curriculum								
3. Has evaluated the instructional program and used the results to plan program improvements								
4. Has knowledge of good teaching methods and assists teachers to improve diagnostic skills and teaching strategies								
5. Has carried out procedures to evaluate and maintain a building climate conducive to learning								

Total points _____ ÷ _____ number of items marked = _____ average marking.

SUPERVISION	Consistently Outstanding						Needs Improvement	NA
1. Has coordinated the work of special and support personnel with the programs of the school								
2. Has conducted a program of faculty and staff supervision that includes periodic visits, conferences, and evaluation of all personnel								
3. Has carried out a procedure for the orientation and supervision of all new personnel								

Continued

SUPERVISION	Consistently Outstanding						Needs Improvement	NA
4. Has developed and implemented procedures to maintain effective school discipline								
5. Has maintained a system of supervision of all after school activities								

Total points _____ ÷ _____ number of items marked = _____ average marking.

SCHOOL AND COMMUNITY	Consistently Outstanding						Needs Improvement	NA
1. Has promoted good relationships between the school and community through positive interpretation and implementation of district policy								
2. Has conducted a comprehensive and effective system of communication with the students of the school								
3. Has conducted a comprehensive and effective system of communication with the parents of the school								
4. Has coordinated and maintained a volunteer program in the school								
5. Has participated in various civic, service, and community groups and functions to help assure public knowledge and understanding of the school program								
6. Has provided support and guidance to PTO, Mothers' Club, and other parent groups								

Total points _____ ÷ _____ number of items marked = _____ average marking.

PERSONAL QUALITIES	Consistently Outstanding						Needs Improvement	NA
1. Has exhibited professional growth through staff development activities, conferences and conventions, membership and participation in professional organizations, and continuing formal education.								
2. Has displayed appropriate decision-making skills by recognizing problems, evaluating facts, and implementing decisions								

PERSONAL QUALITIES	Consistently Outstanding						Needs Improvement	NA
3. Has displayed good personal relationships with administration, faculty, staff, parents, and students								
4. Has evidenced personal and professional ethics in all relationships								
5. Has shown sustained effort and enthusiasm in the quality and quantity of work accomplished								

Total points _____ ÷ _____ number of items marked = _____ average marking.

Building Priorities

Each building priority is rated separately on a combination of the following criteria:

1. Building priorities are identified with input from teachers, students, and/or parents.
2. The design to meet each priority is clearly written with definitive steps and a timetable.
3. Periodic review of progress toward accomplishing each priority is carried out, and necessary adjustments are made during the year.

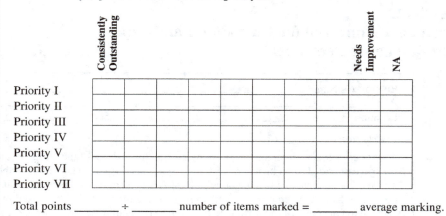

	Consistently Outstanding						Needs Improvement	NA
Priority I								
Priority II								
Priority III								
Priority IV								
Priority V								
Priority VI								
Priority VII								

Total points _____ ÷ _____ number of items marked = _____ average marking.

4. Accomplishment of building priorities involves participation and input from the school faculty and other affected groups when appropriate.
5. Each priority is completed according to the timetable and definitive steps in the original written design. Deviations from that design are stated and explained.

Rating System

1. The *average marking* in each category is multiplied by the percentage weight given that area.
2. The weighted scores for each area are added. The sum will fall in a range from 1 to 9. The total score will be carried out to the third decimal place.
3. The sum of the weighted scores is applied directly to the merit portion of the administrators' salary schedule.

Continued

	Average Marking	Percentage Weight	Weighted Score
Administrative Skills	_____ ×	.10	_____
Instructional Leadership	_____ ×	.20	_____
Supervision	_____ ×	.20	_____
School and Community	_____ ×	.10	_____
Personal Qualities	_____ ×	.10	_____
Building Priorities	_____ ×	.30	_____
		Total	_____

EVALUATOR'S COMMENTS:

ADMINISTRATOR'S COMMENTS:

Evaluator's Signature _____ Date _____
Administrator's Signature _____ Date _____

Appendix C
Performance Appraisal for Custodial, Landscape, and Maintenance Personnel[*]

Employee's Name _____
Position _____
Location _____ School Year _____

Instructions

The supervisor is to complete this form by placing the number of the rating for each item in the space provided. If an item is rated 1 or 2, then a statement is to be written in the comment area clarifying what needs to be done to improve. A form is to be completed at the end of three months on new employees, and a second evaluation is to be completed by June 1 of each year. One copy of the form is to be given to the employee, and a second copy is to be sent to the personnel department for placement in the employee's file.

   I. *Quality of Work*   Rating _____
      Indicators: Neatness, accuracy, consistency of quality.
      5. Exceptionally neat and accurate. Practically no mistakes.
      4. Usually accurate. Very neat. Seldom necessary to check work.
      3. Acceptable. Usually neat. Occasional errors—some supervision required.
      2. Acceptable work if closely supervised.
      1. Unacceptable work. Too many errors.

      Comment: _____

[*]*Source:* Adapted from Lindbergh School District, St. Louis, Missouri, 1985.

II. *Job Knowledge*   Rating _____
   Indicators: Experience, special training, education.
   5. Well informed on all phases of the job.
   4. Knowledge is thorough enough to perform without assistance.
   3. Knows job fairly well.
   2. Requires assistance frequently.
   1. Inadequate knowledge.

   Comment: _____
   _____

III. *Quantity of Work*   Rating _____
   Indicators: Amount of work required under normal conditions.
   5. Exceptional quantity. Rapid worker. Usually good production.
   4. Good volume—will do more than is expected.
   3. Average volume—does what is expected.
   2. Does not always complete expected amount of work.
   1. Slow worker. Frequently does not complete duties.

   Comment: _____
   _____

IV. *Dependability*   Rating _____
   Indicators: Tasks are completed on time.
   5. Work is always completed on time.
   4. Work is almost always completed on time.
   3. Work is usually completed on time.
   2. Work is completed on time only under close supervision.
   1. Work is rarely completed on time.

   Comment: _____
   _____

V. *Initiative*   Rating _____
   Indicators: Develops new ideas, develops efficient ways of doing jobs, takes charge
   when something needs to be done, is self-reliant.
   5. Highly motivated and contributes new ideas frequently. Does other jobs without
      being told.
   4. Very resourceful. Can work on own. Occasionally contributes new ideas and
      methods. Does small jobs without being told.
   3. Does job very well. Will do other jobs when told to.
   2. Rarely volunteers to help in other areas. Usually waits for instructions.
   1. Needs constant supervision. Not motivated. Displays little interest in improving.
      Does only what is told to do.

   Comment: _____
   _____

VI. *Cooperation and Relationship with Others*   Rating _____
   Indicators: How employee works with coworkers, supervisors, subordinates,
   parents, teachers, students, visitors.
   5. Goes out of the way to cooperate with others. Always has a positive attitude.
      Takes and gives instructions easily.
   4. Gets along well with others. Does not complain about others. Good attitude.

Continued

3. Satisfactory relationship with others and only occasionally complains.
2. Shows reluctance to cooperate and complains often.
1. Very poor cooperation. Does not follow instructions. Complains often.

Comment: _____

_____

VII. *Ability to Learn*   Rating _____
     Indicators: Speed of understanding new routines, ability to understand explanations, how well instructions are carried out, ability to retain knowledge.
     5. Exceptional ability to learn assigned work and adjust to new conditions.
     4. Learns rapidly. Follows instructions well. Retains instructions.
     3. Usually understands instructions and masters new ideas reasonably well.
     2. Requires extra instruction. Necessary to repeat instructions.
     1. Very slow to understand instructions. Cannot remember instructions. Very slow to master new ideas.

     Comment: _____

     _____

VIII. *Attendance*   Rating _____
      Indicators: Number of days of absenteeism, number of tardies (consider the reasons for absenteeisms).
      5. Less than three days absent and less than three days tardy.
      4. Three or four days absent and less than three days tardy.
      3. Five or six days absent and less than five days tardy.
      2. Seven or eight days absent and less than seven days tardy.
      1. Nine or more days absent and more than six days tardy.

      Comment: _____

      _____

IX. *Appearance*   Rating _____
    Indicators: Cleanliness, appropriate dress (uniforms where applicable).
    5. Always neat and clean and appropriately dressed.
    4. Almost always neat and clean and appropriately dressed.
    3. Usually neat and clean and appropriately dressed.
    2. Usually neat and clean but not appropriately dressed.
    1. Often not neat and clean and often carelessly dressed.

    Comment: _____

    _____

Directions for Overall Evaluation

1. Add the ratings for all nine categories.   _____
2. Divide by nine.   _____
3. Circle the category that corresponds to the average.

4.6–5.0	Doing an excellent job.
3.6–4.5	Doing a very good job.
2.6–3.5	Doing a satisfactory job.
1.6–2.5	Work needs to be improved.
1.0–1.5	Work is unacceptable.

Employee Comments: _____

_____

_____

_____

_____

_____

_____   _____
Signature of Supervisor   Signature of Employee

_____   _____
Date   Date

Employee's signature indicates the employee has had this form reviewed with him/her. The signature does not indicate agreement. An employee may appeal the decision of the supervisor to the next line supervisor. The decision of the superintendent is final.

CHAPTER 8

Compensation

Focus Scenario

You are the director of employee benefits in a school district that is experiencing a short-age of qualified teachers and other support employees. After conducting informal tele-phone interviews with qualified candidates who did not accept the district's offer of employment or who dropped out of the selection process, it is clear that one of the reasons was that other school districts in the same vicinity have higher salaries and better fringe benefits. Further, the reputation of the district that has been circulated within the larger education community gives the impression that the district does not value its employees. Also troubling is that the district appears to lack support from the community because a bond issue referendum, which was needed to build an addition to the middle school, failed.

The fiscal accountability of the administration was called into question by the local newspaper last year when the teachers were only given a 2-percent salary increase and the fringe benefits package for employees' dependents increased by 18 percent. Also appear-ing in the newspaper, and perhaps the most damaging issue to the district's reputation, was information concerning the superintendent's contract. Per this contract, the superintendent was provided with a district-owned automobile, an annuity, and paid medical and hospital insurance for his wife and children.

Please use both the "Discussion Questions and Statements" and "Suggested Activi-ties" at the end of this chapter to help you develop a way of proceeding in addressing the issues in this section.

Compensation

Before engaging in any activity, most people consider the same question: *What will I get out of this?* Psychologists have long recognized that satisfaction of needs is the motivation behind all actions. This satisfaction or reward might be money, a promotion, recognition, accept-ance, the receipt of information, or the feeling that comes from doing a good job.[1]

This self-interest motive often carries a negative connotation, yet it is a reality of life. People act in ways that they perceive to be in their own best interests. Whether a given act is truly in an individual's best interest is irrelevant; what counts is that he or she believes it to be so. Even if an action appears to be irrational, such as handing in a resignation because of a minor misunderstanding at work, the act may be in keeping with what the individual resigning believes to be in his or her best interest.

From an administrative standpoint, managers can develop a unique compensation system if they understand what their employees believe to be in their best interests. Not all individuals value the same type of compensation. Consequently, a compensation program must be flexible enough to meet the expectations of individual employees. It is also necessary to structure a compensation program in such a way that people realize they are acting in their own best interests when they are acting in the best interest of the school district. This exemplifies the importance of compensation in a *performance-based* model, which uses incentives as the foundation of a compensation program. This is also an approach that minimizes the *membership-based* type of program, which increases compensation for teachers, administrators, and staff members as a result of seniority and credentials. The membership approach extends salary increases and fringe benefit improvement regardless of the level of an employee's performance. Thus, because of this model, several things become clear:

- Compensation must be linked to behaviors that the school system classifies as desirable.
- Employees should recognize that good job performance is compatible with self-interest.
- Employees should recognize that the compensation system will also satisfy their own needs.
- Administrators must analyze and interpret the needs of the employees.

The fourth statement requires further explanation. In recommending that administrators analyze and interpret employees' needs, the major question that arises is how this can best be accomplished.

The most obvious way of learning about an individual's needs is to ask the person. However, some people do not always understand their own needs and self-interests; others find it difficult to put such needs into words. The most immediate way for an administrator to learn about employees' needs is to observe and develop an awareness of employee behaviors. Behavior is usually a stronger indicator than the verbal utterances of employees. Unfortunately, developing skill in interpreting behavior takes time and practice. The only reliable method of identifying needs is through social scientific research aimed at determining patterns of needs, quantified and analyzed through statistical applications. A number of consulting firms are capable of providing this service, and some packaged programs are available that can be administered by staff employees.[2]

Supporting the processes and procedures of the compensation function is cybertechnology, which can provide online information about the amount of salary and wage income that is electronically transferred on a payroll schedule into the accounts of employees at financial institution such as banks, savings and loan companies, and credit unions. These data also include all payroll deductions for fringe benefits and for local, state, and federal withholding taxes. This would also provide a history of the amount of income that is usually provided through pay stubs, which are still mailed to employees of some school districts.

Further, the intranet of a school district is an avenue through which employees can be reminded of enrollment periods for voluntary fringe benefits, such as dental or vision insurance, and of money that can be withheld for pre-tax services, such as dependent care plans.

Email is certainly a method of informing employees of their voluntary and mandatory fringe benefits and explaining the nuances of such plans.

In this context, the school district's intranet can ensure transparency and accountability concerning the salary and wage and fringe benefits programs. Employees can access a wealth of information about how such programs are developed and can be given the opportunity to express not only their satisfaction with such programs but also their dissatisfaction.

Of uppermost importance is how technology can be used to orientate employees to the performance-based compensation programs that are tied to the performance-based evaluation programs. This ensures that all salary and wage increases for individuals and for different categories of employees are equitable. Electronic technology can also be used as a staff development technique to help employees know and understand the criteria on which raises will be awarded.

Finally, it is obvious that all employees can be apprised of the school district's compensation policies and procedures through electronic technology. Thus, the implementation provisions of HIPAA and all other federal and state legislation policies and procedures should be readily available on the school district's Website. Of course, the obvious state legislation involving compensation is workers' compensation for injuries sustained while working.

Variables Affecting Compensation

The main purpose of establishing a compensation policy is to attract and retain qualified employees who will provide the type of service expected by the public. It is essential that employees understand the compensation structure and have confidence in the objectivity by which the system is implemented. Five major variables must be taken into consideration by the administration in constructing and recommending a compensation policy to the board of education for approval: performance, effort, seniority, skills, and job requirements. It is not important how appropriations are allocated for the compensation system; whether through board approval of the budget or collectively negotiated with employee unions, these variables are necessary to the policy.

Performance

The evaluation of performance is concerned with a basic question: Did you get the job done? Compensating individuals requires criteria that define performance. The task of constructing valid and reliable criteria for evaluating performance was discussed in Chapter 7. The use of performance as a basis for compensating employees is critical to all effective compensation systems.

Effort

School districts require teachers to consider the effort put forth by students as a determinant in evaluating student performance. Even if effort does not influence a grade directly, some method is usually used to indicate whether a given student is putting forth his or her best effort. It is ironic, therefore, that school districts have long neglected using the degree of effort put forth by employees as a component in their compensation systems. Yet, without such an orientation, a school district will fall prey to compensating quantity rather than quality, and the end rather than the means. Also, there are some situations in which an outcome is difficult to evaluate, and effort becomes a primary determinant of compensation. Thus, not all curricular innovation programs turn out to be successful as measured by student-demonstrated learning through test scores or projects. However, the effort that goes into investigating, developing, and assessing the effectiveness of instructional programs can be significant. Because teaching and learning are human activities, there is no one way of delivering these activities. Rather, research and development demand a certain amount of risk taking that contribute to educators' understanding of the instructional learning process, and this effort should be rewarded.

This discussion is obviously concerned with a topic much debated in education: performance incentives. There is no one best method for rewarding performance with money; however, the following comments help clarify this issue. Compensation programs for teachers and administrators in school districts tend to be parochial in scope, and neglect some basic considerations for rewarding those who strive for excellence in performance. One indication that a school district is moving toward a performance-based rather than a membership-based approach is paying teachers who demonstrate that their knowledge and skills contribute to improved student outcomes. Other indications are paying proven teachers to mentor less successful teachers and paying teachers more if they are willing to accept difficult teaching assignments.[3]

In a more systematic way, a performance-based approach provides incentives within the following context:

- Entry-level teachers must benefit from a performance incentive program by receiving all salaries as they begin their careers.
- School district citizens must be willing to provide the funding for a performance incentive program by raising their taxes, which can only occur if they recognize that the membership-based approach is no longer in place.
- Performance incentive programs must compensate those with the most-needed skills.
- All teachers and administrators must recognize that those who work the hardest, as measured by normative criteria, receive the most compensation.
- Performance evaluation policies and procedures must be equitable and easily recognized as such by all employees.[4]

Seniority

Length of time in a particular position plays a significant role in compensation systems in the public sector. The civil service system of the United States is the best example of how seniority operates in a compensation program. The master salary schedule approach used by many school districts, incorporating channels for credentials and an incremental dollar amount for years of service, testifies to the influence of seniority in compensation systems. In business and industry, seniority has some impact on the compensation systems collectively bargained by unions. However, for management positions, seniority has little or no effect on rewards.

Seniority has been used by educational organizations to determine financial compensation because it can be applied so easily. A principal may evaluate a given teacher's performance either higher or lower than another teacher's performance, but if both teachers perform within the limits of what is considered satisfactory, both receive the same salary increase if they have served the same number of years in the school system. This relieves the principal of the responsibility of recommending to the superintendent a different amount of compensation for each teacher based on the principal's evaluation of that teacher's performance.

Nevertheless, seniority is a variable to be incorporated into a compensation system because the basic purpose of establishing a compensation policy is to attract and retain qualified employees. A compensation system is ineffective when its sole criterion for rewarding employees is seniority.

The necessity of retaining some form of seniority in a compensation plan that also rewards performance has led to the establishment of what are commonly referred to as *career ladders*. Two of the more frequently discussed programs are the Charlotte-Mecklenburg Schools Career Development Plan and the Tennessee Better Schools Program. The objective of these two and most other programs is to encourage teachers to direct their careers along paths that lead to refined skills and higher levels of responsibility. For example, a person entering the education profession as an apprentice teacher must have performed all the following criteria:

1. Completed a teacher education program offered through an approved college or university
2. Attained a bachelor's degree
3. Successfully completed student teaching
4. Passed the National Teacher Examination

This apprentice teacher could progress to subsequent higher levels of designation such as professional teacher, senior teacher, and, finally, master teacher. The path to these levels requires additional education and the assuming of more and more responsibilities. For example, a master teacher could be expected to serve as a curriculum specialist, seminar presenter in a staff development program, or resource person to apprentice teachers. Each level of attainment could be rewarded with perhaps a more lucrative salary schedule. A bonus on attaining each successive level is another method of rewarding those reaching such levels. Exhibit 8.1 shows the career paths for teachers in Tennessee.

Skills

A common practice in organizations, particularly in the private sector, is allocating compensation based on the skills of employees. Those who possess the most advanced skills receive the highest compensation. When an individual is hired by an organization, his or her skill level is usually a major consideration in determining the amount of compensation to be received.

Competition, therefore, to hire individuals with certain skills becomes an element in the compensation package. The standard as to what constitutes a desirable skill is imposed from either the human resource requirements of the organization or the occupational category itself. If the board of education has mandated having a community education program, individuals possessing the experience and educational qualifications necessary for implementing such a program must have skills that demand a quality compensation package.

EXHIBIT 8.1   Career Paths for Teachers

Apprentice Teacher

Entry Routes

- Completion of a teacher training program and recommendation by an approved institution of higher education
- Trade shop personnel who meet appropriate standards

Qualifications/Requirements

- Student teaching
- Successful completion of the National Teacher Examination
- Bachelor's degree
      or
- Employment standards required for trade shop personnel

Certificate

- Three-year
- Nonrenewable

Contract/State Salary

- Regular school term of 200 days
- State salary schedule based on training and experience

Professional Teacher

Entry Routes

- Three (3) years as an apprentice teacher
- A currently certified teacher with three (3) or more years of experience who wishes to enter the new career paths

Qualifications/Requirements

- Knowledge of subject matter
- Acceptable student achievement
- Participation in professional growth activities
- Observation by evaluating team/teacher interview

Certificate

- Five-year
- Renewable

Contract/State Salary

- Regular school term of 200 days
- State salary schedule based on training and experience *plus* state incentive pay supplement of $1,000

Continued

EXHIBIT 8.1 *Continued*

Senior Teacher

Entry Routes

- Three (3) to five (5) years as a professional teacher
- A currently certified teacher who has eight (8) or more years of appropriate experience

Qualifications/Requirements

- Acceptable student achievement
- Participation in professional growth activities
- Observation by evaluation team/teacher interview
- Exceptional classroom practice
- Evaluations by local supervisors and administrators

Certificate

- Five-year
- Renewable

Contract/State Salary

- Contract for 10 months (200 days)—*current teachers only*—state salary schedule based on training and experience *plus* state incentive pay supplement of $2,000
- Contract for 11 months (220 days)—state salary schedule based on training and experience *plus* state incentive pay supplement of $4,000

Master Teacher

Entry Routes

- Five (5) years as a senior teacher
- A currently certified teacher who has twelve (12) or more years of appropriate experience

Qualifications/Requirements

- Acceptable student achievement
- Participation in professional growth activities
- Observation by evaluation team/teacher interview
- Classroom effectiveness
- Capability and willingness to assume additional duties
- Evaluations by local supervisors and administrators
- Skill in supervising, evaluating, and improving the performance of other teachers

Certificate

- Five-year
- Renewable

Contract/State Salary

- Contract for 10 months (200 days)—*current teachers only*—state salary schedule based on training and experience *plus* state incentive pay supplement of $3,000

Source: Tennessee Better Schools Program (Tennessee Master Teacher-Master Administrator Act, 1983).

Job Requirements

The complexity and responsibility of a job are criteria that often determine how compensation is distributed. A job that is difficult to perform because of stress, unpleasant working conditions, or level of responsibility must also offer higher compensation to attract capable individuals. A major determinant of job difficulty is the degree of discretion a job requires. The greater the discretion, the greater the need for good judgment, and, consequently, the greater the need for commensurate compensation.

Any good compensation system must recognize effort, seniority, skills, and job requirements; performance, however, must also be given a primary emphasis. Quality individuals are attracted to school districts that reward performance, which in turn affects the quality of education offered by a school district.

Types of Compensation

If compensation is to motivate performance, employees must recognize the relationship between performance and compensation. Most school districts have traditionally used non-performance criteria, such as seniority-based salary schedules, for allocating compensation. However, this chapter views compensation primarily as a payoff for performance. This concept is in keeping with the outcry for accountability and, if properly applied, might be the only realistic approach to improving the quality of education. For too long, teachers and other employees of school districts have been placed apart from the rest of humankind by taxpayers who believe that they should be more dedicated to service than concerned about making a living. Teachers and other public employees have fought this long-held belief by engaging in unionism and collective negotiations for wages and fringe benefits. A reasonable compensation system that recognizes quality performance and that is objectively administered could help remedy some of the dissatisfaction voiced by school district employees.[5]

The most obvious kinds of compensation are wages and fringe benefits. However, a truly effective compensation system must be multifaceted, incorporating both intrinsic and extrinsic aspects. Although modern school districts employ people in many different occupational categories, many of the possible rewards are applicable only to particular job positions. For example, teachers, administrators, bus drivers, and custodians receive a salary; administrators, in addition, have greater job discretion; and custodians could receive overtime pay.

Rewarding performance and encouraging higher levels of performance must be fashioned into a comprehensive system that is ongoing and integral to the operation of the school district. Thus, Figure 8.1 has many functions: First and foremost, it demonstrates that compensation can be woven into a complete system for both rewarding performance and creating organizational commitment that encourages improvement of performance.

Intrinsic compensation is a reward that the employee receives from doing the job itself. The employee's job satisfaction is usually increased by the following: participation in the policy-making process, greater job discretion, increased responsibility, and opportunities for professional development.

Extrinsic rewards are divided into *direct* and *indirect compensation*. The most common forms of direct compensation are salary, overtime pay, holiday pay, and merit pay for

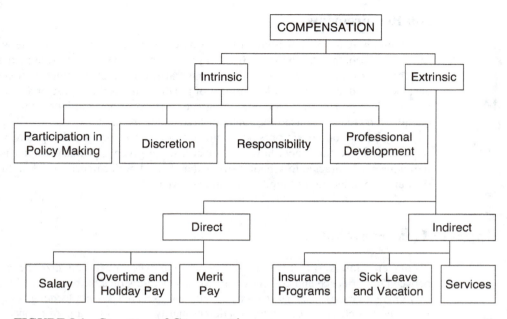

FIGURE 8.1   Structure of Compensation

performance. Direct compensation is also the part of a compensation system that generates the most controversy and disgruntlement among employees. Industrial psychologists have long contended that rate of pay is not the most important determinant of job satisfaction. However, it is an indispensable part of every compensation package and, because of its importance, is treated at length under a separate title in this chapter.

Indirect compensation usually includes insurance programs, pay for time away from work, and services. There is a widespread attitude among human resources administrators that indirect compensation helps retain individuals in an organization rather than motivating them to greater performance. Direct compensation is considered the stimulus to better performance. Because of the complexity and importance of indirect compensation, more frequently referred to as *fringe benefits*, this also is treated under a separate heading in this chapter.

Nonfinancial rewards have begun to appear in some school districts and may either motivate an employee to greater performance or help retain his or her services. The kind and extent of nonfinancial compensation are limited only by the creativity of those responsible for establishing a compensation program. Nonfinancial compensation, however, is effective only if it meets the needs of specific employees. What one person considers desirable might seem superfluous to another. For example, a status-conscious employee might be motivated by a job title, a reserved parking place, the services of a private secretary. Another individual might value working without close supervision. The significant point is that organizations can use a variety of nonfinancial means as part of a total program, and these means may be more appreciated by certain individuals than direct or indirect forms of compensation.[6]

Direct Compensation: Salary and Wage Administration

The basic philosophy underlying pay systems in school districts is compensation for services rendered. However, the subjective nature of administrative judgments, collectively bargained agreements, state and federal pay guidelines, and salary rates in the public and private sectors has a definite influence on actual wage programs. To ensure external and internal wage comparability, a school district must continually gather data on the wage and salary policies of other school districts, as well as those of public and private employers in the community and region. Most organizations are cooperative in sharing information concerning salary programs because they, too, understand that their systems are influenced by others. Surveys by telephone and letter, government publications, and literature published by employee organizations and unions are also valuable resources in gathering information.

Because the principle of compensation for services rendered is somewhat elusive, the following policy should help a school district in developing a salary and wage policy aimed at fair treatment for all employees:

The board of education recognizes the importance of creating a compensation plan for teachers, administrators, and staff members that is equitable and transparent in application to the various job categories in the school district. Thus, the board requires the ongoing evaluation of every job category and individual position in order to determine a justifiable compensation for the skills and talents required to efficiently and effectively carry out the responsibilities of the categories and positions.

As a method of implementing the uniform administration of wages and benefits, all categories and positions in the school district will be arranged in a relative hierarchical order of responsibility with the position of most responsibility at the top. Thereby a gradation system is created that will permit wage and benefit differentiation. Further, the board is requiring the administration to develop a process whereby representatives of the teachers, administrators, and staff members can participate in establishing the gradation system of responsibility.

The board of education is further requiring the superintendent of schools or his or her representative to advise the board on a yearly basis concerning the competitive worth of the compensation plan in relation to other school districts, public agencies, and private business within the state and local community.

The primary focus of this compensation plan is the improvement of performance by teachers, administrators, and staff members. As such, this policy will be effective only if it is amalgamated with the school district's performance-based evaluation policy and procedures. Thus, the graduation of responsibility will be tempered by the quality of performance of each individual employee. In essence, the board of education is also establishing by this policy a performance-based incentive plan that rewards the quality of performance. Consequently, the superintendent of schools, along with the human resources administrator, is being required to establish a uniform and justifiable method of evaluating job performance in collaboration with the representatives of the teachers, administrators, and staff members.

Figure 8.1 presents an array of performance incentives that can be used to encourage all employees to strive for higher levels of performance. The key, of course, is demonstration by human resources administrators that there is a direct link between incentive rewards and the quality of performance.

Effects of Salary on Motivation

An interesting question central to all pay systems is, "Does money stimulate an employee to put forth more effort?" The answer to this question is closely related to individual needs because money in itself is rarely an end but rather a means to "purchasing an end." A $4,000 raise for an employee making $40,000 a year would help that individual maintain his or her standard of living in the face of ordinary inflation. That same raise would considerably improve the standard of living for an individual earning $20,000 a year, but it would have much less effect on the lifestyle of someone earning $80,000 per year. From this perspective, money does have a potential to motivate if individuals are seeking to maintain or improve their standard of living. We rarely find a person who is not concerned when his or her life style deteriorates because salary increases have not been keeping pace with inflation.

Performance-based teacher evaluation, along with performance-based pay incentives, appears to have the most significant impact on motivating teachers and administrators to strive for excellence in their teaching and administering. Performance pay without accompanying performance evaluation does not by itself appear to motivate teachers and administrators because there is no structure within which to encourage excellence in performance.[7] This research suggests that money is important to employees regardless of the job level in the organization or the amount of salary earned. In addition, money has a great deal of symbolic value in our society, even though it has varying degrees of importance to individuals with different backgrounds and experiences.

If money is to motivate an individual within an organization to greater performance, it must be clear that such performance is indeed rewarded with more money. The behavior that is thus rewarded will be repeated, and the behavior that is not rewarded with money will not be repeated. This, of course, is not the *modus operandi* of most school systems in the United States. The common position has been one of emphasizing intrinsic motivation. Teachers and other school district employees are expected to perform to the best of their abilities because of the importance of educating children and because of the status afforded to these individuals. The accountability movement, with taxpayers demanding a return on their dollar from school district employees by way of increased student performance, and the number of teacher strikes for higher wages should dispel the myth that the performance of any group of employees in any organization, public or private, is unaffected by money.

Further, performance-based pay incentives for individual employees are more effective if the school district has clearly defined performance objectives. There are other issues related to group pay incentives. For example, if a group of teachers in a given school or department is signaled out for performance and offered pay incentives, the incentive program may become dysfunctional through the phenomenon of competition. Competition sometimes fosters corner cutting and inflated values in addition to disparaging other employees.[8]

A reasonable conclusion concerning the relationship of money to motivation is that money definitely affects performance under certain circumstances. Unfortunately, most school districts use a seniority-based salary schedule, which does not reward performance, but rather rewards an individual's survival for another year.

However, the development of monetary incentives is limited only by the creativity of the human resources department. For example, giving a double-step increase on the salary schedule to an outstanding teacher is a way of using a traditional salary schedule in an innovative way. Salary bonuses for exceptional performance, longevity pay for a certain number of years that outstanding teachers have spent with a school district, and signing bonuses to encourage excellent teachers to continue teaching in a school district are other examples of performance incentives.

Public Disclosure of Salaries

Because school districts are public agencies, salary schedules and budget information are disclosed not only to school district employees but also to the general public and at times to the news media. However, many school districts consider the salaries of individual employees to be confidential. This situation brings up a number of concerns. First, in public agencies supported by tax money, the public would seem to have a right to know how tax money is being spent and for what. Second, secrecy regarding salaries sometimes leads to misperceptions, which in turn may lead to the dissatisfaction of employees with their pay.

An open salary policy might also affect management effectiveness. If pay information became common knowledge among employees, individuals could compare their salaries, and inequities in the pay system would soon become apparent. Of course, there would also be petty complaints and misperceived inequities. However, an open pay system would demonstrate that the administration has confidence in the management of the pay system, and this might increase the trust individual employees have in the school district's administration. Although few statistical data are available on the preferences of employees concerning an open salary policy, experience suggests that most Americans are sensitive about their wages and would probably prefer to have their salaries undisclosed.

The Equal Employment Opportunity Commission continues to receive cases alleging that women are being paid less than men for doing comparable work. This, of course, is contrary to the provisions of the Equal Pay Act of 1963 and Title VII of the Civil Rights Act of 1964.[9] In like manner, school districts receiving federal funds must disclose wage and salary information to demonstrate commitment to the principles of nondiscrimination action. Further, a company cannot prohibit employees from discussing salary issues during working hours because this is an abridgment of their constitutional rights.

Compensation Packaging

Because individual employees have individual needs, no compensation program will satisfy everyone. A number of corporations, recognizing this fact, have developed compensation programs commonly referred to as *cafeteria plans,* which allow each employee to choose the combination of compensation options most attractive to that person. Thus, an employee is informed that his or her compensation is X dollars, and the employee then chooses a mix of salary and other benefits offered by the corporation that suits his or her particular situation. Such benefits might include any or all of the following:

- Major medical and hospitalization insurance
- Pharmaceutical insurance
- Dental insurance
- Optical insurance
- Flexible spending plan
- Life insurance
- Extended care insurance
- Dependent care plan
- Accidental death and dismemberment insurance
- Long-term disability insurance
- Travel accident insurance
- Adoption assistance
- Annuities

Again, the options are limited only by the creativity of human resources administrators.

The concept underlying this approach is that an employee is motivated toward higher performance if such performance carries a dollar value that can then be "spent" by the individual for compensation tailored to meet his or her needs.

Although it is difficult to generalize, younger employees appear to be more concerned with salary and educational reimbursement programs than with life insurance and retirement plans. Married employees are usually more concerned about life insurance and medical programs than are single individuals; older employees are justifiably interested in retirement benefits.

With this type of compensation packaging, a considerable amount of information must be made available to employees for them to have adequate data on which to base decisions. This will obviously increase the administrative costs of the compensation programs. However, the potential benefit in terms of increased performance and the retention of employees could significantly offset the additional costs.

Equity of Pay and Performance

In any organization, employees tend to compare what they get from their job with what they must put into it. At the same time, they are comparing their pay with their coworkers' pay and productivity. The inevitable outcome of this comparison is that an individual will see his or her compensation as either equal or unequal to that of fellow employees. Those who feel inequality exists may view themselves as under- or over-rewarded.

There are heated arguments about the value and legitimacy of performance-based salary and benefits plans. At the top of the list is the question of fairness. Thus, the criteria that are used in a performance-based evaluation model can create heated debate among teachers, administrators, and the general public in a given school district. In turn, this can cause conflicts between employees, which ultimately leads to mistrust of other teachers and administrators. Often, mistrust leads to confusion about the job requirements. The foundation of an equitable compensation program is adequate funding by the board of education. Less than adequate funding adds fuel to the fire of the equity issue. These issues are exacerbated in small- and medium-size school districts in which all or most employees know each other.[10]

An employee who perceives an inequality may choose unacceptable means of rectifying the situation, which could include avoiding tasks that are not measured by performance standards or criticizing the performance of others. In this context, *fairness* means that the school district compensates each employee in a manner that befits the demands and requirements of his or her position, and that this fairness is recognized by other employees.[11] Administrators must realize that employees are concerned not only about the absolute amount of money they are paid but also about the relationship of that dollar amount to what others are paid. When an inequality is perceived, tension is created. The implication for human resources administrators is very clear: Employees are motivated not only by their absolute compensation but also by the relativity of that compensation. Where employees perceive inequality, quality of performance may diminish, absenteeism may increase, and resignations may rise.

Employee Relations in Salary Management

Employees who believe that they are unfairly compensated will certainly create a morale problem for the administration. However, low wages alone will not necessarily create a morale problem if employees believe that the administration and board of education are doing everything possible to improve wages. Therefore, how salary decisions are presented to the employees is of great importance. The method, of course, varies with each individual school district because of local traditions and the number of employees. Most presentation plans must be formulated with sensitivity to the process used in making salary decisions. However, no plan will work if it is not endorsed by the teachers or their representatives. The involvement of teacher representatives may not be necessary in small- and some medium-size school districts, where the board of education can talk directly to the teachers.[12]

Thus, the administration should analyze the fiscal condition of the school district, formulate a recommendation that appears reasonable, receive approval from the board of education, and inform the school district employees of the decision. This method is the most efficient in terms of time spent by the administration, but it is also the most vulnerable in terms of good staff morale because it is basically a "take it or leave it" approach. Although this method is traditional in education, it is also highly suspected even in those school districts where it is used successfully because it has all the markings of a benevolent dictatorship.

A second process, which is the more defensible, brings administration and employee representatives together to develop a mutually acceptable salary and wage package. In more than half the states, this process is mandated in varying degrees by state collective negotiations legislation. However, the process is certainly valid even in those states that prohibit collective negotiations by public school employees. Where such a prohibition exists, salary decisions remain with the board of education, but the task of formulating a recommendation becomes a concern of both administrators and employees.

This collaborative process is not without its drawbacks. It can be time consuming, and the administration may disagree with the proposals presented by the employee representatives. Chapter 9 discusses in detail the process of collective negotiations as practiced in public school districts.

Whatever process is used, the administration must ultimately present the salary plan and the decision of the board of education to the school district employees. A significant advantage of the bilateral model is that the employees, through their representatives, have some knowledge of the administration's position. The sensitive nature of salary and wage decisions cannot be overemphasized. Wages affect an individual's ability to support his or her family and maintain an adequate standard of living, and a paycheck represents security in a highly materialistic society. Therefore, effective communication is essential in explaining policies and decisions.

There are four basic principles that, if followed, maximize the effectiveness of the presentation of salary and wage decisions to the employees:

1. The board of education must place top priority on paying adequate wages when it draws up and approves the school district's budget.
2. The administration must make complete disclosure of the fiscal condition of the school district.
3. The administration must avoid presenting too many technical details of the financial conditions, which could give the semblance of a "snow job."
4. The administration should prepare a position statement to distribute to all employees and the news media. This document may take various forms, but at a minimum it should contain the decision on salary and wages, the process used in reaching the decision, facts about the financial condition of the school district, and data about wages in comparable school districts and the business community.

It is also effective in minimizing confusion and misrepresentation to invite employees to call a designated office responsible for answering questions about the salary and wage document. The most obvious central office component to take this responsibility, of course, is the business and finance office. However, those districts that maintain a public relations office would more properly place this responsibility with the director of community relations.

A final, yet important, point should be made concerning employee relations in salary management. The building principal is often the last person to be informed about central office and board of education decisions, but he or she is usually the first person contacted by teachers and other building-level employees when they have questions. Therefore, it is both good administrative procedure and good public relations to inform the principal first about salary decisions. This also helps principals identify themselves as members of the school district's administrative team.

Collecting Community Wage Data

A defensible technique in developing wage and salary recommendations is to establish salary parameters compatible with wages paid by other government agencies and by business and industry in the community served by the school system. In metropolitan areas, this includes more than the immediate vicinity; salaries in the surrounding area would probably give a better indication of the adequacy of salary levels within the district. Thus, a school district located in suburban Chicago should be concerned with the wages paid by private business and industry, municipal governments, and other school districts in the entire metropolitan Chicago area.

If salaries are to be competitive and sufficient to sustain a reasonable standard of living for school district employees, they must be relatively comparable to the salaries received by other individuals living in the same community. Also, bear in mind that these corporations and their employees support the school district through taxation; salaries paid by the school district must not be out of proportion to the wages paid and received by these constituents.

A source of information on salaries and wages paid in the community to individuals with occupations similar to non-instructional employees of a school district is the employment agency. Although the quality of such agencies varies, both private and public employment agencies usually have valuable data on wages. The civil service commissions of state and municipal governments also have readily available information on salary systems used in their respective jurisdictions.

The most effective way to gather data on salaries and wages is through a survey, a technique that has the advantage of clarity and precision. If the survey instrument is accompanied by a cover letter explaining its purpose, most agencies and corporations will cooperate with the school district by supplying the data because they usually view this type of cooperation as a public service.

Surveys dealing with instructional and administrative positions generally follow the guidelines set forth next, but substitute the appropriate position titles, salary, and job descriptions:

- Of course, the most important issue is confidentiality. Corporations and agencies are usually reluctant to answer surveys if there is a possibility that the general public and other corporations and agencies will discover who responded to the survey. Competition between corporations and agencies to hire the best employees causes some corporations and agencies to refrain from participation.
- The second most important issue is how the survey questions are formulated. They must be easily understood and elicit, as much as possible, unbiased responses. To ensure objectivity and reliability, the survey is typically administered to a pilot group and the defensibility of the results analyzed.
- Wage and salary information is difficult to analyze if it is not reported as the average for a certain job category. This also eliminates the guesswork that may be needed to determine equivalency between the job categories of corporations and agencies and those in the school district.
- The information must be requested by job categories. The rationale for the survey is to gather information from enterprises that are similar to but different from school districts, such as hospitals and not-for-profit organizations.

Examples of job categories that might be used in a survey for nonteaching positions are *skilled craftsperson*, which could include mechanic, electrician, plumber, and carpenter, and *clerical/secretarial worker*, which might include accounting associate, payroll associate, and administrative assistant.

The job category of maintenance could include groundskeeping and housekeeping. Each maintenance position would have a specific job description as set forth in Exhibit 8.2.

EXHIBIT 8.2   Sample Job Description for Housekeeper

Cleans and keeps work areas and restrooms in an orderly condition in school building or central office. Duties involve a combination of the following: sweeping, mopping, scrubbing, and polishing floors; removing refuse; dusting equipment, furniture, and fixtures; polishing metal fixtures or trimmings; maintaining supplies; and providing minor maintenance services.

The practice of keeping school district wage and salary rates comparable to those paid in the community is becoming imperative not only because teacher shortages exist in some fields but also because increasingly more school district employees are attracted to jobs in business and industry. This, of course, is particularly true of craft and clerical positions because of the ease of transferring from public- to private-sector employment. Administrative assistants, electricians, cooks, and bus drivers are sometimes "in training" with public school districts until an appropriate job becomes available in business or industry. Thus, the principle of like pay for public employees for like work in corporations and other organizations is becoming a necessary human resources policy. Such a policy helps a school district to not only compete with the private sector for quality employees but also retain its employees, thereby reducing the expense involved with high turnover.

The salary rates being offered in the private sector are also attracting instructional and administrative personnel. Mathematics, industrial arts, and science teachers are finding more opportunities in business and industry than ever before. This trend is also reaching into the liberal arts disciplines as corporations recognize that they can train an individual for almost any job if that person is motivated and has a basic college education. Salaries have motivated many teachers to seek employment in the private sector and in jobs where the rewards systems recognize performance.

Thus, collecting data about salaries and wages is extremely important. Although school districts individually gather information through the survey method, many cooperative ventures have also emerged, with most or all of the school districts in a metropolitan area jointly sponsoring salary and wage surveys.

The following guidelines have been developed as a road map for preparing a *wage and salary report* that can be used with boards of education, teachers, administrators, staff members, and the general public:

- It is important to develop the survey questions in such a manner that the data received can be easily fashioned into a report that can be understood and used by people without a background in survey analysis. The ultimate purpose is to have data that are helpful in establishing wage and salary compensation plans for school districts. Because the school district reflects the values and financial situations of the citizens living in the school district community and the businesses that provide goods and services to that community, it is important to establish the wage and salary compensation plans in accordance with the community economic culture. The survey should provide the data in such a manner that they can be compared to the categories of jobs in the school district. Finally, the data must reflect the working conditions that affect salary and wage plans, such as the length of the workday for staff members such as school bus drivers.

- It is important to minimize the use of technical terms used by statisticians in collating, analyzing, and presenting data. Further, it is helpful to have the survey available in an online format, allowing the data to be downloaded directly into data analysis software, which permits statistical analysis.[13]

Salary and Wage Review

Because approximately 80 percent of the budget in most school districts is spent on wages, salary planning and review are an essential part of the entire compensation process. Two methods are commonly used by school systems to review compensation programs: continual salary review and annual salary review.

A continual salary review system is usually tied into a cost of living index. Government agencies use a number of indicators to determine inflation rates, with the Consumer Price Index being the most commonly used. A major problem with such a measure is the fact that it is an average; the actual cost of living in a community may be higher or lower than the average reported.

Under a continual salary review system, adjustments are automatically made on salary schedules as the selected cost of living indicator changes, necessitating a change in the hourly rates for classified employees and the contracts for administrative and instructional personnel. Such a system does not reward performance; it merely adjusts the basic salary of all employees. Merit increases, therefore, are not addressed by the continual review process.

The annual salary review process functions from a much different perspective. Salary schedules are adjusted annually in relation to the prevailing wages in other school districts and businesses in the community. The adjustment may or may not be in keeping with a recognized cost of living indicator; rather, its major focus is on the local community as the appropriate measure. The concern of the annual salary review process is that wages in other school districts and businesses in the community, which continually change, may cause the more talented employees to look for positions there. As with the continual salary review process, the annual review process does not reward performance. Therefore, merit increases must be viewed as a separate component of the compensation program.

The decision by a school district as to which method best meets the needs of the employees must take into account budget constraints. There are two significant differences between public-sector and private-sector financing: First, school districts are financed primarily by tax revenue, which is usually not received on a consistent monthly basis but rather as taxes are collected; and second, in most states, taxes can be raised to meet higher costs only with voter approval, whereas in the private sector, the price of an item can be raised at any time to offset costs. These financial considerations make the continual salary review process difficult to implement in a school district.

Salary Schedule Construction

In the public sector—particularly in the civil service systems of the state and federal governments—salary schedules are divided into a number of grades, each of which has several step rates. The use of salary schedules can have three distinct disadvantages: First, recruitment of personnel can be adversely affected if the beginning salaries are fixed by a salary schedule that has become traditional in a school district. Any move away from that model usually causes teachers and teacher organizations to raise concerns of equity. Second, teachers are sometimes disheartened when they receive the same rate of increase on a salary schedule as an unproductive teacher. Finally, it has become obvious in some school districts that the single salary schedule has not produced teacher effectiveness when compared with compensation systems that provide financial and nonfinancial rewards for teacher performance.[14]

A major decision in establishing a salary schedule involves the appropriate number of steps to be included within a grade. If the steps are numerous and small, employees will be unhappy because salary increases will be small. If the steps are large and few, an employee will reach the maximum within a grade in a relatively short time and, consequently, will have no place to progress to over the long term.

A realistic approach, therefore, could be a compromise that sets up six or seven steps within each grade, with each representing a certain percentage increment. Each grade may be further improved by adding longevity steps to the top and expressing these in even dollar amounts rather than percentages. For example, a salary schedule could grant an employee a longevity increase for every two years of service after reaching the last step within a grade.

Each position in the school district is assigned to one of the salary ranges, and each employee is assigned to one of the steps. As new people are hired, they are placed within the range assigned to that position and on a step negotiated with the administration. Advancement from one step to another is based on performance. Consequently, an employee who is performing unsatisfactorily could remain on the same step until termination or resignation. An employee performing satisfactorily could receive a step advancement that represents a salary increase of a certain percentage. A meritorious employee could be granted a two- or three-step advancement.

Some school districts have initiated a policy of placing a new employee on the first step for a probationary period and then advancing the employee as he or she demonstrates satisfactory performance. For example, an employee might be moved to the second step after six months. This method is usually effective only with classified employees who, unlike teachers, are not working under an individual contract.

Advancement from one salary range to another is usually based on either a promotion or an increase in educational qualifications. A teacher who becomes an assistant principal usually advances to the salary range established for the assistant principalship. In like manner, a teacher who receives a master's degree advances to the salary range established for teachers with master's degrees. This same process is applicable to classified employees. A custodian who is promoted to a head custodial position with supervisory responsibilities over the other custodians in a building would be placed on the appropriate salary level. It is important to note that advancement to a higher salary grade will not necessarily result in a higher wage for an employee. For example, step 5 of the bachelor's degree teacher salary range may be higher than step 1 of the master's degree teacher salary range. Consequently, when moving employees to a higher grade, it is important to place them on a step that ensures an increase in wages for having upgraded their academic qualifications or for taking on greater responsibilities.

Although the types of salary ranges vary from one school district to another, a few examples of common designations follow:
Each designation has a salary range with multiple steps.

Administrative	Instructional	Classified
Central Office Director (*Example: Director of Federal Programs*)	Bachelor's degree	Custodian
	Bachelor's degree plus 30 graduate hours	Head Custodian
Secondary School Principal		Maintenance Employee
Secondary School Assistant Principal	Master's degree	Maintenance Supervisor
Elementary School Principal	Master's degree plus 30 graduate hours	
Elementary School Assistant Principal	Doctoral degree	

Exhibit 8.3 is an example of the type of teacher salary schedule found in most school districts. Five categories correspond to the academic requirement necessary for placement in each category. The categories progress from the bachelor's degree level through the doctoral degree level. The steps in each category are listed down the left side of the schedule. Those teachers in category 1 could receive a step increase with satisfactory performance up through ten steps. At that point, they would not receive a step increase until they earned fifteen hours of graduate credit in their subject area, and thus would move to step

EXHIBIT 8.3   Salary Schedule

Step	Category 1 bachelor's degree ($)	Category 2 bachelor's degree plus 15 graduate hours ($)	Category 3 master's degree plus 2 years' experience ($)	Category 4 master's degree plus 15 graduate hours ($)	Category 5 doctoral degree plus 3 years' experience ($)
1	35,000	36,575		33,150	
2	36,575	38,150		40,425	
3	38,150	39,725	40,512.50	42,700	
4	39,725	41,300	42,087.50	44,975	46,550
5	41,300	42,875	43,662.50	47,250	48,825
6	42,875	44,450	45,237.50	49,525	51,100
7	44,450	46,025	46,812.50	51,800	53,375
8	46,025	47,600	48,387.50	54,075	55,650
9	47,600	49,175	49,962.50	56,350	57,925
10	49,175	50,750	51,537.50	58,625	60,200
11		52,325	53,112.50	60,900	62,475
12			54,687.50	63,175	64,750
13				65,450	67,025
14					70,000
15					72,275
16					74,550
17					76,825
18					79,100
19					81,375
20					83,650

EXHIBIT 8.4   Indices

STEP	INDEX	INDEX	INDEX	INDEX	INDEX
1	1.0000	1.0450		1.0900	
2	1.0450	1.0900		1.1550	
3	1.0900	1.1350	1.1575	1.2200	
4	1.1350	1.1800	1.2025	1.2850	1.3300
5	1.1800	1.2250	1.2475	1.3500	1.3950
6	1.2250	1.2700	1.2925	1.4150	1.4600
7	1.2700	1.3150	1.3375	1.4800	1.5250
8	1.3150	1.3600	1.3825	1.5450	1.5900
9	1.3600	1.4050	1.4275	1.6100	1.6550
10	1.4050	1.4500	1.4725	1.6750	1.7200
11		1.4950	1.5175	1.7400	1.7850
12			1.5625	1.8050	1.8500
13				1.8700	1.9150
14					2.0000
15					2.0650
16					2.1300
17					2.1950
18					2.2600
19					2.3250
20					2.3900

11 in category 2. Therefore, this method encourages teachers to upgrade their knowledge and skills. In fact, this is the case with all categories. Two categories have experience requirements in addition to the academic ones. The master's degree level also requires two years of successful teaching experience; the doctoral degree level requires three years. Thus, a person who is pursuing a master's or doctoral degree on a full-time basis without experience in teaching would be placed in the preceding category until completing the successful teaching requirement.

Exhibit 8.4 indicates the percentages of increase between categories and steps. Such a salary schedule is commonly referred to as an *index system*. The designation *incremental system* refers to those salary schedules that have equal dollar increases between steps, such as $500 between step 1 and step 2, $500 between step 2 and step 3, and so on.

Multiple Salary Ranges

There will probably be multiple salary ranges in most school districts for administrative and instructional positions. These ranges are necessary to recognize the various levels of academic preparation and responsibility. A secondary school principal with a master's degree, usually a minimum academic qualification, should not receive as much compensation as a secondary school principal with a doctorate. When a salary plan for administrative or instructional positions has multiple ranges, it is typically referred to as a *salary schedule*. The teachers' salary schedule usually has a range for each of the following: bachelor's degree, bachelor's degree plus a certain number of graduate hours, master's degree, master's degree plus a certain number of graduate hours, and doctorate. Consequently, it is common to find multiple salary schedules with multiple ranges in most school systems. For these professional positions, it is relatively easy to identify appropriate ranges, which is not the case with classified positions.

The use of negotiated contracts is a new phenomenon taking shape in some school districts across the United States, and particularly in school districts experiencing difficulty finding qualified administrators and teachers. This refers to the practice of providing salary and benefit packages tailored to meet the employment demands of desirable candidates. Such candidates might be applying for superintendent, assistant superintendent, principal, or special education positions. For example, there is great demand for secondary school principals with successful experience in large urban school districts, for teachers and administrators experienced in providing quality services to children with autism, and for assistant superintendents with extensive and successful experience in curricular and instructional planning and assessment.

Compensation packaging could include a salary enticement that extends beyond the usual salary schedules or benefits, which might include annuities, financial allowances for professional development, extended periods of vacation, use of a school-owned vehicle, or an automobile allowance. However, negotiated contracts could have some limitations because of the Internal Revenue Service (IRS) code. In addition, it is always a good practice to make known the terms of negotiated contracts because they are being financed by taxpayer money. Also, public disclosure militates against exaggerated claims that may accompany agreements that are out of the ordinary.

For classified employees, it is necessary to designate job families based on similarity in duties and responsibilities and similarity in qualifications. From time to time, it might be necessary to reevaluate a position to determine whether these criteria are still applicable. An example of a family of jobs with similar responsibilities, duties, and qualifications is the designation *secretarial-clerical*. Not all school district secretaries and clerical personnel have exactly the same working conditions. Therefore, a salary schedule for this designation could be constructed with ranges established to discriminate between the various working conditions, with the highest range reserved for executive secretaries working for the superintendent and assistant superintendents, another range assigned to building secretarial positions, and the lowest range to clerk-typist positions. Similarly, a job family for classified transportation supervisory personnel could include ranges for transportation supervisor, mechanic foreman, and dispatcher, with salary ranges appropriate to these designations.

Base Salaries

Two processes can be used to establish the basic wage for each salary schedule range. The preceding discussion of types of salary ranges illustrates the various methods used to calculate step increases but provides no indication of base salaries.

The first process centers on gathering salary data from other school districts and from the business-industrial community. There is little difficulty in analyzing the data in relation to administrative and teaching positions. Classified positions, however, present a more challenging situation because of the multitude of job categories with responsibilities unique to the individual organization.

A successful method of setting classified salaries involves designating certain job categories, which include a family of job positions, as benchmarks. Thus, a *Maintenance Category* includes school bus mechanics, carpenters, plumbers, and electricians, and an

Information Technology Category includes computer programmers, Web designers, and technical assistants.

Such benchmark categories allow for comparison with other school districts, business and industry, public agencies, and not-for-profit agencies. Survey data obtained from these other enterprises can be analyzed statistically to obtain measures of central tendency such as means, medians, and dispersion data that indicate the relative position of the school district in terms of wage and salary compensation when compared with other institutions and organizations in the community.

The second process involves gathering data from individual employees within the organization concerning the extent of their responsibilities, the tasks they perform, and their qualifications. The data can be analyzed and used to establish salaries as part of the annual review process. The data also provide a vehicle for reevaluating jobs to ascertain whether they are properly assigned to the appropriate salary schedule and in the correct range. The Appendix contains a position description questionnaire that can be used for this position analysis and samples of job evaluation forms. The use of this questionnaire and the evaluation forms is predicated on a procedure that uses a salary review committee.

In most situations where this procedure is used, the salary review committee is composed of administrators, supervisors, teachers, and non-instructional personnel who are not directly employed in the job categories being evaluated but who have knowledge of the working conditions involved. This gives credibility and objectivity to the process. A committee of three or five people is optimal for the evaluation task. Thus, if a secondary school principal's position is being evaluated, the committee could be composed of one or two elementary school principals, one or two secondary school teachers, and the assistant superintendent for secondary education. In like manner, if a building-level secretarial position is being evaluated, the committee could be composed of one or two central office executive secretaries, one or two clerk-typists, and the director of staff development.

Each committee member studies the questionnaire completed by the employee and his or her supervisor. Using a scale of 1 to 5, with 5 indicating the highest requirement, each person evaluates the position in terms of the factors indicated on the evaluation form. Finally, a tally sheet summarizing the evaluations is completed. From these data, the assistant superintendent for human resources or another central office administrator can establish the salary range appropriate to the position.

Payroll Deductions

Making deductions from an employee's salary is such a common practice that most individuals take it for granted. Yet, it has significant consequences because of legal and personal considerations. Therefore, the board of education should have a comprehensive payroll deduction policy covering such areas as the minimum and maximum amounts that may be deducted, the number and types of deductions authorized, deduction procedures, and the opening and closing dates for entering deductions on the payroll records.

No payroll deduction should be initiated without written authorization from the employee unless authorized by law or the courts. Exhibit 8.5 shows a list of payroll deductions that describes not only the commonly accepted categories but also information about procedures.

EXHIBIT 8.5   Categories of Payroll Deductions

1. **Income Tax Deductions.** Government income tax legislation requires each employee to execute a certificate of exemptions to be used as a basis for calculating income tax deductions. In most instances, the certificate will provide the following information:

   a. *Full name.* It is recommended that it be typed or printed for legibility. In the case of married women, use first name, maiden name, and last name.

   b. *Employee account number.* This is needed for identification on payroll tax returns as well as for employee record cards. All employees should be required to show their account card and also to copy the name as it appears on the card. The existing U.S. income tax regulations require a social security (FICA) account number for all employees subject to withholding taxes. If an employee has not filed an account number, he or she should be advised to fill out an application form and send it to the nearest district office of the U.S. Social Security Administration. Forms to obtain lost account cards are also available at the same office.

   c. *Home address.* Print or type this information, including city, state or province, and other identifying postal information.

   d. *Claim for withholding exemptions.* The school district must allow exemptions to each employee on the basis of the withholding certificate. If an employee fails to furnish a certificate, the school district is required to withhold tax as if the employee had claimed no withholding exemptions. A certificate filed by a new employee is to be made effective on the first payment of salary. Once filed with the school district, a withholding exemption certificate will remain in effect until an amended certificate is furnished.

   The following classifications of exemption are usually considered:

   a. *Single.* This refers to persons not married and who desire to claim an exemption. A mark, number, or other designation is made on the form for this claim of exemption.

   b. *Married.* This classification allows one exemption each for husband and wife if not claimed on another certificate. If claim is made for both exemptions, then an indication is inserted on the certificate; if one of the exemptions is claimed, or no exemptions are claimed, this is also indicated on the form.

   c. *Other exemptions.* This classification covers such exemptions as:

      i. Age (older than 65)
      ii. Blindness
      iii. Other relatives who qualify as dependents

   Employees may file an amended exemption certificate, increasing the number of exemptions, at any time. Normally, the deductions are reflected in the next payment of wages.

   School districts will usually find it convenient to determine the amount of income tax required to be withheld from wage bracket tables. Government agencies provide these tables free of charge—commercial tax tables may also be purchased from office supply companies, professional accountants' organizations, and suppliers of tax services. Tax tables are available for various pay periods, that is, weekly, biweekly, semimonthly, monthly, daily, or miscellaneous periods.

   In addition to making payroll withholding as specified by Internal Revenue Service tax tables, a percentage method may be used. Additional amounts may be withheld under

Continued

EXHIBIT 8.5   *Continued*

a written agreement between the school district and the employee. This agreement will be effective for such periods as may be mutually agreed on.

The school district is usually assigned a reporting number for purposes of transmitting and accounting for payroll taxes deducted. Returns are usually rendered monthly or quarterly, and an annual reconciliation is required.

Some cities or local government units require collection of an occupational license or payroll tax. The law serves as the basis for the deduction, and no authorizing action is required of the employee. In most instances, this tax is based on a percentage of gross salary, with no provision for exemptions.

The same employer reporting is required as mentioned previously.

2. **Retirement Deductions.** These deductions usually come under one of three classifications—a government retirement plan for all employees, a program specifically limited to certificated or noncertificated personnel, or a commercial underwriting program. Some school districts may permit certificated employees to participate in all three plans or only one plan. This is usually determined by the school board or a governing board or by law. Deductions are usually based on a fixed percentage of gross salary.

3. **Court-Ordered Deductions.** The problems of deductions relative to garnishments, bankruptcies, levies, and other deductions of this nature are sometimes vexing to school districts. Employees should be encouraged to keep their personal financial affairs in sufficient order to prevent this type of action. Of course, the employee should be given every opportunity to rectify the situation if it is an oversight or an honest error on the debtor's part.

In determining this deduction, care must be taken to note the following important information:

a. Name of plaintiff or debtor
b. Date of garnishment served and received by school district
c. Amount of garnishment
d. Court costs—advisable to verify with court
e. Amount of pay due as of date of garnishment
f. Number of days permitted to answer the garnishment

An information copy of the garnishment or order should be sent to the employee. It is possible that a form entitled "Release" may be obtained by the employee that will alter the sum of money to be deducted from his or her salary. In no instance should the school district accept the word of the plaintiff's or defendant's attorney, or the debtor, relative to reduction in the principal amount of the debt unless a written form is furnished by the court responsible for the original garnishment order.

At this time, it is appropriate to stress these four points:

a. Recover the amount required by the court up to the date of the garnishment. If the salary earned is not sufficient to take care of indebtedness, there is a possibility that a subsequent garnishment will be initiated.
b. File with the court the necessary answer within the specified time permitted. Deduction check should be made payable to the court.
c. Always advise the employee of the garnishment and give him or her every opportunity to rectify the matter prior to actual deduction.
d. Establish a policy relative to number of garnishments permitted, and acquaint all employees with the policy requirements.

EXHIBIT 8.5   *Continued*

4. **Miscellaneous Deductions.** The preceding paragraphs have dealt with deductions that are mandatory in nature and that are based on government regulations or court orders. Reference has been made to the control of deductions through an approved policy of the school district. In this connection, surveys of other school district deduction policies may be made to assist in development of the individual district policy.

   The deductions discussed in the ensuing paragraphs are on a voluntary basis and are usually identified as fringe benefits. The types of deductions are varied in scope. However, only a few are presented here to be used for guidance and direction:

   a. *Health, accident, and hospital plans.* These deductions are based on a predetermined premium made by the underwriting company. Rates are based on the type of coverage desired by the employee—the more coverage desired, the higher the premium. A part of the premium may or may not be paid by the school district, depending on the policy of the board and applicable state laws. Some school districts may pay all of the premiums. In most instances, an application form is required of the employee in which personal information and family health history is indicated. A deduction authorization should also be signed by the employee and may or may not be included as part of the application form. Group insurance certificates or individual policies are usually issued to the employee and confirm the coverage authorized on the deduction form.

   b. *Life insurance plans.* These deductions generally follow the same outline as the plan for health, accident, and hospitalization. Many retirement plans now include life insurance as apart of their comprehensive program.

   c. *Employment association dues.* Deductions for association dues are becoming increasingly popular among school districts. These include such deductions as local unit, state or province association dues that may be paid in one or more installments from the employee's salary. Many associations also provide for other deductions as a part of their overall program. This could include a life insurance program, disability income protection, and personal liability insurance.

   d. *Credit union.* This is becoming a more popular deduction for school district employees. The credit union has as its major purpose the encouragement of savings as well as the providing of a source of financial assistance. It is suggested that the deduction authorization form be worded in such a way that the deduction amount is not identified as either a savings or a loan payment. The treasurer of the credit union should determine the monthly amount to be paid or the savings desired and secure the signed authorization for payroll records. Many credit unions pay for deduction service on the basis of the number of accounts serviced.

   e. *Community fund contributions.* Considerable pressure is exerted on the school districts to participate in various solicitations for the welfare of the underprivileged in the community. Many localities have combined all the campaigns into one, on an annual basis. It is emphasized that every attempt be made to combine these appeals into one amount for deduction purposes. A signed deduction form should be obtained that would indicate the amount to be deducted and the period covered.

Source: Adapted from Charles W. Foster and Jean M. Taylor, eds., *Wage and Salary Administration: A Handbook for School Business Officials*, Association of School Business Officials International, 1968, Chicago, Illinois. www.irs.gov.

Pay Periods

The complexity and size of modern school districts have raised a question for education that was answered many years ago in the private sector: Should salaries be paid on a monthly, semimonthly, biweekly, or weekly schedule? School districts no longer employ just a few people in simple jobs, and their payrolls can no longer be managed by a manual method. The complexity of multiple deductions for numerous employee classifications has mandated computerization of payroll management, and this, in turn, has increased the importance of deadlines. The basic principles for determining pay periods are the type of work done by the employee, the amount earned, and the cost to the school district.

Different classifications of employees have different expectations about how often they should be paid. Custodians, bus drivers, and cafeteria workers are more accustomed to being paid on a weekly basis in the business community, and such employees expect a weekly check when working for a school district. Skilled employees such as plumbers, electricians, and carpenters generally receive higher wages than unskilled workers and are more accustomed to being paid on a monthly or biweekly basis. Finally, professional employees such as administrators and teachers are usually paid on a monthly basis; they normally have individual contracts for a set dollar amount, which is divided into equal payments. Some school districts allow teachers to be paid in either nine or twelve payments, at the discretion of the individual teacher. Some building principals, in like manner, work ten months and are given the option of receiving their salary in ten or twelve monthly payments.

The size of the school district determines the complexity of the payroll process. In larger school systems, of course, more people are employed, which usually increases the number of job classifications having different payroll periods. This demands more computerization as well as deadlines and specific procedures for handling the payroll. More payroll specialists and equipment are needed, which increases the school district's cost of managing the payroll process. In conclusion, the importance of the payroll process to the school system is unquestioned.

Principles for Presenting Salary Recommendations to the School Board

It is assumed that all salary recommendations presented to the board of education will be based on sound wage and salary practices. Previous sections in this chapter outline defensible procedures that, if followed, place the administration in such a position. The next objective, then, is to present the recommendations in a manner that result in approval by the school board. Of course, the financial condition of the school district, along with the agreements with employee unions and associations, also have an effect on salary recommendations.

Fiscal Condition of the School District

In the present economy, salary recommendations usually call for an increase, and in some cases, a substantial increase, in wages. As noted previously, salary appropriations account for 80 percent of school district budgets. Clearly, an increase in salaries will create one of the following situations: Less money will be available for other categories of school operations, the school district will have enough revenue and/or balances to accommodate the salary increases, or the board of education will have to find additional sources of revenue to meet the increases. In most states, additional revenue can be obtained only through a tax levy increase, which, of course, requires voter approval. Inflation has generally created scarcity for most school districts. Therefore, a board of education may be unable to approve a recommendation if the cost is unrealistically high.

Administrative Organization of the School District

Usually, only two administrative structures affect salary recommendations. If a school district does not engage in collective bargaining, the superintendent of schools, with the advice of the school business administrator, is directly responsible for making the salary recommendations. However, if the school district engages in collective bargaining, the board will be asked to ratify a master contract that usually has major sections devoted to salaries and wages. The chief negotiator for the school district, with input from the superintendent of schools, will have negotiated within preestablished fiscal considerations. In this latter situation, the salary recommendations, along with working conditions and fringe benefits, which also have a dollar value, must be evaluated by the board.

Employee Unions and Associations

The American Federation of Teachers, the National Education Association (NEA), and many unions representing non-instructional personnel have official positions on salary and wage policies. Most of these unions and associations seek comparability with the private sector and negotiate for their membership along this line. More recently, these organizations have come to realize that, because of the large numbers of people they represent, they have a great deal of political influence that has had an effect on the election not only of school board members but also of state legislators and even national candidates. An endorsement by a national labor or teacher organization such as the NEA is much sought after by all presidential candidates.

Salary Recommendation Procedures

The procedure for presentation of salary schedules to the board varies with the particular needs of the locality. The following set of procedures is a guide for superintendents in formulating salary recommendations to the board of education:

- The recommendations must be backed by quantitative or qualitative or both types of evidence, and they must have been presented for analysis and review by the representatives of teachers, staff members, and the administration team.
- The recommendations and supporting evidence must be *user friendly*. They can be fashioned into a PowerPoint presentation and stored on a CD that should be available to all interested parties, including the general public.
- These data are meaningful only if presented in comparison with previous data, which should clearly identify the differences from previous years and the rationale for the difference.
- All salary recommendations, covering all employees, should be put forth at the same time. Thus, teacher, administrator, and staff salaries should be packaged together so

that the board of education has a complete picture of the salary requirements. This eliminates the criticism that may be leveled against the administration for favoring one group of employees over others. It also eliminates the speculation that is certain to be a component of the discussion and communication between the various employee groups and their supporters. Secure, when needed, the services of a consulting firm to compile data regarding prevailing salary rates in the community. A consulting firm can also be of assistance in establishing classifications of employees and writing job descriptions.

- All levels of administration should be required to demonstrate through the budget process salary and wage efficiency and effectiveness by having a workflow chart that identifies the number of employees who are responsible for carrying out the various functions in the school district.[15]

Small Business Job Protection Act of 1996

Commonly referred to as the *minimum wage law* because its intent was to increase the take-home wages of employees, the passage and signing into law of the Small Business Job Protection Act of 1996 attracted much attention in the news media. When President Bill Clinton signed the bill in August 1996, the ceremony featured minimum-wage workers and their children, labor union officials, congressional leaders, and Vice President Al Gore. To sign the bill, President Clinton used the desk of President Franklin Roosevelt's Labor Secretary, Francis Perkins.[16]

In July 2009, the U.S. Congress passed the Fair Labor Standards Act, which established the minimum federal per hour pay rate at $7.25. Each increase affected approximately 10 million workers, who received larger paychecks. However, individual states can raise the minimum wage to even higher levels. Further, cities may increase the minimum wage beyond federal and state levels.

Because the law was opposed by many small businesses, Congress included approximately $9 billion in tax breaks for businesses that took effect over a seven-year period. For example, in the year of purchase, the total cost of new equipment that a small business can claim as tax exempt was raised from $17,500 to $25,000. A major implication for school districts, of course, is that budgets must be adjusted to account for the required increase in wages.

Conclusions

A few final comments are appropriate on salary and wage administration. First, executive salaries are usually negotiated on a personal basis and do not fall within the limits of a salary schedule. The executive positions in school districts are relatively few, commonly the superintendency and associate or assistant superintendencies.

Second, it is extremely important to consider each salary schedule as a separate entity. In some school systems, increases to the teacher salary schedule are reflected in an additional percentage increase being applied to the administrator schedule. This, of course, defeats the salary schedule objective, which is to reward performance within salary limits that are competitive with those of other school districts and businesses in the community. This can be done only by analyzing each individual salary schedule.

When collective bargaining is involved, such a tied-in procedure violates the distinction between management and employees. If an administrative salary schedule is affected by an increase to the teacher salary schedule resulting from collective negotiations, the administrators are, in actuality, being represented by the teachers' bargaining agent.

Third, "extra pay for extra duty," which is the common language applied to overtime pay for instructional personnel and overtime pay for classified employees, should be determined by the same procedure used to establish regular salary and wages. The rewards of performance and competitiveness are also primary considerations in overtime compensation.

Fourth, this chapter was written from the viewpoint that salary and wage increases are rewards for performance, not simply rewards for seniority with the school district. Many districts have developed salary schedules with channels reflecting academic preparation (bachelor's degree, master's degree, etc.) and steps reflecting seniority in the school district. The salary schedules recommended in this chapter provide for ranges reflecting job classification with step increases based on performance. The practices in most public school districts, which essentially recommend establishing competitive compensation programs that will attract quality personnel, are not in keeping with the principles set forth in this chapter.

Indirect Compensation: Fringe Benefits Administration

Fringe benefits may be defined as benefits available to all employees resulting from a direct fiscal expenditure. Because fringe benefits are available to all employees and are not contingent on performance, such services are not motivators but are more properly considered maintenance factors. Nevertheless, fringe benefits are commonly considered an important part of an effective compensation program. Retirement programs, medical and hospitalization insurance, and life insurance are only a few of the many fringe benefits offered to employees in school systems. Because these services are essential in our society, the quality of these and other fringe benefit programs can have a significant effect on the ability of a school district to attract and retain good employees. Conversely, absenteeism and employee turnover, which are signs of employee dissatisfaction, can possibly be kept to a tolerable level with good fringe benefit and salary programs.

High employee turnover across the United States costs school districts millions of dollars each year. Turnover should be kept to a reasonable rate to minimize the need to recruit and hire new employees, which creates direct expenditures of money. This factor, however, does not begin to address the problem of meeting the primary objective of the school district to educate students when there is a continual flow of new employees.

Absenteeism costs corporations in the United States an average of $20 billion each year. Although figures on the cost of absenteeism to public education are not readily available, millions of dollars would be a conservative estimate. A substitute teacher must be hired whenever a teacher is absent. The students are still present, and the task of teaching them cannot be passed on to another of the district's regular teachers, nor can it wait until the absent teacher returns.

The key factor in addressing high employee turnover and absenteeism is to establish a positive approach. Attracting individuals with excellent credentials and a desire for excellence in performance, from the outset, ultimately correct high turnover and absenteeism.

Quality fringe benefits attract quality candidates for positions and maintain employee commitment to the school district.

Types of Fringe Benefits

The cost of fringe benefits in the United States has risen to approximately one-third of the total compensation paid to employees. School districts across the country are experiencing severe financial problems. With financial problems continuing to spread, school districts have found that fringe benefit enrichment is an alternative when large wage and salary increases are not feasible. As more school districts develop elaborate fringe benefit programs, greater pressure has been placed on competing school districts to develop similar programs to attract and keep employees.

There is also a growing recognition that fringe benefits are nontaxable, which has been another major stimulus toward their expansion. If a teacher wants a certain amount of life insurance, there are two advantages in having it purchased by the school district: First, the premium will be lower because the school district will be purchasing a large degree of protection; and second, the teacher would pay the premium for the insurance out of his or her net pay, which is the dollar amount left over after paying taxes. However, if the school district pays the premium, the teacher has more wages left to pay for other needs, making this an attractive fringe benefit.

Benefits Required by Law

Certain benefits must be provided by the school district: social security premiums, state retirement insurance, unemployment compensation, and workers' compensation. These benefits provide the employee with financial security and protection at retirement or termination, or when an injury occurs in the workplace; they also provide survivors' benefits to dependents in the event of the employee's death.

The social security program usually covers classified employees. Instructional and administrative personnel are normally included in state retirement program. Social security is the major source of income for U.S. retirees and is financed by the contributions of employees, computed as a percentage of employees' earnings and matched by the employer. Survivors' benefits for the dependents of a deceased employee and disability benefits for an employee who is unable to be gainfully employed are provided through the Social Security Administration.

The Social Security Act is an important aspect of the U.S. government's attempt to care for and protect the elderly by ensuring a minimal standard of living for them. Although social security is often referred to as an "insurance program," this is a misnomer. Rather, it is a *transfer program,* using funds from one generation to support another. We, the currently employed, pay a social security tax used to support yesterday's retired workers, dependents, and the disabled. It is important for human resources administrators to be cognizant of the fact that social security benefits and the program itself are subject to legislation. Thus, changes are certain to occur and must be monitored continually to ensure that adequate budgetary appropriations are available to meet the demands of these potential changes.

Unemployment compensation laws in most states provide benefits to individuals who are without a job. To qualify for these benefits, a person usually submits an application to the state employment agency for unemployment benefits and registers with that agency, indicating a willingness to accept suitable employment offered through the agency. In addition, the person must have worked a minimum number of weeks before becoming unemployed.

Unemployment benefits are derived from a tax levied against employers calculated as a percentage of the employer's total payroll. Benefits received by unemployed workers are calculated from the individual's previous wage rate plus the length of previous employment. Unemployment benefits are provided on a limited basis, typically for a twenty-six–week period. Unemployment compensation also serves the total economy of the United States because it provides stability in spending power during periods of high unemployment, as when a recession occurs.

Workers' compensation programs provide benefits to individuals injured or disabled while engaged in a job-related activity. Benefits paid to employees for injuries are based on schedules for minimum and maximum payments, depending on the type of injury sustained. For example, the loss of a hand is compensated with a higher dollar amount than the loss of a finger. In like manner, disability payments are calculated based on the individual's current salary, future earnings, and financial responsibilities.

The costs of workers' compensation programs are borne entirely by employers. Although the programs are mandated by state laws, the method of obtaining workers' compensation insurance is usually left to the discretion of the employer, who may buy such protection from public or private agencies or provide the protection through a self-insuring program. Like social security and unemployment insurance, workers' compensation is subject to the legislative process. Thus, requirements and benefits will certainly change with the passage of time.

Where mandated by state laws, retirement programs for administrators and teachers generally follow the prescriptions of these other protection programs. Contributions are calculated on the basis of employees' wages and are usually matched by the school district. Benefits based on contributions are paid on retirement, with survivors' benefits being available for the dependents of deceased employees.

In 1986, the U.S. Congress passed the Consolidated Omnibus Budget Reconciliation Act (COBRA), a federal law requiring employers to provide group health plans for their employees and their dependents to offer an extension of the coverage on a temporary basis under certain conditions when coverage would usually end. An employee covered by the group health plan is eligible for continuation of coverage if his or her employment is terminated except in cases of gross misconduct, if he or she is laid off for economic reasons, or if he or she is reduced to part-time employment and thereby would usually lose coverage.

Family members of an employee are entitled to continued coverage under the following qualifying events: death of the employee; divorce or legal separation from the employee; Medicare becoming the employee's primary healthcare coverage; termination, layoff, or part-time status of the employee; and ceasing to be considered a dependent child under the plan.

There are notification requirements under this law, and the employee or family members must pay the premiums for the extended group health plan coverage. Extended coverage may last for eighteen, twenty-nine, or thirty-six months, depending on certain qualifying conditions.

Voluntary Fringe Benefits
This category of benefits may be further divided into insurance programs, time away from the job, and services. Group insurance programs are available for almost every human need; the

most common are major medical and hospitalization insurance, dental insurance, term life insurance, errors and omissions insurance, and optical insurance. The number of such programs made available to employees depends on the fiscal condition of the school district and the wishes of the employees. A school district is usually restricted by state statute to paying insurance premiums only for employees. Therefore, an employee who wants to include dependents under such insurance programs must pay the additional premium for this coverage.

Under federal law and IRS regulations, school districts can design "cafeteria" fringe benefit plans that allow individual employees to choose the benefits that best meet their needs. In addition, if the employee is to bear the cost of some of these programs, the premiums he or she pays can be deducted from his or her gross salary or wages before federal income taxes are levied.

This tax advantage for employees and the opportunity to choose their benefits from a predetermined list are two reasons why such programs are quite desirable. The administrative expense of such a program and the availability of insurance coverage that does not demand a high percentage of participation are problems. For example, a company may offer a dental insurance program to a school district only if there is 60-percent participation by employees.

Federal tax-qualified plans (those exempt from taxation) must not be offered only to highly compensated employees. Beginning in 1997, the definition of a *highly compensated employee* was changed to include an employee who was compensated for the preceding year in excess of $150,000 or who was among the top 20 percent of employees in terms of income.[17]

A fringe benefit that is often taken for granted by employees but that creates an additional expense for a school district is time spent away from work. Therefore, sick leave, vacation time, paid holidays, and sabbatical leave are, in fact, benefits provided at the discretion of the school system. In very large school districts, this amounts to a considerable expenditure.

Corporations have long recognized the value of services in a fringe benefit program. Social and recreational events, employee assistance programs, wellness programs, cultural activities, credit unions, company cafeterias, company-provided transportation to and from work, tuition reimbursements, and child care centers are only a few of the services found in many large corporations.

School systems usually provide much more limited services. Services such as time away from work are seldom recognized by employees as fringe benefits. Those most commonly found in public education are payment of expenses for attendance at workshops, professional meetings, and conventions; tuition reimbursement; and free lunches and coffee. In some districts experiencing a decrease in pupil enrollment and thus a reduction in staff, career counseling is provided to teachers in order to help them prepare for jobs outside education. In large school districts, central office administrators are usually provided with district-owned automobiles to use when engaged in school business, or they receive mileage reimbursement.

Fringe benefits are certainly an important component of all compensation programs, and they are becoming even more important as alternatives to large salary and wage increases.

Managed Healthcare

Healthcare costs continue to increase at an alarming rate. Managed healthcare is an alternative approach to traditional insurance programs that is meant to maintain a high quality of care but at a lower cost and in a more efficient manner.

Managed healthcare coordinates services around the patient and thereby produces a more efficient delivery system. To accomplish this, school districts must employ case management specialists who have the job responsibility of evaluating cases that require extensive and/or expensive medical treatment. As an alternative to hiring case management specialists, a school district can contract with a company specializing in third-party healthcare administration specialists who work with patients and physicians in order to identify alternatives that are medically sound, yet cost effective. A common example is developing a plan that incorporates outpatient care after sufficient inpatient hospital care rather than a prolonged hospital stay. Such specialists should also develop employee programs that encourage healthy lifestyles and the prevention of illness. It would probably be cost effective for a school district to offer mammograms or diabetes testing at a nominal cost to employees.

There are various levels of managed healthcare. *Utilization management* attempts to control the cost of a school district's health benefit plan, best accomplished through catastrophic case management and utilization review. When an employee suffers a catastrophic illness, the case manager begins the process of assisting the patient and his or her physicians in accessing the best treatment at the lowest cost. This could include care in a rehabilitation center, nursing home, or extended care facility or outpatient services in the patient's home. The case manager helps negotiate rates with these facilities.

Utilization review usually includes the reviewing of all inpatient admissions, outpatient surgical procedures, inpatient substance cases, and inpatient psychiatric care. The purpose is to ascertain if such services are medically sound. In addition, before a claim is paid, the case manager reviews the charges for accuracy.

An alternative to hiring case management specialists or contracting with a third-party healthcare administrator is for a school district to join a managed care network. Physicians who are members of the network agree to certain fee guidelines, and medical facilities that belong to the network agree to a certain quality of service and fee guidelines. The network provides the school district with the efficient processing of paperwork and with cost information that helps the school district in its financial planning.

There are various types of networks. One type is called a *preferred provider organization* (PPO). Both hospitals and physicians belong to such a network. Physicians treat patients in their own offices. If a school district employee chooses a physician or hospital outside the network, most PPOs pay a much smaller percentage of the bill. Hospitals and physicians outside the network cannot be monitored to ensure quality care and cost containment.

A second type of network is a *health maintenance organization* (HMO). In this arrangement, each patient is provided with a network primary care physician who controls access within the network to care for the employee and his or her dependents. A prepaid fixed monthly fee for all services is another important feature of the HMO. Typically, HMOs are organized around four models: group, staff, individual practice, and point-of-service. In the *group model,* a group or groups of physicians provide care to patients at one or more locations. In the *staff model,* physicians are actually employed by an HMO and provide services at one or more locations. In the *individual practice model,* an HMO contracts with physicians who practice out of their own offices. In the *point-of-service model,* an HMO allows a school district employee to choose physicians outside the network, but the employee pays a higher percentage of the cost.

Many PPOs and HMOs have prescription drug plans whereby certain pharmacies within a network offer medication at a reduced cost. This kind of network can also be found outside PPOs and HMOs.

Health Insurance Portability and Accountability Act of 1996

There was little media coverage of the Health Insurance Portability and Accountability Act of 1996 (HIPAA) until August 21, 1996, when it was signed into law by President Bill Clinton. The law addresses the needs of approximately 25 million Americans who are denied health insurance coverage because of an illness or who cannot change jobs because they, their spouse, or their dependents would be denied insurance coverage because of a preexisting medical condition such as diabetes. The law became effective at the beginning of the new plan year after July 1, 1997. The following are major provisions of HIPAA:

- Immediate coverage is provided for the employee, spouse, and dependents by the new employer if the employee, spouse, and dependents were covered by the previous employer's healthcare plan for twelve months—or eighteen months if they enter the new employer's plan late.
- Immediate coverage is provided for pregnant women, newborns, and children placed in the employee's home pending adoption.
- The new employer can deny coverage for a preexisting condition for up to one year if the employee, spouse, and dependents were not covered by the previous employer for twelve or eighteen months, respectively. If there was a break in the previous coverage of more than sixty-three days, the waiting period could start over again.
- Employers can limit a new employee, spouse, and dependents to the same coverage they had with the previous employer even if other employees have additional coverage.
- The healthcare plan with the new employer could exclude coverage for certain illnesses and could place a cap on benefit coverage.
- Local and state government healthcare plans may exempt themselves from this law.
- Employers can make premium adjustments to their plans or increase copayments and deductibles in order to offset high claims experience, as long as these modifications are applicable to all employees.
- If the new employer does not provide a healthcare plan, the state in which the school district is located is responsible for providing unrestricted access to a choice of individual health insurance policies to those individuals, their spouses, and their dependents who were covered by a group healthcare plan for at least eighteen months with a previous employer.

The law does not address the needs of people who are uninsured because they cannot afford to pay insurance premiums. In addition, individuals who have insurance for long-term care can receive a tax deduction for the cost of the premium and the cost of the care. Finally, the law authorized a pilot program, medical savings accounts, as an alternative to conventional health insurance policies for self-employed people and for employees of small companies. The law also required medical plans to cover illnesses arising from genetic defects. Further, accidents caused through participation in recreation activities or hobbies such as skiing must now be covered by healthcare plans.[18]

School districts must now require their insurance companies to delete provisions from insurance policies that discriminate against employees, their spouses, and their dependents because of preexisting medical conditions. Small school districts could also be eligible for medical savings accounts.

Medical Savings Accounts

HIPAA established a pilot *medical savings account* (MSA) program in an attempt to control the rising cost of healthcare. The program began in 1997 and continued through 2000, after which time employees of school districts that had already established MSAs were allowed to continue with this program. To qualify, a school district had to provide a healthcare plan with a large deductible and had to meet the *small employer* designation. Under this approach, employees can choose the physicians, hospitals, and treatment options they want. Major illnesses are paid for by the school district's insurance company, while money withdrawn from employees' MSAs is used to pay for minor healthcare costs. Health insurance coverage with a high deductible creates a much lower premium than coverage with a low deductible. A high-deductible plan is one with an annual deductible of at least $1,500, but not more than $2,250 for single coverage or at least a $3,000 but not more than $4,500 for family coverage. Thus, the school district can purchase high-deductible healthcare insurance and use the money it saves to establish an MSA for each employee. Also, the employee can authorize the school district to deduct a certain amount of money from his or her payroll check before taxes are assessed to be placed in the MSA to pay minor healthcare costs for a dependent spouse and/or children. If the deductible is reached, the health insurance company pays for the incurred cost.

A school district that met the small employer designation was one with no more than fifty employees during the preceding or second preceding year. Such a district may continue to establish MSAs for new employees or for employees who previously did not have MSAs until the year following the first year when the district has 200 employees. After reaching this plateau, no new MSAs may be established.

The MSA is under the control of the employee, and each year the employee can make additional contributions to it through the district for his or her dependent coverage. The account should be interest bearing, and unspent funds can grow from the contributions and interest. The employee can make withdrawals for nonmedical purposes, but such withdrawals are taxed and penalized.

It is estimated that only 5 to 10 percent of employees will reach the deductible each year. Former employees on Medicare have an option of receiving health insurance and a large contribution to a MSA from Medicare funds.

The advantages of MSAs are considerable, with the most obvious being the following:

- National reduction of healthcare costs
- Increased savings for employers
- Increased saving for employees
- Retirement savings for health and non-health expenses
- Patients' control of healthcare choice
- Healthcare coverage for people and their dependents between jobs (portability)[19]

Procuring Healthcare and Related Insurance

In large school districts, procuring fringe benefit insurance is usually the responsibility of the purchasing and procurement departments, along with significant involvement of the director of employee benefits, who reports to the assistant superintendent for human resources. In medium-size districts, an assistant superintendent may be assigned this responsibility, whereas in small school districts, the superintendent of schools will probably implement the procurement process. Of course, many school districts hire an insurance consultant or broker (who is not permitted to place a bid) to help in developing the bid specifications and may also oversee the bidding process, including the analysis of the bids.[20]

The healthcare industry has been experiencing a period of significant change and modification. Exhibit 8.6 sets forth the categories of coverage in a typical healthcare program that must be considered when developing such a program.

Insurance Agent and Broker

An *insurance policy* is a legal contract between an insurance company and the school district. The provisions of insurance policies are usually developed by a third party, an insurance agent or broker. The majority of insurance companies do business under the American agency system, whereby they contract with individuals within a given territory. These individuals are referred to as *agents* because they are authorized to issue policies, collect premiums, and solicit renewals. Independent agents represent several insurance companies, whereas exclusive agents represent a single company.

Insurance brokers are not under contract to any specific insurance company, and they act on a freelance basis. Thus, brokers buy insurance coverage for clients. Brokers can

---

EXHIBIT 8.6 Categories of Coverage in a Typical Healthcare Program

Physician and Hospital Selection	Physical Medicine and Occupational Therapy
Annual Deductible	Hospital Services
Copayment	Maternity Care
Preventive Care	Prenatal Care
Routine Physical	Postnatal Care
Gynecologic Exams	Delivery
Eye Exams	Mental Health Benefits
Immunizations	Outpatient
Well-Baby and Pediatric Care	Inpatient
Pediatric Dental Exams	Chemical Dependency Benefits
Health Education	Outpatient
Home Care	Inpatient
Physician Care	Emergency Care
Diagnostic Services (including X-ray and laboratory tests)	Prescription Drugs and Medications
	Away-from-Home Care
Surgery	Maximum Out-of-Pocket Costs to the Employee
Outpatient	Maximum Cost Paid in Claims for the Employee
Consultations and Second Opinions	

purchase insurance directly from an insurance company or place business through an insurance agent. The major difference, therefore, between an *agent* and a *broker* lies in the fact that the agent may act on behalf of the company. If an agent states that the school district is covered by an insurance policy even before the policy is issued, then it is covered. A broker must receive written verification of coverage from an insurance company.

Selecting Insurance Companies

There are literally thousands of insurance companies selling some form of healthcare and related insurance in the United States. Companies differ significantly because of their financial capacity to assure timely and accurate processing and payment of claims. In addition, third-party management companies that process claims for self-insured school districts vary depending on their fiscal solvency and performance.

Thus, when bids are received from healthcare and related services insurance companies or third-party management companies, it is essential to check their performance and financial solvency with well-established rating firms. Among the nationally recognized rating firms are A. M. Best of Oldwick (New Jersey), Duff & Phelps of Chicago, Moody's of New York, and Standard & Poor's of New York. These firms award letter grades to individual insurance provider companies based on their performance and viability. A. M. Best awards a range of grades from a top grade of A++ to a low grade of F; Duff & Phelps uses AAA to CCC; Moody awards range from AAA to C; and Standard & Poor's uses AAA to R. Insurance companies desiring a rating must pay an annual fee to the rating firm, so many of them may not request a rating from every rating firm. Consequently, school districts should request in the bidding process that the insurance companies identify the firm or firms by which they are rated. School districts can then contact the appropriate rating firms directly with the list of insurance companies that have submitted a bid. Rating firms may charge school districts a fee for their services.

The specifications in the request-for-proposals bid package should be written in such a way that the school district can select a single company to provide all the lines of healthcare and related insurance or a group of companies, with each providing a different benefit. In selecting one or more healthcare and related insurance companies or third-party companies, the following criteria should constitute the minimum required: successful experience in providing coverage or management in at least two other school districts with an equal number of employees and similar benefits, written references from other school districts stating that claims were processed accurately and promptly, useful communication literature for employees concerning the coverage and claims process, evidence that the school district will be required to provide only reasonable administrative assistance, affordable premiums for the district and the employees, and evidence that the insurance company or management company will use accurate and appropriate data in establishing future premiums.

Of course, there is a direct relationship between the premium a school district pays for healthcare and related insurance and the claims experience of the group of employees covered by the insurance. When the sum of money paid in claims is high, premiums are correspondingly higher. Most insurance companies are *for profit,* and therefore the premium includes a profit for the company. Premiums also include enough money not only to pay claims but also to build up a reserve for cash-flow purposes. In addition, the premium includes a reserve to pay outstanding claims if the school district takes bids and awards a contract to a different insurance company.

There is a significant financial advantage to the school district if the healthcare and related insurance lines have a deductible that must be paid by the employee before the district's insurance program incurs a claim. There is a direct relationship between the amount of the premium paid by the district and the size of the deductible. For example, if an employee must pay the first $250 in medical costs, the cost of premium paid by the district will be less than if the employee has to pay only the first $100. The reason for this is obvious—a claim is incurred after $100 rather than after $250. Several important reasons why a school district should require a deductible for all premium-related fringe benefits include the following:

- Deductibles encourage employees to retain some responsibility for controlling costs.
- Deductibles avoid nuisance claims.
- Deductibles help preserve a competitive market for the district's insurance program.
- Deductibles help reduce administrative costs.

A *copayment* is an alternative to deductibles that is also a financial benefit to a school district if it is incorporated into the district's healthcare and related insurance program. For example, a district's program could require a $10 copayment for an office visit to a physician; the insurance program would then pay the remainder of the cost for the visit. The copayment approach is more commonly used for prescription drugs and medications. Like deductibles, the copayments encourage employees to be more responsible in controlling health costs.

Even if a school district has self-funded healthcare and related insurance programs, deductibles and copayments can bring about the same advantages cited previously. The single most important reason why a school district would create such a program is to save money, usually in two ways: First, the premium set aside by the district does not include a profit; and second, the money budgeted from the district's revenue for healthcare and related benefits can be invested, and the interest helps reduce the cost of the benefits programs during periods of time without large claims.

Self-funding, however, requires a school district to purchase *stop loss* insurance, the purpose of which is to pay a portion of the cost of claims arising from catastrophic illnesses that would significantly deplete the pool of money set aside to pay claims. Insurance should be purchased for individual claims after a certain amount has been paid through the district's self-funded programs and for claims in the aggregate after a certain amount has been paid. For example, the birth of a premature baby results in a costly hospital bill. Stop loss insurance pays for that portion of the hospital bill more than $100,000 (or any other limit set by the school district). Also, stop loss insurance could pay for claims from all employees taken together that exceed, for example, $3,000,000. The cost of the premium for stop loss insurance depends on the amount of money that the school district pays in claims. Obviously, the more money the school district pays in claims, the less the district pays in premiums.

In those school districts in which employee benefits are bargained collectively, these issues are affected by the master agreement. If a school district and its employees do not bargain collectively or do not include these benefits in the negotiations, it is important for the superintendent to establish an employee advisory committee that should be charged with reviewing the district's healthcare and related programs, making suggestions for improvements in benefits and containing costs, reviewing specifications for bidding benefit insurance, reviewing the analysis of bids, and making recommendations to the assistant superintendent for human resources through the director of employee benefits.

Health Risks in the Workplace

A major issue facing many school districts across the United States is the rising cost of workers' compensation. In the early years of the twentieth century, workers who were injured on the job had to pay for their own medical treatment and probably received no wages during the recovery period. If a worker was seriously injured with an extensive recovery period, he or she most likely would not have a job even when able to return to work. Around 1910, individual states began to adopt various systems of workers' compensation, which required employers to compensate workers injured on the job regardless of who was at fault. In return, the workers were not allowed to sue their employers.[21]

Medical costs associated with workers' compensation have risen dramatically since the early 2000s, probably for three major reasons: First, in trying to contain general healthcare costs, employers have initiated cost-cutting measures such as higher deductibles, copayments, case management, utilization reviews, and the utilization of HMOs and PPOs. Although these measures contained costs in general healthcare, employees are now using workers' compensation, which usually pays the total cost of medical treatment, to receive the same level of benefits prior to initiating the cost-cutting measures. Second, the original *no-fault* approach has deteriorated into a massive legal bureaucracy, where lawyers and judges have become the central figures in workers' compensation cases. Finally, the nature of the workplace has changed dramatically, producing more complicated injuries such as carpal tunnel syndrome.[22]

For school district employees, there are three major categories of health risks:

1. *School facility environmental risks.* Radon gas; lead in the drinking water; asbestos in floor tile and other building materials; tobacco smoke; fungi, mold, and spores; pesticides; and cleaning materials containing various harmful chemicals.
2. *Violence.* Today, teachers and staff members are working with students who have a history of committing violent acts. The emergence of gangs is a contributing factor to the increasing number of violent acts committed against teachers and staff members.
3. *Infectious Diseases.* There is the risk of contracting infectious diseases that comes with working with children. For special education teachers who work with children who are multiply or physically impaired, there is also the risk of back injuries because many of these children must be lifted from one position to another.[23]

Employees need and want health information that will help them manage the work environment in such a way that they can be as health conscious as possible. It is the responsibility of human resources administrators to devise methods for providing this information to employees. Such information could prevent an employee from being injured or contracting disease.[24]

As set forth in Chapter 1, fringe benefit management is a component of the human resources function, and because workers' compensation is such a complicated and expensive fringe benefit, increasingly more school districts have established the position of *risk manager*, who usually reports to the assistant superintendent for human resources and whose responsibilities include identifying and evaluating the school district's exposure to risks. It is possible that the school district's insurance agent or broker or underwriter will assist the risk manager in conducting an audit in order to ascertain the exposure of the district to injuries on the job. Of course, the objective of the audit is to find the potential risk and then to eliminate or minimize it.[25] For example, if a school has a problem with gangs, the most appropriate method of dealing with this issue is to develop a comprehensive security program, which might require hiring security guards, developing gang prevention or self-esteem curricula, targeting at-risk students for special prevention programs, increasing job opportunities and drug education, and strengthening extracurricular and recreational programs. The development of such a security program becomes the responsibility of the director of risk management.[26]

A second example of a method for minimizing or eliminating risk is a comprehensive staff development program. For example, maintenance and custodial staff members use potentially dangerous equipment and hazardous chemicals. The manufacturer's sales representative or distributor of cleaning chemicals is usually available to train employees in the proper use of equipment and supplies.

Finally, if it is impossible to eliminate or significantly minimize a risk, it will be necessary to develop procedures that ensure that the workers' compensation program is effective in meeting the needs of the employees.

Implications for Small- and Medium-Size School Districts

The implications for small- and medium-size school districts are tied to the implications for technology and how it supports the compensation programs of a school district because the requirements of all school districts for salary and wage and fringe benefit administration are the same. Of course, what is different is the number of employees, but the policies, procedures, and requirements have the same impact.

Although a superintendent of schools may have electronic technology skills, he or she will need the assistance of a consultant or consulting firm to set up the computer software that gives compensation information and access to all employees. The access is critical because in small- and medium-size school districts, direct access to payroll and benefit plans allows employees to exercise direct control over their salary and fringe benefits. For example, if an employee gives birth to or adopts a child, adding the new dependent to the medical and hospital insurance program can be readily accomplished by the employee through the school district's intranet.

Knowing and understanding mandatory fringe benefits such as workers' compensation, maternity leave, unemployment compensation, and the provisions of COBRA are obviously important for some employees. Thus, employee rights are protected through technology that makes this information easily accessible.

Impact of Generation Y Teachers and Administrators on Compensation

Generation Y teachers and principals are like other generations in terms of wanting to be justly compensated for their work. However, Generation Y teachers and administrators seem to articulate more often their desire to find purposefulness in their careers. This does not imply that Generation Y teachers and administrators are significantly different from teachers and administrators from other generations, but rather that Generation Y has an intensity in terms of wanting work activities to be obviously purposeful. This presents somewhat of a challenge because, in educating children, it is often difficult to see meaningful progress in the immediate future.

As employees of a school district, Generation Y teachers and administrators definitely want financial rewards for their performance and place a high value on salary and fringe benefits. Thus, they tend to compare their salaries and benefits with those of teachers and administrators in other school districts. If the opportunity arises, they may well be prepared to apply for positions in those wealthier school districts. Salary and fringe benefits can be considered symbolic of the value that a school district places on its employees. The most desired fringe benefits are medical, hospitalization, dental, and life insurance, as well as tuition reimbursement.

In hiring and retaining Generation Y teachers and administrators, it is thus important to make use of their desire for purposeful employment to supplement their desire for higher wages and better benefits by developing nonfinancial rewards. Consequently, Generation Y teachers and administrators will appreciate the opportunity to participate in developing school district policy and to have more discretion and responsibility as they carry out their professional duties. Also, members of Generation Y expect to have the opportunity to advance in their careers and place a high value on professional development activities.

Summary

Psychologists have long recognized that satisfaction of needs is the primary motivation behind all human actions. In satisfying their needs, individuals act in ways that they perceive to be in their own best interests. A manager who understands human motivation and what employees believe to be in their best interests is able to develop a unique compensation system.

School district administrators should create a compensation system that links employee behaviors to the objectives of the school district while helping employees meet their personal objectives.

Five variables must be taken into consideration in a compensation program: employee performance, effort, seniority, skills, and job requirements. The rewarding of performance, however, must be the primary objective of a compensation program.

An effective program must include both intrinsic and extrinsic compensation. Intrinsic compensation consists of rewards that pertain to the quality of the job situation; they may include participation in the policy-making process, increased responsibility, and greater job discretion. Extrinsic rewards are divided into direct and indirect compensation. Direct compensation is commonly referred to as salary or wages; indirect compensation is frequently referred to as fringe benefits. Nonfinancial compensation has begun to appear in some school districts and is limited only by the imagination of the administration. It is tailored to meet the needs of individual employees. For example, a status-conscious employee might consider a reserved parking place as a reward for exceptional performance.

Direct compensation, salary and wages, can be administered effectively only if the following principles are incorporated into the pay policy: skills required in various positions must be recognized, salaries must be competitive, the primary focus of salary increases must be improved performance, and salary schedules must be reviewed annually.

An important question central to all pay policies is, "Does money motivate?" A reasonable conclusion, supported by experience and research, is that money does affect performance if it is clear that performance is rewarded by a salary increase.

A number of other issues are involved in salary and wages management that must command the attention of human resources administrators. These issues have an effect on pay policy development and include public disclosure of salaries, compensation packaging, equity of pay and performance, techniques for collecting community wage data, methods of making salary recommendations to the school board, payroll deductions, employee reactions to salary decisions, appropriate pay periods, annual wage review, and salary schedule construction.

Indirect compensation, or fringe benefits, may be defined as benefits that are available to all employees and that help a school district to attract and retain good employees. Certain fringe benefits are required by law, and include social security, state retirement programs, unemployment insurance, and workers' compensation.

Federal law (COBRA) requires school districts that provide group health plans for employees and their dependents to offer an extension of the coverage on a temporary basis under certain conditions when coverage would usually end.

Voluntary fringe benefits may be divided into insurance programs, time away from the job, and services. Group insurance programs are available for almost every human need and include medical and hospitalization insurance, dental insurance, term life insurance, errors and omissions insurance, and optical insurance.

A fringe benefit often taken for granted by employees is time away from the job, including sick leave, vacation time, paid holidays, and sabbatical leave. In like manner, certain services offered by school districts are, in reality, fringe benefits, and include expenses paid for attendance at workshops, professional meetings, and conventions; tuition reimbursement; and free lunches. Central office administrators are usually given use of a school district automobile or receive mileage compensation. In districts experiencing decreasing enrollments, teachers are being offered career counseling services in order to help them look for a job outside education.

Healthcare costs continue to increase at an alarming rate. Managed healthcare is an alternative approach to the traditional insurance programs and is meant to maintain a high quality of care but at a lower cost and in a more efficient manner. Many school districts hire case management specialists who have the job responsibility of helping contain costs while still providing quality healthcare to employees of the school district. As an alternative to this approach, a district can contract with a third-party healthcare administration company or join a managed healthcare network.

A major issue facing many school districts across the United States is the rising cost of workers' compensation. For school district employees, there are three major categories of health risks: environmental risks, the risk of violence, and the risks such as contracting an infectious disease that come from working with children. Many school districts have created the position of risk manager, whose responsibilities include identifying risks and then developing plans to minimize them.

The director of employee benefits supervises the staff in the fringe benefits department. Of course, the director reports to the assistant superintendent for human resources. Fringe benefits, as an alternative to large salary and wage increases, will continue to play a significant role in compensating employees.

Ⓥ **Self-Check Quiz** Click here to take an automatically-graded self-check quiz.

Discussion Questions and Statements

1. What elements would you include in compensation programs?
2. Describe the variables that affect compensation programs.
3. Define *direct compensation,* and explain what should be taken into consideration in developing that aspect of a compensation program.
4. Identify and describe the most common types of mandatory and voluntary fringe benefits.
5. What is the relationship between compensation and higher levels of employee performance?

Suggested Activities

1. You are the director of employee benefits in a large metropolitan school district with more than 5,000 employees. The state where your school district is located does not have a strong collective negotiations law for public employees. Develop, in writing, a process that you would use to create a voluntary fringe benefits program.
2. Visit the payroll office of a school district and discuss how position control is maintained so that someone inside the organization cannot create a fictitious employee who receives a salary.
3. Ask a human resources administrator in a school district what percentage of the personnel budget goes for workers' compensation claims and discuss whether this is a reasonable amount.
4. Find Websites that deal with health risks in the workplace. Also, interview a human resources administrator about the most effective way to conduct a safety and security audit.
5. Interview a human resources administrator in person or on the telephone and discuss the advantages of managed healthcare.

Focus Scenario Activity

Given that you have read and studied this chapter, how would you proceed to develop a plan of action that addresses the entire compensation package offered to all employees, but with particular focus on teachers?

Endnotes

1. Pamela Babcock, "Find What Workers Want," *HR Magazine,* 50, no. 4 (April 2005): 50–57.
2. David A. DeCenzo and Stephen P. Robbins, *Fundamentals of Human Resource Management,* 9th ed. (Hoboken, NJ: John Wiley, 2007), 286–300.
3. Julia E. Koppich, "All Teachers Are Not the Same: A Multiple Approach to Teacher Compensation," *Education Next,* 5, no. 1 (Winter 2005): 13–15.
4. Arlene Ackerman, "Do the Math: Rethinking Teacher Compensation: Can We Afford Not to Change the Way We Pay Them?" *College Board Review,* no. 208 (Spring 2006): 34–37.
5. William C. Cunningham and Paula A. Cordeiro, *Educational Administration: A Problem-Based Approach,* (Boston: Allyn & Bacon, 2000), 307.
6. Zhijuan Zhang, Deborah A. Verstegen, and Hoe Ryoung Kim, "Teacher Compensation and School Quality: New Findings from National and International Data," *Educational Considerations,* 35, no. 2 (Spring 2008): 25–26.

7. Eileen M. Kellor, "Catching Up with the Vaughn Express: Six Years of Standards-Based Teacher Evaluation and Performance Pay," *Education Policy Analysis Archives*, 13, no. 7 (January 23, 2005): 3–17.

8. DeCenzo and Robbins, *Fundamentals of Human Resource Management*, 296–297.

9. Janet Stites, "Equal Pay for the Sexes," *HR Magazine*, 50, no. 5 (May 2005): 65–69.

10. Marilyn J. Amey and Kim E. VanDerLinden, "Merit Pay, Market Conditions, Equity, and Faculty Compensation," *NEA 2002 Almanac of Higher Education*.

11. DeCenzo and Robbins, *Fundamentals of Human Resource Management*, 288, 297.

12. Edward J. McElroy, "Teacher Compensation: What Can Be Done to Maintain (and Improve) Teachers' Wages and Benefits?" *Teaching K–8*, (August/September 2005).

13. Susan E. Morgan, Tom Reichert, and Tyler R. Harrison, *From Numbers to Words: Reporting Statistical Results for the Social Sciences*, (Boston: Allyn & Bacon, 2002), 1–4.

14. Eric A. Hanushek, "The Single Salary Schedule and Other Issues of Teacher Pay," *Peabody Journal of Education*, 82, no. 4 (2007): 579–584.

15. Ronald W. Rebore and Angela L. E. Walmsley, *An Evidence-Based Approach to the Practice of Educational Leadership*, (New York: Pearson Education, 2007), 6–12.

16. Small Business Regulatory Enforcement Fairness Act of 1996, www.sba.gov/advo/laws/sbrefa (as of 2009).

17. Internal Revenue Service, www.irs.gov.

18. Health Insurance Portability and Accountability Act of 1996, www.hhs.gov/hipaa.

19. Health Insurance Portability and Accountability Act of 1996, "Medical Saving Accounts," www.hhs.gov/hipaa/msa.

20. Rebore and Walmsley, *An Evidence-Based Approach to the Practice of Educational Leadership*, 218–223.

21. DeCenzo and Robbins, *Fundamentals of Human Resource Management*, 318–319.

22. New York State Workers' Compensation Board, www.wcb/nys.gov.

23. Vern Brimley, Jr., and Rulon R. Garfield, *Financing Education in a Climate of Change*, 10th ed. (Boston: Pearson Education, 2008), 341–343.

24. Lin Grensing-Pophas, "Health Education Turns Proactive," *HR Magazine*, 50, no. 4 (April 2005): 101–104.

25. William G. Cunningham and Paula A. Cordeiro, *Educational Leadership: A Bridge to Improved Practice*, 4th ed. (Boston: Pearson Education, 2009), 346.

26. Brimley and Garfield, *Financing Education in a Climate of Change*, 351–353.

Selected Bibliography

Ackerman, Arlene. "Do the Math: Rethinking Teacher Compensation: Can We Afford Not to Change the Way We Pay Them?" *College Board Review*, no. 208 (Spring 2006): 34–37.

Amey, Marilyn J., and Kim E. VanDerLinden. "Merit Pay, Market Conditions, Equity, and Faculty Compensation." *NEA 2002 Almanac of Higher Education*.

Belfield, Clive R., and John S. Heywood. "Performance Pay for Teachers: Determinants and Consequences." *Economics of Education Review*, 27, no. 3 (2008): 243–252.

Buchanan, Larry M. "Agents of Change for Health Care Reform." *Leadership*, 36, no. 5 (May/June 2007): 18–21.

Clark, Robert L., and Madeleine B. d'Ambrosio. "Recruitment, Retention, and Retirement: Compensation and Employment Policies for Higher Education," *Educational Gerontology*, 31 (2005): 385–403.

Condrey, S. E., Facer II, R. L., and Llorens, J. J. "Getting It Right: How and Why We Should Compare Federal and Private Sector Compensation." *Public Administration Review*, 72, no. 6 (2012): 784–785. doi:10.111/j.1540-6210.2012.02664.x.

Cooke, Willa D., and Chris Licciardi. "Principals' Salaries, 2007–2008." *Principal*, 87, no. 5 (May/June 2008): 46–51.

David, Jane L. "Teacher Recruitment Incentives." *Educational Leadership*, 65, no. 7 (April 2008): 84–86.

Durante, Robert, and Jason Willis. "The Benefits Dilemma: Rising Healthcare and Pension Costs Squeezing Education Resources." *School Business Affairs*, (November 2005).

Garvey, Charlotte. "Philosophizing Compensation." *HR Magazine*, 50, no. 1 (January 2005): 73–78.

Goldhaber, Dan, Michael DeArmond, Daniel Player, and Hyung-Jai Choi. "Why Do So Few Public School Districts Use Merit Pay?" *Journal of Education Finance*, 33, no. 3 (Winter 2008): 262–289.

Gratz, Donald B. "Lessons from Denver: The Pay for Performance Pilot." *Phi Delta Kappan*, 86, no. 8 (April 2005): 568–581.

Greene, Jay P., and Marcus A. Winters. *How Much Are Public School Teachers Paid?* New York: Center for Civic Innovation, 2007.

Grensing-Pophas, Lin. "Health Education Turns Proactive." *HR Magazine*, 50, no. 4 (April 2005): 101–104.

Hanushek, Eric A. "The Single Salary Schedule and Other Issues of Teacher Pay." *Peabody Journal of Education*, 82, no. 4 (2007): 574–586.

Jacobson, Linda. "Proposal Seeks Health-Insurance Savings." *Education Week*, 27, no. 6 (October 3, 2007): 20–21.

Joiner, Lottie L. "Life-Saving Lessons: What Have Schools Learned since Columbine about Keeping Students Safe?" *American School Board Journal*, 189, no. 3 (March 2002): 14–18.

Jupp, Brad. "The Uniform Salary Schedule: A Progressive Leader Proposes Differential Pay." *Education Next*, 5, no. 1 (Winter 2005): 10–12.

Kellor, Eileen M. "Catching Up with the Vaughn Express: Six Years of Standards-Based Teacher Evaluation and Performance Pay." *Education Policy Analysis Archives*, 13, no. 7 (January 23, 2005): 1–27.

Kersten, Thomas A., and Mohsin Dada. "Skyrocketing Healthcare Costs: Is There a Cure?" *School Business Affairs*, (October 2005).

Koppich, Julia E. "All Teachers Are Not the Same: A Multiple Approach to Teacher Compensation." *Education Next*, 5, no. 1 (Winter 2005): 13–15.

Landolfi, Emilio. *Alternative Teacher Compensation Systems*. Kelowna, British Columbia, Canada: Society for the Advancement of Excellence in Education, 2003, 1–93.

McElroy, Edward J. "Teacher Compensation: What Can Be Done to Maintain (and Improve) Teachers' Wages and Benefits?" *Teaching K-8*, (August/September 2005).

Progressive Policy Institute. *Better Pay for Better Teaching: Making Teacher Compensation Pay Off in the Age of Accountability*. Washington, DC: Author, 2002.

Siems, F. U., Goelzner, H. H., and Moosmayer, D. C. "Reference Compensation: A Transfer of Reference Price Theory to Human Resource Management." *Review of Managerial Science*, 6, no. 2 (2012): 103–129.

Solomon, Lewis C. "Recognizing Differences: Let's Reward the Good Teachers." *Education Next*, 5, no. 1 (Winter 2005): 16–20.

Stites, Janet. "Equal Pay for the Sexes." *HR Magazine*, 50, no. 5 (May 2005): 64–69.

Taggart, Nina. "A New Competitive Advantage: Connecting the Dots between Employee Health and Productivity." *Benefits and Compensation Digest*, (June 2009).

Taylor, Lori L. "Comparing Teacher Salaries: Insights from the U.S. Census." *Economics of Education Review*, 21, no. 1 (2008): 48–57.

Trainor, Charles K. "Ensuring You're Insured." *American School Board Journal*, 195, no. 1 (January 2008): 40–41.

U.S. Department of Education, Office of Educational Research and Improvement. *Teacher Incentive Programs in the Public Schools*, Washington, DC: Author, 1989.

U.S. Department of Education, Office of Educational Research and Improvement/Educational Information Branch. *Teacher Salaries: Are They Competitive?* Washington, DC: Author, 1993.

Zembylas, Michalinos, and Elena Papanastasiou. "Job Satisfaction among School Teachers in Cyprus." *Journal of Educational Administration*, 42, no. 3 (2004): 357–374.

Zhang, Zhijuan, Deborah A. Verstegen, and Hoe Ryoung Kim. "Teacher Compensation and School Quality: New Findings from National and International Data." *Educational Considerations*, 35, no. 2 (Spring 2008): 19–28.

Appendix

Position Description Questionnaire*

I. GENERAL INFORMATION

1. Your full name: _____ Date: _____
           (First)   (Middle or Maiden)   (Last)

2. Title of your position: _____

   When appointed to this position: _____
                                     (Date)

3. To your knowledge, is this position ever referred to by another title? If so, what title or titles are used? _____
   _____

4. To which major division is your position assigned? (e.g., Division of Business Administration, Division of School Administration, Division of Instruction) _____
   _____

5. To which specific unit (office, department, school) is your position assigned? _____
   _____

6. Regular daily hours of work: From _____ to _____

7. What is the position title and name of your immediate supervisor? (i.e., the person or persons who assign work to you regularly and to whom you report)

            TITLE   NAME

   _____   _____

8. If your immediate supervisor is someone other than your department head, what is the title and name of your department head? (If same person, write "same.")

            TITLE   NAME

   _____   _____

9. What are the position titles and names of the persons whom you supervise directly? (i.e., the persons to whom you give work assignments and from whom you receive reports on work progress. If no one, write "none.")

        TITLE   DEPT. OR DIVISION   NAMES

   _____   _____   _____

   _____   _____   _____

*Adapted from Charles W. Foster and Jean M. Taylor, eds., *Wage and Salary Administration: A Handbook for School Business Officials*, Association of School Business Officials International, 1968, Chicago, Illinois.

---

10. What employees do you regularly train or instruct on the job?

| POSITION TITLE | FREQUENCY | | | ONLY NEW EMPLOYEES |
	WEEKLY	MONTHLY	SEVERAL TIMES A YEAR	JOIN DEPARTMENT
_____	_____	_____	_____	_____
_____	_____	_____	_____	_____

11. To what position, or positions, within the school system would a person normally consider a logical promotion from your position?

_____

12. What jobs or positions within the school system do you feel have responsibilities about equal to yours?

_____   _____

_____   _____

13. What position in the department, bureau, section, or office to which you are now assigned is the next more responsible position?

_____

II. ASSIGNED FUNCTIONS AND RESPONSIBILITIES

1. What is the basic function or purpose of your position? (e.g., to provide typing assistance to the _____ department; to receive all persons entering building and direct them to desired office; to direct and coordinate the instructional program)

_____

_____

2. What regular duties or assigned responsibilities do you perform in your position? (Please list all of the duties you can think of, and be as specific as possible, e.g., clean windows, prepare purchase requisitions, conduct staff conferences.) Indicate frequency of performance by code letters as follows:

Daily or several times weekly   Code "D"
Weekly   Code "W"
Monthly   Code "M"
Occasionally during the year   Code "Y"

DUTIES	CODE
_____	_____

3. What machines requiring special skills do you use in your work?

| | FREQUENCY (CHECK ONE) | | |
	CONTINUOUSLY	FREQUENTLY	OCCASIONALLY
_____	_____	_____	_____
_____	_____	_____	_____

Continued

4. What special non-machine skills do you use in your work? (e.g., bookkeeping, creative writing, higher mathematics, etc.)

FREQUENCY (CHECK ONE)

CONTINUOUSLY	FREQUENTLY	OCCASIONALLY
_____	_____	_____
_____	_____	_____

5. What grade level of education did you complete? (check one)

8th grade (or below)	_____	1 yr. college	_____
9th grade	_____	2 yrs. college	_____
10th grade	_____	3 yrs. college	_____
11th grade	_____	4 yrs. college	_____
12th grade	_____	5 yrs. college	_____
or equivalent to above grade		6 yrs. college	_____
checked in special courses	_____	7 yrs. or more college	_____

Up to

1 year special courses after high school _____
2 years special courses after high school _____
3 years special courses after high school _____
4 years special courses after high school _____

6. If you have completed a college or university program, what degree(s) did you earn and in what major subject area?

_____
_____

7. Have you taken other courses, not covered above, to enable you to qualify for your present position or another position in the school system? (Please explain type of course, length, etc.)

_____
_____

8. Is accuracy or working within close precision limits a requirement of your job? _____
YES OR NO

If yes, which of the following would best describe the effect of errors you might make?

_____ Errors would be corrected early and would not be significant.
_____ Errors might involve small losses of money. Corrections can be made with minor inconvenience to other employees or supervisor.
_____ Errors might involve significant losses of money or would cause considerable delay, confusion, or bad public relations. Can be corrected but with loss of time and expense.
_____ Errors would seriously hamper financial operations of school systems or involve loss of prestige of school board. Difficult and costly to correct.

III. DETAILS CONCERNING RESPONSIBILITIES

1. For what specific activities, programs, and/or services do you have responsibilities for formulating objectives and goals? (Please list.)

_____
_____

2. What is the extent of your responsibilities for objectives? (e.g., formulate and recommend to department head; recommend to school board;)

   _____

   _____

3. Which of the following statements best describes your responsibilities relative to objectives and goals for your program or service? (check one)

   _____ None

   _____ My opinions are sometimes requested

   _____ My opinions are regularly requested

   _____ Formulate and recommend objectives to supervisor or department head

   _____ Formulate objectives for department, program, or service and recommend to division head

   _____ Formulate objectives for division and recommend to superintendent

   _____ Formulate objectives for school system

   _____ Other (Specify) _____

4. For which specific programs and/or services do you have responsibilities for analyzing requirements, and whose requirements are analyzed for each? (e.g., purchasing and warehousing for all schools and services)

   _____

   _____

5. For which departments, programs, and/or services are you responsible for planning the organization, staffing, facilities, or finance? (List and describe your planning responsibilities.)

   _____

   _____

6. For which specific programs and/or services do you have responsibilities for evaluating effectiveness and results?

   _____

   _____

7. Which of the following statements best describes your responsibilities for evaluating the results of programs and/or services? (check one)

   _____ None

   _____ Opinions may be requested

   _____ Opinions are regularly requested

   _____ Participate in evaluation regularly with supervisor or department head

   _____ Responsible for evaluation

   _____ Other (Specify) _____

8. For which specific activities, programs, and services do you have responsibilities for developing and evaluating plans of organization? _____

   _____

9. Approximately how many staff members are included in plans of organization that you develop and evaluate? _____

   _____

10. If you have supervisory responsibilities, what is the nature of the tasks performed by the majority of the persons you directly or indirectly supervise?

    _____ Repetitive tasks

    _____ Semi-routine tasks of moderate complexity, but not of a highly professional or technical nature

Continued

_____ Activities of a highly technical or professional nature

_____ Other (Specify) _____

_____

11. For what specific activities, programs, and/or services do you have staff recruitment and/or selection responsibilities?

_____

_____

12. What type of responsibility do you have for facilities planning? (e.g., recommending amounts and layouts of space) _____

_____

13. What responsibility do you have for supervising the use of facilities and equipment? (e.g., supervising one office and office machines; supervising carpenter shop, saws, joiners)

_____

_____

14. What responsibilities do you have for supervising the care and maintenance of buildings or equipment? _____

_____

15. What kind of financial planning responsibilities do you have and for what programs or services? (e.g., estimating current costs, formulating budget, financial projection)

_____

_____

16. What is total amount of annual budgets for which you have planning responsibility?

_____ None

_____ Less than $100,000

_____ $100,000 to $499,000

_____ $500,000 to $999,000

_____ $1,000,000 or over

_____ Please explain: _____

_____

17. What responsibilities do you have for evaluating the management of finances? For which programs and/or services? (e.g., evaluating expenditures for maintenance or repairs; analyzing program costs)

_____

_____

18. What is the total amount of annual expenditures for which you are responsible to evaluate financial management?

_____ None

_____ Less than $100,000

_____ $100,000 to $499,000

_____ $500,000 to $999,000

_____ $1,000,000 or over

_____ Please explain: _____

_____

19. In performing your job, in what ways do you come into contact with the public, employees in other departments, other department heads, etc.? (Briefly describe.)

20. How would you characterize your contacts with the public, employees, and others, as you have described them? (check one)

_____ Little or no contact

_____ Requires only good manners/no pertinent communication

_____ Regular and frequent contact; manner and attitude are important, but giving and receiving information is not a principal requirement

_____ Includes giving and receiving information; requires ability to handle varied face-to-face situations

_____ A predominant feature of the job, necessitating a high degree of tact, courtesy, and ability to work effectively with individuals and groups

21. What responsibilities do you have for planning the external relations (including public relations) of your service, department, or program? (Please specify to the extent that you contribute to planning, are responsible for planning, or otherwise.)

_____

_____

22. With regard to all of your planning responsibilities, for what period of time are you usually concerned in making plans?

_____ Current academic or fiscal year

_____ Current and next academic or fiscal years

_____ Current and next 4 academic or fiscal years

_____ Current and next 5 to 9 academic or fiscal years

_____ Current and next 10 or more academic or fiscal years

IV. OTHER INFORMATION

1. Are there any other aspects of your responsibilities that are unusual and should be taken into account in evaluating your position?

_____

_____

2. Are there any unique requirements not identified above that should be taken into account in establishing the qualifications of a person to fill the position you now occupy?

_____

_____

3. How would you characterize general working conditions necessitated by the nature of your job?

_____ Work in normal temperatures, clean, comfortable surroundings—normal office conditions.

_____ A few disagreeable conditions exist such as noise, congestion, drafts.

_____ Several disagreeable conditions accompany the job such as abnormal temperatures, humidity, excess noise and dirt, offensive odors and fumes.

4. Are there any personal hazards related to your job? (e.g., work on high ladders, use sharp knives, electricity)

_____

_____

Continued

V. DEPARTMENT HEAD OR SUPERVISOR'S SECTION

(To be completed by immediate supervisor or department head.)

1. I have read the staff member's responses to the attached questionnaire and believe that they accurately reflect the duties, responsibilities, and characteristics of the position with the following exceptions: _____
_____
_____

2. I believe the minimum educational requirement for this position should be: (List grade completion such as 8th grade, 2–3 years high school, high school graduation, A.B. degree, doctoral degree, etc. Be realistic.) _____
_____
_____

3. Which one of the following statements do you feel accurately describes the general work schedule of this position? _____

    _____ Normal work schedule; some gaps in the work cycle
    _____ Little or no pressure
    _____ Steadily paced with occasional pressure
    _____ Frequent pressure of work with almost constant accumulation of tasks
    _____ Very high and unusual pressure created by important decisions or frequent emergency situations

_____
(Signature, Supervisor or Department Head)

SCORE SHEET

JOB EVALUATION COMMITTEE NO. 1
OFFICE, CLERICAL, AND MANUAL POSITIONS

Job Title _____ Department _____

Factors:

Technical Demands	_____
Experience	_____
Complexity	_____
Accuracy	_____
Supervision and Training	_____
Independent Action	_____
Contacts	_____
Mental Effort	_____
Physical Effort	_____
Working Conditions	_____
TOTAL	_____

Date: _____ _____
(Signature of Committee Member)

JOB EVALUATION COMMITTEE NO. 1

OFFICE, CLERICAL, AND MANUAL POSITIONS

TALLY SHEET

Job Title _____

Department _____ Date _____

Committee \ Factors	Technical Demands	Experience	Complexity	Accuracy	Supervision and Training	Independent Action	Contacts	Mental Effort	Physical Effort	Working Conditions	TOTAL

SCORE SHEET

JOB EVALUATION COMMITTEE NO. 2
ADMINISTRATIVE AND PROFESSIONAL POSITIONS

Job Title _____ Department _____

Factors:

      Planning Responsibilities   _____

      Professional and Technical Demands   _____

      Supervision   _____

      Staffing   _____

      Facilities   _____

      Finance   _____

      External Relations   _____

      Evaluating Responsibilities   _____

      TOTAL   _____

Date: _____   _____

                                            (Signature of Committee Member)

JOB EVALUATION COMMITTEE NO. 2

ADMINISTRATIVE AND PROFESSIONAL POSITIONS

TALLY SHEET

Job Title _____

Department _____ Date _____

Factors	Planning Responsibilities	Professional and Technical	Supervision	Staffing	Facilities	Finance	External Relations	Evaluating Responsibities	TOTAL

CHAPTER 9

Collective Negotiations

Focus Scenario

You have been the director of employee relations for nine years in a suburban school district with approximately 300 teachers. The state where the school district is located has an effective collective negotiations law for public employees. The law does not allow, however, for teachers to engage in work-stoppage procedures. The teachers' association represents the teachers in the district, and various other unions represent most other categories of employees.

Nevertheless, during the past six years there have been two brief but illegal teacher work stoppages that resulted in major changes to the agreement with the teachers' association. The school district is experiencing significant financial problems as a result of the inability of the board of education to convince taxpayers to raise the tax levy. Three referendums have been defeated to raise the levy by $1.25 million, which is the amount that the board of education claims is needed to maintain a quality education for the students in the district. Ironically, the school district is composed of many citizens who are members of unions. However, unstable economic conditions have caused major companies to move out of the area, resulting in significant unemployment, a situation that appears to have worked against the passage of the referendums.

The lack of support by the community has also caused a major shift on the board of education in the recent election. Four of the seven board members are newly elected, are unfamiliar with collective negotiations in school districts, and are not members of labor unions. One is dentist, another is the owner of a floral shop, the third new member is an administrative assistant to the chief executive officer of a medium-size technology firm, and the fourth member is a pharmacist. It is now time to begin setting goals and developing strategies to begin the collective negotiations process.

The superintendent of school has asked you to develop a presentation for the board of education that will give members a better idea of how collective negotiations operates in education, the various dimensions of the negotiations process, and what should be done if there is another work stoppage. She has also asked you to organize your presentation around human resources strategies that the board can adopt as its position for the coming negotiations.

303

Please use both the "Discussion Questions and Statements" and "Suggested Activities" at the end of this chapter to help you develop a way of proceeding to address the issues in this section.

Collective negotiations have become an accepted part of American education. The first significant collective bargaining contract was negotiated in 1962 with teachers in New York City; since then, all but four state legislatures have enacted some form of collective negotiations laws. Personnel considerations such as salaries, fringe benefits, and working conditions constitute the major negotiable items. Membership in teachers' organizations has stabilized, and consequently, because of dues, so have the fiscal resources of these organizations. Because human resources expenditures constitute approximately 80 percent of school budgets, virtually every aspect of education has been influenced either directly or indirectly by the phenomenon of collective negotiations.

Experience indicates that the underlying consideration in collective negotiations is participation in the decision-making process. It is a natural evolution in our democratic society that individuals continually look for more significant ways to participate in governance, whether in the political sphere or in our employing institutions. It is important for teachers, administrators, and school board members to understand that collective negotiations is about fostering workplace democracy and providing a way for people to be heard. Thus, it is a political process.[1]

Furthermore, as a process, collective negotiations work successfully in both the private and public sectors. This chapter deals with the major components of the collective negotiations process as it operates in education.

The attitudes of teachers, administrators, and members of the board of education are critical to the success of collective negotiations because their attitudes affect the relationship between the negotiating parties.[2] If teachers and representatives of the school district approach the negotiating process with a sense of respect for each other, resentment will be diminished, and the prospect of reaching an acceptable agreement will be enhanced.[3]

As of the date of this writing, thirty-four states and the District of Columbia have legislation that requires boards of education to engage in some form of collective negotiations with teachers unions or organizations. In addition, there are eleven states that permit boards of education to engage in collective negotiations with teachers. Virginia, North Carolina, South Carolina, and Georgia prohibit all forms of collective negotiations for teachers.[4] The terms *collective bargaining* and *collective negotiations* have been used with various shades of meaning when referring to this process in public education. To avoid confusion, and because the process is invariable, we use these terms interchangeably.

When representatives of an organized group bargain collectively over salaries, fringe benefits, and working conditions for their membership with management, the group is in essence a labor union. Therefore, we also use the terms *labor union* and *professional association* interchangeably when referring to the involvement that teachers' organizations have in the negotiations process. This definition holds true for administrator associations when they engage in collective negotiations, which appears to be a trend in public education.

Historical Perspectives

Collective Bargaining in the Private Sector

Collective actions by employees have a history going back to the medieval guilds and have always been influenced by the economic, political, and social conditions of the times.[5] Such influences are even stronger today because the technology of the news media allows daily updating on economic, political, and social trends.

Four major congressional acts provide legal guidelines for collective bargaining in the private sector: the Norris–LaGuardia Act of 1932, the National Labor Relations Act of 1935 (Wagner Act), the Labor Management Relations Act of 1947 (Taft–Hartley Act), and the Labor Management Reporting and Disclosure Act of 1959 (Landrum–Griffin Act). We discuss each in turn here.

The Norris–LaGuardia Act was the first general public policy position on labor unionization. The act supported the concept that workers have a right to organize, if they so desire, into unions. Particularly, the act restricted the U.S. courts from issuing injunctions that would restrict labor activities. It also outlawed the *yellow dog contract,* an agreement that employers required employees to sign as a condition of employment stating that they were not members of a union and would not join a union as long as they worked for that company.

The Wagner Act is perhaps the most important piece of labor legislation. It guaranteed workers the right to organize and join labor unions for the purpose of collective bargaining with employers. The act also prohibited employers from engaging in the following unfair labor practices:

- Interfering with an employee's right to join a labor union and bargain collectively
- Interfering with the formation or administration of a labor union
- Discriminating against an employee due to his or her union activity
- Discharging or discriminating against an employee who filed charges or gave testimony under this act
- Refusing to bargain with representatives chosen by employees

The National Labor Relations Board (NLRB) was established and given responsibility for conducting elections to determine union representation and for applying this law against the stated unfair labor practices.

The Taft–Hartley Act was passed to amend the Wagner Act and to prevent unfair labor practices by unions. It sought to protect a worker's right not to join a union and to protect employers from mistreatment by unions. The Taft–Hartley Act specifically outlawed the *closed shop,* in which membership in a union was a condition for being hired and for continued employment. The act allowed the federal government to seek an injunction preventing work stoppages for eighty days in a strike defined as injurious to national welfare, prohibited the use of union funds in connection with national elections, and required union officers to swear that they were not members of the Communist party. The Taft–Hartley Act also required unions to file financial statements with their membership and the U.S. Department of Labor, allowed the states to pass right-to-work laws, and made it illegal for any collective agreement to contain a clause requiring compulsory union membership.

The Taft–Hartley Act also prohibited unions from engaging in the following unfair labor practices:

- Refusing to bargain collectively with an employer
- Causing an employer to discriminate against an employee who was refused membership in a union or expelled from a union
- Engaging in secondary boycotts, which is exerting pressure on an employer not directly involved in a dispute
- Causing an employer to pay for services that were not rendered
- Engaging in a conflict between two or more unions over the right to perform certain types of work
- Charging excessive or discriminating initiation fees

The Landrum–Griffin Act was passed as a result of internal corruption in some unions. This act contained a bill of rights for union members, including freedom of speech at union meetings, use of a secret ballot on proposed dues increases, and protection against improper disciplinary action. It also established the conditions to be observed in electing union officers.

The Landrum–Griffin Act, in addition, contained the following amendments to the Taft–Hartley Act:

- Repealed the requirement that union officials take a non-Communist oath
- Gave states authority over cases outside the jurisdiction of the NLRB
- Prohibited picketing by a union when a rival union had been recognized to represent employees or an NLRB election had taken place within twelve months
- Guaranteed the right of a striker to vote in union representative elections for twelve months
- Prohibited agreements by which an employee could seek to bring economic pressure on another employer by refusing to handle, sell, use, or transport his or her products
- Authorized union shops in the construction industry and required membership after seven days of employment rather than the traditional thirty days

Collective Negotiations in the Federal Government

In 1962, President John F. Kennedy issued Executive Order 10988, which affirmed the right of federal employees to join labor unions and bargain collectively. It required federal agency heads to bargain in good faith, defined unfair labor practices, and established a code of conduct for labor organizations. However, it prohibited the union shop and banned strikes by federal employees.

In 1968, a presidential committee reviewed employee management relations in the federal service and recommended improvements to the provisions of Executive Order 10988. As a consequence, in 1969, President Richard Nixon issued Executive Order 11491, which superseded the previous directive.

The objectives of Executive Order 11491 were to standardize procedures among federal agencies and to bring federal labor relations more in line with those in the private sector.

It gave the assistant secretary of labor the authority to determine appropriate bargaining units, to oversee recognition procedures, to rule on unfair labor practices, and to enforce the standards of conduct on labor organizations. Executive Order 11491 also established the Federal Labor Relations Council, which has the responsibility of supervising the implementation of this executive order, handling appeals from the decisions of the assistant secretary of labor, and ruling on questionable issues.

Collective Negotiations in Local and State Governments

Although some professional organizations support passage of a federal teacher collective bargaining law, most educators see this as a state issue. In fact, public school employees are working for a state agency operating at the local level, the school district.

Forty-six states have permissive or mandatory statutes governing the rights of public school employees to organize, negotiate, exercise sanctions, and strike. There are, of course, substantial differences among these state laws. In a number of states, legislation covers all public employees; in others, a specific law covers only school employees.

Model Board of Education Policy on Collective Negotiations

The following is a sample policy on collective negotiations:

> The board of education believes that collaborative decision making is the most effective way to govern a school system. If school district employees have the right to share in the decision-making process affecting salaries, fringe benefits, and working conditions, they become more responsive and better disposed to exchanging ideas and information concerning operations with administrators. Accordingly, management becomes more efficient.
>
> The board of education further declares that harmonious and cooperative relations between itself and school district employees protect the patrons and children of the school district by assuring the orderly operation of the schools.
>
> This position of the board is to be effectuated by:
>
> (1) Recognizing the right of all school district employees to organize for the purpose of collective negotiations.
> (2) Authorizing the director of employee relations to negotiate with the duly elected employee representatives on matters relating to salaries, fringe benefits, and working conditions.
> (3) Requiring the director of employee relations to establish administrative procedures for the effective implementation of the negotiations process. This is to be accomplished under the supervision of the assistant superintendent for human resources, who reports directly to the superintendent of schools.
>
> On successful completion of the negotiations process, the board of education will enter into written agreements with the employee organizations.

Emanating from this board of education policy is the following definition for *negotiation:* Collective negotiations are the process by which representatives of the school board meet with representatives of the school district employees in order to make proposals and counterproposals for the purpose of mutually agreeing on salaries, fringe benefits, and working conditions covering a specific period of time.

Recognition and Bargaining Unit Determination

In labor history, most of the violence that occurred in the private sector centered on the query, "Who represents whom?" Unions fought each other for the right to represent workers against management. The prize was power. In education, the prize is still the same, but the contest is usually nonviolent.[6]

Recognition is defined as the acceptance by an employer of some group or organization as the authorized representative of two or more employees for the purpose of collective negotiations. Without recognition, each teacher is left to make his or her own arrangements with the school board, which is the antithesis of collective negotiations.

There are two basic types of representation in education—multiple and exclusive. Multiple representation does not occur in many school districts because of the inherent problems when two or more organizations or unions represent a specific bargaining unit. Before collective negotiations elections, it was typical for multiple organizations to be accorded equal representational rights by the board of education. There are still school districts in which more than one organization claims the right to represent a segment of the professional staff.

In multiple representation, recognition is usually granted by the board of education on the basis of organizational membership. This recognition is operationalized by one of the following methods: The board meets with representatives of each union separately; the board meets in joint sessions with an equal number of representatives from each union; or the board meets in joint sessions with a proportional number of representatives from each union. For example, if union A has 500 members and union B has 250 members, A is entitled to twice as many representatives on the negotiating team as B.

Exclusive recognition occurs when a single union represents all members of a bargaining unit. The technical designation for the union in this role is bargaining agent. The *bargaining unit* consists of all the employees whose salaries, fringe benefits, and working conditions are negotiated by the bargaining agent. The paramount importance of exclusive recognition is that the employer cannot negotiate with anyone in the unit except through the designated bargaining agent.

Exclusive recognition is the most accepted form in education for three reasons: First, it is supported by both the National Education Association (NEA) and the American Federation of Teachers (AFT); second, exclusive recognition is mandated by law for the public sector in many states and widely accepted in most communities, even in the absence of state legislation; and finally, private business and industry are witnesses to the fact that this is the most effective form of recognition.

Recognition procedures take various forms in education. The three most commonly used are membership lists, authorization cards, and elections. If a union can demonstrate that 51 percent of the employees in a bargaining unit are members or if 51 percent of the employees in a bargaining unit present their signatures on a card authorizing a certain union to represent them, the board may recognize this union as the exclusive bargaining agent.

A more common practice is the *representation election*, which is also necessary in the absence of membership lists or authorization cards that signify majority support. Most school boards prefer an election as a requisite to recognizing a union as the exclusive bargaining agent for a number of reasons. Some teachers who join a union may not want that union to represent them in negotiations. Teachers join certain unions for social, professional, or other reasons that have nothing to do with negotiations. In some cases, a teacher may be a member of more than one teachers' union.

The representation election poses several questions that must be addressed by both the school board and the unions seeking recognition:

- Who conducts the election?
- Who pays the costs for the election?
- What are the ground rules for electioneering?
- Who is eligible to vote?
- Who certifies the results?
- What is the duration of the certification?

There are no correct answers to these questions. Rather, they must be answered within a framework that takes into consideration the variables affecting local situations. A cardinal principle is that the board and unions must maintain credibility, and therefore, a third party is often requested to intervene in finding a workable answer to these questions. The Federal Mediation and Conciliation Service (FMCS) and the League of Women Voters are examples of two independent agencies with the public image necessary to act as the appropriate third party. In many states with collective bargaining laws, recognition procedures and bargaining unit determination are mandated by state legislation. This discussion pertains to those states without legislation and to those states where the law allows latitude on these issues. Some states have public employee relations boards that conduct the elections and make a determination on who belongs to the bargaining unit.

It is necessary to more closely define the term *bargaining unit*. School districts employ not only teachers of many different subjects and levels but also a wide variety of specialists such as psychologists, nurses, social workers, and attendance officers.

In addition, there are non-certificated employees: cooks, custodians, bus drivers, maintenance workers, administrative assistants, and clerks. To have collective negotiations, there must be a determination on what specific category of employees is represented by the bargaining agent who wins the representation election. In practice, this determination must occur as part of the recognition process because only those employees in a given bargaining unit are allowed to vote on which union will represent them. The most commonly accepted definition states that the bargaining unit is composed of all those employees who are covered by the negotiated agreement or master contract.

The fundamental criterion for determining who belongs to the bargaining unit is formulated on the community-of-interest principle. Although it may sound elusive, the principle is not difficult to implement. Employees have a community of interest if they share skills, functions, educational levels, and working conditions. Elementary school teachers of all levels, secondary school teachers of all subjects, and guidance counselors clearly have a community of interest and should belong to the same bargaining unit. Clerks and administrative assistants, however, could not be represented effectively by such a unit and should constitute a separate unit. It is conceivable that medium to large school districts might have the following units bargaining separately with the representatives of the school board:

- Certificated educators exclusive of supervisors and administrators
- Building-level administrators
- Subject-matter coordinators
- Administrative assistants and clerks
- Cooks and cafeteria workers
- Bus drivers
- Custodians
- Maintenance workers

Each of these bargaining units should have a separate agreement or master contract that specifies salaries, fringe benefits, and working conditions, and that could be quite different from the others.

Besides community of interest, there are two additional considerations determining a bargaining unit. Size of the group is important. An extremely small unit of five or ten employees has little impact acting alone; in this case, the employees have a more strategic base from which to bargain if they combine with other categories of employees. In a small school district, for example, there might be two bargaining units: a certificated employees' unit, including teachers, nurses, psychologists, and so on, and a non-certificated employees' unit, including cooks, custodians, maintenance personnel, and others.

A final consideration in determining bargaining units is effective school administration. An unreasonably large number of units would be unworkable. For example, if guidance counselors, classroom teachers, speech therapists, music teachers, physical education teachers, and safety education teachers were each covered by different agreements specifying different working conditions, a building principal would have a difficult job of supervising the staff.

Two other issues have an influence on future negotiations—the agency shop and administrator bargaining units. *Agency shop* is a term borrowed from industry and is used when referring to a question of equity: An employee who is a member of a given bargaining unit may choose not be a dues-paying member of the union that is the bargaining agent. If the negotiated agreement with the school board includes an agency shop clause, such an employee would be required to pay a fee, usually the equivalent of dues, to the union. Although the employee would not be allowed to participate in internal union affairs, he or she would be allowed to participate in such unit activities as attending meetings called by the negotiating team and voting on ratification of an agreement.

A growing number of educational administrators, particularly building principals, are organizing into unions and negotiating with school boards, for reasons that include decreasing autonomy and power and economic concerns. It appears that this trend will continue and that school board representatives will be negotiating with increasing numbers of administrator bargaining units.

Scope of Negotiations

Scope of negotiations refers to those matters that are negotiable.[7] In some school districts, negotiations are limited to salaries; in other districts, literally hundreds of items are discussed. Negotiations must be focused on those issues that the local board of education and teachers consider to be important, or the process will be considered a failure by both boards and teachers. Behind this last statement must rest a critical perspective concerning the ultimate purpose of the negotiating process, which is student achievement. However, this objective is achieved only through negotiating items that the board of education and teachers consider to be in the best interest of the school district and the best interest of the professional concerns of the teachers.[8] Thus, what constitutes an important item is dictated by local circumstances. A school board might only be willing to negotiate on salaries and refuse to consider such items as a grievance procedure or a reduction-in-force policy. Experience indicates that some of these nonmonetary items are just as important to teachers as salaries. Therefore, it is extremely important to place only mandatory limitations on the scope of negotiations. These limitations refer to items that are illegal by reason of state and federal constitutions and laws and to items that are contrary to the policies of a given state board of education.

Most state laws on collective negotiations stipulate that negotiations must be confined to "working conditions." However, this phrase usually refers to salaries, fringe benefits, and working conditions. The meaning of *salary* is self-evident, but there is some confusion over what is meant by the terms *fringe benefits* and *working conditions*.

A *fringe benefit* may be defined as a service made available to employees as a direct result of a fiscal expenditure by the school district, and may include major medical insurance, hospitalization insurance, pension benefits, sick pay, dental insurance, and professional liability insurance.

Working conditions pertain to the quality of the employment situation. Teaching for a particular school district might be more desirable than teaching for other districts located in the same geographic area because that district has desirable policies concerning class size, duty-free lunch periods, preparation periods, sabbatical leave, and so on.

A major concern in defining the scope of negotiations for a particular situation centers on the concept of educational policy. School boards are required by state law to set educational policy. Although many teachers are deeply interested in educational policy and believe that they should be consulted in formulating such policy, it is commonly understood that such policy is not subject to negotiations.

The following are examples of policy issues:

- Should the school district provide a foreign language program in the elementary grades?
- Should statistics be offered in the high school mathematics program?
- Should extracurricular activities be sponsored or supported by district funds?

The obvious problem is that virtually all educational policy decisions have implications affecting working conditions. For example, funds expended to introduce a foreign language program in the elementary grades could leave less money available to lower class size. Therefore, it is often impossible to decide issues pertaining to policy apart from those pertaining to working conditions.

Bargaining

This section analyzes those factors that influence the "at-the-table" process of negotiations[9] because it is critical for the negotiating teams to understand and appreciate the necessity of developing a collaborative attitude toward the negotiating process.[10]

Selecting the Negotiating Team

The first issue that must be addressed is the composition of the school board's negotiating team. There is no universally accepted practice in forming a negotiating team; however, the size of a school district appears to have a significant influence on the makeup of the team. In small school districts, a committee of school board members usually negotiates directly with a team of teachers. In medium to large districts, the assistant superintendent for human resources, along with other central office or building-level administrators, may be designated by the superintendent to negotiate with the teachers' union. In some large districts, a chief negotiator is employed on a full-time or ad hoc basis.

In keeping with the model presented in Chapter 1, medium to large school districts should employ a director of employee relations who has responsibility for managing the entire process of collective negotiations and who acts as the chief negotiator on the board's team. The size of the team is relative, but it should have an odd number of members to avoid a deadlock in making strategy decisions; therefore, a team of three, five, or seven members would be appropriate. Experience also dictates that a team composed of more than seven members impedes decision making.

Membership on the team may be by job description, appointment, or election. This author prefers a team of five members. The chairperson and chief negotiator is the director of employee relations by virtue of job position. Additional membership on the team should include building-level principals because they are the first-line supervisors who manage the master agreement. Also, many principals have been critical of school boards for "negotiating away" their authority. On a five-member team, one principal from each level (elementary school, junior high or middle school, and high school) elected by the other principals gives the team high credibility among building administrators. The final member of the team should have some specific expertise and knowledge of the district's financial condition; thus, the assistant superintendent for administrative services or the business manager is an appropriate appointee.

This team must function as an entity over the entire academic year. As discussed later in this section, the development of strategies and the construction of proposal packages cannot be accomplished during only a few months of the year. Although a major portion of work falls to the director of employee relations, the team is required to devote a great deal of time. However, it is helpful to the collaboration necessary for the teachers' and board's teams to meet throughout the year. Consequently, it is advisable to provide those principals who serve on the team with compensation such as a stipend or with additional administrative assistance in their buildings.

A final issue concerning the board's negotiating team must be addressed. The current trend, especially in large urban school districts, is for building administrators to organize, form a bargaining unit, and elect a bargaining agent to represent them concerning salaries, fringe benefits, and working conditions. In this case, the same structure for the board's negotiating team may be maintained with the substitution of assistant superintendents for principals. Because each bargaining unit negotiates a separate master agreement that reflects salaries, fringe benefits, and working conditions for employees in a given job category, it is not inconsistent with good administration for principals to negotiate for the board on the one hand and against the board on the other.

The negotiating team for the teachers is, of course, composed of teachers. Sometimes the officers of the local association or union act as the team; in other situations, a negotiating team is appointed by the union officers or elected by the teachers. If the local is affiliated with a national union, experts in the bargaining process are made available to advise union officers.

Developing Strategies

The school board's negotiating team is responsible for the entire bargaining process, which must begin with strategy development. This entails two activities: assessing the needs of the school district and establishing goals for negotiations. It is always important to enter into negotiations from the perspective that there must be give-and-take on both sides.[11]

Needs assessment may take various forms, but certain tasks must be completed:

- Review the current master agreement to determine if its provisions meet the goals of the district and if they allow for effective administration.
- Study the previous negotiating sessions to determine whether the ground rules provide for effective negotiations.
- Analyze the formal grievances filed by both the union and the administration.
- Study the arbitration decisions rendered on these grievances.
- Meet with school district administrators to gather input concerning the provisions of the current master agreement.
- Meet informally with the union to ascertain its concerns over the current agreement.
- Confer with the board of education and superintendent to learn their concerns and to establish fiscal parameters.

From this information, the team sets the goals and objectives for negotiations that are formulated into operational language in the proposal package.

Setting the Ground Rules

With the advice and consent of the negotiating team, the chairperson should meet with the union negotiators to determine rules for the "at-the-table" process. A significant observation in setting the ground rules is that no two school districts are alike, and this holds true for the teachers and staff members engaged in the negotiating process. Negotiators on both sides of the table will find it important to pay attention to the culture or cultures operating in the schools.[12] Key points that must be determined include the following:

- Time and place for the sessions
- Number of participants who will sit at the table

- Role of each participant
- Manner in which each side presents its proposals
- Target date for completing negotiations
- School district data needed by each side
- Conditions governing caucuses
- Provisions for recording the sessions
- Method to be used in recording counterproposals and agreements
- Policy on press releases
- Types of impasse procedures that will be employed and when
- Format for the written agreement
- Procedure for agreement approval by the school board and union membership
- Procedure used in publishing the ratified agreement

Conducting at-the-Table Sessions

There are two objectives for being at the table. First, through making proposals and counterproposals, the negotiating teams should be able to ascertain what issues are critically important to each side. Second, each team should be able to assess the other side's *bargaining power,* or the ability to get the other team to agree on an item or the entire proposal package based on your terms. Thus, the bargaining power of the school board's team can be viewed in terms of what the cost would be to the teachers' team of disagreeing with the terms of the school board versus what the cost would be of agreeing with the terms. In like manner, the bargaining power of the teachers' team can be viewed in terms of what the cost would be to the board's team of disagreeing with the terms of the teachers versus what the cost would be of agreeing with the terms.

Political pressures, negotiating skill, and psychological elements are important sources of bargaining power. Although it is impossible to measure bargaining power exactly, it is apparent that, at some time, the overall advantages of agreement outweigh the overall disadvantages of agreement. During the bargaining sessions, it is important to keep the board and the entire administrative staff informed of the progress being made. If this is not accomplished effectively, rumors may adversely affect the bargaining power of the board's team.

When an agreement is reached by the negotiating teams, ratification by the respective governing bodies is the final step in the process. The board's team meets with the superintendent and board of education to explain and recommend the agreement. In like manner, the union's team meets with the bargaining unit membership to explain and recommend the agreement. Formal ratification occurs when a majority of school board members vote to accept the agreement and when a majority of the bargaining unit membership similarly votes approval.

Because negotiating is an art rather than a science, it is extremely difficult to develop a formula for success. Nevertheless, a number of practical hints may be in order. The following are recommendations made to local boards of education by the Ohio School Board Association:

- *Keep calm—don't lose control of yourself.* Negotiation sessions can be exasperating. The temptation may come to get angry and fight back when intemperate accusations are made or when "the straw that broke the camel's back" is hurled on to the table.

- *Avoid "off the record" comments.* Nothing is "off the record." Innocently made remarks have a way of coming back to haunt those who said them. Be careful to say only what you are willing to have quoted.
- *Don't be overcandid.* Inexperienced negotiators may, with the best of intentions, desire to "lay the cards on the table face up." This may be done in the mistaken notion that everybody fully understands the other and utter frankness is desired. Complete candor doesn't always serve the best interests of productive negotiations. This is not a plea for duplicity; rather, it is a recommendation for prudent and discriminating utterances.
- *Be long on listening.* Usually, a good listener makes a good negotiator. It is wise to let your "adversaries" do the talking—at least in the beginning.
- *Don't be afraid of a "little heat."* Discussions sometimes generate quite a bit of heat, so don't be afraid of it. It never hurts to let the "opposition" sound off even when you may be tempted to "sound" back.
- *Watch the voice level.* A wise practice is to keep the pitch of the voice down even though the temptation may be strong to let it rise under the excitement of emotional stress.
- *Stay flexible.* One of the skills of good negotiators is the ability to shift position a bit if a positive gain can thus be accomplished. An obstinate adherence to one position or point of view, regardless of the ultimate consequences of that rigidity, may be more of a deterrent than an advantage.
- *Refrain from a flat "no."* Especially in the earlier stages of a negotiation, it is best to avoid giving a flat "no" to a proposition. It doesn't help to work yourself into a box by being totally negative too early.
- *Give to get. Negotiation* is the art of giving and getting. Concede a point to gain a concession. This is the name of the game.
- *Work on the easier items first.* Settle first those things that generate the least controversy. Leave the tougher items until later in order to avoid an early deadlock.
- *Respect your adversary.* Respect those who are seated on the opposite side of the table. Assume that their motives are as sincere as your own, at least until proved otherwise.
- *Be patient.* If necessary, be willing to sit out tiresome tirades. Time has a way of being on the side of the patient negotiator.
- *Avoid waving red flags.* There are some statements that irritate teachers and merely heighten their antipathies. Find out what these are and avoid their use. Needless waving of red flags only infuriates. For example, nothing agitates teachers more than stating that they only work nine months for their salaries while taxpayers work twelve months.
- *Let the other side win some victories.* Each team has to win some victories. A "shut out" may be a hollow gain in negotiation.
- *Negotiation is a way of life.* Obvious resentment of the fact that negotiation is here to stay weakens the effectiveness of the negotiator. The better part of wisdom is to adjust to it and become better prepared to use it as a tool of interstaff relations.

Considering Third-Party Negotiations

In recent years, some parents and other school district patrons have been clamoring for an active involvement in collective negotiations. Proponents of this position have eagerly sought an extension of the sunshine laws to require negotiations sessions to be open to the public. Other forms include trilateral negotiations, by which a citizen group becomes an equal participant with the board's team and the union's team in the negotiating process; public response to proposals before an agreement is reached; and public referendum, by which proposals are voted on by the citizens of the school district. There are other variations on this theme. However, the ultimate objective is the same—citizen participation in the bargaining process.

Collective negotiations demand refined skills of those sitting at the table. Citizens generally do not possess these skills. Furthermore, a third party will bring confusion and can interfere with the employment relationship between the board and the employees. In addition, school board members have been elected to represent the interests of parents, students, and district patrons.

Impasse Procedures

In considering impasse procedures, it is important to understand what could be the cause of an impasse. The most common cause is a lack of "good faith" in the bargaining process, which is the product of a closed mind-set before the process begins.[13]

It is extremely difficult to define the term *impasse*. Negotiators often have trouble knowing when an impasse has been reached. However, for this discussion, an *impasse* is considered a persistent disagreement that continues after normal negotiation procedures have been exhausted.

Impasse must be expected to occur from time to time, even when both parties are negotiating in good faith. There are, unfortunately, no procedures that are guaranteed to resolve an impasse. Some procedures have been more successful than others, and the objective of this section is to outline these procedures. Also, it must be kept in mind that improperly used impasse procedures can aggravate rather than resolve a disagreement. Therefore, a working knowledge of procedures is essential to all participants in the negotiating process.

Twenty-two of the states that have passed collective negotiations laws also have established public employee relations boards. Each board is charged with implementing the law and, in most cases, with administering impasse procedures, including mediation, fact finding, and arbitration.

Mediation

Mediation is usually the first procedure used when an impasse has been reached.[14] The negotiators for both labor and management must agree on the need for third-party assistance. The role of the mediator is advisory, and consequently, the mediator has no authority to dictate a settlement. Some mediators use the tactic of first meeting with both parties separately and thereby attempt to ascertain what concessions each party might be willing to make in order to reach an agreement. This procedure has been most effective when one or both parties consider making concessions to be a sign of weakness. Meeting jointly with both parties is also helpful, particularly in assessing the actual status of negotiations and in obtaining agreement from the parties on the importance assigned to each unresolved issue. Most mediators use a combination of separate and joint meetings to facilitate an agreement.

Mediators usually refrain from recommending a settlement until they are sure that their recommendations will be acceptable to both parties. Up until the time of recommendation, the mediator acts only as a clarifier of issues and, through the process attempts, to defuse the antagonism between the parties, which is frequently the cause of the impasse. A mediator may be called into a dispute at any time. In some cases, the mediator may even practice preventive mediation by making suggestions useful to the parties early in the negotiations. Because mediation is a voluntary process, in the stages preparatory to the actual negotiations, the parties must decide who will mediate and what the mediator's role will be. In approximately one-third of the states, this issue is settled by statute, and a formal declaration of "impasse" is all that is required to put the process in motion. Often, a master agreement contains provisions outlining impasse procedures to be followed in negotiating the agreement. When mediator services are not provided by a government agency, the fee for a private mediator is borne equally by both parties to the dispute.

Fact Finding

Fact finding is the procedure by which an individual or a panel holds hearings to review evidence and make recommendations for settling the dispute. Like mediation, the fact-finding process is governed by a state statute, provided for in a master agreement, or established by both parties before negotiations begin.

The formal hearing is usually open to the public. Parties having a vested interest in the dispute are given the opportunity to offer evidence and arguments on their own behalf. Fact finders are sometimes requested by both parties to mediate the dispute and avoid the formal hearings.

The fact-finding report and recommendations are usually made public. The process is voluntary, and the parties may reject all or part of the report. To a certain extent, the action of the parties depends on the public's reactions, which in turn depend partly on the prestige of the fact finders.

Arbitration

Arbitration is the process by which the parties submit their dispute to an impartial third person or panel of persons that issues an award the parties are required to accept.[15] Arbitration can be either compulsory or voluntary. Compulsory arbitration must be established by statute; nineteen states have such legislation. The voluntary use of arbitration has gained some acceptance in the public sector for handling grievances arising from the interpretation of master agreements.

The Federal Mediation and Conciliation Service

The FMCS is an independent agency of the federal government created by Congress in 1974, with a director appointed by the president of the United States. The primary purpose of the FMCS is to promote labor management peace. To carry out this mission more effectively, the agency has established regional offices and field offices staffed by professional mediators. The FMCS works to resolve disagreements arising out of collective negotiations in the public sector, which amounts to approximately 8 percent of the agency's caseload annually.

Federal labor laws do not cover employees of state and local governments. However, if state legislatures fail to establish mediation services for public employees, the FMCS may voluntarily enter a dispute. The FMCS also has an Office of Arbitration Services in Washington, DC, that maintains a roster of arbitrators located throughout the United States. On request, the FMCS furnishes a randomly selected list of arbitrators from which the parties to a dispute may choose a mutually acceptable arbitrator to hear the dispute and make a decision.

In summary, it is too difficult to promote one impasse procedure as the most effective approach to handling all persistent disputes that arise at the bargaining table or in grievances over master agreement interpretation. It is more appropriate to think in terms of sequence. Mediation should be used first, followed by fact finding, and then, where permitted by law, arbitration. This sequence places the initial responsibility for resolving the dispute on the parties themselves. Experience teaches that better and more effective agreements are reached when the parties can resolve their own disputes. Yet, when disputes cannot be resolved and when it is mandated by law, arbitration curtails strikes, which always have a devastating effect on school districts.

Work–Stoppage Strategies

Scope of Strikes

Nothing is more disruptive to a school district than a strike. As board members, administrators, teachers, and support personnel engage in heated and public argument, schisms occur that often last for years. Community groups also become divided over who is right and who is wrong. When a strike occurs, the administrative team has the responsibility of keeping the schools open; to protect students who report to school; to protect school property; and to maintain communications with parents, teachers, and the public.

Work stoppages by public school employees are made illegal, or at least limited, by most state laws. However, this has not prevented strikes from occurring each year in many states. The news media daily remind us of the magnitude of this issue. There is also no indication that strikes will go away as school employees, administrators, and teachers become more proficient in the negotiations process.

In past decades, most teachers believed that strikes were not in keeping with their professional status. This thinking has vanished, and the personal traumas once associated with this type of action are also gone. Today, teachers engage in strikes over many issues, including recognition of their unions, salary increases, curriculum control, reductions in force, and lack of community support. Teachers also have honored strikes by nonteaching personnel and have attempted to get their unions to support them in their work stoppages.

School Employee Strike Tactics

A strike by school employees is usually the result of failure at the bargaining table. The objective of all strikes is to gain as favorable a settlement as possible from the board of education within the shortest period of time.

A few key issues have been used by teachers' unions to rally support for a strike. These include the pupil/teacher ratio; planning time, particularly for elementary school teachers; and extra pay for extra duty, particularly for secondary school teachers. With the onslaught of the accountability reform movement, the rallying call centers around job security and compensation issues.

Teachers' unions have almost unlimited resources from state and national affiliates at their disposal in a strike. In sensitive strikes, as many as a hundred field staff members may be available to help the local union. A careful examination of several strikes verifies the following as some of the tactics most commonly used by teachers unions:

- Inundating the community with the reasons for the strike. Handbills, advertisements in the local press, and news coverage are the mainly used vehicles.
- Placing the blame on a specific person such as the superintendent of schools or board president, thus channeling the pressure exerted by parents and the community.
- Encouraging local and state politicians to become involved in the dispute. School employee groups represent a sizable number of votes.
- Working diligently to gain support from other unions in the community.
- Staging a strike in the late spring because this interferes not only with graduation but also with state aid, which is usually calculated on a certain number of days in attendance before the end of the school year.

Although some strikes do occur spontaneously because of unexpected developments, most teacher work stoppages are well orchestrated. Teachers' unions are generally aware weeks or even months in advance that certain negotiation demands are strike-producing issues.

Administrative Strategies

If a school system finds itself in the middle of a strike without an adequate plan of action, the administration and the board of education have not been paying attention to the tenor of the times or the situation in their own school district. In fact, the superintendent and his or her cabinet should have a carefully developed strike plan that should operate at both the district and the building levels, even in the most tranquil of school settings. Exhibit 9.1, fashioned after a plan that was developed by the American Association of School Administrators, contains a series of steps that can serve as a guide for administrators in establishing their own district plans.

When the administrative control center recommended in Exhibit 9.1 is established at the central office, duties are assigned by the superintendent of schools with the advice of his or her cabinet. Central office administrators are assigned specific tasks to be performed during a strike. The director of labor relations could be given the task of notifying staff members of the state law and board policy concerning strikes. The director of community relations would have the responsibility of notifying the news media of the manner for providing daily information concerning a strike. In like manner, the building principal and, if it is a large school, his or her administrative team are responsible for implementing the building-level provisions.

EXHIBIT 9.1   Sample Strike Plan

Before a Strike

District Level

The board of education should develop an overall district plan well in advance of an anticipated strike. Such a plan should include the following provisions:

- Notifying the news media, parents, teachers, and staff of the likelihood of a strike
- Notifying teachers and staff members of applicable state laws and school board policies concerning a strike
- Establishing provisions for an administrative control center, where administrators can deal with issues that arise in a strike
- Contacting emergency responders such as the police and fire departments about the possibility of a strike and establishing a method of contact in an emergency
- Developing electronic emergency communication systems for ongoing information to all constituencies
- Having the board of education pass the legal resolutions required to deal with a strike, such as restraining orders and injunctions

Building Level

The principal should develop an overall building plan in conformity with the district plan well in advance of an anticipated strike. Such a plan should include the following provisions:

- Securing backup personnel for each building principal to act in his or her stead during the strike
- Making provision for a daily, early morning report to the administrative control center setting forth the names of teachers and staff members who reported for duty and the number of pupils in attendance at the school
- Making provision for continuity of communications if the usual means of communication are disrupted in the school
- Making provision for each building principal to have specific guidelines and authority to close the school when the safety and health of the pupils are threatened or when it is impossible to carry on an educational program
- Making provisions for building security

After a Strike

District Level

The board of education should develop an overall district plan that contains the following provisions:

- Notifying constituencies that the strike has ended
- Holding information sessions for administrators and board members
- Holding information sessions for building principals in preparation for the return of teachers
- Providing information to other constituents about the details of the strike settlement
- Developing a plan to defuse "anti-climactic" emotions

Building Level

The principal should develop an overall building plan in conformity with the district plan that contains the following provisions:

- Making plans to not allow teachers who participated in the strike to return to the classrooms until all substitute teachers are out of the school
- Making plans to focus major attention on the educational program and learning environment for students

Administration of the Master Agreement

Collective negotiations are ineffective unless the agreement reached by a board of education and a union or organization is codified in writing. Thus, a detailed written master agreement becomes the policy statement governing the board and union or organization in relation to the issues and rights of the parties that were agreed to. If the agreement is not reduced to writing, there is a likely possibility, and even a probability, that controversies will arise. Also, the master agreement becomes a tool to be used in communicating with all constituents in the school district, which is so critical because of the focus on transparency in the collective negotiating process.[16] The types of articles and appendices that operationalize master agreements can be found in the sample table of contents in Appendix A of this chapter.

Most master agreements include the salaries, fringe benefits, and working conditions that were negotiated. Some of the articles listed in Appendix A are universal and should be included in all master agreements:

- General Purpose and Duration of the Agreement
- Recognition
- Fair Practices Provisions
- State Employee Rights
- Redirection of the Contract
- Ratification and Final Disposition
- Grievance Procedure
- Description of Employees in the Bargaining Unit
- Impasse Procedures

The style and format of the master agreement are sometimes dictated by state statutes; however, in the absence of legislation, school boards and unions must look elsewhere for help. In many cases, teachers' associations affiliated with national unions have access to model master agreements that can be adapted to local situations. In fact, some models are complete in every detail except for filling in the blanks with the proper data.

Implementing the Master Agreement

It is the responsibility of the administration to interpret and implement the provisions of the agreement. Furthermore, the administration is limited only by the specifics of the master agreement, which is commonly referred to as *management prerogative*.

In the day-to-day interpretations of the agreement, it is certainly possible for violations to occur. Most written agreements, therefore, provide for a grievance procedure by which individuals or the union can allege that the master agreement is being violated or misinterpreted. Most grievance procedures contain the following elements:

- A detailed, descriptive definition of the term *grievance*
- A statement of the purpose of the grievance procedure
- A clause stating that a person alleging a grievance or testifying in a grievance will not face prejudicial treatment by the other party

- A clear outline of the appropriate steps to be taken in a grievance and the time allotments for each step
- In the case of arbitration, clauses stating who will bear the costs of arbitration and what qualifications are required for an arbitrator

The grievance procedure used in the Dade County (Florida) School District is reproduced in Appendix B of this chapter because it is an excellent example of how these provisions can be put into operation.

Labor Management Relations Committee

In an attempt to diffuse the adversarial relationship that sometimes exists between the board of education/administration and unions, labor management relations committees have been organized in some school districts. The charge to these committees is to work through concerns, problems, and issues before they appear at the table in the next round of negotiations. In a large school district, the director of employee relations has the responsibility of chairing the board/administration team, which should include first-line supervisors. In smaller districts, an assistant superintendent or even the superintendent may want to assume this responsibility. Shop stewards or other representatives of a given union constitute labor's membership on the committee.

The approach to labor management relations committee meetings should be informal, with the emphasis on mutual interests and collaboration. Compromise is the key to a successful relationship, as is true in at-the-table negotiations. A win–win strategy should also prevail, with each party attempting to come away with something that it wants. Whatever is agreed to at these sessions should be put in writing because this helps avoid confusion at a later time.

Of course, a labor management relations committee should not deal with monetary and fringe benefits issues but rather with working conditions issues. If this committee is to be successful, it must meet throughout the term of the master agreement.

Win–Win Approach to Collaborative Negotiations

In the mid-1980s, a movement began with the hope of defusing the hostility that sometimes accompanies collective negotiations, resulting in a derivation of the collective negotiations model presented in this chapter. In win–win collaborative negotiations, the overall goal is to develop a non-adversarial climate that allows interested parties to form consensus on issues related to salary, fringe benefits, and working conditions. Instead of a team composed of an employee category such as teachers sitting across the bargaining table with representatives of the administration, there is only one team, composed of teachers, board members, and administrators, whose mission is to solve problems and issues. This approach is sometimes termed *interest-based bargaining* because the interests of each person on the team are of equal value as that of all the other members.

As part of the process of the win–win approach, the members of the team attend a training program that includes communication skills, problem-solving skills, creative thinking skills, orientation to the collaborative approach, development of group agreements, and development of superordinate goals. Someone is usually elected by the team to be the convener. A group recorder who is not a member of the team should also be provided. Finally, a process observer who acts as a consultant to the effective use of the win–win approach is usually hired to provide the training. Many professional organizations have identified consultants who are skilled in process.

In win–win collaborative negotiations, there are three important hallmarks: First, it is an evidence-based approach, especially in relation to budgetary issues as set forth in detail later. Second, transparency is essential because hidden agendas ultimately hinder the process. There can be no secrets. Third, civility in communication creates the environment within which the process can be effective.

Superordinate goals such as "enhancing teaching and learning" are highly valued, attainable, and commonly sought after by the group members. These goals provide the framework within which the various issues are addressed and solved. Consensus is the essence of the decision-making process. However, the win–win approach usually requires more time than the traditional model. It can be a very effective approach, especially if the traditional model has resulted in overt hostility. However, it is important to approach the win–win collaborative approach with caution; it is not a panacea.

Evidence-Based Support for Collective Negotiations

In keeping with what has been stated in preceding chapters, the amount of information that is now available has changed the negotiations planning process for boards of education, the administration, and teachers' unions and organizations. Further, the scope and analysis of data have also changed the at-the-table negotiating process. These dimensions of collective negotiations have moved the process into a more complete, focused, evidence-based approach to decision making.

In many school districts, the skepticism caused by faulty or incomplete data that dominated many negotiating sessions in the past has ceased to exist. Of course, this evidence-based approach to decision making can be successful only if two board of education or administrative policies are adopted and adhered to firmly: First, there must be a culture in the school district that values and uses data in all decision making; and second, there must be complete transparency in terms of the school district's budgeting process. Revenues and expenditures must be available on the district's Website for everyone to review.

For example, salary information should be available that sets forth the number of teachers in each of the various categories and levels of the salary schedule. Administrator salaries, in like manner, should be available.

School districts using an evidence-based approach to administrative functions can make available data that give a complete picture of the school district's financial situation. This is critical in collective negotiations. For example, it is possible to generate reports on fringe benefit usage such as medical and hospital insurance, sick-day leave, and extracurricular compensation. School districts' Websites permit a school district and teachers' union or organization to garner comparative data from other school districts on all aspects of budgeting—not only salaries and fringe benefits but also expenditures that impinge on working conditions such as class size and the number of teacher assistants.

The evidence-based approach to negotiations also provides the board of education, the administration, and teacher's unions and organizations with the opportunity to keep all constituents apprised of progress in the negotiations process.

Implications for Small- and Medium-Size School Districts

Of course, there are many school districts that do not have full-time directors or assistant superintendents for human resources administration or employee relations. In fact, the superintendent of schools and members of the board of education may be the negotiators for the school district designated to meet with the teachers' representatives. There may only be one bargaining unit that represents both teachers and staff members, and no formal ground rules for the negotiating process. Impasse procedures may be limited to time away from the negotiating table waiting for parents to demand that the board of education and teachers' union or organization return to the table. There may be no requirement in the state in which the school district is located to formalize the final agreement with the teachers into a master agreement. However, boards of education, administrators, and teachers are engaged in collective negotiations in forty-six states across the United States.

This chapter provides the reader with the maximum amount of information on the most advantageous manner in which to engage in collective negotiations. It is understood that each person will take from this chapter the material that will be most helpful given his or her current situation. However, regardless of the size of the school district or the legal requirement to engage in some form of collective negotiations, the following elements of the negotiations process should be adhered to:

- The teachers and staff members should be represented by the union(s) or organization(s) that they designate through a formal process of selection.
- Negotiations should be centered on salaries, fringe benefits, and working conditions.
- Those charged with representing the board of education and the teachers and staff should agree on a set of ground rules for how the at-the-table meetings will take place.
- The representatives of the board and the teachers and staff should agree on data that the district should provide for the negotiating process.
- The final agreement must be ratified by the board of education and the teachers and staff in the aggregate through a formal vote.
- Work stoppage should be avoided at all costs.

Impact of Generation Y Teachers and Administrators on Collective Negotiations

Generation Y teachers and administrators are concerned about being treated with equity and fairness, financially supporting themselves and their families, saving money for retirement, and participating in governance to the extent that they can affect policy.

These characteristics are addressed in the collective negotiations process, which typically includes bargaining for improved working conditions, better fringe benefits, and higher salaries. At the foundation of these characteristics is the search for security usually manifested in having a decent job with an adequate salary and the opportunity for career advancement, accompanied by good fringe benefits. It is what Samuel Gompers always answered when asked about what he wanted from management—*more*. Generation Y teachers and administrators are usually supportive of professional associations such as the NEA and AFT because these associations are supportive of participation in the policy-making process, which is the ultimate purpose for engaging in collective negotiations.

Members of Generation Y also tend to be activists in the political process at all levels, which certainly includes supporting candidates for the board of education who are supportive of teachers and administrators to the extent that they need and deserve better working conditions, fringe benefits, and salaries. Working conditions of interest to Generation Y teachers include those that recognize the importance of balancing professional and personal responsibilities, such as job sharing and daycare services in the school district for teachers and administrators with preschool-age children. Like other younger teachers and administrators, Generation Y employees are greatly concerned about having a salary that helps them as they start their families, whereas teachers and administrators from other generations are probably more concerned about fringe benefits.

A final characteristic of Generation Y employees is their desire to get ahead faster than teachers and administrators from other generations. Thus, staff development opportunities and assistance with tuition for graduate education are also concerns of Generation Y.

Summary

Collective negotiations have become an accepted part of American education, as evidenced by the fact that more than three-fourths of the states have enacted collective negotiations laws affecting teachers. The consideration underlying collective negotiations is participation in the decision-making process, which is a natural extension of our democratic lifestyle.

Teachers and administrators want input concerning the priorities established by the school board when these affect their salaries, fringe benefits, and working conditions. *Collective negotiations* may be defined as the process by which representatives of the school board meet with representatives of the school district to make proposals and counterproposals for the purpose of agreeing on salaries, fringe benefits, and working conditions for a specific period of time. To operationalize this process, it is necessary for the board of education to adopt a policy that gives the administration authority to implement negotiations.

Collective actions by employees have a long history in the private sector, reaching back to the time of the medieval guilds, and are directly affected by the economic, political, and social conditions of life. Four major congressional acts provide legal guidelines for collective bargaining in the private sector: the Norris–LaGuardia Act of 1932, the

National Labor Relations Act of 1935, the Labor Management Relations Act of 1947, and the Labor Management Reporting and Disclosure Act of 1959. Executive Orders 10988 and 11491 affirm the right of federal employees to organize and bargain collectively, but strikes are forbidden.

Public school teachers are state employees working in a local unit, the school district. As such, they are covered not by federal legislation, but rather by the acts of state legislatures. There are substantial differences in those state statutes granting collective negotiations rights to teachers.

There are six aspects to the collective negotiations process: recognition and bargaining unit determination, the scope of negotiations, the bargaining process, impasse procedures, work stoppages, and the administration of the master agreement.

Recognition and bargaining unit determination answer the question, "Who represents whom?" *Recognition* is the acceptance by an employer of a bargaining agent as the authorized representative of a bargaining unit. There are two types of recognition: *multiple* and *exclusive.* Experience indicates that exclusive recognition is more effective. The three most commonly used recognition procedures are membership lists, authorization cards, and elections. In an election, a third party such as the FMCS should be engaged to handle the mechanics of the process.

The bargaining unit is composed of all employees to be covered by the negotiated master agreement. The criteria for deciding who belongs to the unit include a community of interest among the members, effective bargaining power, and effective school administration.

The scope of what is negotiable usually includes salaries, fringe benefits, and working conditions. A major problem in defining the scope is the fine line between *educational policy,* which is the prerogative of the school board, and *working conditions,* which are negotiable.

The at-the-table bargaining process must begin with the formation of a negotiations team for the school board. An odd-numbered team composed of the director of employee relations, building principals, and a central office fiscal administrator has the greatest potential for being effective. This team is responsible for developing strategies, formulating goals, setting the ground rules, preparing proposals, and participating in negotiating sessions. Once an agreement is reached, the team makes a recommendation to the superintendent and school board members, who formally ratify the agreement.

If there is persistent disagreement at the table after normal negotiations procedures are exhausted, an *impasse* has been reached. The three procedures usually employed in an impasse are mediation, fact finding, and, where permitted by law, arbitration. *Mediation* is the voluntary process of bringing in a third party who intervenes to end the disagreement. *Fact finding* is a procedure by which an individual or panel holds hearings for the purpose of reviewing evidence and making a recommendation for settling the dispute. *Arbitration* occurs when both sides submit the dispute to an impartial third person or panel that issues an award that the parties are required to accept.

Nothing is more disruptive to a school district than a *strike,* a tactic sometimes used by unions when negotiations reach an impasse. Although strikes by teachers are illegal in most states, a number of strikes occur each year throughout the United States. It is extremely important, therefore, for the administration to develop a strike plan, even in the most tranquil of school settings.

The process of collective negotiations is usually ineffective unless the agreement reached is put in writing, thus formalizing the basic rights governing the parties and reducing potential controversy. It is the responsibility of the administration to interpret and implement the master agreement. Furthermore, the administration is limited only by the specifics of the agreement, which is commonly referred to as *management prerogative*.

In the day-to-day interpretation of the master agreement, it is certainly possible for violations to occur. Most written agreements, therefore, provide for a grievance procedure by which individuals or the union may allege that the agreement is being violated. In some school districts, labor management relations committees have been formed for the purpose of working through concerns, problems, and issues before they appear at the table when the existing master contract is renegotiated.

An innovative approach to collective negotiations was developed in the mid-1980s. Called *collaborative bargaining*, its purpose is the defusing of the hostility that sometimes accompanies the traditional negotiations process. In this process, there is one team composed of teachers or other categories of employees reflecting the bargaining unit, administrators, and board members. The goal of the process is to solve problems, and its essence is reaching consensus.

The amount of information that is available because of technology has changed the negotiations planning process for boards of education, administrators, and teachers' unions and organizations. Further, the scope and analysis of data have changed the at-the-table negotiating process. These dimensions of collective negotiations have moved the process into a more complete, focused, and evidence-based approach to decision making.

Self-Check Quiz Click here to take an automatically-graded self-check quiz.

Discussion Questions and Statements

1. What are the significant differences between collective negotiations in the public and private sectors?
2. What provisions do you believe should be included in a state statute on collective negotiations for teachers?
3. Explain the differences among the impasse procedures of mediation, fact finding, and arbitration, and further explain which procedures would be the most effective in collective negotiations with teachers' organizations.
4. Should public school employees have the right to strike?
5. Explain the differences between a *master contract* and an individual person's *employment contract*.
6. Explain how the labor movement in the United States has affected teachers' unions and organizations.

Suggested Activities

1. You are the director of employee relations in a small suburban school district with approximately seventy-five teachers. The state where the school district is located has a strong collective negotiations law for public employees. Create, in writing, a process for conducting collective negotiations from a central office perspective that meets the principles in this chapter.

2. Write a board of education collective negotiations policy that you believe meets the needs of employees for a school district in a state with a weak collective negotiations law for public employees.

3. Review the statutes in the state in which you live on collective negotiations for public employees, and write a comparison of these statutes with the principles in this chapter.

4. Interview a human resources administrator in person or on the telephone, and discuss the implementation of the policies in his or her district concerning collective negotiations.

Focus Scenario Activity

Given that you have read and studied this chapter, how would you proceed to educate the members of the board of education about collective bargaining and how it pertains to your school district? Also, recommend the human resources strategy that you would like adopted by the board and superintendent.

Endnotes

1. Kathryn Tyles, "Good Faith Bargaining," *HR Magazine*, 50, no. 1 (2005): 51.
2. P. D. V. Marsh, *Contract Negotiation Handbook*, 3rd ed. (Burlington, VT: Gower, 2001), 224.
3. Ibid.
4. North Carolina School Boards Association, www.ncsba.org.
5. David A. DeCenzo and Stephen P. Robbins, *Human Resource Management*, 7th ed. (New York: John Wiley, 2002), 418–422.
6. Ibid., 422–426.
7. Emily Cohen, Kate Walsh, and RiShawn Biddle, *Invisible Ink in Collective Bargaining: Why Key Issues Are Not Addressed*, (Washington, DC: National Council on Teacher Quality, 2008).
8. Charles Taylor Kerchner and Julia E. Koppich, "Negotiating What Matters Most: Collective Bargaining and Student Achievement," *American Journal of Education*, 113, no. 3 (March 2007): 349–365.
9. C. Daniel Raisch and Charles J. Russo, "How to Succeed at Collective Bargaining," *School Business Affairs*, (December 2005).
10. Linda Kaboolian, "Table Talk," *Education Next*, 6, no. 3 (Summer 2006): 14–17.
11. Susan Black, "Bargaining: It's in Your Best Interest," *American School Board Journal*, (2008).
12. Paul Hewitt, "Bargaining within the School Culture," *Leadership*, 36, no. 5 (May/June 2007): 26–30.
13. Todd A. DeMitchell, "Unions, Collective Bargaining, and the Challenges of Leading," in *The Sage Handbook of Educational Leadership: Advances in Theory, Research, and Practice*, (Thousand Oaks, CA: Sage, 2005), 545–546.
14. Roberto Martinez-Pecino, Lourdes Munduate, Francisco J. Medina, and Martin C. Euwema, "Effectiveness of Mediation Strategies in Collective Bargaining," *Industrial Relations*, 47, no. 3 (July 2008): 480–495.

15. Kevin P. Brady, "Bargaining," in *Yearbook of Education Law 2007*, (Dayton, OH: Education Law Association, 2007), 100–107.

16. Howard Fuller and George A. Mitchell, "A Culture of Complaint," *Education Next*, 6, no. 3 (Summer 2006): 18–22.

Selected Bibliography

Bennett, Ron, and John Gray. "Principal-Centered Negotiations." *Leadership*, 36, no. 5 (May/June 2007): 22–24.

Brady, Kevin P. "Bargaining." In Charles J. Russo, ed., *The Yearbook of Education Law, 2007*, Dayton, OH: Education Law Association, 2007, 100–107.

Fuller, Howard, and George A. Mitchell. "A Culture of Complaint." *Education Next*, 6, no. 3 (Summer 2006): 18–22.

Garfield, Timothy K. "Governance in a Union Environment." *New Directions for Community Colleges*, 2008, no. 141 (Spring 2008): 25–33.

Godshall, Clark J. "Managing Success: Collective Bargaining." *School Business Affairs*, 68, no. 4 (April 2002): 2–3.

Grossman, Robert F. "Unions Follow Suit." *HR Magazine*, 50, no. 5 (2005): 46–51.

Hewitt, Paul. "Bargaining within the School Culture." *Leadership*, 36, no. 5 (May/June 2007): 26–30.

Holley, William H., Kenneth M. Jennings, and Roger S. Wolters. *The Labor Relations Process*. Winfield, KS: Southwestern College Publications, 2007.

Kaboolian, Linda. "Table Talk: The Case for Collaboration." *Education Next*, 6, no. 3 (Summer 2006): 14–17.

Kerchner, Charles Taylor, and Julia E. Koppich. "Negotiating What Matters Most: Collective Bargaining and Student Achievement." *American Journal of Education*, 113 (March 2007).

Losey, Mike, David Ulrich, and Sue Meisinger, eds. *The Future of Human Resources Management: 64 Thought Leaders Explore the Critical HR Issues of Today and Tomorrow*. New York: John Wiley, 2005.

lutins, allen. (2013, February 26). "An Eclectic List of Events in U.S. Labor History." www.lutins.org/labor.html.

Marsh, P. D. V. *Contract Negotiation Handbook*, 3rd ed. Burlington, VA: Gower, 2001.

Martinez-Pecino, Roberto, Lourdes Munduate, Francisco J. Medina, and Martin C. Euwema. "Effectiveness of Mediation Strategies in Collective Bargaining." *Industrial Relations*, 47, no. 3 (July 2008): 480–495.

Murphy, John F. "The Thanksgiving Dinner: An Allegory of the School Negotiation Process." *School Business Affairs*, 68, no. 4 (April 2002): 9–11.

Raisch, C. Daniel, and Charles J. Russo. "How to Succeed at Collective Bargaining." *School Business Affairs*, (December 2005).

St. Antoine, Theodore J. *The Common Law of the Workplace: The Views of Arbitrators*. Arlington, VA: Bureau of National Affairs, 2005.

Stover, Del. "State of the Unions." *American School Board Journal*, 195, no. 4 (April 2008).

Tyler, Kathryn. "Good Faith Bargaining." *HR Magazine*, 50, no. 1 (2005): 48–53.

U.S. Department of Labor. www.dol.gov.

Zorn, Robert L. "Information-Based Bargaining for a New Age." *School Administrator*, 63, no. 7 (2006): 44.

Appendix A
Sample Master Agreement Table of Contents

Appendix B
Dade County (Florida) School District Grievance Procedure

A. Purpose

It is recognized that complaints and grievances may arise between the bargaining agent and the employer or between the employer and any one or more employees concerning the application or interpretation of the wages, hours, terms, and conditions of employment as defined in this agreement. The employer and the bargaining agent desire that these grievances and complaints be settled in an orderly, prompt, and equitable manner so that the efficiency of the County Public Schools may be maintained and the morale of employees not be impaired. Every effort will be made by the employer, the employees, and the bargaining agent to settle the grievances at the lowest level of supervision. The initiation or presentation of a grievance by an employee will not adversely affect his or her standing with the employer. No reprisals of any kind will be made by the School Board or its representative or any member of the administration against any party in interest, any Union representative, or any other participant in the grievance procedure by reason of such participation. All documents, grievance forms, communications, and records dealing with the processing of a grievance shall be filed separately from the personnel files of any party in interest, including final disposition, except for and exclusively for awards resulting from arbitration.

B. Definitions

1. *Grievance.* Formal allegation by an employee and/or the bargaining agent that there has been a violation, misinterpretation, or misapplication of any of the terms and conditions of employment set forth in this contract, or its appendices.

2. *Bargaining agent.* The bargaining agent shall mean the employee organization certified as the exclusive bargaining agent pursuant to State Statutes.

3. *Aggrieved employee.* The aggrieved employee shall mean any full-time or part-time teacher and such other persons who are members of the bargaining unit as certified pursuant to State Statutes.

4. *Party in interest.* A party in interest is any person who might be required to take action or against whom action might be taken in order to resolve the grievance.

5. *Supervising administrator.* The individual having immediate administrative authority over the aggrieved employee(s).

6. *Immediate superintendent.* The area, assistant, or associate superintendent having immediate administrative authority over the supervising administrator.

7. *Days.* As referred to in the time limits herein, days shall mean working days.

8. *Letter of inquiry.* Request in writing on the proper form, from the bargaining agent to the Division of Legislative and Employee Relations, seeking clarification of the Public Schools rules, state law, or this agreement.

Source: Appendices A and B were adapted from the Successor Contract between the Miami-Dade County Public Schools and the United Teachers of Dade (Miami: Miami-Dade County Public Schools, 2006), www.dade-schools.net/employees/labor_union/UTD/entire.pdf.

C. Special Provisions

The time limit set forth herein may be extended and/or modified by mutual agreement, using the stipulated Grievance Form.

In the event a grievance is filed at such time that it cannot be processed through all steps in the grievance procedure by the end of the aggrieved employee's contract year and, if left unresolved until the beginning of the following year, could result in irreparable harm to a party in interest, the time limits set forth herein will be reduced so that the grievance procedure may be exhausted as soon as practicable.

If the employer violates any time limits, the bargaining agent may advance to the next step without waiting for the employer response.

The parties acknowledge that as a principle of interpretation, employees are obligated to work as directed while grievances are pending.

The employer and the bargaining agent shall have the right of free choice in designating representatives for the purpose of resolving grievances. Aggrieved employees, or employees who are called as witnesses, will be allowed released time without loss of pay to process or assist in the processing of a grievance.

The bargaining agent in accordance with its own nondiscriminatory internal rules shall have the sole and exclusive right to determine whether any grievance warrants processing through this procedure. In the event the bargaining agent determines at any step of the grievance procedure that a grievance does not warrant processing, a written notification of that determination, using the stipulated Grievance Form, shall be sent to the Special Counsel for Legislative and Employee Relations and to the employee(s) involved who shall then be free to process it themselves or through legal counsel.

If the bargaining agent has declined to process or further process any grievance presented to it, and if any employee or group of employees desires to process it or further process it through this procedure, the bargaining agent shall be sent copies of all written communications sent by the employer or the employee(s) involved. Further, nothing herein contained shall be construed to prevent any public employees from representing, at any time, their own grievance in person or by legal counsel to the employer and having such grievance(s) adjusted without the intervention of the bargaining agent, provided however, that the adjustment is not inconsistent with the terms of the collective bargaining agreement then in effect, and provided further that the bargaining agent has been given notice and a reasonable opportunity to be present at any meeting called for the resolution of such grievances.

The bargaining agent shall not be responsible for any costs attendant to the resolution of any grievance it has not processed.

The parties acknowledge that multiple grievances may be combined with mutual agreement of the employer and the union.

One set of School Board rules at each work location shall be made available to Union building representatives for the purpose of reference and information as well as for the purpose of expediting the provisions of this grievance procedure.

The use of tape recorders or other mechanical devices is expressly forbidden.

D. Letter of Inquiry

Either the immediate superintendent or the bargaining agent may send a Letter of Inquiry on the stipulated Letter of Inquiry Form to the Special Counsel for the Division of Legislative and

Employee Relations for the purpose of seeking a clarification of the Public Schools rules, state law, and/or terms and conditions of employment as set forth in this agreement.

The Division of Legislative and Employee Relations shall respond within ten (10) working days of receipt of the Letter of Inquiry. If the interpretation of the Letter of Inquiry is not satisfactory, a formal grievance may be filed.

E. Implementation

Step I

1. The grievance shall be filed within thirty (30) days of the alleged violation, misinterpretation, or misapplication of the terms and conditions of employment set forth in this agreement.

2. The grievance shall be filed in writing stating the specific article, section, and language alleged to have been violated, misinterpreted, or misapplied to the supervising administrator of the aggrieved employee(s). It is further understood and agreed that the aggrieved employee(s) shall be granted released time to attend formal proceedings, as described herein, that are held during working hours. No County Public Schools employees, other than the aggrieved employee(s), shall be granted released time to either represent the aggrieved employee(s) or to observe the proceedings as representatives of the bargaining agent.

3. The supervising administrator shall note the date of receipt of the grievance and shall seek to meet with the aggrieved employee(s) at a mutually agreeable time within five (5) working days of receipt of the grievance.

4. The bargaining agent for the unit shall be advised in writing as to the date of the proposed meeting and shall have the right to send one (1) observer to the proceeding if the bargaining agent is not involved in the actual representation of the aggrieved employee(s).

5. Within five (5) working days of the meeting, the supervising administrator shall render a decision and shall immediately communicate that decision in writing to the aggrieved and the appropriate immediate superintendent or his or her designee. Additional copies of the decision shall be sent to the Division of Legislative and Employee Relations and to the exclusive bargaining agent.

6. The aggrieved employee(s) and/or the bargaining agent may appeal the decision of the supervising administrator within five (5) working days of its rendering.

7. The notice of intent to appeal shall be communicated in writing to the immediate superintendent. Failure to appeal the decision of the supervising administrator within five (5) working days shall constitute acceptance by the aggrieved employee(s) and the bargaining agent of the decision as being a satisfactory resolution of the issue raised.

Step II

1. If the aggrieved employee(s) appeals the decision, the immediate superintendent shall schedule a meeting to take place at a mutually agreeable time not more than ten (10) days after receipt of the notice of appeal. The immediate superintendent shall immediately communicate the notice of appeal to the Division of Legislative and Employee Relations.

2. The exclusive bargaining agent shall be advised in writing as to the date of the proposed meeting and shall have the right to send one (1) observer to the proceedings if the agent is not involved in the actual representation of the aggrieved employee(s).

3. Within ten (10) working days of the meeting, the immediate superintendent shall render a decision and shall immediately communicate that decision in writing to the aggrieved employee(s). Copies of the decision shall be sent to the Division of Legislative and Employee Relations and to the exclusive bargaining agent. A copy is to be retained by the immediate superintendent.

4. The aggrieved employee(s) may appeal the decision of the immediate superintendent within five (5) working days of its rendering. The notice of intent to appeal shall be communicated in writing to the Special Counsel for Legislative and Employee Relations. Failure to appeal the decision of the immediate superintendent within five (5) working days shall constitute acceptance by the aggrieved employee(s) and the bargaining agent of the decision as being a satisfactory resolution of the issue raised.

Step III

1. If the aggrieved employee(s) appeals the decision, the Superintendent or his or her designee shall schedule a meeting to take place at a mutually agreeable time not more than twelve (12) days after receipt of the notice of appeal.

2. Within twelve (12) working days of the meeting, the Superintendent or his or her designee shall render a decision and shall immediately communicate that decision in writing to the aggrieved employee(s). Copies of the decision shall be sent to the supervising administrator, the immediate superintendent, and the exclusive bargaining agent.

3. Failure to appeal the decision rendered in Step III.2 within five (5) working days by filing a notice of intent to submit to arbitration shall deem the decision at Step III.2 to be final, and no further appeal will be pursued.

F. Arbitration

If the employer and the aggrieved employee(s) and/or the bargaining agent fail to resolve the grievance, the grievance may be submitted to final and binding disposition by an impartial neutral mutually selected by the parties. Nothing contained in this Appendix or elsewhere in this agreement shall be construed to permit the Union to file an issue for arbitration, unless by mutual consent, that has not been processed through applicable steps of the grievance procedure.

1. Notice of intent to submit the grievance to arbitration shall be communicated in writing to the Special Counsel for Legislative and Employee Relations within five (5) working days of the decision at Step III.2.

2. Prior to the submission of the appeal to arbitration, the arbitrator may hold a prehearing conference to consider and determine

    a. The simplification of the issues,

    b. The possibility of obtaining a stipulation of facts and documents that will avoid unnecessary proof,

    c. Such other matters as may aid in the disposition of the grievance, and

    d. Matters of jurisdiction or applicability.

3. In the event that an employee desires, on his or her own behalf, to process the grievance to arbitration, the bargaining agent reserves the right to intervene in the arbitration proceeding up to and including the full right to participation as a party. Should the bargaining agent intervene, it shall bear half the employee's cost.

4. Within ten (10) days after written notice of submission to arbitration, the parties will attempt to agree upon a mutually acceptable arbitrator and obtain a commitment from said arbitrator to serve. If the parties are unable to agree upon an arbitrator or to obtain such a commitment within the specified time, a request for a list of arbitrators may be made to the Federal Mediation and Conciliation Service by either party. The parties will be bound by the rules and procedures of the Federal Mediation and Conciliation Service in the selection of an arbitrator and the holding and conduct of an arbitration hearing.

5. The arbitrator, selected by the parties or pursuant to the rules of the Federal Mediation and Conciliation Service, will issue a decision not later than twenty (20) days from the date of the close of the hearings, or if oral hearings have been waived, then from the date final statements and proofs are submitted. The arbitrator's decision will be in writing and will set forth findings of fact, reasoning, and conclusions on the issue submitted and where permitted by law may include a monetary award. The arbitrator will be without power or authority to make any decision that requires the commission of an act prohibited by law or that adds to, subtracts from, modifies, or alters the terms of this collective bargaining agreement. The decision and award of the arbitrator shall be final and binding.

6. All arbitration costs, including the cost of stenographic reporting of the arbitration hearing, if agreed to by the parties, shall be divided equally between the employer and the bargaining agent or, if the bargaining agent has determined not to process the grievance through arbitration, between the employer and the employee(s). Each party will pay the cost of presenting its own case; however, the aggrieved employee(s) or the employee(s) called as witnesses for an arbitration hearing will be allowed released time to process or to assist in the processing of their own grievance or to testify.

7. It is understood and agreed by the employer, the members of the unit, and the bargaining agent that the resolution of complaints that are grievable or litigable shall be pursued through the grievance procedure until such remedy is exhausted. At that time, the employer, the aggrieved employee(s), and/or the bargaining agent may seek other legal remedies as are available.

Refusal to discuss a grievance in good faith shall constitute an Unfair Labor Practice and shall be subject to the penalties provided for in State Statutes.

8. Both parties agree to negotiate and mutually agree to the rules and procedures that govern arbitration. In the event mutual agreement cannot be reached, the American Arbitration Association will be utilized to process arbitration cases.

CHAPTER 10

Legal, Ethical, and Policy Issues in the Administration of Human Resources

Focus Scenario

You are the director of risk management in a large metropolitan school district serving approximately 30,000 students. In conducting the yearly safety and security audit, you and your staff have found a number of safety hazards and security needs in many of the district's schools. The audit report is a written document presented to the assistant superintendent for human relations. However, she has informed you that the facilities budget has been reduced by 10 percent because of a shortfall in state aid again for a second year that will keep many of your safety and security recommendations from being implemented.

Shortly after you were told that the money was not available for building repairs, a loose ceiling tile fell on a student, causing a laceration to her head that required plastic surgery. The parents of the student have retained an attorney who has filed a lawsuit alleging negligence by the school district. The assistant superintendent for human resources talked with you about the incident and reminded you that the employee responsible for the maintenance of the building where the accident occurred is an at-will employee without a contract and that he can be terminated for neglecting the necessary repairs. She further indicated that the audit reports are internal documents that do not need to be made available to the public.

You set forth in writing to the assistant superintendent that the policy of the school district requires a thorough investigation by the school district's attorney when a lawsuit is filed in order to determine the material facts before a defense strategy can be formulated. This is the second year that the annual audit report has included the identification of loose ceiling tiles. You have the distinct impression from the assistant superintendent that she wants you to find a way to minimize the potential for the district to lose the case in court.

Please use both the "Discussion Questions and Statements" and "Suggested Activities" at the end of this chapter in order to help you develop a way of proceeding in order to address the issues in this section.

This final chapter is concerned with legal, ethical, and policy issues in the administration of human resources. An understanding by current and future human resources managers of contract management and the nuances of litigation has become more important within the past decade because of the ever-increasing societal emphasis on legal rights and responsibilities. Human resources managers are as vulnerable to litigation as teachers and principals. In fact, with the multitude of federal and state laws, regulations, and procedures that impinge on human resources functions, defensibility and accountability must be continuing concerns in the human resources department.

Relevant, concise, and clear personnel policies become the foundation on which the eight human resources functions rest. Administrative processes and procedures operationalize these policies and provide the internal structure necessary to accomplish the school district's primary mandate—to educate children. Consequently, this chapter has been written with these issues in mind and should provide direction to all persons concerned with human resources administration, including boards of education, superintendents, assistant superintendents, and human resources managers.

It is also important for human resources administrators to promote the positive cultural history of their school districts through the development of certain personnel policies. This is also true in relation to balancing the gender make-up of the professional and support staffs. For example, in urban school districts composed primarily of African American citizens, the board of education, superintendent of schools, and human resources personnel must make a concerted effort to have a significant number of African Americans represented in all employment categories. In like manner, a goal of the human resources department should be to have a significant number of females represented in all employee categories. This approach to human resources policy development reflects the ethical and legal responsibilities of human resources administrators.

Contract Management

Teachers and administrators usually work under the provisions of an individual contract; classified personnel such as clerks, bus drivers, and custodians are employed at an hourly rate or for an annual salary. In school districts where a master contract has been negotiated by a union, teachers and/or administrators belonging to the bargaining unit do not have individual contracts, but rather work under the provisions of the master agreement. There are exceptions to these general statements; however, for all practical purposes, these are the methods by which employees are hired to work in a school system.[1]

The question may legitimately be asked, "What is the purpose of issuing individual contracts to teachers and administrators?" Whereas the purpose varies in different states, the most accurate response is "tradition." As professionals, teachers and administrators are employed to perform a service for which they receive a certain amount of financial compensation. The performance of the service may require a teacher to take student projects home to be graded or to remain after the school day to talk with the parents of a student having problems. The time it takes to perform the service and the amount of work involved are not considerations under the contract method of employment.

Classified employees also are paid to perform a service, but the time and work involved do make a difference in the amount of money received. When such employees are required to work after the regular eight-hour day, they receive overtime pay. When they are required to perform a task not specified by the categories outlined in their job descriptions, they receive additional compensation.

Those professional employees who are covered by the terms of a master agreement have a closer identity to classified employees than to teachers and administrators with individual contracts. Their working conditions are spelled out in the master agreement.

Board of education policies sometimes address working conditions, but these policies are usually not as specific as the terms of a master agreement. Teacher and administrator handbooks\may also contain references to working conditions, but these are usually more concerned with internal procedures.

Although using individual contracts for teachers and administrators is a matter of tradition, it is also mandated in some states such as Missouri. Individual contracts also distinguish an employee's working conditions from those of employees who are termed *classified*. A teacher's or administrator's contract must meet the requirements of general contract law. Because school districts are legal entities with a corporate character, they may sue and be sued; purchase, receive, or sell real and personal property; and make contracts and be contracted with. The contracts entered into by a school district must conform not only to state statutes governing contracts, but also to the precedents established through case law. An individual contract is an agreement that, in order to be valid, must possess five basic components: offer and acceptance, competent persons, consideration, legal subject matter, and proper form.

Offer and Acceptance

A valid contract must contain an offer and an acceptance. In the selection process, therefore, it is poor procedure to notify unsuccessful job candidates that the position has been filled until after the prospective employee has accepted the offer of employment. If the board of education approves a contract for a specific person to teach high school English, no agreement exists until the contract is executed, which constitutes acceptance.

A few other facts about the legal nature of an agreement must be kept in mind: First, an offer can be accepted only by the person to whom it was made. For example, the husband of a candidate for a teaching position cannot accept the offer for his wife. Second, an offer must be accepted within a reasonable time after it is made. If an individual does not sign and return a contract within a few weeks in the hope that another job offer will be made by a different school district, the board of education may offer the contract to another candidate. Finally, a newspaper advertisement is not an offer of a position, but rather an invitation to become a candidate for a position.

Competent Persons

A contract is not valid unless it is entered into by two or more competent parties, meaning that the persons have the legal capacity to enter into a contract. As a corporate entity, a school district has the power, through the legal action of the school board, to enter into a contract. Certain classes of individuals, however, have a limited capacity to contract. The most commonly identified classes include minors, persons with mental illness, and individuals who are intoxicated. If a person was mentally ill or intoxicated to the extent that he or she did not understand the significance of the action at the time of entering into a contract, he or she may have the contract set aside because there was no acceptance, which is essential to the validity of every contract.

Consideration

For a contract to be valid, it must be supported by *consideration,* usually defined as something of value. The type of consideration found in an employment contract is referred to as "a promise for an act." For example, in a teacher's contract, the board of education promises to pay an individual $40,000 to teach third grade for one year. The teacher receives the promised consideration when he or she teaches during the designated time period.

Legal Subject Matter

In all fifty states, an individual may teach only if he or she possesses a teaching license issued by the respective state department of education. Consequently, if a board of education enters into a contract with a person who does not possess a license to teach the third grade, such a contract would involve illegal subject matter and would be invalid.

Proper Form

For a contract to be enforceable, it must be in the form required by law. The courts recognize both oral and written contracts. However, most states have statutory provisions that require teachers' and administrators' contracts to be in writing, and even specify the proper wording for the contracts.

Litigation in Human Resources Management

Sovereign immunity is the common law principle that protects government officials from lawsuits resulting from the performance of their duties. School districts are subdivisions of the state government operating on the local level, and thus school board members have been protected from such lawsuits. However, school districts have experienced an increase in litigation partially because sovereign immunity has been abrogated to varying degrees by nineteen state legislatures and the District of Columbia.

The ripple effect from this situation has caused human resources administrators to become more vulnerable to judicial review of their decisions and actions. Even if human resources administrators act in good faith and with reasonable deliberation, they may find themselves defending their actions in court. Therefore, it is imperative that all administrators have a rudimentary understanding of the U.S. judicial system and be capable of carrying out their daily responsibilities in such a manner that they can legally defend themselves if they are sued. The following discussion is meant to provide future human resources administrators with a better understanding of their potential liabilities.

U.S. Judicial System

There are two systems of law. The first, known as *civil law*, is descended from Roman law; the rule of law in this system is established through statutes enacted by a legislative body. The second system, known as *common law*, is the basis of law in England and was adopted in theory by most of the states in our country. Under this system, the decisions rendered by a court become a guide or precedent to be followed by the court in dealing with future cases. The system of law found in the United States today is a mixed system, using both civil and common law principles.[2]

Sources of Law

Three major sources of law form the foundation of the U.S. judicial system: constitutions, statutes, and case law. Two additional sources of law—administrative law and attorney general opinions—affect education even though they are not primary sources.[3]

Constitutions

Constitutions are bodies of precepts that provide the framework within which government carries out its duties. The federal and state constitutions contain provisions that secure the personal, property, and political rights of citizens. School districts have been continually confronted with constitutional issues, many of which have resulted in lawsuits. Some of these suits have dealt with racial discrimination in hiring practices, due process rights for individuals faced with employment termination, and the privacy right of employees in relation to their personnel records.

Statutes

Statutes, more commonly called *laws*, are the enactments of legislative bodies. Thus, the U.S. Congress or a state legislature may enact a new law or change an old law by the passage of legislation. A statute is then subject to review by the federal or appropriate state court to determine whether it is in violation of the precepts set forth in the federal or state constitution.

The presumption is that laws enacted by legislative bodies are constitutional, and they are proven otherwise only through litigation. Thus, if a state legislature passes a law that gives school administrators the right to terminate tenured teachers without a hearing before the school board, a teacher or group of teachers could initiate a lawsuit asking the state's supreme court to consider the constitutionality of the new law. The basis for the lawsuit might be a provision in the state constitution citing general due process rights.

Because public schools are state agencies, the legislature of every state has created statutes governing school districts. School operation, therefore, must be in compliance with such state statutes, and it is the responsibility of the board of education and the superintendent of schools to ensure compliance. Further, the board of education cannot establish policies that are in conflict with acts of the U.S. Congress or state statutes; in addition, the policies must not be in conflict with either the federal or state constitution. If a school board, for example, created a policy prohibiting the employment of individuals with disabilities as teachers, this policy would violate federal law—in particular, the Rehabilitation Act of 1973 and the Americans with Disabilities Act of 1990, and probably the due process clause of the Fourteenth Amendment to the U.S. Constitution. It might also violate a given state constitutional provision stipulating that all citizens have a right to employment opportunities.

Case Law

The third source, common law, is more properly called *case law* because it is derived from court decisions rather than from legislative acts. Past court decisions are considered to be binding on subsequent cases if the material facts are similar. This is the doctrine of *precedent*. Lower courts usually adhere to the precedent (rule of law) established by higher courts in the same jurisdiction. The U.S. Supreme Court and state supreme courts can reverse their own previous decisions and thereby change the rule of law. Thus, a state circuit court may apply a rule of law established by a state supreme court as to what constitutes due process in the termination of a tenured teacher. In a later case, the supreme court may redefine what constitutes due process and thus change the rule of law.

Administrative Law and Attorney General Opinions

Administrative law has developed through the creation of state and federal boards and commissions charged with administering certain federal and state laws. In carrying out their responsibilities, these boards and commissions establish rules and regulations. For example, school employees are likely to be affected by the regulations of the Social Security Administration, the Employment Security Administration, or the Workers' Compensation Commission. Of course, the actions of these boards and commissions are subject to review by the courts.

A second and frequently initiated legal procedure is the requesting of an opinion from a state attorney general on the interpretation of a state statute. In the absence of case law, this opinion can be used by educators in addressing legal issues.

Human resources administrators must continually research professional journals that speak to significant court decisions and legislation. Most state departments of education also notify school administrators concerning recent state court decisions and laws that affect school districts' human resources practices and policies. The agencies of the federal government are diligent in notifying school districts across the United States about regulations with which they must be in compliance.

Major Divisions of Law

There are two broad classifications of law: criminal and civil. *Criminal law* is concerned with protecting the rights of society, and as such, the state, representing the people, is responsible for prosecuting wrongs committed against society by individuals or corporate entities. *Civil law* is concerned with protecting the rights that exist between individuals, between an individual and a corporate entity, or between two corporate entities. Most of the litigation that arises out of human resources management, of course, deals with civil law. Civil law embraces many areas, including contracts, wills and estates, corporate law, divorce, and torts. Human resources administrators are most vulnerable in lawsuits dealing with contracts and torts.

Court Structure

The federal court structure has three levels: the federal district courts, the circuit courts of appeals, and the U.S. Supreme Court.[4] The district courts are courts of original jurisdiction where all suits involving federal law are filed. Civil suits that involve agencies of the U.S. government also are heard in the federal district courts. A case heard in a district court may be appealed to the appropriate circuit court and then to the U.S. Supreme Court. Human resources administrators should be familiar with the nuances of the federal court system because of the multitude of federal employment laws, which are potential areas of litigation.

The state court structure is analogous to that of the federal system. The court of original jurisdiction is termed the *circuit court* in most states and is where all civil lawsuits are filed. Cases involving tenure and contract management will be heard in the circuit court. The decisions of the circuit court may be appealed, usually to an appellate court and finally to the state supreme court. Once again, it must be stated that human resources administrators should become familiar with the workings of the state court system because of the high incidence of litigation involving state laws as they relate to human resources management.

The municipal court structure is of little or no concern to human resources administrators. These courts are usually concerned with enforcing the ordinances of municipal governments, which include housing and building codes and traffic ordinances.

There is a distinction in the manner by which certain courts can hear cases, which is an important distinction for human resources administration. Certain issues are traditionally tried in *equity* by the state circuit courts and federal district courts. The most familiar to human resources administrators are *injunctions*. For example, if there is a state statute prohibiting strikes by teachers, a school district may go to a state circuit court to ask for an injunction directing a group of teachers to leave the picket lines and return to their classrooms. If the parties named in an injunction fail to obey the court order, they are in contempt of court and may be punished by a fine or by jailing.

Role of the Attorney in Human Resources Management

A common misconception about the role of the school district's attorney in a lawsuit against the district is that he or she will completely handle the litigation. An attorney's expertise centers around his or her ability to take the material facts in a case and research the statutes and the precedents of other court cases for the purpose of organizing a reasonable defense. An attorney must begin with what you, the human resources administrator, can offer by way of documentation. The defense is only as strong as the level of accountability that has been demonstrated through human resources procedures and policies. Consequently, a good indication of the workability of procedures and policies is whether they were a help or a hindrance in previous lawsuits.

Anatomy of a Lawsuit

Although lawsuits do not follow a set pattern, there is enough commonality in litigation to make a few general observations (Figure 10.1). The plaintiff files a petition with the appropriate court, setting forth the cause of action, which is the *allegation*. A summons is

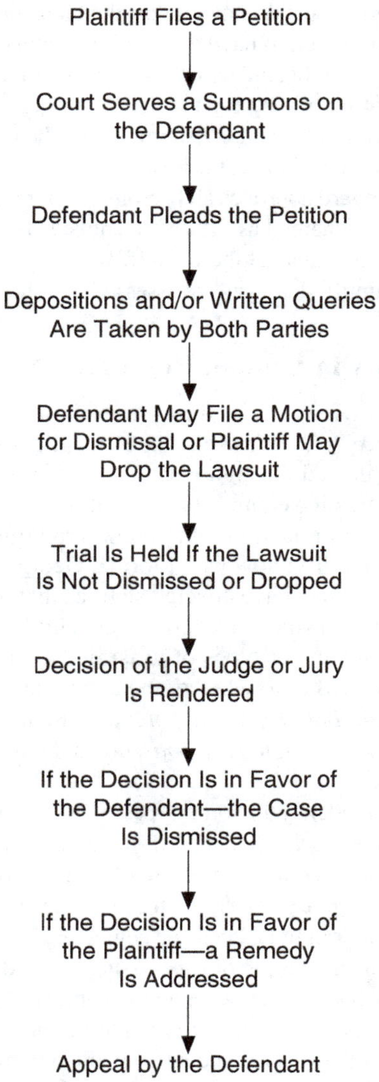

Plaintiff Files a Petition

↓

Court Serves a Summons on
the Defendant

↓

Defendant Pleads the Petition

↓

Depositions and/or Written Queries
Are Taken by Both Parties

↓

Defendant May File a Motion
for Dismissal or Plaintiff May
Drop the Lawsuit

↓

Trial Is Held If the Lawsuit
Is Not Dismissed or Dropped

↓

Decision of the Judge or Jury
Is Rendered

↓

If the Decision Is in Favor of
the Defendant—the Case
Is Dismissed

↓

If the Decision Is in Favor of
the Plaintiff—a Remedy
Is Addressed

↓

Appeal by the Defendant

FIGURE 10.1   Anatomy of a Lawsuit

Source: Rebore, Ronald, *Educational Administration: A Management Approach,* © 1985, p. 69. Reprinted and electronically reproduced by permission of Pearson Education, Inc., Upper Saddle River, New Jersey.

then delivered by the court to the defendant, who is required to appear in court on a given date to plead to the petition.

The next step involves clarifying the allegation and the material facts supporting it. This may be accomplished by the taking of *depositions,* a formal procedure in which the parties to the lawsuit answer questions posed by the respective opposing attorneys. Also, written queries may be required in lieu of or in addition to the depositions.

If the material facts do not support the allegation, then the school district's attorney will probably enter a motion to have the petition dismissed. If the judge does not dismiss the petition, a trial date is set. In civil cases involving tenure, a contract, or a tort, the defendant usually has the option of requesting a jury trial or relying on the judge to make a decision. Who the defendant is in a civil lawsuit is determined by the nature of the petition and the material facts. In a tenure or contract dispute, the board of education as a corporate body is usually the defendant because the board approves all personnel contracts. If it is a tort, an individual or a group of individuals may be named as the defendant because the petition may allege that a civil wrong has been committed against the plaintiff by one person or a group of persons. In a judgment favoring the plaintiff, damages are assessed in dollar amounts to be paid by the defendant.

Tort Liability in Human Resources Administration

A *tort* is a civil wrong, other than a breach of contract, committed against a person or a person's property.[5] Tort law emanates from common law, which is composed of those principles established through court cases that are usually referred to as *precedent.* The acts of legislatures have either broadened or narrowed these common law principles. For example, at common law, an individual wrongfully causing the death of another person incurs no civil liability; however, Florida, Georgia, Missouri, New Jersey, New York, and other state legislatures have enacted statutes that impose civil liabilities in favor of certain persons, including a surviving spouse and children.

There are two major types of torts: intentional torts and negligence. *Intentional torts* are further classified as to whether the action interfered with a person or with the person's property. *Assault, battery,* and *defamation* are the most common torts associated with personal interference; *malicious trespassing* is the most common interference with respect to property rights.

There is a tendency in some types of civil lawsuits—and particularly in tort suits—to take a shotgun approach when identifying defendants. If a student is injured as a consequence of using gymnastics equipment, the teacher might be sued for being negligent in supervising the student or for not properly instructing the student on how to use the equipment. The building principal might be sued for neglecting to properly evaluate and remove the teacher who allegedly did a poor job of supervising the student. The superintendent might be brought into the lawsuit because he neglected to remove the principal who inadequately supervised the teacher. The board of education might be sued because the members neglected to supervise and monitor the superintendent in evaluating the performance of the principal. This path follows the chain of command in a school district and ensures that the responsible party or parties are identified by the court.

This same type of situation is applicable to human resources management. A case could be made alleging that a given teacher's references were not investigated properly by the assistant superintendent for human resources or other human resources staff members, which eventuated in the hiring of an unqualified applicant.

It goes without saying that human resources managers may carry more legal vulnerability than other school district employees. Therefore, it is important for human resources managers to be well informed about tort liability. With this knowledge, they are better able to establish human resources processes and procedures that accomplish the objectives of the human resources department and are also easier to defend in court.

In human resources management, *defamation of character* is a potential area of litigation with regard to giving references and communicating the contents of an individual's personnel file. *Defamation* occurs when false information is communicated either by word of mouth (*slander*) or in writing (*libel*), brings hatred or ridicule on a person, and produces some type of harm to the person. With regard to the human resources function, the harm produced by defamation might be the loss of an employment opportunity or a job promotion.

To protect against such litigation, established procedures should outline who is responsible for writing references and under what circumstances the contents of an individual's personnel file can be released. Although each situation varies, the following guidelines should be observed:

1. The employee has a right to review the contents of his or her personnel file in the presence of a human resources administrator.
2. The supervisor of an employee has a right to review the contents of an employee's file in the presence of a human resources administrator.
3. Only official and approved documents (e.g., attendance records, payroll records, performance evaluation forms) may be added to an employee's file.
4. No document may be removed from an individual's personnel file without notifying the employee, who has the right to question the removal.
5. The contents or partial contents of an employee's personnel file (e.g., attendance records being requested by a potential employer) may not be released to other parties without the written permission of the employee.
6. Under no circumstances should a human resources administrator discuss over the telephone information in an employee's file.

Negligence is the type of tort that involves some form of injury to another person as a result of conduct that falls below an established standard. It is the duty of the assistant superintendent for human resources and other human resources administrators to establish processes and procedures that do not violate federal and state laws and that accomplish the objectives of the human resources function. Therefore, in the recruitment and selection of new employees, affirmative action procedures must be followed so that the rights of protected groups are not violated. A human resources administrator who neglects to properly initiate or follow such procedures could be guilty of a tort if a minority applicant is denied an opportunity to be interviewed for a position and, as a result, loses a job opportunity. In this case, a charge of discrimination will probably be filed with the Equal Employment Opportunity Commission (EEOC); however, there is also the possibility that the applicant will bring a civil lawsuit against the individual administrator.

In a tort lawsuit that involves a question of negligence, the court applies the standard of the "reasonable person" to determine liability. This concept has a specific application and definition, as well as some limitations in an increasingly pluralistic society.[6] The *reasonable person* is someone who

1. Possesses average intelligence, normal perception, and memory
2. Possesses such superior skill and knowledge as the defendant
3. Possesses the same level of experience as the defendant
4. Possesses the same physical attributes as the defendant

The conduct of the human resources administrator involved in a lawsuit is compared against the conduct of a mythical reasonable person. If a reasonable person could have prevented the consequence, the administrator will be found negligent by the jury. The moral of this example is that all administrators should examine their professional responsibilities to determine whether their conduct in fulfilling these responsibilities can withstand the test of the reasonable person.

In a civil lawsuit resulting in a judgment favoring the plaintiff, the defendant is usually required to pay *actual damages,* which is the amount of money that the injury cost. The plaintiff's loss of a job opportunity has the potential to cost the defendant a considerable amount of money—conceivably hundreds of thousands of dollars. If it can be demonstrated in court that the defendant deliberately caused the injury, punitive damages may also be levied. This dollar amount is a punishment for intentionally bringing about a civil wrong. In some cases, punitive damages may equal or surpass the actual damages assessed by the court. A human resources administrator who publicly disagrees with the concept of affirmative action and who tells ethnic jokes to fellow employees might be laying the foundation for an allegation that he or she deliberately neglects to follow affirmative action procedures.

Crisis Event Management

Crises have been a concern in schools and school districts throughout the history of public education. However, the tragic violence that took place at Columbine High School in Littleton, Colorado, in 1999 brought to the attention of the U.S. public not only the issue of student violence but also the issue of crisis event management. In terms of risk management, violence is one of an entire range of crises that must be addressed in all schools and school districts. Crises occur because of a variety of situations such as the following:

- *Accidents:* Arise out of human error, equipment malfunction, or inadequately maintained facilities
- *Misconduct:* Includes bullying of students and staff members, theft, threats, sexual harassment, and immoral public behavior
- *Natural disasters:* Include earthquakes, droughts, floods, landslides, tornadoes and hurricanes, and storms
- *Technology malevolence:* Includes sabotage of computer equipment and software, unauthorized entry into computer programs, and breach of the confidentiality of computer records
- *Violence:* Ranges from self-inflicted deadly physical injury, as in suicide, to the injuring and killing of others

Of course, these are neither the only nor the full range of possible crises facing school administrators. However, they do represent some of the more common occurrences that require the attention of the director of risk management.

When a crisis occurs, it is usually without warning, and the response required to manage the event is time sensitive. Immediate action is required that could catch administrators off guard in the unprepared school district. If a school district has a director of risk management, he or she should have the responsibility of managing the entire crisis event. He or she needs the assistance of other administrators, including the assistant superintendents and other central office administrators and staff members who should have specific responsibilities in a crisis. For example, the director of maintenance and custodial services could be responsible for notifying public services such as the police and fire departments. The director of community relations could be responsible for contacting the news media and for issuing statements and other communications about the crisis. The director of employee benefits could be responsible for making certain that injured staff members and students are receiving proper medical attention. If the event occurs in a school, the building principal, along with the counselor and other professional staff members, is responsible for communicating with parents and students. The director of transportation could be responsible for evacuating students and staff members from the crisis scene. Securing the facility and equipment could be the responsibility of the maintenance or custodial supervisors.

Errors and Omissions Liability Insurance

It should be clear from this presentation that every human resources administrator should be protected by errors and omissions liability insurance. Sources for such coverage include professional organizations and the school district's insurance carrier.

Many professional educator associations offer this type of insurance as a part of their regular membership benefits. Many of the large insurance companies are happy to provide such protection under a group policy for all central office administrators or for any other group of employees. The members of the board of education may also be included in this coverage and, in fact, should be covered in those states where sovereign immunity has been abrogated. Finally, it should be remembered that most errors and omissions liability insurance policies do not cover punitive damages because this would amount to condoning an act that was deliberately perpetrated.

Ethical Considerations in Human Resources Management

People in the United States have become increasingly aware of the vulnerability of those who occupy leadership positions in private business, government, churches, and public education. It is a topic that is on everyone's mind because of the major scandals that have plagued American society and culture. A pervasive attitude among the American people is mistrust of leaders in all segments of our society.[7] The news media constantly reveal crimes committed even by those who hold not only leadership positions but also positions of significant trust.

The central issue in this treatment is the fact that all people must make decisions on a daily basis where the lines of appropriate behavior are somewhat blurred, the gray area. Human resources administrators are legally vulnerable because their decisions affect people in one of the most important areas of life—employment. Students are also affected because the quality of their education depends on the quality of the people employed by a school district.

The basis for making ethically sound decisions is usually grounded in religious beliefs or philosophical assumptions. The Judeo-Christian-Islamic tradition sets forth norms of appropriate conduct that are accepted by most U.S. citizens. Many of these religious beliefs and philosophical assumptions are contained in the documents on which the United States, as a nation, was founded. However, espousing the principles found in these religious and philosophical traditions and documents does not guarantee that the practices of a school district will support human development. Thus, the proof is in the formulation of strategies and procedures that ensure social justice.[8]

The American Association of School Personnel Administrators has adopted the Statement of Ethics for School Administrators, which was developed by the American Association of School Administrators. Although this statement is appropriate, it is intended for all categories of administrators and does not go far enough to provide guidance in the many diverse and complicated situations that face contemporary school human resources administrators. There are three principles gleaned from the preceding sources that constitute the foundation on which the responsibilities in Exhibit 10.1 have been developed.

EXHIBIT 10.1   Responsibilities for the Ethical Management of the School

School districts have a moral and legal obligation to provide children and young adults with the best education possible given the human and financial resources available to them. The quality of education depends on the quality of personnel who directly or indirectly provide the educational service. Consequently, boards of education and superintendents of schools must be diligent in the selection of human resources administrators who manage the human resources function. Once employed, human resources administrators will be held accountable for the following responsibilities:

Responsibilities to the School District and Its Staff

The responsibilities to the school district and its staff are to

- Support and implement the policies of the board of education in a positive and effective manner
- Support and implement administrative processes and procedures in a positive and effective manner
- Through appropriate means, pursue changing board polices and administrative processes and procedures that are not consistent with sound practice

- Project a positive image of the school district to the community-at-large and the education community
- Promote the equitable treatment of individuals, groups, and companies
- Help colleagues and subordinates fulfill their obligations and aspirations
- Help subordinates achieve their maximum potential
- Treat colleagues and subordinates with dignity and fairness
- Maintain confidentiality in carrying out the obligations of a school human resources administrator
- Promote adherence to all local, state, and national ordinances and laws

Responsibilities to the School Human Resources Profession

The responsibilities to the school human resources profession are to

- Promote membership in and the activities of school human resources professional associations at the local, state, and national levels
- Accept leadership roles in school human resources professional associations

EXHIBIT 10.1 *Continued*

- Promote research in school human resources administration that enhances the effectiveness of the profession
- Promote professional development activities that enhance the performance of school human resources administrators

Personal Responsibilities

Personal responsibilities are to

- Fulfill the obligations of a school human resources administrator in an open manner
- Seek consultation from colleagues or other professionals when faced with an ethical or professional problem for which there appears to be no appropriate solution
- Continue to grow as a person and as a school human resources professional through attendance at conventions, seminars, or conferences, or through university coursework
- Develop the virtues of prudence, honesty, and justice so your behavior enhances not only your integrity as a person but also the integrity of the school district in which you work and the school human resources profession that you represent

First, over time, making decisions in the course of exercising these responsibilities helps an individual determine the sort of person and human resources professional he or she wants to become. Any given decision does not usually determine an individual's central ethical orientation unless it is a decision of monumental significance such as deliberately committing a felony. Rather, a person is constantly in the state of becoming either a better person and professional or a person who gradually loses his or her integrity. Even inappropriate decisions about issues that might appear to be rather insignificant can chip away at the edges surrounding a person's central core of integrity.

Second, the decisions of school human resources administrators have a definite effect on school districts as institutions. This effect is either positive or negative, depending on the motivation for the decision and its magnitude. For example, an assistant superintendent for human resources who attempts to influence the hiring of a candidate solely because that person is his or her friend has made a decision that will have a negative effect on the school district in which the assistant superintendent is employed. If this type of action is repeated over time, the school district could take on a negative image that could affect morale among other employees and among other educators in the surrounding school districts. In a similar manner, the decisions of human resources administrators have a positive or negative effect on the school human resources professional associations to which they belong or in which they have positions of leadership. Human experience indicates that it is virtually impossible to keep inappropriate actions from becoming common knowledge.

The third principle is taken from the Declaration of Independence: "[A]ll men are created equal, . . . they are endowed by their Creator with certain unalienable Rights, that among these are Life, Liberty, and the pursuit of Happiness." Any action by a school human resources administrator that constitutes preferential treatment of certain people, groups, or companies is contrary to this principle. The human resources administrator has a duty to ensure that such rights are afforded not only in the daily actions of employees but also in the policies and procedural processes of the school district.

Ethical Responsibilities of School Human Resources Administrators

The responsibilities set forth in Exhibit 10.1 are grouped under three separate headings: those pertaining to the school district and its staff, those pertaining to the school human resources profession, and those pertaining to the human resources administrator as a person. This approach has been selected over the more traditional approach, wherein a list of prohibitions is presented as a code of ethics. The emphasis here is on carrying out responsibilities that will have a positive effect on the school district, the human resources profession, and the human resources administrator. Also, because every human is constantly in a state of becoming either a better person or a person of decreasing integrity, just avoiding certain types of actions is not enough to steer the process in a positive direction. Each person must be proactive. This is why, in this presentation, the ethical administrator is portrayed as a person who seeks to fulfill responsibilities.

Responsibilities to the School District and Its Staff

This first group of ten responsibilities clearly addresses the communal aspect of public school administration and, in particular, the communal aspect of school human resources management. School human resources administrators have obligations to the institution for which they work—the school district. Further, they have obligations to their colleagues and subordinates. Thus, loyalty to the board of education, superintendent of schools, colleagues, and subordinates becomes the vehicle for fulfilling these responsibilities. Sometimes, it happens that a certain human resources administrator cannot ethically accept the policies or practices of the school district for which he or she works and thus must seek other employment. However, in practice, the overarching responsibility is to help establish an ethical culture in the school district through implementing ethical human resources systems. Thus, in marketing, recruitment, selection, placement, induction, staff development, performance evaluation, compensation, and collective negotiations, the goal should be publicly defensible processes and procedures that ensure social justice. In this manner, the human resources function becomes a vehicle for promoting ethical sensitivity in all dimensions of the school district.[9]

Responsibilities to the School Human Resources Profession

The next group of responsibilities defines the professional obligations of the human resources administrator. Emphasis is placed on participating in professional associations and working within these associations to enhance the profession. This is particularly important in the areas of research and professional development.

Personal Responsibilities

The final group of responsibilities is concerned with the personal growth of the human resources administrator. This growth is nurtured through professional development activities. The practice of certain virtues, particularly the virtue of honesty, should help administrators avoid conflicts of interest, and the virtue of prudence should help avoid even the appearance of such conflicts. Thus, accepting gifts, services, or anything of value because of an act performed or withheld certainly violates the virtue of honesty. Accepting gifts, services, or anything of value even though "no strings" were attached violates the virtue of prudence. Honesty is also violated when administrators use their position in a professional association for personal gain. When an employee receives preferential treatment simply because of friendship with a certain administrator, the virtue of justice is violated.

All people need help at times. Consulting with other professionals when the need arises is viewed here as an obligation. Therefore, to continue an inappropriate practice or to persist in behavior that could bring derision on the school district, the human resources profession, or the administrator is a violation of this obligation. Thus, ethical literacy should be a focus of all staff development programs in school districts, and the case study approach is appropriate for practicing human resources administrators and staff members.[10]

Human Resources Policy Development

Chapter 1 enumerates the advantages of having board of education policies. Now that the eight human resources functions have been elucidated in detail, it should be clear that well-defined human resources policies are absolutely necessary. In fact, creating such policies is a major task of the human resources department. The difference between board of education policies and administrative procedures should also be kept in mind. A *policy* is usually a broad statement of direction, whereas a *procedure* is a sequence of steps to be followed in implementing a policy. In practice, however, there is a fine distinction in some situations between the wording of a policy and the wording of the procedure that makes it operational. Appendix A presents two example policies created by the author. Appendix B lists policies that might be included in an employee personnel manual.

Technology: Legal, Ethical, and Policy Issues

The advent of information technology and the Internet forever changed the way school districts carry out the administration of human resources. On a daily basis, human resources administrators and staff members access, analyze, create, and distribute information throughout schools and school districts. These administrators and staff members have an obligation not to abuse technology resources and to respect the rights of teachers, other administrators, and other staff members in the school district community.

With this mind, it is recommended that every school district create a policy covering the proper use of technology. Such a policy should clearly identify what technological components it covers. Exhibit 10.2 describes a model policy that incorporates those provisions that this author deems necessary in order to encompass the legal, ethical, and policy dimensions of the proper use of technology.

Certainly, individual school districts will modify the preceding model policy based on their culture and board policies. Further, job descriptions should clearly set forth the technological responsibilities of each employee required to use such technology.

EXHIBIT 10.2   Sample Technology Policy

The board of education, the superintendent of schools, and the administration and staff of the human resources department recognize that the effective administration of human resources functions depends on the full and proper utilization of technology in formulating human resources procedures and policies. This policy is applicable to all human resources employees of the Goodville School District, regardless of their authorization to use or not to use certain technologies owned by the school district. Those technological components that are covered by this policy are computers, databases, data storage, networks, printers, related equipment, and software. This policy is also applicable if such employees engage technological systems owned by the school district on a private computer.

This policy is being enacted to ensure that the school district's technology systems are available, reliable, and used only for the human resources purposes for which they were created and made available. Thus, the following activities by authorized human resources administrators and staff members are prohibited:

- Accessing and modifying elements of the system for which they are not authorized
- Accumulating information for unauthorized purposes
- Impeding or interfering with the authorized use by other employees of technological systems
- Using the technological systems for purposes, such as political activities, that violate the public status of school districts
- Attempting to override the security component of the systems
- Using the systems for illegal purposes such as sexual harassment, racial and ethnic harassment, or promiscuity
- Impersonating others in technological communication
- Modifying the technological equipment
- Violating the license agreements of hardware or software

In like manner, the following basic employee rights are ensured for human resources administrators and staff members:

- Free inquiry and expression in relation to carrying out employment responsibilities
- Maintenance and security of personal passwords
- Proper registration of equipment
- Minor personal use of the systems, such as receiving emails of a personal nature, when such usage does not impede the performance of responsibilities

The board of education recognizes that the superintendent of schools may authorize access to the systems without the consent of the authorized users for the following purposes:

- To diagnose and repair the systems
- When required by federal, state, and local courts and agencies
- When reasonable evidence exists that there has been a violation of policy or law
- To protect public health and safety

Each employee of the human resources department has certain responsibilities that are associated with the improper use of the school district's technological systems that should be reported to the superintendent of schools:

- If an employee believes that his or her personal integrity has been compromised
- If an employee observes that others are violating policy or law

Penalties for such infractions may include temporary or permanent suspension of access and termination of employment. The employee so penalized has the right to appeal such penalties to the board of education.

Implications for Small- and Medium-Size School Districts

Only large school districts can afford to have a legal department staffed by attorneys specializing in school law. However, every school district has no choice but to hire an attorney to represent the school district when the district is involved in a lawsuit. Further, when a lawsuit arises in relation to the human resources function, it is imperative to hire an attorney who has expertise in the legal dimensions of human resources administration. The vetting process for hiring the attorney depends on a number of variables, the most important of which is to have sufficient financial resources in the school district's budget to hire the best-qualified attorney.

Other considerations include the following:

- It is better to hire a legal firm rather than a single attorney because other attorneys from the firm can take over a case if the lead attorney is unable to continue with his or her responsibilities due to illness or other obligations.
- It is better to hire a firm that has had experience in school law cases.
- It is better to hire a firm that has attorneys who have handled other human resources–related cases.
- It is better to hire a firm that has a fee structure in keeping with the financial constraints of the school district's budget.
- It is better to hire a law firm on a retainer basis for a set period of time, perhaps one to three years. Then the school district can respond to a lawsuit more easily and quickly, and does not have to find legal counsel on an immediate-need basis.
- The law firm should also be able to provide the administrative staff with guidance in terms of administrative practices and policies that provide the school district with a proactive rather than a reactive approach to carrying out administrative responsibilities.
- It is not good practice to hire a law firm only on the basis of its fee structure rather than its success in representing clients in lawsuits. Thus, instead of "taking bids," the school district should seek portfolios from interested law firms that include the types of cases with which the firm has been involved, the success of the firm, and the firm's fee structure.

The location of the school district is another consideration in seeking portfolios because there may not be attorneys practicing law in the vicinity of the school district who have experience with the type of lawsuit facing the district. The experience of the law firm is of paramount importance.

Obviously, the size of a school district has no bearing on the ethical responsibilities of the administrators who are responsible for the human resources functions. Thus, the material on ethics presented in this chapter is applicable to all administrators and staff members.

Finally, the responsibility of the school district to develop policies that are defensible, appropriate, and proactive is also a responsibility of all human resources administrators regardless of the size of the district. Significant policy resources are available to school districts from state and national professional associations such as the National School Boards Association.

Impact of Generation Y Teachers and Administrators on Legal, Ethical, and Policy Issues

Generation Y teachers and administrators tend to be rather conservative in their approach to legal, ethical, and policy issues. To understand this conservatism, it is important to remember the signs of the times during which they have moved into adulthood with significant responsibilities to themselves and their families. Rightfully so, the news media have brought to their attention many concerns, including the misconduct of religious, business, government and military, and law enforcement leaders; fiscal instability of business and financial institutions; controversial life issues such as the cloning of human organs and other genetic engineering issues; threats to civil rights in dangerous times; lack of universal access to medical and pharmaceutical services and products; environmental deterioration; and terrorism.

Perhaps the ultimate issue for Generation Y teachers and administrators is trust. Who can they trust? Of course, the issues discussed here are not the only concerns but they are also ethical issues, and most have legal ramifications. Further, there are implications for school district and particularly human resources policy development. Most Generation Y employees want some voice in the governance function manifested in policy development, which is witnessed in the collective negotiations process. Also, they want supervisors whom they can trust and admire, and who are professional in their conduct. Thus, Generation Y teachers and administrators expect transparency, accountability, and equity as the hallmarks of human resources policies and procedures.

Summary

This chapter is concerned with legal, ethical, and policy issues in human resources administration. These issues have become important within the past decade as a result of the increased emphasis on legal rights and responsibilities.

Teachers and administrators usually work under the provisions of an individual contract; Classified personnel are employed at an hourly rate or for an annual salary. Using individual contracts for teachers and administrators is a matter of tradition that is also mandated by law in some states and that distinguishes a professional employee's working conditions from those of classified employees.

Teachers' and administrators' contracts must meet the requirements of general contract law, state statutes, and the precedents established through case law. A *contract* is an agreement between two or more competent persons for legal consideration on a legal subject matter in the form required by law. The five basic components to every valid contract are, therefore, offer and acceptance, competent persons, consideration, legal subject matter, and proper form.

School districts have experienced an increase in litigation. In addition, the actions of human resources administrators are far more vulnerable today to judicial review than was the case previously. It is imperative, therefore, that administrators have a rudimentary understanding of the American judicial system and be capable of making decisions that are legally defensible.

There are basically two systems of law. The first, known as *civil law*, is established through statutes enacted by a legislative body. The second, known as *common law*, is the basic approach to law in England and was adopted in theory by most of the states in our country. Under this system, the decisions rendered by a court become precedent to be followed by the court in dealing with future cases. The system of law in the United States today is a mixture of both civil and common law.

There are three major sources of law that form the foundation of the American judicial system: constitutions, statutes, and court cases. *Constitutions* are bodies of precepts that provide the framework within which government carries out its duties. *Statutes* are the enactments of legislative bodies; they are more commonly called *laws*. As stated previously, common law emanates from the decisions of courts rather than from the acts of legislative bodies. There are two additional sources of law that affect education, even though they are not traditionally considered primary sources: administrative law and attorney general opinions. *Administrative law* consists of those regulations set forth by agencies established by Congress and state legislatures. In the absence of case law, the state attorney general may be requested to render an opinion on the interpretation of a state statute.

The two broad classifications of law are criminal and civil. *Civil law* is concerned with protecting the rights of individuals and corporate entities; *criminal law* is concerned with protecting the rights of society.

The judicial system is composed of federal, state, and municipal courts. There are three categories of federal courts: district courts, courts of appeals, and the U.S. Supreme Court. In like manner, most states have three categories of courts: circuit courts, courts of appeal, and supreme courts. The U.S. judicial system also preserves the concept of equity. The state circuit and U.S. district courts may handle both law and equity issues. Certain issues are traditionally tried in equity, with the most common equitable remedy being injunctions.

Human resources administrators should become familiar with the nuances of the state and federal court systems because of the great number of laws affecting employment and the resulting potentiality for tort lawsuits.

In human resources management, it is also extremely important to understand the role of the attorney. The attorney takes the material facts in a case and researches the statutes or laws and precedents of court cases for the purpose of organizing a reasonable defense. The defense is only as strong as the level of accountability that has been demonstrated through human resources procedures and policies.

A *lawsuit* begins with the filing of a petition, setting forth the allegation in the appropriate court of original jurisdiction. The next step is clarifying the allegation and the material facts. The final step is the trial.

A *tort* is a civil wrong, other than a breach of contract, committed against a person or a person's property. The two major types of torts are classified as *intentional torts* and *negligence*. Assault, battery, defamation, and trespassing are the most common types of intentional torts. In human resources management, *defamation* is a potential area of litigation with regard to giving references and communicating the contents of an individual's personnel file.

Negligence is a tort that involves conduct falling below an established standard that results in some type of injury to another person. Negligence, therefore, implies neglect of a duty. The duty of human resources administrators is to establish processes and procedures that do not violate federal and state laws and that meet the objectives of the human resources department. A human resources administrator who neglects to initiate or follow such procedures could be guilty of a tort if a minority applicant is denied an opportunity to be interviewed for a position and, as a result, loses a job opportunity.

Crises occur because of a variety of situations, including accidents, misconduct, natural disasters, technology malevolence, and violence. Crises are time sensitive and require immediate action. The director of risk management should be responsible for managing the entire crisis event, but must have the assistance of other administrators.

In a civil lawsuit resulting in a judgment favoring the plaintiff, the defendant may be assessed actual damages and even punitive damages if the injury was deliberately perpetrated. Every human resources administrator, therefore, should be protected by an errors and omissions liability insurance program.

People in the United States have become increasingly aware of the fallibility of those who occupy leadership positions. All people must make decisions on a daily basis when the lines of appropriate behavior are somewhat blurred. Human resources administrators are particularly vulnerable because their decisions affect people in one of the most important areas of life—employment.

The basis for making ethically sound decisions is usually grounded in religious beliefs or philosophical assumptions. There are three principles that have been gleaned from these beliefs and assumptions: First, making decisions in the course of exercising these responsibilities will, over time, help an individual determine the sort of person and human resources professional he or she wants to become. Second, the decisions of school human resources administrators have a definite effect on school districts as institutions. The third principle comes from the Declaration of Independence, which states that all people are created equal and have certain unalienable rights, among which are life, liberty, and the pursuit of happiness.

The ethical responsibilities of school human resources administrators are grouped around responsibilities to the school district and its staff, responsibilities to the school human resources profession, and personal responsibilities.

Effective policies are the key to effective human resources management. Boards of education should take a deliberate approach to policy development that ensures defensible human resources operations.

Self-Check Quiz Click here to take an automatically-graded self-check quiz.

Discussion Questions and Statements

1. Explain the elements that must be considered in creating an individual employment contract for teachers.
2. In what ways are human resources administrators vulnerable to lawsuits, and what are the guidelines that help protect them?
3. Identify the common stages in the development of a lawsuit.
4. What are the ethical responsibilities of human resources administrators?
5. How does the "reasonable person" concept influence the practice of human resources administration?

Suggested Activities

1. You are the director of risk management in a large metropolitan school district serving approximately 30,000 students. In conducting the yearly safety and security

audit you and your staff have found a number of safety hazards and security needs in several of the district's schools. The assistant superintendent for human resources has informed you that the facility's budget has been reduced by 10 percent due to a shortfall in state aid, which will keep many of your safety and security recommendations from being implemented. Given this situation, set forth in writing your ethical and legal responsibilities and what you would do.

2. Write a policy dealing with an issue in human resources administration that can serve as a model for policy construction.
3. Attend a state court proceeding concerning a school personnel issue, and write a reflection paper about your observations.
4. Interview an attorney, in person or on the telephone, who specializes in school law, and discuss with him or her the role and function of a school district's legal counsel.
5. Interview a human resources administrator in person or on the telephone about the process he or she uses when the school district is sued concerning a personnel issue.

Focus Scenario Activity

Given that you have read and studied this chapter, how would you proceed to maintain your legal and ethical integrity when working with the school district's legal counsel concerning the lawsuit?

Endnotes

1. Charles J. Russo, *Reutter's The Law of Public Education*, 6th ed. (New York: Foundation Press, 2006), 434–436.
2. Ibid., 1–2.
3. Ibid., 2–14.
4. Ibid., 15–24.
5. Ibid., 375–408.
6. Moran Mayo, *Rethinking the Reasonable Person: An Egalitarian Reconstruction of the Objective Standard* (New York: Oxford University Press, 2003), 315–316.
7. Robert M. Fulmer, "The Challenge of Ethical Leadership," *Organizational Dynamics*, 33, no. 3 (2004): 303–317.
8. Paul Miller, "Strategy and the Ethical Management of Human Resources," *Human Resource Management Journal*, 6, no. 1 (1996): 5–18.
9. M. Ronald Buckley, Danielle S. Beu, Dwight D. Frink, Jack L. Howard, Howard Berkson, Tommie A. Mobbs, and Gerald R. Ferris, "Ethical Issues in Human Resources Systems," *Human Resources Management Review*, 11, nos. 1–2 (2001): 11–29, www.nipc.ir/uploads/p11214_7642.pdf.
10. Diana Winstanley and Jean Woodall, "The Ethical Dimension of Human Resource Management," *Human Resource Management Journal*, 10, no. 2 (2000): 5–20.

Selected Bibliography

Adjibolosoo, S. "The Evolution and Implications of Human Resources Regulations and Policies: A Critical Human Factor Analysis." *Review Of Human Factor Studies*, 17, no. 1 (2011): 90–134.

Brown, Trevor L., and Matthew Potoski. "Contract-Management Capacity in Municipal and County Governments." *Public Administration Review*, 63, no. 2 (2003): 153–164.

Buckley, M. Ronald, Danielle S. Beu, Dwight D. Frink, Jack L. Howard, Howard Berkson, Tommie A. Mobbs, and Edwin C. Darden. "School Law: Responsibility and Obligation." *American School Board Journal*, 119 (August 2007): 42–43.

Dutton, Marcy. "A Good Contract Only Starts with the Signing." *School Administrator*, 64, no. 6 (June 2007).

Essex, Nathan L. *School Law and the Public Schools: A Practical Guide for Educational Leaders*, 3rd ed. Boston: Allyn & Bacon, 2005.

Ferris, Gerald R. "Ethical Issues in Human Resources Systems." *Human Resources Management Review*, 11 (2001): 11–29.

Fullan, Michael. *The Moral Imperative of School Leadership*. Thousand Oaks, CA: Corwin Press, 2003.

Fulmer, Robert M. "The Challenge of Ethical Leadership." *Organizational Dynamics*, 33, no. 3 (2004): 303–317.

Looney, Susan D. *Education and the Legal System: A Guide to Understanding the Law*. Upper Saddle River, NJ: Merrill/Prentice Hall, 2004.

Mayo, Moran. *Rethinking the Reasonable Person: An Egalitarian Reconstruction of the Objective Standard*. New York: Oxford University Press, 2003.

Miller, Paul. "Strategy and the Ethical Management of Human Resources." *ProQuest LLC* (2008).

Rebore, Ronald W. *The Ethics of Educational Leadership*. Upper Saddle River, NJ: Prentice Hall, 2001.

Rebore, Ronald W. *A Human Relations Approach to the Practice of Educational Leadership*. Boston: Allyn & Bacon, 2003.

Russo, Charles J. "Letters of Recommendation: A Legal Update." *School Business Affairs*, 68, no. 7 (July/August 2002): 30–33.

Schimmel, David, and Matthew Militello. "Legal Literacy for Teachers: A Neglected Responsibility." *Harvard Educational Review*, 77, no. 3 (Fall 2007): 1–14.

Starratt, Robert J. *Ethical Leadership*. San Francisco: Jossey-Bass, 2004.

Winstanley, Diana, and Jean Woodall. "The Ethical Dimension of Human Resource Management." *Human Resource Management Journal*, 10, no. 2 (2000): 5–20.

Zirkel, P. A. "Paralyzing Fear? Avoiding Distorted Assessments of the Effect of Law on Education." *Journal of Law and Education*, 35 (2006): 461–495.

Appendix A
Sample Human Resources Policies

Conflict of Interest in Human Resources Administration

It is the policy of the Goodville School District that the administrators and staff members who have human resources responsibilities will be held to the highest standards of conduct and integrity. A conflict of interest occurs when a human resources administrator's or staff member's decisions or actions for the school district also produce a personal advantage for the administrator or staff member, or a disadvantage for the school district.

A conflict of interest occurs in the following situations:

- When a human resources administrator or staff member, directly or indirectly, has a financial interest in outside companies that provide or intend to provide goods or services to the school district (e.g., companies that design and sell the school district recruitment brochures or companies that provide third-party administration of fringe benefits).
- When a human resources administrator or staff member provides consultative or other services to a company that provides or intends to provide goods or services to the school district (e.g., assisting companies in developing competitive proposals in order to bid on providing health and hospital insurance).
- When a human resources administrator or staff member provides information about the operations of the school district to friends or relatives who are seeking employment with the district.
- When a human resources administrator or staff member receives gifts or entertainment from companies providing goods or services to the school district or from potential employees of the district.

Each year, human resources administrators and staff members will be required to sign a disclosure statement affirming that they have not engaged in conflict of interest decisions or actions. If an infraction of this policy takes place, disciplinary action will be taken by the superintendent of schools that may include leave without pay or termination of employment.

Human Resources Administration Policy on Evidence-Based Decision Making

The administrators and staff of the Human Resources Department recognize that the effective administration of human resources functions depends on the full and proper utilization of both quantitative and qualitative data in formulating human resources procedures and in making decisions about human resources.

To facilitate this responsibility, the board of education mandates the ongoing collection and analysis of both qualitative and quantitative data by human resources administrators in the areas of human resources planning, recruitment of personnel, selection of personnel, placement and induction of personnel, staff development, evaluation of personnel, compensation of personnel, and collective negotiations.

The assistant superintendent for human resources, under the direction of the superintendent of schools, is directly responsible for the collection and analysis of data. He or she must involve all members of the Human Resources Department, including the director of employee relations, director of staff development, director of affirmative action, director of employee benefits, and director of risk management in fulfilling this responsibility.

The assistant superintendent for human resources is expected to develop a schedule for the collection and analysis of data by July 1 of each year. The annual human resources report will be presented to the superintendent of schools and the board of education by April 1 of each year in order for the superintendent and the board to be able to utilize the report in developing the annual budget.

The report will not only set forth data along with an analysis, but also clearly identify the methodology that was used to collect data. Further, the report will set forth what statistical and qualitative treatments were used in the analysis process.

Appendix B
Contents for an Employee Personnel Manual

GOODVILLE SCHOOL DISTRICT

Employee Personnel Manual

This manual constitutes the human resources policies and regulations for employees of the Goodville School District. Accountability for the implementation and maintenance of this manual is delegated to the assistant superintendent for human resources. The policies contained in this manual may be deleted or amended, and additional policies may be included by action of the board of education. Regulations contained herein may, in like manner, be deleted or amended, and new regulations may be included by administrative memorandum. Each employee will receive a copy of this manual and is expected to become familiar with its contents.

CONTENTS

Continued

EPILOGUE

This book has covered a lot of material in relatively few pages, describing the various dimensions of the human resources function. The reader who has just finished this book must keep in mind that politics and the human condition in general affect the processes, procedures, and techniques used in human resources administration. For example, a human resources administrator may recommend the employment of a teacher who is turned down by the board, whereas another person with fewer qualifications is hired. The human resources administrator may never know why this occurred. There are always hidden agendas!

There is no issue more important in our contemporary times than ethical behavior. This is true not only for teachers and educational administrators but also for government officials, business people, and the clergy. The media continually focus on illegal and unethical conduct. Although professional educational administrators have always recognized the necessity of being aboveboard, the climate in contemporary society is such that administrators must be able to demonstrate that their actions are based on a system of ethics. It is for this reason that I developed the section in Chapter 10 dealing with ethics in school human resources management, along with a corresponding set of responsibilities. It is vital that every administrator learn to carry out his or her professional responsibilities in such a manner that his or her integrity cannot be questioned. Short-term solutions and arbitrary decisions, therefore, must be judiciously avoided.

Technological advances present educational administrators with unique opportunities and significant challenges. Administrators must continue to use technology as an ordinary manner of conducting the educational enterprise. Administrators must continue to refine and expand the application of technology in performing the usual tasks of pupil scheduling, attendance reporting, grade reporting, inventory reporting, and fiscal accounting, as well as the management of the various dimensions of the human resources function. Some larger school districts already have sophisticated information management systems that make for more efficient and accurate human resources management. The dimensions are carried forward in identifying how the material in each chapter applies to small- and medium-size school districts, and consideration is given to how Generation Y employees affect human resources administration.

To balance involvement in the new technologies, human resources administrators must also become more humanistic. Technology tends to isolate individuals from one another and emphasizes solitary activities. What happens, in essence, is that information collection, storage, and use increase, while human interaction decreases. In the final analysis, we know more but understand less, with an accompanying decrease in human relations skills.

The human resources administrator, therefore, must see the necessity of developing innovative ways to interact with teachers and staff members. Using a collaborative approach to human resources management, as set forth in this book, provides such an opportunity.

Human resources administrators of the future must be scrupulously ethical. At the same time, they must understand and make use of technological advances, as well as appreciate the necessity of creating ways to improve human interaction.

GLOSSARY

Acquired immunodeficiency syndrome (AIDS) A viral infectious disease; those who contract it are protected under Section 504 of the Rehabilitation Act of 1973 and the Americans with Disabilities Act of 1990. Fear of contagion by itself does not permit federal agencies and federally assisted employers to discriminate against employees infected with the AIDS virus.

Administrative service organization (ASO) A third-party administrator under contract to a school district and responsible for monitoring and processing claims when a school district is self-insured.

Advertisement A technique used to communicate a position vacancy; also important verification of a school district's efforts to promote affirmative action and equal employment opportunity.

Affirmative action The detailed and results-oriented programs whose objective is compliance with the equal employment clauses found in most civil rights legislation.

Age Discrimination in Employment Act of 1967 A federal law, as amended, that promotes the employment of workers between the ages of forty and seventy based on ability rather than age. This statute makes it illegal to discriminate against older workers in all areas of employment.

Agency shop The situation in a school district when certain employees are not members of the union that is the bargaining agent for the bargaining unit to which they belong; as a result, these employees are required to pay a fee to the union.

Alternative certification programs College and university programs designed for people with bachelor's degrees that give them the opportunity to become licensed as teachers in a relatively short period of time. These programs have been designed in many states where there is a shortage of teachers.

Americans with Disabilities Act of 1990 (ADA) The most comprehensive legislation ever passed protecting the rights of individuals with disabilities. This legislation extends the Rehabilitation Act of 1973 in that it pertains to the private sector and to local and state government agencies that receive no federal monies. Both the U.S. Department of Justice and the Equal Employment Opportunity Commission have been given jurisdiction to enforce the ADA.

Apprenticeship training The oldest form of training, whereby a person understudies a master worker for a given period of time or until the trainee acquires the necessary skills.

Arbitration An impasse procedure by which a board of education and an employee union agree to be bound by the decision of a third party in the bargaining process or in a grievance.

Assessment center A place where candidates for jobs can be observed as they work through a series of simulations, usually taking the form of case studies and decision-making exercises dealing with administrative problems.

Assistant superintendent for human resources The chief human resources administrator in a school district who is charged with developing the strategies and implementing the policies, processes, and procedures necessary for the effective management of the human resources function. Alternative titles are *director of personnel* and *director of human resources*.

Asynchronous   The experience of using technology independent of real-time constraints. Thus, a person can log on to a school district's Website and process a medical claim after normal working hours.

Automatic patch management software   Computer security software patches for programs and systems. The most promising patches detect unidentified viruses by recognizing virus-like patterns.

Bargaining power   A favorable balance of influence that can compel the other party's agreement with a proposal or entire proposal package because of the consequences accompanying disagreement.

Bargaining process   At-the-table engagement of representatives from the board of education and an employee union concerning salary, fringe benefits, and working conditions.

Bargaining unit   Those employees who are organized into a category because they have a community of interest for them to be represented in collective negotiations.

Bargaining unit determination   The process of determining which employees have a community of interest so they can be organized into a category for the purposes of collective negotiations. Size of the group and effective administration are additional considerations.

Board of education   The elected or appointed policy-making body of a school district.

Career ladder   Advancement to a higher level of recognition and financial rewards due to attaining a higher level of professional proficiency.

Catastrophic case management   When an employee, his or her spouse, or his or her dependent suffers a catastrophic illness, a case manager assists the patient and his or her physician in accessing the best treatment at the lowest cost.

Certification of bargaining agent   The designation by an authorized state agency or the board of education that a certain organization or union is representing a bargaining unit as its exclusive bargaining agent.

Civil law   Law concerned with protecting the rights that exist between individuals, an individual and a corporate entity, or two corporate entities. Most of the litigation that arises out of human resources management concerns civil law.

Civil Rights Act of 1964   Title VII of this federal law, as amended, provides that a person cannot be denied a job or fair treatment on a job because of race, color, religion, gender, or national origin.

Civil Rights Act of 1991   A federal law that extends compensatory and punitive damages and jury trials to employees who have been discriminated against because of race, national origin, gender, disability, or religion.

Collective negotiations   The entire process of negotiations, including recognition and bargaining unit determination, the bargaining process, impasse procedures, and master agreement administration.

Common law   Also called *case law* because it is derived from court decisions rather than from legislative acts. Past court decisions are considered to be binding in subsequent cases if the material facts are similar, known as the doctrine of *precedent*.

Community of interest   The common skills, functions, levels of education, and working conditions shared by a certain group of employees.

Compensation packaging   The distribution of an individual employee's compensation into a certain amount of salary and into certain fringe benefits based on his or her expressed desire and needs.

Conditions of learning The stimulus, response, reinforcement, and motivation techniques used by an instructor to facilitate learning, which is a change in human capability.

Consolidated Omnibus Budget Reconciliation Act of 1986 (COBRA) A federal law that permits an employee, his or her spouse, and his or her dependents to continue healthcare coverage through the school district's group insurance programs under certain conditions when the employee is no longer employed by the district.

Constitution A body of precepts that provide the framework within which government carries out its duties. The federal and state constitutions contain provisions that secure the personal, property, and political rights of citizens, which is a concern in developing human resources processes and procedures.

Contract An agreement between a school district and an employee that requires an offer and acceptance, competent persons, consideration, legal subject matter, and proper form.

Copayment The amount of money an employee pays for medical services in addition to that paid by the school district's medical plan; usually a significantly smaller amount than the district's portion.

Court injunction An order from a court to perform or to cease performance of an activity. An example is a court order requiring a group of striking employees to return to work.

Criminal background investigation The process used by school districts to check both the references and credentials of job candidates and the records of law enforcement agencies to identify any candidates who might have been convicted of a criminal act.

Criminal law Law that is concerned with protecting the rights of society; thus, local, state, and federal governments representing the people are responsible for prosecuting wrongs committed against society by individuals or corporate entities.

Cyberethics The study of how technology has affected public policy through computing and communicative electronic techniques.

Data mining The use of an array of analytical applications to identify patterns in a database.

Data warehouse A school district–wide database designed to support the activities of the entire district. It is usually batch-updated and provides rapid online information and summaries.

Decision support system An interactive, computer-based system that allows a user to solve problems through data-based modeling.

Deductibles The amount of money that an employee must pay for medical and hospital services, usually within a calendar year, before a school district's insurance programs begin to pay the remaining cost of the services.

Direct compensation That part of a compensation program composed of salary, overtime pay, holiday pay, and merit pay.

Drug-Free Workplace Act of 1989 A federal law that gives employers the choice of rehabilitating or dismissing employees working in federal grant programs who are convicted of drug abuse offenses in the workplace.

Due process Procedures enacted to safeguard the rights of an employee, including the right to a fair and impartial hearing on allegations of noncompliance with the policies, goals, objectives, rules, and regulations of a school district.

Education The process of helping an individual understand and interpret knowledge through the development of reasoning processes that allow him or her to analyze the relationship between variables.

Employee organization An organization or union that represents employees in the collective negotiations process concerning salary, fringe benefits, and working conditions.

Employee relations   Strategies, policies, processes, and procedures used in collective negotiations that implement the preparatory phase for negotiations, at-the-table bargaining, management of the master agreement, and grievance management.

Employment agency   A private company that helps clients search for employment opportunities and charges either the client or the hiring school district a fee for this service.

Employment termination   The cessation of a person's employment for cause based on documentation that can stand up against legal scrutiny.

Employment test   Intelligence, aptitude, ability, and interest tests constitute the usual battery of tests that are used in the selection process for certain types of jobs.

Enrollment prediction   An estimate of the number of students who will attend specific schools at specific grade levels over a five- to ten-year period of time. The cohort survival method is commonly used in many school districts.

Equal Employment Opportunity Commission (EEOC)   Established by Title VII of the Civil Rights Act of 1964 and strengthened by the passage of the Equal Employment Opportunity Act of 1972, this agency investigates charges of discrimination, attempts conciliation, and can litigate cases.

Equal Pay Act of 1963   A federal law that requires employers to pay males and females the same salary or wage for equal work.

Errors and omissions liability insurance   Insurance that pays for the defense of an employee and the actual damages arising out of a civil lawsuit.

Ethics   Human conduct norms that provide a guide for administrators in the practice of human resources management.

Evaluation instrument   A formal document used by supervisors in evaluating the performance of personnel in relation to behavior traits and/or goals and objectives.

Evaluation process   In human resources administration from a central office perspective, refers to the development of policies, procedures, methods, and instruments used in evaluating the performance of personnel, with an emphasis on legal and due process considerations.

Exclusive representation   The situation in which an organization or union is the exclusive representative of a bargaining unit. Such designation is usually given by a state agency or the board of education after a recognition procedure has been carried out.

Executive orders   In the federal government, the presidential orders that have the force of law. They have been issued by several presidents to address issues of employment discrimination.

Expectancy model   A model for compensating employees by which they can readily understand that, when they act in the best interest of the school district, they are acting in their own best interests.

Extrinsic compensation   Usually divided into direct and indirect compensation.

Fact finding   An impasse procedure in which testimony from interested parties is taken and information is gathered and analyzed in order to formulate a recommendation for resolving a grievance or an impasse in the bargaining process.

Fair share fee   Usually, the equivalent of dues proportioned to cover the service that is rendered by a union or an organization in the collective negotiations process. This fee is paid by nonunion or non-organization members because they are benefiting from the representation.

Family and Medical Leave Act of 1993   A federal law, the fundamental purpose of which is to provide eligible employees with the right to take twelve weeks of unpaid leave per year for personal or family health reasons and for first-year parenting purposes.

Federal Mediation and Conciliation Service (FMCS)　An independent agency of the federal government created by Congress in 1974 for the purpose of promoting labor management peace. The agency is staffed by professional mediators.

Fringe benefits　Benefits available to all employees resulting from a direct fiscal expenditure; usually classified as insurance programs, paid time away from work, and services.

Garnishment　A court order requiring an employer to deduct a certain amount of money from an employee's salary for remission to the court in order to satisfy a creditor.

Generation Y　Often referred to as the *Millennial Generation* and composed of people born in or after 1980, who, as discussed in this book, are old enough to be seeking post-collegial professional employment as teachers and administrators in school districts.

Grievance procedures　The procedures for resolving an allegation by an employee or an employee organization or union that a school district or an administrator of the district misapplied, misinterpreted, or violated a provision of a master agreement.

Health Insurance Portability and Accountability Act of 1996 (HIPAA)　A federal law guaranteeing certain health insurance coverage to employees, their spouses, and their dependents, even if they have preexisting medical conditions.

Health maintenance organization (HMO)　In this approach to healthcare management, health insurance and the delivery of healthcare are combined. Physicians receive a salary for providing services, or they receive, through a contract, a fixed per-patient payment regardless of the number of visits.

Hostile environment sexual harassment　The harassment that occurs when unwelcome sexual conduct interferes with an employee's job performance.

Human resources administration　Management of the processes, procedures, and techniques necessary to implement the following dimensions of the human resources function in a school district: planning, recruitment, selection, placement and induction, staff development, performance evaluation, compensation, and collective negotiations.

Human resources forecasting　Estimating future human resources needs, usually established through expert estimates, historical comparison, task analysis, correlation, and modeling.

Human resources inventory　The human resources profile for the school district, generated from such employee information as age, job title, education and/or training, placement, gender, special skills, and certification.

Human resources planning　The process whereby a school district ensures that it has the right number of people, with the right skills, in the right place, and at the right time in order to carry out its goals and objectives effectively.

Immigration Reform and Control Act of 1996　A federal law that makes it unlawful to knowingly hire an unauthorized alien, continue the employment of one who becomes an unauthorized alien, or hire any individual without first verifying his or her employability and identity.

Impasse　The formal designation by the representatives of the board of education and the representatives of the employees of the situation in which agreement cannot be reached on an issue or issues in the at-the-table bargaining process. Initiates predetermined impasse procedures.

Indemnity healthcare plan　A traditional healthcare insurance plan that allows the employee, his or her spouse, and his or her dependents to choose any physician and hospital in order to receive services.

Independent practice association (IPA)　A group or network of physicians in which the physicians remain independent while contracting with HMOs.

Indirect compensation   That part of a compensation program that includes protection programs, pay for time away from work, and services.

Induction   The process designed to acquaint both newly employed and newly assigned employees with their job positions, the community, and their colleagues. With newly employed individuals, an orientation to the school district is most beneficial.

Insurance company ratings   Ratings of insurance companies according to their performance and financial solvency; prepared by nationally recognized, independent rating companies such as A. M. Best of Oldwick (New Jersey), Duff & Phelps of Chicago, Moody's of New York, and Standard & Poor's of New York.

Interstate New Teacher Assessment and Support Consortium (INTASC)   A national consortium that has developed standards considered to be best practice for the licensure of teachers in many states.

Intrinsic compensation   The satisfaction that accompanies the successful performance of job responsibilities through participation in the policy-making process, job discretion, responsibility, and opportunities for staff development.

Job analysis   The process of gathering information about a given job that centers on the job's parameters; how tasks are carried out; the job's skills, education, and training requirements; physical and environmental conditions of the job; and the job's relationship to other jobs.

Job description   A formal job designation that includes the job title, duties, authority and responsibility, and specific qualifications.

Job vacancy announcement   Based on the job description; provides potential candidates with sufficient information to decide whether to apply for a position.

Labor management relations committee   A committee composed of administrators and employees from a school district who meet on a regular basis to resolve concerns, problems, and issues related to working conditions.

Lawsuit   A petition filed with an appropriate court of original jurisdiction setting forth a cause of action.

Libel   Defamation committed through communicating false information in writing that brings hatred or ridicule on a person and produces some type of harm to him or her.

Managed healthcare   An approach to coordinating services around the patient and thereby producing a more efficient healthcare delivery system, which is also more cost effective.

Management approach   An approach to human resources administration that centers on developing strategies and carrying out processes, procedures, and techniques.

Management rights   Those responsibilities that are endemic and necessary to the administration of a school district.

Mandatory fringe benefits   Benefits that are required by law and constitute a direct cost to a school district. All states require districts to contribute to employee retirement, unemployment, and workers' compensation programs.

Master agreement   Provisions arising out of the collective negotiations process that have been approved by both the board of education and the employees and that have been put into writing. The provisions set forth in the master agreement have the force of board policy.

Mediation   An impasse procedure whereby a third party meets together or separately with the representatives of the board of education and the employees to help them resolve an issue arising during collective negotiations or from a grievance. Mediation is always a voluntary measure.

Medical savings accounts (MSAs)   Established by HIPAA in an attempt to manage the rising cost of healthcare. Under certain conditions, employers can place the savings that are realized through establishing high medical deductibles into an employee MSA, which can be supplemented by employee contributions in order to pay minor healthcare expenses.

Mentoring   The practice of pairing newly employed teachers, staff members, and administrators with experienced colleagues to provide support and encouragement.

Merit pay   Financial compensation in addition to a person's salary as a reward for above-average job performance.

National Association of State Directors of Teacher Education and Certification (NASDTEC)   A professional organization that promotes the role and function of state certification officials and maintains the Teacher Identification Clearinghouse.

National Council of Chief State School Officers   The professional organization that supports the role and function of state commissioners and superintendents of education.

National Labor Relations Board (NLRB)   A federal agency, created by Congress in 1935 through enactment of the National Labor Relations Act, that has jurisdiction to conduct union representation elections and to apply this act against unfair labor practices in the private sector.

Negotiated agreements   Agreements developed by school districts that have difficulty in recruiting and hiring highly qualified administrators and teachers. Such districts are designing compensation packages that are tailored to meet the employment demands of desirable candidates.

No Child Left Behind Act (NCLB)   Federal legislation signed into law by President George W. Bush in 2002. The law requires all children to be proficient in reading and mathematics by 2014. Other provisions mandate improved communications with parents and improved safety at school for children.

Off-the-job training   Various training techniques such as lectures, seminars, workshops, case studies, programmed instruction, and simulations.

Omnibus Transportation Employee Testing Act of 1991   The provisions of this federal law allow certain employers to conduct preemployment, postaccident, random, reasonable suspicion, and return-to-duty alcohol and controlled substances testing on persons in safety-sensitive jobs.

On-the-job training   Training in which employees are placed in the actual work situation in order for them to learn by doing but are monitored by a supervisor.

Online analytical processing   An interactive, computer-based system that allows a user to reframe multidimensional data gathered from various sources and stored in a data warehouse; allows data to be organized into many different representations.

Online application   The use of the Internet to post job vacancies on a school district's Webpage and to receive applications and resumes via email. Through a district's intranet, an administrator can check the status of an applicant in relation to the selection process or search the human resources database to find a candidate whose profile fits a certain job description.

Online recruitment   The use of the Internet by school districts to post job vacancies, provide information about the districts, provide information about a given job, and indicate how to apply for positions.

Open-ended interview   A type of interview that encourages the candidate to talk freely and at length about the topics introduced by the interviewer(s).

Organizational change   An organizational learning theory that is implemented in school districts under two rubrics. First, all stakeholders are identified with the organization; second, an organization must be focused on a vision that gives it direction.

Out of network   A physician or hospital not under contract to an HMO or a PPO network. If an employee, spouse, or dependent accesses the services of such a physician or hospital, the healthcare plan pays a smaller portion of the costs that result from receiving the services.

Personal adjustment   The aspect of an induction program that focuses on helping a new employee establish professional relationships with colleagues and others with whom he or she is required to interact; also, helping the employee acquire a sense of job satisfaction.

Personnel administration   An alternative designation for human resources administration.

Placement   Job assignment of an employee based on the best judgment of the superintendent of schools or a designee in relation to the school district's programming, staff balancing, and welfare of the students.

Point of service (POS)   An HMO plan that permits a member to access healthcare services outside the HMO. However, the HMO plan usually imposes a high deductible for such services and pays a much smaller portion of the cost after the deductible is reached.

Policy   Guidelines setting forth the authority and general means of attaining the goals and objectives of a school district or a division, department, or other administrative component of a district.

Preferred provider organization (PPO)   An organization of individual healthcare professionals, hospitals, healthcare organizations, or groups of healthcare organizations that provides services to employees, their spouses, or their dependents at a discount.

Pregnancy Disability Amendment   An amendment to Title VII of the Civil Rights Act of 1964 that makes it illegal to discriminate against pregnant women in all employment-related situations, including hiring, promoting, assigning, granting medical benefits, and receiving seniority credit.

Primary care physician   A healthcare professional who acts as a gatekeeper, making the referrals that are required by the managed care plan for the patient to receive healthcare services.

Professional learning community   A school or school district with four focuses: learning rather than teaching, collaboration, viewing all members of the community as learners, and self-accountability.

Program design   The process of matching needs with available resources through an effective delivery method.

Progressive discipline   Corrective action taken by a supervisor when an employee does not meet socially acceptable standards or does not comply with the rules and regulations of a school district. The severity of such corrective measures depends on the type of behavior exhibited by the employee and the number of incidences.

***Quid pro quo* sexual harassment**   Harassment that occurs when personnel decisions are made based on an employee's submission to or rejection of an employer's or supervisor's sexual advances.

Reasonable person concept   A criterion in tort litigation to which the actions of the defendant is compared. The "reasonable person" is someone who possesses average intelligence; normal perception and memory; and the same level of skills, knowledge, experience, and physical characteristics as the defendant.

Recognition   Acceptance by the board of education of an organization or union as the authorized representative of certain employees for the purpose of collective negotiations.

Recruitment   The process used to ensure that a school district has qualified candidates for positions that become vacant due to retirements, resignations, terminations, and enrollment growth.

Recruitment brochure   A specialized type of advertisement commonly used to recruit principals and superintendents that provides extensive information about the school district, position, community, and application process.

Reduction in force (RIF)   The process required when decreasing student enrollments produce a surplus of teachers in a given school district. The reduction can be humanely carried out through attrition, early retirement incentive programs, enhanced curricular programs, and help for employees to acquire new skills or find other positions.

Rehabilitation Act of 1973   Title V of the Rehabilitation Act contains five sections: four relate to affirmative action for people with disabilities, and one deals with voluntary actions, remedial actions, and evaluation criteria for compliance with the law.

Relational database   A database that permits the sharing of information from multiple files, which can be linked or related.

Representation election   A recognition procedure that identifies an employee organization or union as the exclusive representative of a defined bargaining unit. The organization or union receiving a majority of the votes is the exclusive representative.

Results evaluation   A method of evaluating the performance of an employee based on objectives that were developed by the employee and agreed to by his or her supervisor.

Risk management   The strategies, policies, processes, and procedures that are necessary for implementing a health and safety program for a school district, and that include safety and security audits, training and education, monitoring, and crisis event management.

Role of the attorney   An attorney's expertise centers around his or her ability to analyze the material facts in a case, research the statutes and precedents of other court cases, and set forth the position of the plaintiff or defendant in a reasonable manner.

Salary and wage administration   The management of direct compensation, which includes compensation research and development, payroll management, position control, and salary determination.

Salary schedule   A method of calculating an individual teacher's salary based on either an incremental or an index schedule that credits seniority, number of graduate course hours, and academic degrees.

Scope of negotiations   The subject matter of collective negotiations, usually consisting of salary, fringe benefits, and working conditions; commonly a bargained issue.

Selection criteria   Those ideal characteristics that, if possessed by a person to a minimal degree, ensure successful performance of a given job.

Selection interview   A structured conversation with direction and format between one or more interviewers and a candidate for a job in order to generate information about the person being interviewed; learn about the candidate's opinions, beliefs, and attitudes; and experience the candidate as a person.

Selection process   The process designed to hire people who will be successful on the job; includes developing a job description, establishing selection criteria, advertising the job vacancy, interviewing candidates, checking reference and credentials, making the job offer, and notifying unsuccessful candidates.

Services   A component of indirect compensation that provides a benefit to employees, such as a wellness program, tuition reimbursement, an employee assistance program, and paid attendance at workshops or conventions.

Sexual harassment   In 1980, the EEOC declared sexual harassment to be a violation of Title VII of the Civil Rights Act of 1964. There are two types of sexual harassment: *quid pro quo* and hostile environment harassment.

Slander   Defamation committed through communicating false information by word of mouth that brings hatred or ridicule on a person and produces some type of harm to him or her.

Small Business Job Protection Act of 1996   Commonly referred to as the *minimum wage law* because it increased the take-home wages of employees.

Social justice   The concept that people have certain rights and responsibilities simply because they are members of a given society.

Social Security   The U.S. government's attempt to care for and protect the aged by ensuring them a minimum standard of living through a monthly allotment of money from a trust fund that is transferred from one generation to the next.

Staff development   Because of knowledge expansion and advances in technology, every employee must acquire new information, understanding, and skills in order to meet the goals and objectives of a school district. The staff development dimension consists of conducting needs assessments, establishing staff development goals and objectives, designing programs, implementing delivery plans, and evaluating the programs.

Synchronous   The experience of interacting with another person through technology in real time. Thus, a retiree may be communicating through email with a staff member in a school district's benefits office during normal working hours.

Teacher center   A place where teachers determine their own staff development needs and, on their own initiative, implement staff development programs.

Teacher Identification Clearinghouse   A national database of all teachers who have been denied certification or whose certification has been revoked or suspended for moral reasons.

Theories of occupational choice   A set of theories concerning the interaction among a person's psychological makeup, his or her vocational and occupational choices, the availability of appropriate jobs, and the culture of various communities.

Third-party healthcare   Healthcare in which a company hired by a school district manages the district's healthcare program, including cost analysis, cost projection, case management, catastrophic case management, utilization review, and claims management.

Title IX   Title IX of the Education Amendments of 1972 prohibits discrimination against women in educational programs and activities, including employment, when an educational agency receives federal financial assistance.

Tort   A civil wrong, other than a breach of contract, committed against a person or a person's property. Libel and slander are types of torts committed against a person.

Total quality management (TQM)   An approach to administration based on the philosophy of W. Edwards Deming, which views all employees as stakeholders and empowers them to make strategic decisions about how to meet the goals and objectives of an organization.

Training   The process of learning a sequence of programmed behaviors that can be broken down and analyzed in order to determine the best way to perform certain tasks. Training is most effective in learning routine tasks.

Trait evaluation   A method of evaluating the performance of an employee against a predetermined set of performance indicators.

Transcendental leadership   A leadership theory predicated on the premise that a person acts from the totality of who he or she is as a human. The theory requires administrators to reflect on the fact that their decisions are prompted by more than just the immediate circumstances and have an effect that goes beyond the present situation.

TRICARE   The Department of Defense's health insurance plan for military personnel and their families (formerly the Civilian Health and Medical Program of the Uniformed Services, or CHAMPUS). When employees are called up for active military service, they are immediately covered by this military helathcare system. Their dependents may be covered by TRICARE depending on certain conditions, including length of mobilization.

U.S. judicial system   A mixed system that uses principles of both civil and common law.

U.S. Training and Employment Service   The federal government agency that supervises state employment agencies that provide services to people who are without employment, including the management of unemployment benefits and job searches.

Unemployment compensation   A program established by state law that provides benefits to individuals who are without a job if they comply with certain regulations.

Union   An organized employee group whose representatives meet with the representatives of the board of education for the purpose of collectively negotiating salaries, fringe benefits, and working conditions.

Union shop   The result of an agreement between the board of education and a union whereby an employee is required to become a member of a bargaining unit as a condition of employment and to remain a member during the term of the bargained agreement.

Vietnam Era Veterans Readjustment Assistance Act of 1974   The purpose of this federal law is affirmative action for veterans with disabilities, especially those who served in the Vietnam War.

Voluntary fringe benefits   Indirect compensation programs provided to employees by a board of education, usually in the form of insurance programs, time away from work, and services.

Win–win bargaining   An approach to collective negotiations having the goal of producing a non-adversarial climate that allows both sides to form consensus on issues related to salary, fringe benefits, and working conditions.

Work stoppage   Commonly referred to as a *strike*; occurs when employees of a school district refuse to perform their responsibilities as a protest against the actions of the board of education, usually in relation to the collective negotiations process.

Workers' compensation   A state program that provides benefits to an individual injured or disabled because of a job-related activity.

Workflow   The technological capability to initiate multiple transactions through a single data entry.

INDEX